The Tale of a Comet
and Other Stories

the Tale of a Comet

of a

Comet

and Other Stories

Helen M. White

Being a Collection of True Accounts of Diverse People and Events Relating to the State of Minnesota, Embracing **COMETS**, a **CIRCUS**, the **SKI-SPORT**, **MILITARY OFFICERS** of Fort Snelling and the Civil War, **REINDEER PEOPLE**, a **TRUTH-TELLING VEGETARIAN REFORMER**, and an **INDIAN HISTORIOGRAPHER;** Together with an Account of the Remarkable and Curious **EVENTS OF 1883**

MINNESOTA HISTORICAL SOCIETY PRESS • ST. PAUL • 1984

Minnesota Historical Society Press, St. Paul 55101
© 1984 by Minnesota Historical Society. All rights reserved
International Standard Book Number 0-87351-169-7

MANUFACTURED IN THE UNITED STATES OF AMERICA

10 9 8 7 6 5 4 3 2 1

Library of Congress Cataloging in Publication Data

White, Helen McCann, 1916-
The tale of a comet and other stories.

Subtitle: Being a collection of true accounts of diverse people and events relating to the state of
Minnesota, embracing comets, a circus, the ski-sport, military officers of Fort Snelling and the
Civil War, reindeer people, a truth-telling vegetarian reformer, and an Indian historiographer,
together with an account of the remarkable and curious events of 1883.
Includes bibliographical references and index.
1. Minnesota — History — Addresses, essays, lectures.
2. Middle West — History — Addresses, essays, lectures.
I. Title.
F606.5.W45   1984   977.6   83-25086

Contents

Preface

THIS IS A BOOK of stories — not fiction, but true stories, as true as I could make them. They take place, for the most part, in the 19th century. They are about various subjects and diverse people, all of them relating to Minnesota and the Midwest: an officer who drank too much at Fort Snelling in the 1820s; a farmer, vegetarian, and radical reformer; a chaplain and artist in the Civil War; a newspaperman interested in Indian history; a stranded circus and circus performers in the 1870s; two brothers who were champions of the ski-sport in its early days; a Minnesota author who wrote about comets; the extraordinary year of 1883; a missionary who imported reindeer from Siberia and Lapland to Alaska; and other men and women who brought reindeer and Santas to cities across the United States at Christmas time.

I was originally attracted to these topics by a number of elements — curiosity, sentiment, sympathy, personal experience, chance remarks of friends, a reference to a famous book or an unidentified object. In short, I cannot explain clearly why these story ideas were appealing, but I remember very well *how* they came to me.

First in order of discovery were Phineas Andrews and Nathaniel S. Harris, central characters in "A Soldier 'Disguised.' " Twenty years ago the Minnesota Historical Society, planning to restore Fort Snelling, asked me to search for source materials on the fort's first buildings in the National Archives in Washington, D.C. There in the records of the Judge Advocate General I found the file of Phineas Andrews, court-martialed for drunkenness. As I scanned the 200 manuscript pages for references to fort buildings, my eye caught the name of Don Quixote. The idea that someone at the fort in the 1820s had been reading Cervantes intrigued me, and I made a brief note for a file I labeled "Ideas." Some day when I had time I wanted to learn more about the officer who read Cervantes.

Dr. Oliver Wendell Holmes, then director of the National Historical Publications Commission (NHPC) at the National Archives, gave me another idea for my file. Because he knew that my husband, Gilbert, worked for the U.S. Department of the Interior and was interested in the

Arctic, Holmes thought we should know about Sheldon Jackson, a former Interior employee. Records of Jackson's career were in the National Archives and in the Presbyterian Historical Society in Philadelphia. Someone, Holmes said, ought to use them and write about Jackson's role in introducing reindeer to the North American continent. Why didn't one or both of us do it?

A few years later, on the north shore of Lake Superior, I thought more seriously about Jackson and the reindeer. I was at Tofte, interviewing Chris and Matelda Tormondsen for the Minnesota Historical Society's North Shore Fisheries project, when Chris mentioned that one year during hunting season he saw a reindeer near Cross River wearing a red ribbon with a bell around its neck. Where did the reindeer come from? Did it have some connection, he wondered, with a former north shore resident who worked with reindeer in Alaska? To mark the trail of the belled reindeer, I put another note in my file; I later traced Jackson's career and that of a handful of memorable characters associated with reindeer for "The Alaskan Reindeer Service" and "The Christmas Reindeer Shows," both part of the "Reindeer People" story in this book.

The idea of the ski story originated with my husband, a devoted skier who was curious about all aspects of the sport. When he retired, he began research on the early history of the ski-sport in the Midwest. After his death I gathered up his notes and continued his work; the result was "Ski-Sport Heroes from Norway."

I found other story ideas in the Ignatius Donnelly and Alexander Ramsey papers when I was editor and director of the society's NHPC-funded project to publish microfilm editions of those collections. Donnelly and Ramsey, themselves remarkable men, corresponded with many other unusual people. One of them was Frans H. Widstrand of Wright County and Litchfield. Dean Theodore C. Blegen, then a research associate for the society, was intrigued, as I was, by this highly intellectual and exasperating man, and he speculated about whether Widstrand had played any part in the Kensington rune stone story. My own investigation led me to deny Widstrand a role in the rune stone event, but I could not forget him. I wanted to find out why he had so much trouble with his brothers and neighbors, to trace what happened to his Farist colony, and to recall his happier years among his books and strawberry beds.

Another Ramsey-Donnelly correspondent who appealed to me was the irrepressible and opinionated Dr. Thomas Foster. I watched for his flourishing signature in the correspondence files, wanting to know more about his adventures in territorial Minnesota and his career as a fighting editor in Duluth. But I was more curious about his Indian historiography project in Washington. Was it in any way related to the beginnings of the Smithsonian Institution's Bureau of American Ethnology? Notes on both Widstrand and Foster were tucked into my Idea file along with those for Andrews, the reindeer, and the ski-sport.

These and a dozen other ideas, some dating back to the 1950s when I did research on the Montana gold rush, filled my file to overflowing.

I had no time for research or writing and I was growing older by the minute. In 1970 I decided to retire from the Minnesota Historical Society and explore some other byways in the field of history. I bought and restored two buildings in what is now the Angels Hill Historic District of Taylors Falls. Then a friend and I started the *Dalles Visitor*, an annual newspaper in which I hoped to prove that the general public would read and support any amount of scholarly historical writing if it were written in an interesting manner. Although producing articles for the *Visitor* somewhat depleted my Idea file and partially satisfied my urge to do research and write, it also suggested a number of new ideas that found their way into other stories for this book.

One day while researching for the *Visitor* in the Chisago County Courthouse I found in a court docket a list of cases involving the Great Australian Circus. Forgetting what I had come to do, I spent the afternoon reading the case files. One item, a clown's contract with the circus, became the starting point in tracing Lem Quillin's career and in the writing of "A Circus Gone Up."

During a short stint as librarian of the Taylors Falls Public Library I found another story idea. On the west wall of the hundred-year-old library building, not far from the librarian's desk, hangs an oil painting of a St. Croix River rock formation against a setting sun. The picture is signed in the lower right corner, in red, "EEE." Curious about the artist, I searched the library's early newspaper files and discovered that he was Elijah E. Edwards; that he had been minister of a local church; and that he and others who had served in the Civil War had lived in houses still standing on Government (now Angels) Hill, not far from my home. An article on him in the *Visitor* and further research led to the discovery of other Edwards paintings and papers and to the two parts of his Civil War journal — one at the Minnesota Historical Society and the other in the Edwards Papers in the DePauw University Archives at Greencastle, Indiana. This journal furnished the major source materials for "Elijah E. Edwards, Civil War Chaplain."

Finally I come to Donnelly's "Tale of a Comet." In working on the Donnelly Papers, I had noted that *Ragnarok*, Donnelly's tale of a comet, was not as well known today as its companion volume, *Atlantis*. Perhaps it should be re-examined, I thought, but I was not seriously interested in comets or any other flying objects and did not think of taking on the task. My attitude changed in March, 1978, when unidentified flying objects passed over my house. I did not see them, but many of my neighbors did, and newspapers reported the event. I began to wonder whether any other UFOs, meteors, comets — or whatever — had traveled over my house in its 130-year history. Research in local newspapers yielded references to a remarkable assortment of objects in and falling from the sky over the St. Croix Valley, and I published a catalog of some of them in the *Visitor*.

As a result of what appeared to be my interest in the unexplained, readers of the *Visitor* told me many tales of haunted houses, out-of-body experiences, and other inexplicable events in the sky. Friends introduced me to a vast literature — scientific and otherwise — concerning such phenomena. Reading these publications, and the more substantial but controversial writings of Immanuel Velikovsky, Frederick Jueneman, Ivan Sanderson, and Charles Fort, was no more than a diversion until I chanced on Fort's statement in *The Book of the Damned*: "I have records of 31 extraordinary events in 1883. Someone should write a book upon the phenomena of this one year — that is, if books should be written."

The idea of writing a story about 1883 appealed to me. As I began to read the *New York Times* and other newspapers published that year, and as comets and meteors proliferated in the skies, my thoughts turned again to Donnelly. I decided I wanted to tell the comet story against a background of other remarkable events of the 1880s.

The year I searched the newspapers for the 1883 story was undoubtedly a trying one for my friends at the Minnesota Historical Society. Week by week during my enthusiastic search, I learned and passed on to them more information than anyone ever wanted to know about that year. Fortuitous discoveries, however, helped to quiet their fears that I had abandoned all scholarly decorum to join the world of phenomena fanatics and persuaded them that the comet and catastrophe story deserved a respectable place in a book of history. After all, the Rochester tornado (and the beginnings of the Mayo Clinic), the catastrophic explosion of Krakatoa (and other associated disasters), and the meeting in Minneapolis of the American Association for the Advancement of Science all occurred in the same month of 1883. Moreover, members of that very same scientific association convened almost a century later to discuss a "new" theory that a close encounter with a heavenly body may have caused the wholesale destruction of dinosaurs and other forms of life at the end of the Mesozoic era.

Well before this time I had sorted through my Idea file and decided that I wanted to write a book of stories. Encouraged by the success of the *Visitor*, I listed subjects that I thought would appeal to such people as those who read that newspaper. If at first glance my techniques looked scattershot or my subjects seemed trivial, I could invoke Lytton Strachey to help me justify them. He described the subtle strategy that the wise historian would use in depicting the Victorian Age: "He will attack his subject in unexpected places, he will fall upon the flank, or the rear; he will shoot a sudden, revealing searchlight into obscure recesses, hitherto undivined. He will row out over that great ocean of material, and lower down into it, here and there, a little bucket, which will bring up to the light of day some characteristic specimen, from those far depths, to be examined with a careful curiosity."[1]

I took the list to June D. Holmquist, the Minnesota Historical Society's director of publications. I told her I wanted to write stories, not biographies or essays or sketches, but true stories. I wanted them to be long enough to cover the subject well, but not so long as to be boring. Ideas of significant and even profound importance would possibly be lurking in the stories, but I did not want to rub the reader's nose in them. Let him or her discover and meditate on the profundities.

June liked the book plan. She thought it would be fun for me to write and for the society to publish, but she wanted a better mix of people and places. We went over the original list, crossing out, substituting, adding, and combining in a process continued after June's death by her successor, Jean A. Brookins, and her publications staff. Like Dr. Foster's historiography, the stories "widened" as I worked on them; despite my own strictures, each one became far too long. Careful cutting and revisions under the direction of the book's talented editor, Ann Regan, have I am sure made the stories more enjoyable to read.

When I was writing the stories, June secured for me a grant from the National Endowment for the Humanities and a supplementary grant from the Minnesota Historical Society to help meet the expenses of my research. June, Jean, Ann, and many, many others have helped me in this project. At the beginning of the notes section for each story I have acknowledged the assistance of many, but there were others who found books, checked files, answered questions by letter and phone, and offered suggestions and encouragement. I am grateful to all who helped me — in particular to the staff of the Minnesota Historical Society — and I hope that they will feel that their efforts were worthwhile.

HELEN M. WHITE

THIS BOOK HAS BEEN MADE POSSIBLE IN PART
BY GRANTS FROM THE NATIONAL ENDOWMENT FOR THE HUMANITIES
AND THE MINNESOTA HISTORICAL SOCIETY.

⧿1⧿

A Soldier "Disguised"

An Officer
at Early Fort Snelling
is Court-Martialed
for Drunkenness

LIEUTENANT Phineas Andrews, Company B, United States Fifth Infantry, had few friends among his fellow officers at upper Mississippi army posts in the early 1820s. Many avoided his company. One of them compared Andrews to the "filthy yahoo" of *Gulliver's Travels* who "befouls every one who comes within smelling distance of him." Others criticized the man's professional behavior, accusing him of conduct unbecoming an officer, neglect of duty, and unfitness to command. Beneath all the accusations lay one major charge, that Andrews drank too much — a common enough practice during leisure time in the frontier army. But when Phineas Andrews appeared on duty seeming to be under the influence of whisky his "vice" became a military offense. He was observed to stagger, hiccup, and slur his speech, and a 17th-century phrase was used to describe his condition: he was a man "disguised with liquor."[1]

Alcohol was readily available to enlisted men and officers alike. An army surgeon said in 1827 that the upper Mississippi River posts were "afloat" in an "empire of drunkenness." Isolated from home and family (only a few of the men had wives and children with them), they drank to forget their loneliness. Because frontier military life was rarely distinguished by deeds of daring or glorious battles nobly fought, they drank to relieve monotony. For many the temporary release from misery did not interfere with their completion of a respectable tour of duty. For some, it ruined their lives.[2]

Officers found to be under the influence of liquor while on duty could be punished by confinement to quarters, and enlisted men could be placed in solitary incarceration in the post's "black hole" on a diet of bread and water. In 1826 Colonel Josiah Snelling, commanding officer of the Fifth Infantry, ordered that men whose deaths could be associated with drunkenness were to be buried without military ceremony. In a less publicized move against alcoholism, some officers with drinking problems were encouraged to resign quietly from the service. Others who drank to excess had friends in high places who, finding mitigating factors, intervened to keep them in the army. The treatment Phineas Andrews received was quite different. Of the numerous victims of drunkenness in the regiment, he was an officer chosen for public punishment — some said as a scapegoat.[3]

Andrews, in fact, was not well. He suffered from an injury incurred under honorable circumstances during the War of 1812. The pain was alleviated by the use of drugs and liquor prescribed by army doctors. Andrews insisted that it was the injury that caused him to walk at times with a staggering gait. The debility resulting from his long illness brought on other symptoms interpreted by some as evidence of drunkenness. Because his equals shunned him, Andrews sought the help (and perhaps the company) of men in the ranks. His purported fraternization with enlisted men and noncommissioned officers further alienated him from the officer class, but it seemed to one of his supporters that it was his treatment by officers that forced him to find friends elsewhere. It seemed as though despite mitigating factors, he was sacrificed to "atone for the prostration of the many at the shrine of Bacchus." The sacrificial ceremony was the court martial of Andrews at Fort Snelling in 1826.[4]

Phineas Andrews, born about 1783 in Hartford, was descended from an early Connecticut family and from the famous Miles Standish. At the turn of the 19th century his family moved to New York. But during the War of 1812, when Andrews was about 30 and a painter by occupation, he joined the Connecticut Militia. In February, 1814, he enlisted as a sergeant in the regular army, marching with the Twenty-fifth United States Infantry to a camp near Buffalo, New York. There he was assigned to headquarters duty in the adjutant's office. When the Twenty-fifth Infantry fought at the Battle of Chippewa in July, 1814, Andrews carried a regimental standard. Crossing a large log, he stumbled and fell, receiving a severe rupture in the right groin that was later diagnosed as a strangulated hernia. For meritorious action in battle, he was commissioned a second lieutenant. In the spring of 1815 he was transferred to the Sixth Infantry, where he remained until leaving the service the following fall.[5]

Little is known of Andrews' life during the next five years. Although he was then considered "a fine specimen of a man, gentleman and soldier, and exceedingly captivating in his manners and address," there is no record of a marriage. There may be truth in a story that he had been "crossed in love" when he first joined the army. In his mid-thirties, he was five feet seven and one-half inches tall and had a light complexion, blue eyes, and dark hair. Soon after leaving the military he suffered a "lung affection" that was said to have aggravated the hernia. He lived for a time in New York before moving back to Connecticut, where he worked as a sergeant of the guard in Newgate, the state prison at Simsbury. A later acquaintance once commented that Phineas served "in the office of retailer of drams to the convicts."[6]

Military records indicate that in 1819 Andrews received a pension of $15 a month, retroactive to June, 1815, for the total disability that prevented him "from procuring his living by manual Labour." For his war

2

service he was also given a warrant for 160 acres of military-bounty lands. A year after receiving the pension, despite his disability, Andrews rejoined the army with his former rank of second lieutenant. He was sent with his company of the Fifth Infantry to Fort Edwards on the western frontier in Illinois. Thus he entered the second phase of his military career, a six-year period that was to end tragically.

By 1823 Andrews had been transferred to Fort Crawford at Prairie du Chien, Wisconsin; the following year he was promoted to first lieutenant. During much of 1824 and early 1825 he served as acting post adjutant under Lieutenant Colonel Willoughby Morgan, commanding the post, who was satisfied with his work.

Andrews' troubles began in the spring of 1825, when he came into conflict with Lieutenant James McIlvaine of Delaware. Like Andrews, McIlvaine had served in the War of 1812 and walked with a limp, the result of a broken leg sustained at Fort Snelling in 1822. The fuss began about the middle of March, when Andrews, as post adjutant, received and transmitted verbal orders from Lieutenant Colonel Morgan to send a private in Company K to plow the field behind the post. The soldier had been "turned out" three or four days on this special duty under the supervision of Lieutenant Joseph M. Baxley when he was mistakenly reassigned by Sergeant John Bailly to a normal turn at guard.[7]

The next morning, when Lieutenant Baxley sought out the private for plowing, the mixup was reported to Lieutenant McIlvaine, who charged Andrews with carelessly handling his duties as post adjutant. The verbal order had not been proper, McIlvaine insisted hotly, and Andrews "should know it had not." McIlvaine carried his protest to the commanding officer, only to be told that verbal orders were indeed acceptable at the post. In the interest of harmony, Andrews scratched off a penciled order directing the private to report to Baxley for daily duty. The next morning, the soldier was presumed to be out in the back field again "a ploughing." McIlvaine was not pleased.

Andrews left Fort Crawford on temporary duty about April 1, 1825, ordered to pursue Private Patrick Cavan of Company K and Sergeant Roderick Westernra of Company G, who had deserted. Gossip at the fort predicted that the sergeant, who was "a notorious rascal," would never be captured. Westernra was a friend and boon companion of Andrews and, the story went, had loaned the lieutenant money that had not been repaid.

It was assumed that the deserters would head south toward more civilized country. So Andrews pursued them down the Mississippi on the steamboat "Putnam" bound for St. Louis. On April 2 the boat stopped briefly about 180 miles below Fort Crawford at Fort Armstrong in Illinois. Andrews went ashore to report his mission. He spoke to, or was observed by, various enlisted men at the fort. He resumed his journey aboard the "Putnam"; the two fugitives were caught soon afterward and thrown into the Fort Armstrong guardhouse. News of their capture was sent to Andrews at St. Louis, so he simply stayed aboard the "Putnam" and returned upriver.[9]

3

At Fort Armstrong, Andrews was assigned a guard of four to convey the prisoners back to Fort Crawford. The men had already been put in chains by Sergeant William W. Burns, who had permission "to iron them in a way he thought most secure." Burns put cleves on each man's legs, attached to chains that were from five to seven feet long. An observer who watched the prisoners being marched from the guardhouse to the boat said they looked "tolerably confined."[10]

Sergeant Burns and three other men (two named Cook and Stewart; the third was unnamed in the record) comprised the guard. Andrews saw that they were furnished with guns and ammunition, and Burns escorted the prisoners to the upper deck of the "Putnam." Andrews' quarters and a cabin for the guards were on the second or lower deck. A yawl, or small boat, was aft of the second deck, but at about this time, Andrews said, he "caused it to be moved" forward to the bow "for security."[11]

As he watched the prisoners dragging along in their chains, Andrews remarked to Burns that "he had a mind to take the irons off the prisoners after the Boat started." Accordingly, soon after the "Putnam" left Fort Armstrong, Andrews appeared with a file and hammer and had the shackles removed. He later gave several reasons for doing so. It was difficult for the men to go up and down the ladder, and the extreme measure of chaining the prisoners was not necessary, since they were guarded by armed men. The two were under arrest, it was true, but they had not yet been convicted and sentenced. And furthermore "two gentlemen whose ladies [were] in a delicate condition . . . were annoyed by the clanking of the chains."

Andrews' right to make the decision was never questioned. His judgment in making it was. Lieutenant McIlvaine later commented sarcastically that it was better for a gallant man to betray his duty than to annoy ladies "whose nerves, poor souls, could not endure the jingling of the chains . . . through a deck three inches thick." Still, the prisoners remained fastened together by a rope — that is, until it somehow became untied.[12]

Andrews went to the upper deck frequently during the afternoon and evening to check the prisoners. Between 8:00 and 11:00 that night Stewart and the unnamed guard retired to their cabin. Shortly afterward, Cook, the third guard, went below and forward to help the crew weigh anchor, leaving Burns alone with the prisoners. It was said that Westernra wanted to use the "necessary" and Burns allowed him to go down. A few minutes later Cook, who was still forward, saw Westernra wandering around and took him to the stairway. Cook said that he watched Westernra ascending toward Sergeant Burns, who was standing at the head of the stairs.[13]

Cook then returned forward. After the anchor was raised the "Putnam" drifted toward shore. The boat was near the Missouri side of the river at the Rock Island Rapids. One man said the water there was swift but "not the strongest." The crew dropped anchor again, six rods —

4

more or less — from shore. About this time one of the ship's crew, a "black fellow," hauled the yawl back to the stern.[14]

Some 20 minutes later, after Cook had seen Westernra ascending the stairs, Andrews appeared on the upper deck asking Burns about the prisoners. Cavan was in place but Westernra was not beside him. Burns said that he was on the lower deck with Cook. When Cook was questioned, he said Westernra had gone up to Burns. Burns and Cook roused the other two guards. Where was Westernra? No one knew. In the search it was discovered that Westernra's baggage, a rifle, a bag of bread, and other items were missing. In the meantime, when the anchor was dropped the captain had ordered the yawl sent ashore to tie up for the rest of the night. The yawl, too, was missing! Thus the "means of conveyance" for pursuing Westernra was gone.[15]

In the confusion many questions were asked, but few of them were clearly answered then or later. Could Westernra have escaped without the assistance of the guard or other persons on board? Did the "black fellow" help him? Andrews was in his cabin on the second deck, not far from where the yawl was normally kept. Could he have assisted the fugitive? Did Burns or Cook connive at the prisoner's escape? Sergeant Cook admitted that they could have been more vigilant. "We had no suspicion of his going away and therefore did not look out so sharp for him, where we were lying out in the stream," he said. Each of the witnesses defended his actions, but all agreed that Westernra's escape would have been nearly impossible had he remained in irons.[16]

Back at Fort Crawford, when Lieutenant Colonel Morgan asked Andrews why he had permitted the removal of the prisoners' chains, the lieutenant said simply that "the chain was too short to enable them to go up and down the ladder." Although Morgan apparently attached no criminality to Andrews' actions on the "Putnam," Lieutenant McIlvaine did.[17]

About June 1, 1825, Andrews left Fort Crawford under orders transferring him to Fort Snelling. Gossip said that McIlvaine was determined to "ruin" him. Certainly the months at the new post were unhappy ones for Phineas Andrews. In August he became ill, and Captain (Brevet Major) Thomas Hamilton, his immediate superior, put him on sick report. Because there was no surgeon at the post, Corporal William Cole, the hospital steward, was called to treat the patient.[18]

Cole found the lieutenant "labouring under excrutiating [sic] pain," so great as to produce delirium. Andrews told Cole that his suffering was caused by a hernia. Cole administered "external anodyne applications" and gave him a laxative. He then instructed Andrews' servant to bathe the lieutenant with a mixture of laudanum and whisky every half hour. The treatment was continued day and night for four or five days. It gave temporary relief, Cole said, but "did not subdue the disease." The steward was reported to have said that Andrews was drinking too much and should abstain. Cole later denied having said any such thing, asserting that Andrews' illness was not "occasioned by a too free use of whiskey."[19]

5

Fort Snelling, 1830. *MHS*

Private Robert W. Sayres, the enlisted man who was Andrews' "waiter" or servant, tended the lieutenant night and day. After staying with him three nights in a row, Sayres said "it was out of my power to set up any longer without help." Another enlisted man chopped wood for the stove and eased his labor somewhat. At times, with Andrews' permission, Sayres gave the other soldier a little grog "as other Gentlemen were in the habit of doing." Then he went to the quarters of Company B in search of someone to spell him on night duty. At least seven different noncommissioned officers and two privates "sat up" nights with Andrews during his illness.[20]

During the first weeks of his illness Andrews lay in bed in the back room of his quarters. He had few visitors other than the men of lower rank who stayed with him at night. Captain Hamilton came to see him once or twice. Lieutenant St. Clair Denny stopped in about that often to ask "how he came on." Lieutenant Dudley W. Allanson visited several times. None offered to sit with him, nor did the sick man ask them to do so. It was suggested that he preferred the company of enlisted men. Andrews later said that he would gladly have availed himself of the company of fellow officers had that been possible.[21]

Sayres was sitting on a chest beside the bedroom door one night when Hospital Steward Cole arrived. Another private was present, and both men testified that they heard Cole tell Andrews that none of the officers "cared" for him except Lieutenant Colonel Morgan who, on occasion, came up from Fort Crawford to take command when Colonel Snelling was absent. The only reason Denny visited, Cole went on, was to see

6

whether Andrews was really sick or only pretending, to avoid duty. Allanson, whom Andrews considered one of his few friends in the garrison, may also have been mentioned by Cole in this regard.[22]

Surgeon Benjamin F. Harney reached the post about September 1 and called on Andrews at his quarters that day. The patient was still feeling miserable. He showed Harney a skin discoloration a little below the navel, extending to the hip, which he said was very painful and sore to the touch. Andrews spoke of "costiveness" (constipation) and pain in his stomach or chest. Dr. Harney did not examine him. What he had heard from the hospital steward and perhaps others at the post, as well as from Andrews in his rambling, rather incoherent explanation of his sickness, convinced the doctor that Andrews was intoxicated.[23]

Harney "assented" to continuing the treatment initiated by Cole. He prescribed "spirits" for internal use, and renewed the prescription, possibly three or four times — not a quantity large enough, in his judgment, to cause intoxication. The doctor then directed that Andrews' bed be made on the floor of his front room, nearer the fire. Harney saw no need for anyone to remain with the patient at night. He was annoyed when Sayres continued to ask him to attend the lieutenant, and to insist that

Fort Snelling, 1825. *MHS*

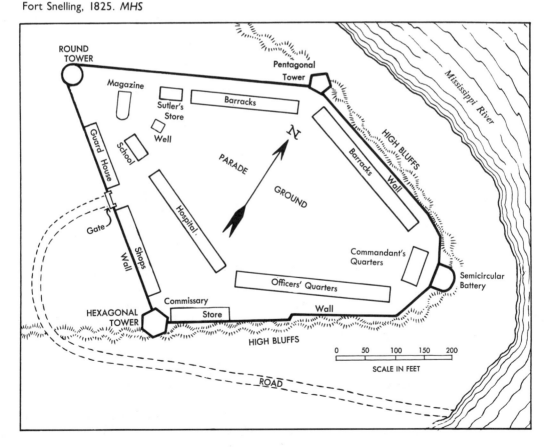

people should stay with Andrews. Sayres, too, was frequently drunk, Harney said. Nevertheless, Sayres continued to recruit people to sit with Andrews. For the most part, they testified that Andrews stayed on his bed; he did not drink liquor; he did not play cards; and he did not associate "familiarly," or "in a free and companiable [sic] manner" with those who stayed in his quarters.[24]

The night Sergeant Joseph Adams and another sergeant sat with Andrews, Lieutenant Allanson passed by. Through a closed window of Andrews' quarters he thought he saw one of the sergeants shuffling a pack of cards and laughing. He was talking to someone. Allanson could not see the face or hands of the person in bed (he did not say whether the bed was on the floor), but since it was Andrews' room, he assumed that the legs visible on the bed belonged to Andrews. Adams said that Andrews did not leave his bed (on the floor) that night, nor did anyone drink any liquor.[25]

William G. Camp, a former officer of the Fifth Infantry attached as a civilian to the sutler's store at Fort Snelling, called on the patient September 2. Andrews mentioned to him that Lieutenant Denny had come to "ascertain whether he was sick or simulated sickness to avoid duty." Camp repeated this gossip to Denny. In the meantime Cole was reported to have talked to Allanson and to Doctor Harney who, he said, ought to advise Andrews to abstain from liquor, or words to that effect. Denny had done his share of gossiping, too, it was reported, and he had forbidden the men of his company to go to Andrews' quarters, "for it was a common grog shop." When Denny heard Camp's story, however, he was more concerned with the aspersions on his own honor than with Andrews' drunkenness or sobriety.[26]

On the night of September 5, as Andrews lay on his bed by the fire, Denny came storming in with Camp, demanding that Andrews name the person who had accused him of spying. Had he, Denny, *ever* visited Andrews except on business unless specifically requested to call? In the angry dialogue that followed, it emerged that Sayres, Andrews' waiter, had encountered Denny, with other officers, not far from Andrews' quarters. The waiter had asked Denny to call on Lieutenant Andrews. It was before the dinner drum the previous day; Denny had declined then, but arrived later. Had not Andrews sent the request for Denny to call? Denny turned to the waiter for an answer. The discomfited Sayres pointed to Andrews, saying "there is the Gentleman he will answer for himself." Denny advanced toward Sayres in a threatening manner and ordered him to answer. Sayres, thoroughly intimidated, answered, yes, that Andrews had ordered him to speak to Denny, an answer he later repudiated under oath.[27]

Denny turned to Andrews, who was lying on the floor, and again demanded the name of the person who had accused him of spying. Andrews said he was not at liberty to give it. Denny said he would either be given the name or have it disclosed by a court martial. Andrews again tried to put him off. He felt too ill to go into the matter. If Denny would come back in the morning, Andrews would then "reveal the whole to

8

him and give him his author." Denny would not wait. Andrews said it was his duty to protect his inferiors. Denny brushed such sentiments aside.

Finally Andrews was browbeaten into saying that the story had come from Cole, the hospital steward. When Cole was brought to Andrews' quarters and confronted by the angry Denny, he "denied the whole," although both Sayres and another witness insisted that the story had originated with him. The frustrated Andrews said that had he the strength, he would punish Cole "on the spot for his insolence in denying what he knew he had stated to him [*Andrews*] before." And why, Andrews wondered afterward, had he allowed Denny, a lower-ranking officer, to behave in so overbearing a manner? He should have deprived Denny of his sword "for attempting to degrade his superior officer in the eyes of his own company."

After the confrontation between Denny and Andrews on September 5, a handful of officers and an assortment of soldiers of lower rank provided fragments of gossip, rumor, and firsthand evidence of Andrews' behavior during the summer and on earlier occasions at other posts. Lieutenant Platt R. Green, adjutant of the regiment, drew up charges and specifications for a court martial. Neglect of duty, lying, conduct unbecoming an officer, drunkenness on duty, association in a familiar way harmful to discipline and contrary to the deportment of a gentleman with enlisted men and noncommissioned officers — the charges ran on. They were serious enough to forward to army headquarters and to cause Andrews' arrest.[28]

He was ordered out of his quarters and sent under arrest to a small dwelling near the army sawmill at the Falls of St. Anthony, some ten miles north of the fort. His waiter, Sayres, left him at the end of October, and Private John W. Stone took his place. The orders for Andrews' trial by court martial were issued late in October by Major General Winfield Scott at Louisville, Kentucky. Court was to be convened at Fort Snelling as soon as Colonel Snelling could arrange matters.[29]

For Andrews, it was a long, cold, lonely winter. Not until February 8, 1826, did court convene in Colonel Snelling's office. For his court martial duties Lieutenant William E. Cruger, special judge advocate, was issued 12 quires of paper, 50 quills, 50 wafers of ink, six ounces of paper, and half a cartridge of sealing wax. Colonel Snelling was president of the panel; Lieutenant Green read the charges. For four days 12 witnesses gave testimony about Andrews and answered questions put by him in his own defense. Another witness, Corporal Alexis Leger, appeared in court "in a state of intoxication" on February 10 and 11 and was unable to testify. "For the want of other witnesses who were absent from the post," court was recessed on February 11. The trial was expected to resume on the arrival of the witnesses, the coming of spring, and the opening of river transportation. Until then Andrews would remain confined to the small house at the falls.[30]

There he stayed until May, when Lieutenant McIlvaine arrived from Fort Crawford with "a platoon of witnesses and a greenbag of charges

9

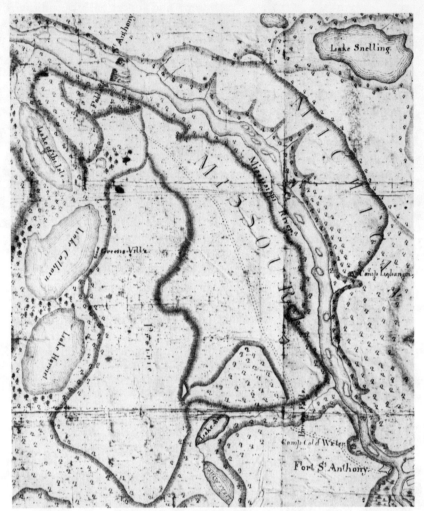

Topographical view of the site of Fort St. Anthony, later Fort Snelling, on the border between Michigan and Missouri territories, about 1823. *MHS*

and specifications" to add fresh fire to the trial. Snelling reconvened the court on May 3. When that day at last arrived, Andrews appeared to be very sick. Lying in his bed at the falls and "groaning," he wondered how he would be able to cross swollen Minnehaha Creek to go to the fort. He told his waiter, Private Stone, that he wanted to attend the trial if he could manage it. Stone did not think it advisable for Andrews to attempt the journey. The spring runoff after the unusually severe winter had earlier raised the waters of the Mississippi 20 feet or more above normal; the creek was still reported to be impassable, and no canoe or boat was available to ferry the lieutenant over.[31]

When Andrews did not appear, court was adjourned until the following morning. Colonel Snelling ordered Dr. Edwin James, on tem-

10

porary duty at the post, to visit Andrews and report on his condition. James swam his horse across the creek, got thoroughly wet, and reported to the court that Andrews had declined to appear "on account of ill health." What was the nature of Andrews' indisposition? "Debility," said James. And the cause of the debility? "I think it must have resulted from intemperance," answered the doctor. Snelling then ordered either Dr. Harney or Dr. Robert Wood, assistant surgeon at the post, to visit Andrews daily. They were to report in writing the state of his health and their judgment of his ability to attend court. The lieutenant was to be removed from the house at the falls to the garrison as soon as a room could be prepared for him.[32]

Andrews attended court on May 4, but he was in poor shape. For the first time he was confronted by Lieutenant McIlvaine in his self-assumed role as prosecutor. The session was quickly adjourned, however, for the court decided that "the prisoner[']s state of debility was such as to render him unable to remain." McIlvaine said Andrews was intoxicated, no more no less. As a result of the events of May 3 and 4, additional charges and specifications were preferred against Andrews to which the prisoner pleaded "general illness." The court met May 11 and on four more days that month.[33]

Outside the courtroom some of the witnesses were having their own difficulties. Lieutenant Allanson was placed under arrest. Lieutenant Denny was arrested and confined to his quarters. Sayres, Andrews' former waiter, was arrested for drunkenness, tried, found guilty, and sentenced to solitary confinement on bread and water. Gossip about the Andrews case traveled unchecked around the post. Two of the guards on the "Putnam," who had come upriver with McIlvaine, conversed about the court martial. Sergeant Burns, it was said, had bragged that he "put Lieut. McIlvaine up to a dozen things" against Andrews that McIlvaine had not known before; Burns denied having done so. McIlvaine, too, discussed the trial out of court. He warned Sergeant Bailly not to let himself be "pumped" by men of the garrison about his testimony.[34]

Toward the end of May both Andrews and McIlvaine requested more witnesses to support their positions. Andrews asked that Thomas Stewart, one of the guards on the "Putnam," and 12 other witnesses be summoned to testify. Among other requests, Andrews also wanted, as essential evidence, the Fort Crawford orderly book for 1825; the detail book or a certified copy "bearing Col. Morgan[']s signature," which listed the detailing of men for daily duty; and the regimental orders (or copies of them) from August 30 to September 5, 1825, "in order to prove whether I was for duty or not during that period, and also the date of my first reporting sick."[35]

The court considered Andrews' letter and granted only his first request — to call Thomas Stewart from Fort Armstrong. It also agreed to let Prosecutor McIlvaine summon several civilians employed at Fort Crawford. At the end of May it adjourned temporarily.

About June 8 Andrews went aboard the steamboat "Eclipse" at the

Fort Snelling landing. His actions that evening provided fuel for further damning charges against him. Captain Clark, Lieutenant Baxley, and Camp saw Andrews on the boat. All described his behavior.[36]

When Clark went on board, he found Andrews talking to the boat's captain about buying butter. Andrews' "articulation" and his "difference in walking" indicated to Clark that the lieutenant was intoxicated. Clark observed this behavior "with deep regret," both on Andrews' account and because it "might reflect dishonor or discredit to the Army." Did Clark think the captain of the "Eclipse" noticed that Andrews was drunk? "I can't say," Clark replied, "for I thought him intoxicated also."

Lieutenant Baxley went aboard the "Eclipse" to make some purchases at about the same time. Andrews was conversing with the captain in his cabin, and turned to talk to Baxley about butter, the voyage, and such matters. Baxley thought Andrews was "very much affected by liquor." After half an hour in the same room with him, Baxley said, "my opinion was strengthened." Andrews seemed "too much affected by liquor to do business of any kind." His "gestures, hiccuping, manners, conversation and appearances" all indicated drunkenness to Baxley, who had remarked to the clerk of the "Eclipse" that Andrews was "not a specimen of the Gentlemen on the hill."

Camp, too, went aboard the "Eclipse," where he saw Andrews and thought him intoxicated. After leaving the boat, the two walked up the hill to the lower entrance of the commissary and climbed the steps. Camp said Andrews staggered "considerably" on the way. Andrews countered by saying that *his own* friendly arm had saved *Camp* in that gentleman's "windings through the worse than Cretan Labyrinth of the commissary's store." As a result of these reports, McIlvaine quickly added more charges to the case against Andrews, alleging that he was "in such a state of intoxication as to be a disgrace to the Army of the United States and the Regiment to which he belonged." To the new charges Andrews pleaded "general illness."

A week after the incident on the "Eclipse" Dr. Wood reported to Colonel Snelling that Andrews' whisky allowance must be stopped, or he would never recover. The commissary officer and the sutler were directed to sell Andrews no more liquor. Cut off from alcohol and from human society, Andrews must indeed have felt abandoned.[37]

AT THIS POINT fate intervened in the person of Lieutenant Nathaniel S. Harris, who publicly and voluntarily assumed responsibility for Andrews' defense. As Andrews said in his official defense, the court — and surely the regiment — knew that "untill Lieut. Harris tendered his assistance on my trial, the labour of conducting it fell solely upon myself, and that no other [help], save what intelligence could be found in the ranks[,] was at my command." Now Harris attempted to salvage something from the wreck.[38]

Harris was barely 20 years old, the youngest officer at Fort Snelling, and on his first assignment after graduating from West Point less than a year before. The son of a Presbyterian clergyman, Harris was said to be related to one of the "most respectable" families of New Jersey. He left West Point with a creditable if not brilliant record, and was well schooled in the classics, in military law, the obligations and duties of a soldier, the dignity of man, and the mission of the army. At Fort Snelling he had already performed a number of unpleasant tasks. He had made winter trips to Traverse des Sioux and to Prairie du Chien. On the orders of Colonel Snelling he had seized a supply of illegal whisky from Alexis Bailly, a local fur trader. He had been ordered to reorganize the post library, left in chaos by Lieutenant Allanson.[39]

There is reason to suppose that Harris had interested himself in the Andrews case about a month earlier, and that he had suggested some strategic moves to help the lieutenant in his defense. His sympathy was undoubtedly genuine; he thought Andrews had been unfairly treated, and he saw the wretched lieutenant as more sinned against than sinner. Yet with all Harris' good will, intelligence, and dedication, the task he assumed was formidable. Lieutenant McIlvaine observed that for Harris to attempt "in defiance of publick opinion to patch the ragged reputation of his client . . . was an effort as hopeless as singly to pump a ship with half her bottom shot out and which the very rats have deserted."[40]

As Harris prepared for the last days of Andrews' trial, he studied the record page by page and conferred with the accused. From his well-stocked mind or from reference books probably in the post library, with which he was by now intimately familiar, Harris found literary allusions, bits of Latin, and snatches of poetry to dignify and embellish the defense. Thus prepared, Harris was at Andrews' side when the court reconvened in Snelling's quarters on July 24.[41]

The defense called 14 witnesses. Some offered new evidence; others were cross-examined on previous testimony. Colonel Snelling admitted that it was usual for officers to "avail themselves," when ill, of the attention and services of enlisted men. He said that no censure was attached to the practice. Private Thomas Stewart, whom the defense had hoped would clarify some of the events that occurred on board the "Putnam," gave Andrews little comfort. A member of the guard, he was asleep in his cabin, he said, when the prisoner Westernra escaped. While he had little to say about the escape, Stewart's testimony on other points tended to support that of the other guards and to cast doubt on Andrews' sobriety that night.[42]

The defense questioned the credibility of two former witnesses, Sergeants William Burns and Charles Smith. Captain Hamilton took the stand to say that Burns had served in his command between 1812 and 1814 and appeared to be a "perfectly correct and upright man." When it was made known that Burns had enlisted in the army under two different names, he was recalled. He said that he had joined while under age without the knowledge of his parents. When he re-enlisted, he used his full and proper name.[43]

The veracity of Sergeant Smith, who had testified that he saw Andrews stagger while on duty at Fort Crawford, was then called in question. Another sergeant told the court that Smith had said "he did not believe one word contained between the lids of the bible." Called to speak for himself, Smith was asked to say whether he believed "in God, the obligation of an oath, and a future state of rewards and punishments." Smith said he did. Was he a Roman Catholic? No, said Smith. Was it not true that he considered himself "relieved from the obligation of an oath if the ceremony of kissing the cross be neglected in its administration"? Smith said, "No, I do not."

There was little more to be said that had not already been spoken and transcribed into the official record, now numbering 121 pages. Court was adjourned July 26, to meet again on August 2. Andrews and Harris had a week to prepare the prisoner's final defense.[44]

In the interval before the court convened again relations between Colonel Snelling and some of his junior officers came to a boil and the fearless young Lieutenant Harris, while preparing Andrews' defense, took on another unpleasant duty for a friend. The immediate cause of trouble was the commanding officer's high-handed assignment of a waiter from Lieutenant David Hunter's company to Lieutenant Baxley, without notifying Hunter — an action contrary to military regulations.[45]

Hunter, Harris' friend, and others at the fort had heard Colonel Snelling say that if officers were dissatisfied with the way he conducted his command, he was at all times ready to give them personal satisfaction. In other words, contrary to military law, he would accept a challenge to a duel. Snelling's behavior in the Baxley affair was only one of a series of actions Hunter found so reprehensible that they "would make the Blood of a Slave Boil." At the boiling point, Hunter took Colonel Snelling at his word and, in a private letter that he entrusted to Lieutenant Harris, challenged him to a duel. Harris delivered the letter to the colonel at the end of July.

Snelling ignored the challenge but showed his extreme displeasure with Hunter by confining him to his quarters under arrest. When it was clear that there would be no duel Hunter requested a court martial. Since he had violated military regulations in challenging the colonel to a duel, he would be tried on those grounds. Hunter hoped that in a court martial "good might Result from having the machinations of our Colonel in some Small Measure Exposed." So the pot simmered a few more days before it boiled over again.

On the morning of August 2 Harris again stood before Colonel Snelling and the court to read some 70 hand-written folio pages without interruption. The defense statement opened with allusions to Andrews' previously unstained record in the army, recalling his enrollment in the rank and file as a man of humble but honorable station who rose "unaided by the kind offices of the great; uncheered by the smiles of the principal." Harris noted that somehow the lieutenant had "excited the displeasure and roused the vindictive passion" of fellow officers. His accusers, instead of remaining silent until the court established his guilt or innocence, had spread poisonous talk about him until even the "antidote of an acquittal" would not bring back the friendship and sympathy he had lost.[46]

Colonel Josiah Snelling. *MHS*

In several general statements the defense quoted the military "doctrine of trials" concerning what constituted the best evidence. For
example, in support of allegations that Andrews had neglected his duty,
the prosecution should have presented orders and duty rosters. In the
matter of his supposed drinking and playing cards with enlisted men in
his quarters, the men were there, the cards were there, the liquor was
there, but evidence of their presence in the room was not proof of their
misuse or abuse.

As to the noncommissioned officers — Burns, Bailly, Smith, and
others — the defense analyzed their evidence. Harris maintained that
Sergeant Smith, despite his protestations, was "loose" in his beliefs. Sergeant Bailly had said he thought Andrews incapable of performing his
duties at Fort Crawford. Should his testimony on this point be accepted?
If the testimony of noncommissioned officers on their officers' abilities
were allowed to stand, said Harris, "the commissions of one half the officers of the regiment" would be in jeopardy. Furthermore, if neither
Lieutenant Colonel Morgan nor Lieutenant Baxley were willing to
accuse Andrews of being intoxicated on duty, why should the court believe Bailly? The testimony of the guards on the steamboat "Putnam"
was flawed because they dared not admit what orders Andrews had
given them. To acknowledge their duties would be to admit their dere-
lictions. They remembered only what was damaging to Andrews, drawing inferences unfounded in fact, seeing what could not be seen on a
dark night, and hearing what at a distance could not be heard.

The defense then took up the credibility of seven officers who had

participated in the trial, pointing out that at least three of them —
Allanson, Baxley, and Green — as well as ex-officer and civilian Camp
might themselves have been intemperate. Was Allanson sober when he
identified legs on a bed without seeing the body to which they were
attached? Green, who had lodged the original charges against Andrews
(it was presumed, to be sure, less on his own account than at the request
of other officers), was described as a man of "rubicund visage." It was
shameful, said Harris, that an accusation of intoxication should have
come from one with his alcoholic tendencies. As for Camp, it was
Andrews, the defense reminded the court, who had kept Camp from
falling on the commissary steps after the two left the "Eclipse." Of the
doctors who attended Andrews, Harney's prejudices were notorious. He
visited Andrews already convinced of what he would find, and he was
unwilling to be persuaded otherwise.

Baxley's testimony was equivocal in most respects, said the defense.
Although Baxley said that Andrews drank more than any other officer
at Fort Crawford, he himself had been known to drink excessively. He
had told the court Andrews was drunk on board the "Eclipse"; the defense recalled a time not far gone when Baxley, weaving across the snow
to his quarters, had come upon what he took to be three enlisted men
in threatening poses. Harris likened Baxley to the "knight of the rueful
countenance," Don Quixote, whose supposed giants became windmills:
in the pale dawn, Baxley had discovered that his foes were merely
wooden posts.

The defense was ambivalent about Lieutenant Denny, characterizing him as an honorable man of "unimpeachable" character who had
been misled by gossip. Harris chided him for uncharitable, discourteous,
and unkind behavior toward Andrews. His angry demands that the sick
man reveal the tale-telling man's name were contrary to the military
obligation of officers to "conduct, direct and protect inferiors of every
rank." Denny, in his better moments, should feel regret and embarrass-
ment for insulting Andrews in the presence of enlisted men. Only youth
and inexperience excused his behavior, said the young Harris.

More kindly words were reserved for Captain Clark, who had testified "with deep regret" about Andrews' actions on the "Eclipse." His
statement, the defense gratefully acknowledged, was the only public
manifestation of sympathy offered to Andrews during the 12 months of
his incarceration and trial.

Finally the defense trained its biggest guns on Lieutenant McIlvaine.
Without that officer's additional charges and specifications, and without
his active prosecution of the case, the trial would have ended months
before. Indeed, it might not have occurred at all. No sooner had one
charge been answered, the defense said, than McIlvaine introduced
more charges and permutations of charges. The Andrews case was like
Hydra, that many-headed monster of mythology; for every head cut off,
two new ones grew.

The defense attacked McIlvaine in bitter terms as a malicious man
intent on destroying Andrews' career, characterizing him as a self-

appointed Hercules, a soldier with no other "prediliction for the service than a *sordid attachment* to its pay and emoluments," and an officer who had a "grovelling appetite for the peccadilloes" of others. Testimony against Andrews was hardly credible coming from one so corrupt, proclaimed Harris.

It was equally insupportable to persecute Andrews for the "vice of drunkenness" when men all around him were similarly guilty — McIlvaine himself, for example. Why did he limp? "We both have that imperfection in our gait," said Andrews' defense. "The cause of mine I am proud to say, I have with me from the plains of Chippewa," while McIlvaine's "resulted from the eager and rather too precipitate descent of this hill, in quest of egg-nog." In other words, McIlvaine limped because he had broken his leg while searching for liquor. A SOLDIER "DISGUISED"

By this time the strategy of the defense was becoming apparent. Andrews and Harris were speaking not solely to the small group of officers in Snelling's quarters, but to the outside world, especially to Washington, D.C., where a final decision in the case would be made. The judge advocate general of the army would see the transcript, and the president himself would affirm or deny the court's decision. Moreover Harris had in mind an even wider audience, for he planned to release a copy of Andrews' defense to the press.[47]

McIlvaine, who was also much aware of the larger world and higher powers, could not allow the defense to go unanswered. He requested and was granted three days to prepare a "replication." In his 20-page reply, delivered August 5, 1826, he assailed Harris and Andrews as bitterly as the defense had attacked him. The counsel for the defense, McIlvaine said, had delivered a long harangue, graced with all the flowers of rhetoric, in a "nasal twang" at times reminiscent of "the cant of a strolling Methodist preacher, or of the drone of a bagpipe." Had Harris forgotten, as he lectured the court on higher points of military law, asked McIlvaine, that the members of the court were in the army when he was "muling and puking in his nurse's arms?" Equally distasteful to McIlvaine were the attempts of Harris, that "pretty person," to impress heaven in his "precious, preposterous production" with scraps of Latin and poetry. Far from evidence of erudition, the rattling quotations were merely "pilfered from a common place book of reference."[48]

Beneath McIlvaine's distaste for Harris lay more than hard words and "dog Latin." Drawing a clear distinction between himself, a man of years and practical experience, and an upstart new to the service but full of book learning, McIlvaine attempted to "strip the cackling daw of his borrowed plumes." Harris should have tarried at home until his beard had grown. Reaching out to the nation's taxpayers and to old army men who had never benefited from a West Point education, the prosecutor asserted that it had "cost the good people of the United States more than two thousand dollars to teach" such a one as Harris. It was to be hoped that riper years would correct his follies and that ultimately he would prove to be no discredit to his country and his family, McIlvaine intoned piously.

McIlvaine, having thus discredited Andrews' defender, now turned to the testimony offered at the trial. More than enough had been said, in his opinion, to show unequivocally that the prisoner was unfit for his situation in the army. While it was true, McIlvaine said, that the enlisted men who testified against Andrews were, like Andrews himself, of humble origin, they were by contrast above reproach in character. If Stewart, the guard, offered ambiguous or conflicting testimony, it was only because he was "confounded and perplexed" by the "piebald jargon" of Harris. Burns, in particular, was warmly supported. When Burns said that Andrews was "highly intoxicated," what he meant to say was "beastly drunk." When Burns had used two names, he was no more guilty than Andrews, who "When he was barkeeper in Newgate [prison] . . . spelled both his christian names otherwise than he does at present," said the prosecutor.

McIlvaine admitted that he had not been able to substantiate some of his charges. Civilians beyond the reach of military law had refused to travel to the fort to testify. Other witnesses should have been able to prove (but did not) that Andrews played cards and drank in his room with men from the ranks. McIlvaine suspected that they had been suborned.

Nevertheless, when all was said and done, McIlvaine concluded, Andrews was guilty of the "vice" of drunkenness. "Hernia" and "debility" were an unacceptable "convenient cloak" for that vice. Nor could the excuse be accepted that Andrews was in any measure less guilty because others drank. He could not escape blame by thrusting himself into the crowd, for in so doing he was drawing down censure on the whole regiment, said McIlvaine. Were Andrews to be acquitted, the prosecutor promised, in a final extraordinary burst of rhetoric aimed at his Washington audience, "henceforward I will write rogue to my name, walk the streets of the capital with a haltar [sic] round my neck and think it no disgrace."

After McIlvaine completed his replication, the defense asked permission to make a rejoinder. The request was denied and court was adjourned on August 5, 1826, to meet once more two days later to announce its decision in the case of Lieutenant Andrews.

In those two days the Fort Snelling pot boiled over again, and there followed one of the strangest episodes in the long Andrews affair.[49]

It began after court adjourned. Lieutenant Hunter, under arrest and confined to his quarters, had heard what transpired in court that day. He saw William Joseph Snelling, the colonel's 22-year-old son by his first marriage, passing by and called him into his rooms. Snelling, whose father "adored" him, was a civilian; he had been dismissed from West Point for some breach of discipline; he, too, suffered from intemperance. His position in the Andrews affair is unclear, but he may have been a witness against Andrews in the charge of drunkenness on duty: Harris said "the evidence touches only on that [testimony] of Snelling, a guard." If the younger Snelling gave testimony at the court martial, it must have been expunged, since none appears in the record. But somewhere, either in court or out, he had said something about Andrews that Hunter found highly objectionable. Hunter accused the colonel's son of lying. He was making this opinion clear to Snelling when Harris walked into the room. Harris agreed with Hunter; he, too, thought Snelling had lied. Angry and insulted, Snelling immediately went to report the incident to his father.

A few minutes later the hot-tempered colonel, the events of the day fresh in mind, stormed into the office of Lieutenant Baxley, the acting post adjutant, and told him to summon Harris to the messroom. Nothing was said about Hunter. Someone, sensing trouble, quickly called Captain Clark, a kindly, even-tempered man who might perhaps prevent further difficulty. Reaching the messroom, Clark, Baxley, and at least one enlisted man heard much of the conversation between the angry colonel and his subaltern.

Baxley and Clark later agreed that the colonel spoke with "some degree of warmth" about Harris' conduct toward his son. The colonel had the impression that it was Harris who had called the younger Snelling into Hunter's quarters. Harris insisted that he had found Snelling already there and had only agreed with what Hunter said. The colonel then criticized Harris personally. The lieutenant was no gentleman; he lied; his oath was worth nothing before the court. Snelling also made a sarcastic remark about Harris' youth. The lieutenant thought he heard the colonel say "the beard had scarcely sprouted" on Harris' chin, a remark reminiscent of one made by McIlvaine in court earlier that day. Among other harsh words, Snelling may have called Harris "stupid" and a "blockhead."

Harris asked Snelling if his words were to be interpreted as coming from the commanding officer or an individual. Snelling ordered Baxley to arrest Harris, and, in answer to the question, said that Harris could interpret the remarks any way he pleased. Resigned to his arrest, Harris started out the door. Snelling then had second thoughts; Harris was not "worth arresting" after all, or he was "too mean for an arrest." Snelling told Baxley to release Harris and say that "if Harris felt himself offended he might take such measures as he pleased, or words to that effect." Officers Clark and Baxley agreed that Harris had gone to the messroom obedient to command and had acted properly toward his commanding officer, while the colonel's manner was "*marked* with violence and menace," said Clark. For the moment Harris did nothing.

On August 7 the court martial rendered its verdict. Of all the original charges regarding Andrews' conduct at Fort Snelling while he lay sick during August and September, 1825, he was judged not guilty. Of the charges rising out of his drunkenness in court, in his quarters, and on the "Eclipse," and his failure to appear in court, he was judged guilty but "with no criminal intent." But at Fort Crawford and on the steamboat "Putnam," while guilt was not proven in each specification, his behavior was sufficiently damning in the eyes of the court to warrant a

19

final verdict of guilty. Andrews was sentenced to dismissal from the army, but in a compassionate gesture, the court postponed his final separation until the following spring.

Harris' subsequent actions were undoubtedly influenced by disappointment at the decision against Andrews and outrage at Colonel Snelling's behavior toward himself and Lieutenant Hunter. If Andrews were not to be dismissed until spring, and if the colonel's son had lied about him, perhaps another court proceeding could bring to light facts not revealed in the present record. Harris' course was more prudent than that of Lieutenant Hunter. He did not challenge the colonel to a duel, but he asked for a court of inquiry into Colonel Snelling's behavior toward him on August 5 when the colonel had used "language of insult and abuse" and had ordered Harris arrested in an "unofficerlike manner." Perhaps Harris felt the braver for knowing that he would soon be beyond the colonel's jurisdiction, for he was under orders to join the Third Infantry Regiment under the command of Colonel Henry Leavenworth, where he was not apt to suffer reprisal for his action. The lieutenant's request was granted, and the order was issued in September. It was not carried out, however, until the following May, too late to be of any help to Andrews.

In the meantime the inspector general, who visited the post in August, observed: "That harmony so desirable at every post & especially so at a frontier one, seems not to prevail here. The Officer in command & some of his jun[io]r officers are at variance. He gives his orders, they obey them, tho' not without some grumbling & questioning of their correctness." So far, the general conceded, there was discipline "as defined in the Book of Regulations." The inspector general did not mention Harris or the Andrews case, but he did discuss Andrews' immediate superior, Captain Hamilton, whom he had observed enough to consider "a confirmed sot." Nevertheless, in an action that deviated greatly from the harsh treatment Andrews had received, Hamilton was commended to leniency because he had a "large & interesting family," was poor and old, and had seen long service.[50]

The transcript of the court-martial proceedings of Phineas Andrews did not reach the Washington office of the judge advocate general until October 2, almost two months after the verdict was read at Fort Snelling. After the document was reviewed in the department, it was forwarded to President John Quincy Adams. His small, neat signature and his brief assent to the verdict are dated November 15, 1826. Phineas Andrews was ordered dismissed from the army. But the decision no longer mattered to Andrews. Three weeks earlier his long ordeal had ended. On October 21, 1826, he died "at the River St. Croix." Was he alone? Was he then "disguised with liquor"? Was his death an accident or the result of illness? Where was he buried? Military documents are silent on these points. There is no record of ceremonies honoring him and no tombstone marked his grave.[51]

In death Andrews suffered yet another indignity at the hands of his superiors. According to military custom and regulation his personal effects should have been sold at the post in the spring six months after his death. An undated "Account of sales of the effects of Lt. P. Andrews" in Colonel Snelling's journal records the items sold, the prices paid, and the names of the buyers. Sergeant Adams bought an old sash, one old pack, one striped cotton coat and overalls, two cotton shirts, one brass candlestick, one broken "bake" kettle, one gridiron, and two bearskins. Sergeants Adams and Rose together bought an inkstand and six shirts; Rose also acquired a tin kettle. Lieutenant Baxley purchased an old uniform coat and wings, a sword, and a belt. Among other effects sold were an old trunk, a pistol, shoes, vests, clothes brushes, spurs, iron candlesticks, tin pans, a basin bowl, dish, plate, a hand "vice," and "one small bundle of trinkets." A total of $26.79 was realized from the sale, but that amount does not appear in the final settlement of Andrews' account with the army. According to the auditor's report, Andrews died indebted to the government for $33.47. The proceeds from the sale of his effects could very nearly have balanced his account.[52]

Andrews' champion, Lieutenant Harris, remained in the Third Infantry until 1835. For a time he served on the faculty of the military academy. He left the army to study for the ministry in the Protestant Episcopal church. Ordained in 1838, he served churches in Philadelphia and Chester, Pennsylvania, Baltimore, Maryland, and Hoboken, New Jersey, and was secretary and general agent of the domestic missions program of his denomination. In the latter capacity he traveled west once more. His account of the conditions and challenges facing the church in its work among the Indians was evidence in the older man of the forthrightness and compassion the young Harris had revealed in the Andrews case. He died in 1886 at the age of 80.[53]

At Fort Snelling in 1827 time was running out for Colonel Snelling. Officials in Washington could no longer ignore what Harris, Hunter, and other young officers of his command were saying about him. In October, 1827, the quartermaster officer at the fort wrote to his superior in Washington that Snelling refused to account for many supplies that may have been lost or diverted to improper uses. It was said that "not three officers in Snelling's regiment entertain a good opinion" of him. It was well known that he permitted a number of duels to be fought. Furthermore, he had taken for "Safe Keeping" and never returned large sums of money from men of the regiment.[54]

Lieutenant Hunter said that Snelling did not reward regular habits and attention to duty but gave his approval to those who were most ready to drink with him, to laugh at his "Obscene tales and Stale Jests." He implied that Snelling, too, drank more than he should have. Sergeant Adams' wife, who was a servant in the Snelling home, spoke of the colonel's deplorable "convivial" spells, and one historian has said that Snelling's death may have been hastened "by habits of intemperance." Did the colonel, then, bear some responsibility for implicitly, if not explicitly, encouraging such officers in his command as Andrews to indulge too freely in alcohol?[55]

Events of Snelling's last days at the fort suggest that at this point in his career he was in no position to censure others. On September 10, 1827, contrary to military law, Snelling accepted the challenge of Lieutenant Baxley to a duel. While he was willing to waive any privilege of rank, the colonel would not agree to a reconciliation or shaking of hands, saying, "When I think a man is a rascal I never take his hand." On or about September 14, when the combatants met on the dueling field, Snelling (according to testimony later given by Hunter) was "in such a beastly state of intoxication as to be unable to hold or direct a pistol properly." In fact, said Hunter, during the whole month of September the colonel was "so habitually drunk . . . as to be unable to perform his duties."[56]

Early in October Snelling left the fort honored with his name for the last time — burdened with debts, his command in disarray, his younger officers near mutiny. He traveled downriver to St. Louis, where evidence in the court martial of Hunter raised grave questions about his conduct of regimental affairs. He proceeded to Washington where he tried unsuccessfully to settle his accounts. In May, 1828, he was confined to jail for non-payment of debts. Other serious charges against him, filed the previous November by three junior officers of his command, finally reached Washington in mid-summer. The court martial that would undoubtedly have resulted was never held. Snelling died in Washington at the end of August, 1828, and was given an honorable burial in the Congressional Cemetery.

2

Truth Teller
at
Lake Constance

*A Swedish-American Reformer
Publishes a Controversial Newspaper and
Tries to Found a Utopian Colony
in Wright County, Minnesota*

H OW PLEASANT it was on the shore of the little lake in Wright County, Minnesota, on the spring day in April, 1856, when Frans Herman Widstrand took possession of his new land! The lake, which he named Constance (some said in memory of a lost love), covered some 163 acres and was nearly triangular in shape, its south side about a mile long. Deeper than 30 feet in places, its waters were full of fish, and in season white water lilies bloomed on its surface.[1]

Widstrand, the first white man to settle beside this lake in Buffalo Township, had carefully chosen a quarter section on the northwest shore for his new home. There grassy hay meadows were intermixed with woodland, and the land gently sloped to the water, not too low, not too steep. Wild flowers bloomed under tall trees. With the help of a hired man, the new owner built a house and a tool shed and cleared land around them. The buildings were sheltered from the north wind and open to the sun; Widstrand hoped someday to trap its rays to fuel a solar engine.

The soil was good; clear water was available in the lake and in a well he dug near his house; and wood was plentiful enough for building purposes and fuel. Widstrand planted fruit trees, bushes, and a garden. After patient cultivation his orchard numbered 150 apple trees, his vineyard three kinds of cultivated grapes. He grew gooseberries, rhubarb, red and black raspberries, currants, strawberries, various grains, and domesticated flowers. In his vegetable garden he raised tomatoes, melons, squash, corn, asparagus, cucumbers, onions, radishes, and beans.

How peaceful it was in those days! No quarreling neighbors. No hogs or cattle or horses or marauding dogs. No unruly children; no "human brutes." Only trees and meadows, clear water, wild flowers, garden, orchard, and vineyard.

Widstrand, the pioneer, lived by Lake Constance in "antediluvian innocence, simplicity and ignorance of fear." He was three and a half miles from the town of Buffalo and seven from Monticello on the Mississippi; yet he was an exile, a condition forced on him by his brother and

23

arising from events of some years earlier in Sweden. Frans Herman Widstrand was the son of Jocob Isaacson Widstrand, a Lutheran clergyman, and his wife Gustava (Annell) Widstrand, the daughter of another clergyman. Frans, the eldest child, was born in Stockholm on October 10, 1824. In later years he attached some mystical significance to the fact that his birth occurred "10 minutes past 10 p.m. on a sunday, and that [was] the 10th day of the 10th month of that remarkable year 1824." In "genealogy," learning, "and everything else" he considered himself not only similar but superior to the renowned mystic scientist and theologian, Emanuel Swedenborg. When Frans was about a year old he became ill with a disease affecting one of his hips; in consequence one leg was left shorter than the other. Only after a long convalescence was he able to walk without crutches.[2]

Frans's parents had two other sons and four daughters; one daughter died in infancy, another at age ten. Until Frans was nine, the family lived in Stockholm, where Jocob was a teacher and then curate of St. Jocob's parish.

In 1835 Jocob was called to a large country parish seven miles from Orebro City. The two elder brothers, Frans and Claes, were educated at the Orebro school, the Strengnais gymnasium, and the University of Uppsala. At home the brothers tutored their sisters until the girls were old enough to go to a private school in Orebro.

When Jocob died suddenly in 1849, he left only a meager estate, which provided little support for his family or for the education of the younger children. Frans, however, was well situated in Stockholm. For several years, Gustava Widstrand kept house for him and her two youngest children, but she and the children later moved to Kungshor, where she bought a small house with a garden.

In 1843 Frans had taken examinations at the University of Uppsala preliminary to studies for a doctorate in philosophy. His courses ranged from classical and modern languages, theology, anthropology, history, geography, various branches of science and mathematics to law, jurisprudence, and political economy. In preparation for a government career he served an apprenticeship in a number of government departments and continued independent study in Stockholm. By 1849 he was employed in a position of responsibility in the Bank of Sweden.[3]

Since the days of his boyhood Widstrand had developed strong democratic sympathies, influenced by his studies and perhaps in part by his father's example (although their religious views were apparently very different). In 1849 Frans joined the first working men's organization in Sweden. He became editor of its weekly paper, *The Demokrat*, and spent his own time and money in promoting the organization. His antimonarchical tendencies were well known. He had read the United States Constitution and on July 4, 1852, which was the birthday of the king of Sweden, he and his friends chose to celebrate instead the American Independence Day.[4]

In those days he lived well. He had "decent company" and took his meals "at the best establishments in Stockholm." Yet he saw little prospect in Sweden of realizing the ideals of the working men's society or of achieving a more democratic government. "Thinking only liberty was needed to make people good and happy," he began planning to emigrate to America, where he would promote those reforms he thought could not be introduced in Sweden. He ignored disquieting hints that America was not so wonderful as he imagined. A book by a former Swedish diplomatic official who had served in the United States described the prevailing morality in America as "horrible." Widstrand could not believe him. More impressive to him was Fredrika Bremer's account of her two years of travel in the New World. Her enthusiastic picture of Minnesota Territory, the "new Scandinavia," undoubtedly influenced Widstrand, despite her words of caution: "Yet seriously, Scandinavians who are well off in the Old Country ought not to leave it."[5]

Widstrand called on Miss Bremer at her rooms on Nerrlands Street in Stockholm to discuss his plan for emigrating. The famous little lady found time to talk to Widstrand, but she was not able to dissuade him from leaving Sweden.

It was true that Frans was well situated at home, but other members of his family were not. The thought that his brothers and sisters would find greater opportunities in America under his guardianship provided practical as well as ideological reasons for emigrating. Because his brother Claes had been in some kind of difficulty at home, Widstrand arranged for him to go first. He entrusted Claes, 27, with funds from their father's estate to invest for the minor children and other money to buy land for Frans. Claes sailed on the brig "Ellida" on a 35-day voyage from Hamburg to New York. He reached St. Paul in June, 1854, carrying with him three letters of introduction from Miss Bremer to Minnesotans she had met on her visit. Claes, a talented musician, found work as an organist and piano teacher in St. Paul and in 1855 moved to St. Anthony where he served as an organist for several churches. He became a teacher and piano tuner and, later, a bookkeeper for a business firm. He is said to have been one of the first Swedes to settle in Minneapolis.[6]

On September 6, 1855, Frans, then 30, sailed for Boston with his sister Emma, 21, and their young brother Carl, 12, who in America became Charles. Left behind were their mother, whom they would not see again, and their younger sister, Ulla, 15, who followed them to the United States 13 years later.

Widstrand remembered vividly his disillusioning experiences in Boston. Shortly after arriving, he saw on a Boston street some "white devils [nearly] knocking out the eye . . . [of] a black man." A second upsetting incident was the sight of "an elegantly dressed woman falling drunk in the street." Widstrand took some "clothes, bed clothes, carpets, etc.," to a freight office in Boston to send on to Minnesota. He never saw them again.

More disheartening experiences awaited him in Minnesota. Claes had not handled the money entrusted to him as Frans would have liked, and the two quarreled. It is not clear in what specific ways Claes disappointed his brother, but the enmity between the two was bitter. Frans claimed that he had been "better than a father" to Claes, but Claes did not agree. When Frans gave him a book of essays on morality to read, Claes burned it in a fit of temper. Their quarrel reached a point where Claes tried to have Frans arrested. Although Frans offered no resistance, the sheriff, after inquiry, refused to make the arrest. Frans blamed Claes for "hypocrisy, deceptions, and other rascalities towards me whom he thought he could maltreat with impunity for my lameness, free thinking and . . . ignorance of the English language &c." Frans considered himself much abused, and the younger brother and sister were reluctantly drawn into the dispute. Charles, who was then Frans's ward, thought that he showed "a relentless and unforgiving disposition" and chose to stay with Claes in Minneapolis during the next few years. Sister Emma lived at times with each of her older brothers.[7]

In Minneapolis Frans had purchased and built a home on two acres of land where Eighth Avenue South now crosses Tenth and Eleventh streets. But Claes's behavior, Frans wrote, "if it did not make me insane, still gave me a horrible shock, depressed me awfully, and took my time for several years, caused me to leave Minneapolis and go out in the wilderness, where I have endured hardships not possible fully to describe and on which I can not think without horror." Widstrand claimed that his exile in Wright County kept him from doing as much good in the world as he would like to have done.

Yet he found many outlets in the pioneer community for his reforming zeal. In 1861 he became a naturalized citizen and thereafter was active in Republican party affairs and at conventions, caucuses, and town meetings. He was elected a justice of the peace, town clerk, and a delegate and secretary of the Wright County Republican convention and was a candidate for the state legislature. When Republicans supported Ignatius Donnelly for election to Congress, Widstrand had some constructive advice for him. Costs of government were far too high, Widstrand told him, and congressmen should lead the way in economizing. A congressman was paid $3,000 a year — far too much. He should be paid, say, $2 a day for time actually employed, with not more than $15 a month contingent expenses, but mileage and other per diem should be paid only for "actual and necessary cost." For these expenses a congressman should be accountable to the district that had elected him. Widstrand convinced the convention to support some of these ideas, but Donnelly did not take them seriously.[8]

Although Widstrand believed the republican form of government was certainly better than a monarchy, he thought it needed improvement. The "social machinery is left in the hands of old tricksters," and the laws were too complicated. In his disillusionment he found them "generally nothing better than the rotten stuff taken from the tottering English monarchy." In America he became "highly disappointed in my expectations," finding as much ignorance and superstition in native-born people as he ever had seen in Sweden.

Life at Lake Constance was not easy for Widstrand and his early-day neighbors. The same forests that gave them building materials covered the land they wanted to farm, and had to be cleared. Constructing roads and bridging the many streams of Wright County was difficult and expensive in comparison to the costs of public improvements on prairie lands. But with few taxpayers in the sparsely settled county, the public budget could provide only a minimum of improvements.[9]

Adding to the difficulties of life in Wright County was a series of disasters — natural and man-made — which caused numerous early settlers to abandon their farms. In 1856 and 1857, grasshoppers devoured the flourishing crops. In the summer of 1862 came more devastating trouble. Wright County settlers heard reports that on August 17 Dakota Indians had killed people in Meeker County and were moving eastward. Realizing their isolated homes made them vulnerable to attack, Widstrand and his neighbors sought safety to the east. Some fled to Fort Snelling, Minneapolis, or St. Paul; others gathered at Monticello and Rockford, where hastily constructed stockades guarded by armed volunteers offered protection closer to their farms. Returning to their homes in September, many settlers found their crops ruined and their buildings vandalized, either by belligerent Indians or by white men who took advantage of their absence. Widstrand discovered that his bedding, clothes, dishes, and tools had been stolen — probably by whites. Although he would not claim for himself damages from the Indians for white men's thefts, he agreed to help his foreign-born neighbors and the families of soldiers away in the Civil War to file such indemnity claims. A second Indian scare caused an even greater exodus the following June, when a band of Indians killed members of the Amos W. Dustin family west of present-day Howard Lake.

Although the Indian scares caused short-term absences for most county residents, many men left for longer periods to fight in the Civil War. Two of the Widstrand brothers, no less patriotic, offered their services to the war effort. Charles enlisted in the Second Company of Minnesota Sharpshooters and was wounded at the battle of Antietam. Frans, barred from the army because of his disabled leg, wrote to Senator Alexander Ramsey in May, 1862, requesting that he be allowed to serve the government in some capacity. As an abolitionist, he said, he wanted the slaves to be free, but he was willing to allow owners some compensation. Whatever the job, he told Ramsey, he would work for the same pay ($13 a month) that army privates received.[10]

Actually, Widstrand's appointment paid considerably more. In November, 1863, he took a position in the second auditor's office of the Treasury Department in Washington, which he held until the end of the war. Earning $1,400 a year, Widstrand — never a liberal spender — was able to save a substantial amount. At first he stayed at the National Hotel, but he soon found cheaper lodging. For 30 cents a day he ate nourishing meals of fresh and preserved fruits — apples, pears, peaches, strawberries, dates, figs — supplemented with nuts, cakes, crackers, and bread.[11]

His devotion to frugal living was not appreciated by his associates, who felt that they were underpaid. When Treasury Department employees asked for an increase in pay, Widstrand refused to sign their petition. He was not willing to ask for higher wages while soldiers fought on the battlefield for much less.

Widstrand's diversions in Washington were varied. He kept in touch with Wright County neighbors and asked them to watch over his farm, repair and replace the fences around his clearing, and plant some crops to keep down the weeds; he even sent them new kinds of seeds. To local men serving in the army, he sent reading matter. During leisure, Widstrand wrote articles for the *Women's Journal*, a Philadelphia publication. He met, and was much impressed by, black leader Frederick Douglass. And with a friend he attended the seances of a medium who was said to have communicated with the spirits of Utopian reformers Étienne Cabet and Robert Owen. The spiritualist vowed that he saw the initials "R O" on Widstrand's forehead, and the spirits of both reformers encouraged Widstrand's idea of founding a Utopian colony.

For years he had read about communitarian experiments and visited a number of them — one of the Shaker colonies, the Oneida colony in New York, the Swedish Jansonist Bishop Hill colony in Illinois, and the Icarian colonies in Iowa and Illinois, which were established by followers of Étienne Cabet, the little-known French Utopian philosopher and author of *Le Voyage en Icarie*. Widstrand believed that Cabet's ideas of a society in which men and women lived in peace and plenty without class distinctions were "better than anything in that line in the english language, better than Plato[']s Republic and More[']s Utopia." Although he did not visit the Amana Society in Iowa, he liked its philosophy and thought it "pretty near what it ought to be economically."[12]

Fruitlands, A. Bronson Alcott's attempt to establish heaven on earth near Harwood, Massachussetts, was another of the Utopian experiments which appealed to Widstrand. He admired the vegetarianism, frugality, and self-sufficiency of the community's members. He understood, too, that "They did not bring any children into this horrible world. They were not hypocrites or deceivers. Their place was beautiful but the soil was poor and they failed financially and the noblest of them lost all." With the Fruitlands and Icarian philosophies guiding him, Widstrand began using the money he saved on his frugal vegetarian diet to promote his own proposed colony. He had hopes of recruiting as many as 400 people, and he was encouraged when more than a dozen government clerks indicated an interest in joining. All would be brought to Lake Constance or some other place where he would persuade Congress to grant land for his Utopia.[13]

In his ideal community, men and women would have equal rights and they would wear the same sort of clothing — a simple costume that he later called a Liberty dress. Disdaining the female clothing then popular, he said that "As long as women wear the dress now generally used it is no wonder that thoughtless persons considered them fit for nothing else than propagation." Rather than reproducing themselves, members of his colony could adopt poor children and soldiers' orphans. Until mankind became fully happy, no other children ought to be brought into the world; there would be no marriages in his colony until that day.

All members of the colony would work for one and one for all; necessary purchases would be made in bulk for a common store. What was produced would be sold for everyone's benefit. Food would be prepared on a large scale for all, with meat served only when other foods were not available. No tobacco or intoxicating drinks would be permitted.

Despite its communitarian aspects, his society would guarantee individual rights and individual privacy. Every person would have two comfortably furnished rooms and opportunities for quiet meditation and study. The society would be governed not by the majority or by might or fraud but by "the rule of right."

The society Widstrand envisioned needed a new name. It was not simply a co-operative, nor was it "communism in the vulgar sense of that word." It was more like Christianity "as on the day of Pentecost," but not like any of the sects "now called Christians, not methodists, baptists, roman catholics, etc." The name he coined to describe his Utopia was "Farist." But for various reasons, Widstrand's plans for his Farist heaven on earth were postponed for more than ten years.

Before leaving Washington, Widstrand discharged his duties as guardian of his brother Charles, who had re-enlisted in the regular army after recovering from his battle injuries. With help from Frans and Representative Donnelly, Charles was assigned as a printer to the surgeon general's office, where he earned $1,200 a year. In 1864, when he reached the "age of discretion" at 21, Charles rejected the brotherly advice of his guardian. Like Claes before him, Charles was unable to meet the high expectations Frans had for his siblings. Frans, on the other hand, found Charles ungrateful for the opportunities he had provided him. The rift that developed between the brothers was never repaired, and the sisters too were eventually alienated from Frans.[14]

Widstrand resigned from his government position in April, 1865, and returned to his home on Lake Constance where he devoted the next decade to farming and politics. The first two years after his return were not good ones for farmers. Spring arrived late in 1866 and 1867 because of unusually wet weather. Rivers and lakes overflowed, roads became impassable, and fields were so waterlogged that many Wright County settlers could not plant crops. Two years of adversity made many destitute. Private collections augmented county funds to aid the needy, but it was difficult to deliver food to them over roads deep in mud. Somehow Widstrand and his neighbors survived this difficult period, and for him, at least, there was hope that the community, if not the weather, could be improved.[15]

Political activities, however, proved to be disillusioning experiences for him. Just before the election on November 8, 1866, Widstrand went to Monticello to speak to the county attorney, Hanford L. Gordon, who was a candidate for the state senate. He found the hot-tempered, controversial Gordon sitting in an office at a table some four or five feet from where Widstrand stood. The two men exchanged heated remarks about

29

political matters. Gordon later claimed that Widstrand "had done something wrong in Electioneering" but would not say anything more about it until after the election. Widstrand later said that he was not sure of his response to Gordon. "I think I shook my hand but not my fist." Whereupon Gordon stood up, hit Widstrand on the nose, and pulled his beard. Widstrand's nose was not broken, but it hurt for some time.[16]

The angry victim then left the room in search of the local justice of the peace. He swore out a warrant for the arrest of the county attorney, charging him with assault "unlawfully, wrongfully and maliciously and with force and violence . . . against the peace and dignity of the State of Minnesota." The justice had the county attorney arrested and tried the same day. After hearing the case the justice concluded that Gordon was guilty of the charges and ordered him to pay costs and a fine of $5.

Gordon did not dispute the facts but announced that, on legal grounds, he would appeal the case to the district court. Apparently neither Widstrand nor the justice of the peace realized what the grounds for appeal would be. Gordon, as county attorney, prepared the notice of appeal and the deputy sheriff, who also served as Gordon's "security recognizance," delivered it to plaintiff Gordon and to Widstrand.

When the case came before District Judge Charles E. Vanderburgh in April, 1867, he cited the law: "In criminal cases tried before a justice of the peace the justice should not proceed to trial without a jury unless the defendant waives a trial by jury." On these grounds he reversed the lower court's decision. Gordon had not asked for a jury trial, but neither had he waived the right to one. And so justice was done in the case of the State of Minnesota v. H. L. Gordon. Gordon, who had won the election, served a term in the senate, while Widstrand was more than ever convinced that the court system was in much need of reform: "The weak, lame, halt, poor and good are robbed, insulted, assaulted, belied, and if they try to 'go to law' they are fleeced in a horrible way."[17]

For Widstrand, worse times were yet to come. Like many of his neighbors he was short of funds and allowed his taxes to become delinquent. A land transaction in which he hoped to exchange 40 acres at Lake Constance for property in nearby Buffalo caused him more trouble. He soon learned that Jackson Taylor, local businessman and Buffalo postmaster, held a lien on the Buffalo property. In the meantime the buyer of his Lake Constance acres resold them before he had paid Widstrand. As a result Widstrand was left without a clear title to either piece of land.[18]

Perhaps it was not surprising that in such frustrating circumstances Widstrand took refuge in his dream of a happier society. Early in 1868 he and six of his neighbors signed a petition to the state legislature. It was a reasonable first step in reviving his idea of a Farist colony, and it expressed the petitioners' belief that there could be no lasting remedy for the "faulty" condition of society without co-operation and "unity of interests." What they wanted was legislation that would give communities or associations founded on the principles of communism the same rights that were bestowed on corporate bodies — rights of perpetual succession, to buy, sell, and hold "all manner of property," and to make laws, to elect officers, and to make and enforce contracts. The muddled *St. Paul Pioneer*, which published their petition, compared the signers to the founders of the "free love" Oneida colony, perhaps because two women were numbered among them.[19]

Nothing seems to have come of the petition, and Widstrand took on other challenges. He was elected secretary of Grange 16, a newly organized branch of the Patrons of Husbandry, and he was one of the first members of the Wright County Agricultural Society established in 1870. When one of his neighbors was cheated by a register in the United States Land Office, Widstrand's letters of complaint on his friend's behalf reached Washington and forced the officer "to disgorge." Widstrand sent other letters far and wide to public officials, to French, Swedish, Norwegian, and English publications, and to newspapers from Boston to St. Louis. He wrote about inequities in the land system, about civil service, tax and language reform, right living, and useless work. Many of his contributions to publications were printed unsigned.[20]

In August, 1869, Widstrand offered himself as a candidate for the position of county register of deeds. He sent a long autobiographical sketch of himself to the *Northern Statesman* (Monticello), suggesting that the paper publish it and similar biographical information about all other candidates for office. The editor of the *Statesman* replied that the register of deeds was only a "second-rate county office" and its candidates were not entitled to so much free publicity. It was not a bad idea, he admitted, but Frans had forgotten to send at least $10 to pay for the advertising space. The *Statesman* could not undertake "to blow each one's horn for him gratis." Widstrand lost the election.[21]

Shortly afterward, the *Statesman* gave him front-page space for a letter on a subject of popular interest to many in the county. Widstrand wrote about a young immigrant from Rockford who got drunk in a Buffalo saloon and died in a ditch on the road home. "Is not the man that sold him the intoxicating drink a murderer?" he asked. He affirmed his support for legislation to prohibit drinking or, better still, for reforms in education and society "that there will be no temptation to do wrong."[22]

During the same year he campaigned for register of deeds, Widstrand was left homeless. On the "wild, desolate and fearful night" of July 9 and 10, 1869, a tornado blew down Widstrand's fences and tool shed and destroyed his crops. Lightning struck his house, and it burned to the ground. Widstrand was at home but miraculously escaped injury. Although his house and furniture were said to be insured for $500, he received only $240 to cover the loss.[23]

To help rebuild, Widstrand hired his neighbor, Olof Nilson, who claimed to be a carpenter. Nilson wanted to buy some land from Widstrand, who agreed to accept the labor as partial payment. But Nilson turned out to be a poor carpenter, or at least one who could not meet Widstrand's standards; he worked only sporadically, doing "more harm than good," and became a constant annoyance to his employer. At the same time, because his tool shed had been destroyed, Widstrand's tools lay out in the open and were stolen.[24]

Somehow, despite these difficulties, the house and tool shed were rebuilt, but because of financial stringency Widstrand again allowed his taxes to become delinquent. Like many other farmers of his day he lost part of his land at a sheriff's sale. It was bought by Thomas A. Perrine, a lawyer and Republican party activist who held office as county superintendent of schools and judge of probate.[25]

Although Perrine was described by the Monticello *Northern Statesman* as a "gentleman of fine scholarly ability," others held him in lower esteem. Like many other men who profiteered on the misfortunes of others, Perrine bought Widstrand's land for a fraction of its value. For this or other sharp practices a fellow Granger at Monticello called him a thief. In 1871 Perrine bought the *Northern Statesman* and changed its name to the *Wright County Times*. During his tenure as "an enterprising publisher and an interesting and able editor," the *Times* was ranked by some as "one of the best county newspapers in the state." In the pages of the *Times*, native-born and educated Perrine treated the scholarly Widstrand with indulgent amusement. Quoting from the Swede's own pronouncements on social and governmental reform, more often than not out of context, Perrine fostered the idea that Widstrand was deranged, idiotic, crazy, or lunatic — but harmless. It was easy for those who knew Widstrand only through the *Times* to believe what Perrine said. Others who met Frans found him a sincere, inoffensive, kindly, and often hospitable man.

After Widstrand's home was rebuilt, he invited refugees from a fire in Chicago to stay with him. It turned out to be a traumatic experience for Widstrand, and perhaps for his guests as well. They were a family of eleven, whose children Widstrand found to be lazy, impudent, and disorderly. He said he had to wait on them. The refugees did not pay for what they were given. They pilfered other things and even replaced the cornhusks he preferred in his mattresses with hay, "the effect of which is felt every night." One of the children died while the refugees were at Lake Constance and was buried in Widstrand's woods. Finally the visitors moved on to a new home in Sherburne County.[26]

In possession of his home again, Widstrand continued his farming and scholarly pursuits. He wrote to the press and to public officials about his ideas, but his letters were often ignored. He began to think that one needed to hold public office in order to be taken seriously as a reformer.[27]

In 1875 Widstrand decided to run for a seat in the United States Senate. The Minnesota legislature, responsible for electing senators at that time, made headline news during the first months of its 1875 session with the political struggle over the choice. Besides Widstrand the candidates included incumbent Alexander Ramsey, Ignatius Donnelly, then a member of the state legislature, Governor Cushman K. Davis, and State Supreme Court Justice Samuel J. R. McMillan. In all, 48 nominees were considered by the legislature for the position during six weeks of voting and political maneuvering.[28]

At the end of January Widstrand went to St. Paul to advance his candidacy. Money for his trip was said to have been provided by Scandinavian friends in the legislature, although the *Times* implied with some skepticism that perhaps the county actually paid since Widstrand had received county welfare funds that year. Widstrand checked in at the Metropolitan Hotel and met with Scandinavian legislators to present his platform. The editor of the *St. Paul Dispatch* interviewed him, and on February 18, the day before the long political struggle was over, the newspaper published a feature about him entitled "Fun in the House."

The day before, said the *Dispatch*, Representative Luther L. Baxter had introduced a communication from Widstrand that the house clerk was instructed to read aloud. Baxter said that his action was motivated by "a spirit of kindness toward the old gentleman who would be pleased with the recognition." On the other hand, Representative John S. Irgens of Wright County objected to the proceedings and wanted it clearly understood that Widstrand was "insane." Another Scandinavian and former editor is said to have told Irgins (as Widstrand remembered the story) that Widstrand had more sense in his little finger "than Ramsey, Donnelly, Davis, and all the other senatorial candidates together." (Widstrand later commented immodestly that the statement "may not be an exaggeration no matter how much or little wisdom [is] in that finger.")

Widstrand's views on the need for frugality in government and daily life were given in detail in the *Dispatch*. Estimating that it cost the state about $4 a minute for a legislative session, Widstrand urged public officials to shorten their talk and to elect a senator who would be satisfied (as all public officials should) to earn $1,000 a year, as long as the majority of the people earned no more. "Why in the name of common sense," Widstrand asked, should the governor or any other official earn $3,800 annually? He also thought that giving the governor $800 for house rent was robbery. "He has good rooms in the Capitol," Widstrand wrote, "and can have a bed there to sleep in." Neither the governor nor any other official should take his wife with him to the capital when serving in public office, Widstrand added. Men who went from Wright County to the logging camps in winter did not take their wives with them, and in fact, the loggers probably did better work when their wives were not around. As for the governor, said Widstrand, he "should buy a barrel of Graham crackers, a barrel of apples, a box of teas, get some corn cakes, and he could have plenty of good food to eat for about ten cents per day, or even if he should eat for twenty cents per day, — and he could probably not eat more, — the food would not cost over $75 a year. The clothes, washing, &c., do not need to cost more than $75 a year. He may have to ride in the street cars occasionally, for say $25 a year. Books may cost $25 a year, and other expenses may be $100-$300."

Widstrand set a good example: his own expenses for food during his five-day stay in St. Paul amounted to $1, with which he bought fruit, crackers, and cakes. It was all he needed, he said, and was more satisfy-

33

ing than if he had been at a table in any of the best hotels. Furthermore, he noted, during that time he had worked as hard as any member of the legislature.

Widstrand also spoke particularly about the need for judicial reform and the importance of having judges who could speak other languages as well as English. He had advocated courts of reconciliation since 1867, and for details of such courts as organized in Denmark, he referred interested persons to page 84 of documents of the United States Department of State, 1868–69, a volume which could be found in the library of the Minnesota Historical Society, "under the Senate Chamber, in the capitol at St. Paul, on a shelf near the door." In such courts of first resort, people involved in disputes would meet together with the judge. Only after the disputants, without witnesses or lawyers, tried to solve their problems would they be permitted access to higher courts.

Samuel J. R. McMillan was chosen United States Senator, and Widstrand returned to Lake Constance, his brief time in the limelight soon gone. Also ignored and forgotten were the many letters he wrote on various subjects. The reformer realized he needed a more effective way of spreading his ideas; he decided to start a newspaper. He did not question the need to continue fighting for reform: "If we do not fight with the word there will be fight with the sword by and by." But it seemed clear to him that fighting for democracy and republican principles alone was not enough. In the "levelling downwards" of humanity, Widstrand observed too many people incompetent to govern or to choose wisely others to govern them. His newspaper would be devoted to raising standards, to excellence, to the achievement of good. He named it the *Agathocrat*, a borrowing from the Greek, which he translated as "government of the good." Government by the people should become "government by *good* people." The *Agathocrat* promoted good education, the abolition of poverty, ignorance, and wickedness, all comprehensive measures that would help to enlarge the population of good people. "GOODNESS MUST BE MADE FASHIONABLE," he wrote, and "Whoever attempts to lower the standard of morality, shoot him down on the spot."[29]

Early in 1876 Widstrand invited a traveling printer to stay with him at Lake Constance. While the printer produced a small Norwegian paper of his own, Widstrand published the first few issues of the *Agathocrat*. By April the printer had left, taking his type and small job press with him. Widstrand put out another issue at Becker, Minnesota, and in the meantime made more permanent arrangements for his publication. He ordered his own supply of type and taught himself how to set it. He made by hand much of the equipment needed for printing — the cases, composing stick, tweezers, shooting stick, bodkin, planer, mallets, reglets, and so on.

He then set his copy in type, locked the type in forms, and inked the forms. His problems in inking the type evenly are evident in the one set of the *Agathocrat* that has survived. Indeed, some lines and sections of pages are almost illegible. Then he printed by laying sheets of paper on the type and rolling over them with a handmade rolling pin — he did not, as the *Times* reported, pound the sheets with the palm of his hand. Once printed, the pages were dried, folded, and wrapped, and the editor-publisher then addressed them. Before daybreak, carrying a satchel stuffed with papers, he walked three and a half miles to the Buffalo post office and put them in the mail. In this way the Lake Constance reformer reached out into the world.

Widstrand was aware that postal regulations defined a newspaper as a "printed publication issued in numbers and published at short intervals of not more than a month"; that it should convey intelligence of passing events, and that "the dissemination of such intelligence must be the prevailing characteristic and purpose of the publication in order to entitle it to pass in the mail at pound rates." The editor planned to publish regularly (first at two-week intervals and later, as money permitted, weekly), and to deal with many newsworthy events. He believed that his publication was a "newspaper of the best kind." It had not entered his mind that others would view it as anything less.[30]

Widstrand printed 80 copies of the first issue and perhaps as many as 400 of some later issues. In 24 issues published between August, 1876, and December, 1877, he estimated that he had printed and distributed a total of 10,000 copies. The newspaper cost from $2 to $3 per issue, a sum spent largely for paper, ink, and postage. Widstrand did not intend to make money; for him the paper was a labor of love and dedication. He sent the paper to individuals in every state and territory of the union and in other areas of North and South America, Asia, Africa, Europe, and Australia. Copies for resale were consigned to Truebner and Company in London. Twenty-five copies went to readers in Buffalo and 33 to Monticello.[31]

He maintained a casual attitude toward subscriptions and advertising as potential sources of income. Readers could subscribe at the rate of 25 cents for six months or 50 cents for a year; the wholesale price was 20 cents for six copies. Those who had no money could send a postcard expressing interest in subscribing and the editor would send the paper, asking the buyers to pay when able. Other newspaper publishers could receive the *Agathocrat* free in exchange for their publications. Seasonal fringe benefits to subscribers were strawberry and rhubarb plants at special prices. As income permitted, the editor promised, he would send subscribers "agathocratic" tracts that he hoped to publish later. The advertising rate was ten cents a line, but only on carefully outlined terms. "Those who have anything useful to advertise," he offered, "should send it for inspection and it will be advertised pay or not."[32]

Widstrand's first issue was eight pages; thereafter the paper comprised only four. In his opinion "A publication should be valued according to the good thoughts in it; not according to its size. People, generally, have no time to read large sheets." Furthermore, he observed from his own experience as printer-writer-editor that "If authors had to set up their articles in type, and were not paid by the line, they would write shorter and nothing useless." When newspapers paid by length for what they published, inevitably they wasted paper and money. "The more intellect a person has got the more simple he can afford to be," he said. And those who wrote at length should remember that "EVERY IDLE WORD MUST BE REPENTED OF AND ATONED FOR. What will then become of the big newspaper editors, the priests, preachers, long speech makers, gossips, big book makers etc?" he wondered.[33]

In paragraphs scattered throughout the *Agathocrat*, Widstrand presented his thoughts about government reform, repeating, revising, and illustrating his proposals as time and space permitted. He defined the best government, as did the Athenian lawgiver Solon, as one wherein the least injury done to the humblest individual is considered an insult to the whole constitution. He proposed a reorganization of the highest government offices, beginning with the president of the United States. In his view no president alone could intelligently perform the duties of his office, so Widstrand proposed a supreme council — a council of quality — to tell him what to do. For election to this council he suggested author Ralph Waldo Emerson; the founder of Fruitlands, A. Bronson Alcott; the feminist leader Lucretia Mott; and other persons of similar stature. He envisioned the council as a service organization selflessly devoted to the public good, somewhat in the manner of the Catholic Sisters of Charity.[34]

Reiterating his views about economy in government, he advocated ceilings on public employees' salaries, keeping government expenditures in line with tax income, and tax reform. He argued that the income tax — the most equitable of all forms of taxation and the least expensive to collect — should be a graduated tax that would exempt all who had incomes of less than $600; for others the tax rate should rise at the rate of 1 per cent for every $500 of income.[35]

His proposals also included those for government insurance to compensate the victims of crime as well as those who suffered from loss by natural disasters such as hail, tornadoes, and grasshoppers; public storehouses to maintain supplies of food for sufferers from crop failure; government ownership of railroads; changes in the way government land was sold; deeds written in simple language; and decentralizing the federal government by moving some departments west and building model cities "therefor." His ideas about civil service reform included preference in public hiring for women and handicapped persons. To aid in the education of the public he proposed that laws, reports, and messages be printed by the government and distributed to everyone at public expense or perhaps with a certain amount of private advertising to defray part of the cost. And repeatedly he advocated the establishment of courts of reconciliation based on the Danish system.

Widstrand's ideas for improving the government postal system included the free delivery of mail to citizens in rural areas as well as in cities (a dream not to be achieved for another generation), with basic low costs for slow mail and higher rates for faster mail. He proposed "Government by Postal Cards," both for voting in elections and to communicate with public officials. "If every decent person sent a postal card to presidents, governors, congress members, legislators, officeholders or other persons, reproving them when doing wrong and telling them what to do, here would be a better state of affairs," he wrote.[36]

Language, especially English, also ranked high on Widstrand's list of needed reforms. Like many other foreigners in America, he felt he had been handicapped, and made to appear ignorant, because he could not "jabber English as natives." He read the language well before emigrating to America, and after 20 years he could write it "like fury," but he still had trouble speaking "the infernal English." He felt that foreigners had difficulty gaining "a proper hearing" and finding work. "It is a great impudence," he once complained to Ignatius Donnelly, "to ask people to learn anything so foolish as the English language." He considered it one of the relics from old England that the American republic should be rid of. It was, he said, "a disgrace to the human intellect, a product of ignorance, mishearings and misunderstandings, a hellish waste of time for children and others." Just to learn to spell it correctly took "more time than needed to raise food." In 1874 he sent Alexander Ramsey a memorial which favored abolishing English and offering a reward for the invention of a better language. When the good senator introduced the memorial in the United States Senate, he said that it came from "a gentleman of learning, and research."[37]

Far superior to English, or for that matter any other language Widstrand knew, was the Vidal language, described by its inventor in a book printed in Paris in 1844. It was a simple, regular language based on a small number of roots with easy grammar and was pronounced as written. In Vidal all words beginning with "b" were the names of animals; all "z" words were reserved for plants. Adjectives were always words of one syllable beginning and ending with consonants, and so on. Widstrand promoted Vidal as a universal language and praised its merits in the *Agathocrat*. Still later, he sent a letter about it to the *Scientific American*, where it was published in 1885.[38]

Central to Widstrand's philosophy of a more rational individual and social life were his proposals for reformed eating habits and diet. From his long experience as a vegetarian, he spelled out the advantages of a basic diet of corn or oatmeal with fruits and vegetables. As he had demonstrated in Washington and St. Paul, one could live adequately at low cost on a vegetarian diet. Fifty pounds of oatmeal or cornmeal, a month's supply, cost $30 or less. "People who are not willing to use cornmeal or middlings instead of fine flour for bread, ought to starve," he wrote, adding that only the simplest cooking was required for cakes made of cornmeal and water.[39]

To raise animals for food was an immense waste of time and money, said Widstrand. Animals required costly fences (and their owners incurred additional costs in lawsuits about the fences); animals trampled the ground, making cultivation of crops more difficult; additional costs in time and money were required to care for the animals, to slaughter them, and to process and cook the meat. Having animals made people brutish and cruel and caused trouble between neighbors. Moreover, "if all had to butcher . . . there would not be so much meat eating." Dining

37

on selected meat like beef and pork was irrational. It was "no worse to
eat rats and dogs than cattle or hogs." Widstrand quoted Benjamin
Franklin in support of his vegetarianism: "You cannot repress a man who
can live on bread and water." Substitute dry cornmeal for the bread, said
Widstrand, it is cheaper and better. And finally, "When the mind is
occupied with noble thoughts, the body does not crave irrational food."

Widstrand's views on religion related closely to his vegetarianism. If,
as he believed, all creatures everywhere were part of one whole, then for
men to damage each other or to kill animals was a great wrong. The
"knowledge of universal solidarity [should] induce all to treat well and
prevent suffering for all human beings as well as for other animals and
all sentient being[s]. This should also prevent eating other animals."[40]

It was evident to Widstrand that Americans — not all Americans, he
conceded, but "the most conspicuous" — had no religion. They were
nominally Christians who devoted much time to church going, church
building, long prayers, and other hypocritical observances, but they
ignored the teachings of Jesus of Nazareth and they did not obey the ten
commandments or live by the golden rule. Through centuries, influenced by stupid greed, wretchedness, irrational creeds, and ignorance,
people had murdered each other either "bodily" or "mentally" in the
name of religion. They had acted far worse "than heathens, slaves,
savages, brutes." In the light of such miserable examples, life seemed at
times hardly worth living.

Yet there was hope that perfection could arise out of imperfection.
"When we consider what human beings — alone or assisted by other
known or unknown, beings — under miserable social organizations, difficulties and obstacles, as well as opposition from others, have discovered
and done with nature, we may justly expect that with co-operation and
its rational consequences and savings as also better kinds of food and
clothes[,] it may be so arranged, that there will be no unpleasant earthquakes or thunderstorms, lightning, tornadoes, epidemic or epizootic
diseases, no failure of crops &c., and no smashing up generally as now
expected; but it must be remembered for that purpose unity, righteousness and knowledge are necessary. Neither must be wanting. The human
army, fighting against nature, if fight there must be, must be so placed,
so arranged, that it does not fight against it self [sic]; that nobody shall
be tempted to hurt another."

Pared down to its essential elements, Widstrand's religion was "Anything that will unite people, [and] make them behave well," and he
defined God as simply "the great final product of evolution or development." Working in harmony with nature, since "every particle of matter
is affected by every other particle, not only on this earth but every-where
else," superior beings might develop, who "have not only will to do
good, . . . but also wisdom and power enough" to prevent suffering.
Until that day "the good must unite to protect each other, prevent the
bad from doing harm and punish them as far as possible, as a warning
to others." Nothing less than right living would put human beings in harmony with this noble vision.

Widstrand's views about women, marriage, and family life were more controversial than almost anything else he promulgated. He had long expressed reservations about marriage — some said because of an early disappointment in love. Whatever his personal experience with women, he staunchly championed their rights and thought it "disgustingly ridiculous" to keep human beings "from doing what good they are able and willing to do, on account of sex." To his way of thinking, women had the same inalienable rights as men (including full voting rights), but those rights were not sufficient to guarantee them equality. Therefore he advocated giving women special preference in public employment but pointed out that greater opportunities awaited women who remained single. If they wished to have children they could get together with other women and adopt them. "Honor to old Maids and Bachelors," he proclaimed.[41]

Those who would marry should be warned that, in the words of an old German proverb, "Marriage tames the Democrat." When a young man who wanted to be a reformer decided to marry, he would find that "hard work, debts, disease, doctor bills, sleepless nights, suffering of wife and children, baby tending, 'nastiness' quarrels, scoldings, fights, desertions . . . lawsuits, divorces, death" would distract him from his noble purposes.

If, in spite of all, people would marry (as the Apostle Paul suggested, it was better to marry than to burn), Widstrand proposed reforms that would minimize harmful results. To marry, people should be at least 35 years old and have been acquainted for five years. They should sign a written marriage contract, give proof that they owned a house, and contribute $200 to the local school fund. Their houses should have single beds and separate rooms for men and women. In a poem about domestic life, he wrote, "Double beds are for the silly / and behoove good people illy." Divorce should be granted without a stated cause and second marriages prohibited. Rape either within or without marriage should be punished by law. The state had a right to adopt laws relating to marriage and to forbid "improper propagation" just as it had the right "to prevent cholera and small pox."

Love, said Widstrand, is "a kind of craziness induced by education or fashion," and marriage generally "only legalized licentiousness or prostitution of women who do not know the consequences of marriage, to the brutal lusts of rude men." While he deplored "sinning without conceiving," far worse, in Widstrand's view, was "the procreation of children by unfit parents." If or when children were conceived, it should be by "only the best looking persons, the most perfect mentally, morally, physically, economically, and in every other respect." This was a child's inalienable right. "Abortions, foeticides, preventions &c, bad and disgusting as they are, are not so horrible as a whole life of misery, suffering, disease, deformity of soul or body."[42]

On a related subject, the *Agathocrat* offered practical suggestions for reform in dress, elaborating on ideas Widstrand had proposed in his Farist colony circular. Woman's lot would be improved if outward dis-

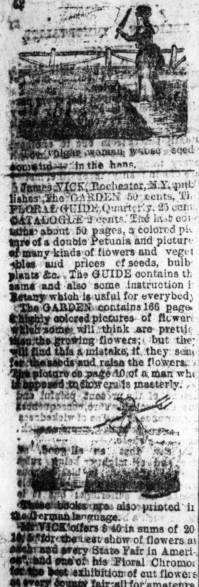

The vulgar woman whose seed come up—in the hens.

James VICK, Rochester, N.Y. publishes The GARDEN 50 cents, The FLORAL GUIDE, Quarterly, 25 cents, CATALOGUE 2 cents. The last contains about 50 pages, a colored picture of a double Petunia and picture of many kinds of flowers and vegetables and prices of seeds, bulbs, plants &c. The GUIDE contains the same and also some instruction in Botany which is usful for everybody. The GARDEN contains 166 pages of highly colored pictures of flowers which some will think are prettier than the growing flowers; but they will find this a mistake, if they send for the seeds and raise the flowers. The picture on page 10 of a man who is opposed to flowers is masterly.

These books are also printed in the German language. Mr. VICK offers $ 40 in sums of 20 &c. for the best show of flowers at each and every State Fair in America, and one of his Floral Chromos for the best exhibition of cut flowers at every county fair, all for amateurs. If you send $1, you may order seeds for $1.10 and get the Guide a year.

The Lady in LIBERTY dress whose seeds come up and grow well.

THE FREE FLAG, weekly, published in Minneapolis, Minn. by J.S. RANKIN, a veteran reformer, $1.50 a year, advocates co-operation. If the people of Minn. had known enough, they would have elected Mr. Rankin to Congress rather than Bill King, E. Wilson and all others; but the people are horribly fooled. By and by they may, however, electricize the foolers.

The Eclectic and PEACEMAKER, monthly, 50 cts, New York, S. LEAVIT also an old reformer, advocating co-peration.

The BATTLE AXE, monthly, 75 cts, Worcester, Mass, well worth reading by all who dare to think.

Mrs Henderson (DOT), St. Louis, has published a cook book which is to aid to abolition of poverty and wickedness. A better one will be published by and by. Send 15 cents to the AGATHOCRAT for that.

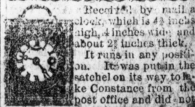

Received by mail a clock, which is 4½ inches high, 4 inches wide and about 2½ inches thick. It runs in any position. It was put in the satchel on its way to Lake Constance from the post office and did not stop. It is made by S.B. JEROME & CO in New Haven, Conn. and on receipt of $2 they will send it by mail and pay the postage. It runs 30 hours and has a detached lever escapement.

From the *Agathocrat*, January 31, 1877. Captions for the illustrations at top read: "The vulgar woman whose seed come up—in the hens" and "The Lady in LIBERTY dress whose seeds come up and grow WELL."

tinctions in dress between men and women were removed. Women should not "ape the dress of the prostitutes in Paris." Instead, he advocated for both men and women a Liberty or neuter dress "made of waterproof cloth, without lining, ravishing or prettiness." For this rational, natural, unisex costume he suggested a four-piece basic pattern — a tunic or blouse that reached to the knees, sleeves, collar, trousers, and possibly a vest on which to fasten the trousers. The advantages, both social and economic, of wearing such a costume were clear to him; he saw no more reason for differences in dress for men and women than for male or female harnesses for horses. In fact, if the dress did not indicate the sex, much temptation would be prevented, for "many men are very weak."[43]

Carried away by enthusiasm, Widstrand went on: "The unnecessary expence and work on dress would soon pay the national debt — and all other debts — and abolish poverty, ignorance and wickedness. One may well say that women's fashionable dress is worse than tobacco and whiskey, causes more sufferings to themselves, to men, children and other animals — birds plucked alive to get their feathers, cruelties of other kinds worse than committed by the worse savages; perpetuates their own slavery and low state."

Widstrand was indebted to Benjamin Franklin for the idea that one should not need to work more than four or five hours a day for clothing, food, or the necessities of life. To work longer in order to make more money to buy unnecessary frills and furbelows was dishonorable. One could live very well with little and honorable work, supply all bodily wants, and have time for cultivating the mind. His long poem, "WORK MADE EASY in a Philosophical Community" published in the *Agathocrat*, celebrated the advantages of working only 20 minutes a day. It was his answer to Sophia Lloyd's poem, "Work Goes Wrong," which portrayed the endless round of housework necessary for a woman to meet the demands of her family. Widstrand planned to publish for 25 cents a small book on "How to Behave," in which he would explain in more detail how one could live well with little work. Work made easy was an important part of his plan for a Farist community at Lake Constance. While he published his newspaper, however, he must have often worked longer hours than his ideal.[44]

Part of the problem lay with his neighbors, the Ryans, Quinns, Kellys, and Nilsons, who made his daily life miserable. Month by month he grew more exasperated with them. Winter was relatively quiet, but even then the neighbors, their children, and their livestock wandered onto Widstrand's land. In the spring and summer their encroachments were nearly intolerable. Nilson, his nearest neighbor and a major offender, lived on the lake directly north of Widstrand's property line. Nilson's "shanty" was too close to Widstrand's house and gardens for comfort.[45]

The neighbors were legally responsible for keeping their stock at home, but to claim indemnity for their encroachments Widstrand had to catch the offending animals, an almost impossible task for a disabled

41

man. Once he tried to have the neighbors arrested for stealing his strawberries, but neither the justice of the peace in Buffalo nor the county
attorney would help him with the legal proceedings. A year later he
went to Monticello to ask for the arrest of neighbor Quinn for attacking
him with a pitchfork. The *Times* reported the encounter with a different slant: "To protect his strawberries, vegetables, &c, against their [*the*
animals'] incursions he [*Widstrand*] keeps a pitchfork with a rope attached to the handle. He wields this highly effective weapon as sailors
use the harpoon — throwing it at the game and drawing it back with the
rope, and is said to have acquired such skill in handling it, that he will
pierce a steer's flank every shot at a distance of several rods. The other
day while on the look out for cattle he was surprised by his neighbor
Quinn who, report says, disarmed the philosopher of his pitchfork and
proceeded to 'put a head on him.' " The county attorney, said the *Times*,
was "not disposed to interfere in the endless war which is waged between the half-crazy Ishmaelite and the 'white savages' by whom he
represents himself to be surrounded." Again the justice of the peace refused to issue a warrant, saying that Widstrand had no witnesses and
Quinn could "swear himself free." Without legal recourse, Widstrand
relieved his frustrations with tongue and pen, which only enraged the
marauding neighbors and provoked more damaging incursions.[46]

Not the least of Widstrand's irritations were the sounds emanating
from the Nilson farm — the swearing, shouting, screaming, crying, and
pounding, the clatter of cowbells, and the noises of sheep, hens, and
other fowl. All of these distracted him from thinking, studying, or writing. He thought the Nilsons very unpleasant and disliked even the sight
of them.[47]

His bitterness came out: "See O. Nilson[']s wife how she looks when
running, almost naked, after cattle in deep water in marshes like one of
the Furiae, and you must think that, if this is civilization, we need something far better. See that man with a dungfork on his shoulder[,] a nasty
pipe in his mouth, nastiness all over, walking through the flower or garden beds — and so many like him! Better, far better, that they [had] never
been born!"

And again: "See the children, girls and boys, promiscuously, nearly
naked, hunting . . . cattle in the woods at dusk or after, and you must
pity both the children and the other animals, if your heart is not of stone.
How would you like to go barefoot and ragged t[h]rough . . . flies,
rain, briars . . . brush, snakes, woodticks and other vermin, and be
whipped if you don't find the cattle; tied to the fence and whipped over
again, and compelled to go on another hunt in the dark, and if you run
away, be brought back to be whipped again?" He added: "Put your self
in their place! No wonder that they are suspicious, treacherous, cruel,
stealing, lying and deceiving."

Ryan's cattle and oxen, Quinn's cattle and sheep, Nilson's bull, cattle,
calves, hogs, and even the cattle of his friend John Varner trampled
Widstrand's garden and meadow. They ran through the strawberry bed,
walked among the radishes and other vegetables, and broke down

fences. The children ran after the animals, threw stones at Widstrand's house and broke windows, damaged his boat and oars, and stole his ripe strawberries and Clinton grapes. They, or someone, tried to set fire to his house, tore down his gate, smashed his front door, and drove an ax into a window frame.

When he was not responding to such harassments, many other duties as farmer, housekeeper, editor, and publisher occupied Widstrand's time at Lake Constance. He wrote numerous articles for his newspaper and long letters to correspondents; he read books, pamphlets, laws, and some 30 exchange newspapers; and he printed his paper and delivered it to the post office. He also sawed wood, washed floors and dishes, baked and cooked (among his lesser activities, since he ate much of his food raw), made and mended clothes and sometimes shoes, repaired doors, windows, roofs, stoves, chairs, and pans, and in the summer worked in his garden. Worst of all was chasing his neighbors' livestock from his property day and night. The neighborhood warfare took its toll of Widstrand. By August, 1877, his weight had gone from 130 to 110 pounds.[48]

Despite unlovely neighbors there were lovely days. Once "good visitors" came to see him; twice friends shortened his long walks to and from Buffalo and Monticello by offering him rides. No doubt other acts of friendship brightened his life, but they remained largely unrecorded, for unfortunately he devoted more space in his paper to his enemies than to his friends.[49]

When Nilson's daughter drove horses into Widstrand's garden one day he threatened to drive them back, but the girl said, "YOU A'N'T ABLE." From this remark Widstrand surmised that the neighbors persecuted him because he was crippled. When the children picked his strawberries and trampled in his garden he heard them call him "son of a bitch" and say that they would come into his house and kill him with a revolver, or they would put a knife through his heart, or if they had a rope they would hang him. Widstrand was a "d--d cripple," said Quinn. Infuriated by what Widstrand had written about them in his newspaper, the Nilson boy shouted down at Widstrand from a hill, "You white pup. . . . First time you put me in the paper again, you are a gone fellow."[50]

It was too bad to have such people so near. "Seeing them is enough to make me sick," Widstrand wrote. "Still, in the unwise order or disorder on this horrible earth, someone has to see them descend to hell to know what they are and describe them, so as to induce others to prevent the existence of such anywhere."[51]

Widstrand did not expect any immediate helpful results from his chronicle of tribulations (the *Times* called them "Lamentations"). He hoped, however, that it would point up the need to reform the judicial system and the property laws that had permitted the sale of his land at ridiculous prices for delinquent taxes and thus allowed Nilson to live so close to him. He promised further details of these matters in a forthcoming book he entitled "The Pioneer's Shanty or Life Among White Savages."[52]

43

During some of the worst days of tribulation Widstrand took refuge in spirit communications, which he reported in his newspaper. In the land of his visions people wore costumes similar to his Liberty dress. The spirits called him Truth Teller, comforted him, and predicted that Perrine would eventually give up his press and type to him. Several guardian angels and a lady spirit protected him and his home. Since they were "not a bit afraid" of his tormentors, the spirits would drive them away.[53]

He took some small comfort, too, in the idea that the people who tormented him would be punished in a terrible way even before they were dead. Widstrand remembered an Old Country custom of nicknaming someone for a crime. Once a boy stole a steer, and for the rest of his life he was known by his deed and everyone despised him. So perhaps "Oar Mike" and "Boat Pat" and "Strawberry Andrew" would be punished in their lifetime for having wronged him.[54]

On April 20, 1877, the *Agathocrat* had become the *Truth Teller*. With his jackknife Widstrand cut a new masthead out of type metal, but despite the new name the appearance of the paper was not materially improved. The press Widstrand had ordered nearly a year before was held in the express office in Delano for want of $25 to pay shipping charges. Still printed by the rolling pin method, the paper was ink-blotched, as if "it were suffering from small pox," said the *Times*. Widstrand had ordered more type, but he needed $18 to pay for it. So far, his income from subscriptions and sales amounted to less than $5, and most of that sum had been used for postage.[55]

Because his gloomy financial condition was made worse by the United States postal service, Widstrand did not publish *Truth Teller* in June. He explained the problem in his July issue. Jackson Taylor, the Buffalo postmaster, who said that Widstrand's paper was "unfit for families," had refused to send for the stamps required to mail the periodicals, and Widstrand was forced to mail from the Monticello post office — twice as far for him to walk. On the day in May that he mailed *Truth Teller* at Monticello, he received a letter from that town's postmaster, who wrote: "In regard to Postage on you[r] Paper I will say that Mr. [Jackson] Taylor Rote to the Department and sent a coppy of your paper to the P.M. General and he desided that it was not a Newspaper and that it coulnot [*could not*] Be sent throu the mails at the pound Rates but must be paid as second clas[s] mat[t]er one cent an ounce and Fracken thereof. yours Respectfully G. W. Gerrish P.M."[56]

Widstrand appealed the decision. He wrote to the postmaster general and sent him ten issues of the paper. He sent letters and a circular about his paper to other editors, to President Rutherford B. Hayes, and to some of his subscribers. By the end of June he had no indication that anyone had received what he sent or was concerned with his problem. There had been no cries of indignation at this blow to freedom of the press.

Neither of the local postmasters, in Widstrand's opinion, was qualified to judge his paper, which he insisted was greatly needed for "guarding families, [and] preserving purity." No one should be a postmaster — or hold any other office, for that matter — who did not know some other language than English "to benefit immigrants," since, "other circumstances being the same, a person who has lived in two countries, must know more than one who has lived in one." Furthermore, said Widstrand, referring no doubt to Gerrish, "It would also look well if postmasters etc could write and spell the english language tolerably well."

In July, as though it were a completely new idea to the department, the postmaster general's office wrote Widstrand asking for sample copies of *Truth Teller*. What, Widstrand wondered, had happened to the copies sent the office in May? Had the local office not forwarded them? To guard against a possible recurrence of the loss, Widstrand sent sets of *Truth Teller* from three different post offices — Buffalo, Monticello, and Delano. All were directed to the acting first assistant postmaster general, the functionary who had written to him most recently. In exasperation *Truth Teller* quoted the publisher of the *Floral Guide*, who said "the postal laws were concocted by a congress of lunatics."

By August 21, the first anniversary of Widstrand's newspaper, only 22 issues had been printed; that no more had been published, Widstrand said, was not his fault but should be blamed on the postmaster general. But Widstrand was not yet ready to surrender, and the dispute with the postal service dragged on through the fall. Whatever the final decision about the rate he should pay for postage, he needed more money. On October 3 he issued number 23 and he told his readers that he was willing to accept any amount from a "cent to millions of dollars or wheat or rags or anything else that can be turned to use."[57]

Far from being discouraged, he enjoyed the coming of autumn and the turning of the leaves. There was yet no frost; in spite of grasshoppers and other human and animal marauders the harvest was abundant, and Widstrand was moved to poetry.

> Hubbard Squash as nice as honey,
> Better than big piles of money;
> Many kinds of rich tomatoes
> And some Early Rose potatoes.

Then he looked ahead to other endeavors that would expand the *Truth Teller*'s mission. He announced that he would give two or more acres of land with a fine view of Lake Constance for a Union Meeting House which would be open to all denominations and parties. Lectures could be held there and "Instruction" given; it would have reading rooms and a library containing the hundreds of newspapers and magazines that he received in exchange for *Truth Teller*. Anything that could be used in any way for the meeting house would be welcome — money, books, lumber, windows, brick, desks, shelves, stoves, lamps, clock, sink, harness, tools, and so on. Some day maybe people would travel to Widstrand's center of learning as to Mecca, and the good people would drive away the bad neighbors, if the spirits had not already done so.

In the meantime, if "nothing prevents," Widstrand would branch out

TRUTH TELLER.

No. 17 ... **1877**

Dedicated to Abolition of Poverty, Ignorance and Wickedness, Advocating Goodness, Education, Justice, Co-operation, Universal Wellbeing.

Lake Constance, (Buffalo P.O.) Wright Co, Minnesota, July 21, 1877. Published twice a month or oftener, 50 cts a year. Frans Herman Widstrand, Editor.

A letter has just arrived from the Postmaster general asking for copies of the TRUTH TELLER; which indicates that he did not get what I sent 22 May, a letter and 19 numbers of the paper. Who took them?

We must form a supreme government of J.B.Alcott, L.M.Child, R.W. Emerson, L.Mott, and others.

Their duty shall be to tell the president and others what to do and not to do; their orders must be followed.

The president travels too much. On his travels he does not learn the opinions of unperverted citizens; they are generally turned out of his way by rascals.

FANNY WRIGHT, when very young, hearing some people tell about another what was not correct, stepped up and corrected them.

How many, old or young have courage or goodness to do so now?

"His very refinement of thought weakens his grasp of practical questions". Not likely. It is that others lack refinement and prevent what is most practical.

It is great need of legislators with ideality, goodness and wisdom who would enable people to go forward, not prevent them as now.

"Purity can not rest beside impurity without resorting to means of purification." M.S.W.

You can not repress a man who can live on bread and water. Franklin

Dry cornmeal is cheaper, better.

Few can comprehend unselfishness - they think a person who has that is crazy, sick; they are so themselves.

"CHILDRENS RIGHTS" will be printed separate, Sent by mail 10 cts.

How infernally ridiculously mean the people of the U.S. appear to decent persons in stealing from and fighting a few Indians!

Stop it. Let the Indians have all they want; they never asked too much.

The trouble in Oregon is caused by the government — contractors &c.

A lot of rascals now try to rob the well educated Indians in the Indian Territory of their land. It is horrible.

The whole world looks with merited contempt on these U.S. now, as formerly with great expectations. Are there not honorable persons enough to prevent a shameful ruin?

A knife you sharpen on a poor mans fingers will cut off your own hand.
(Russian proverb.)

To require workmen in government employ or elsewhere to work ten or more hours a day while government clerks, who have more pay and easier work, stay at the office only 6 or 7 hours is a damnable injustice which no human being should submit to.

Better live on dry cornmeal, abstain from having children, work for reform and join a rational community.

Those persons who come in possession of a great truth and attempt to convince others of its value, are generally set down as first class lunatics.
True Republic, N.Y.

In Renville Co Minn. a man settled on land justly, but not technically, belonging to another. The neighbors told the intruder to leave or they would have nothing to do with him. Serve Periue O Nilson so!

In each nr of U.S. RECORD & GAZETTE have been 20 @ 30 Postal Decisions, some of them very stupid and contradictory &c. On the following page is something in regard to postal affairs which will be continued.

From the *Truth Teller*, July 21, 1877.

TALE OF A COMET AND OTHER STORIES

46

in another direction as a lecturer on "How to Live Well with Little Work," "Law and Justice," "Money," and "THE WORKING MEN'S PARTY." He offered to deliver these lectures in one of four languages — English, Swedish, French, or German — at from $50 to $100 each, depending on the locality.[58]

Strong of heart, with zeal unabated, Widstrand reaffirmed his commitment in the December issue of *Truth Teller*. His paper was "dedicated to the abolition of poverty, ignorance and wickedness." It advocated justice, goodness, education and co-operation and a better way of living "whereby all kinds of sickness will be evitiated and sufferings from grasshoppers, weeds, fires, winds, floods[,] thieves, . . . etc. greatly diminished or abolished and less than 4 hours work a day [will be] needed to supply all bodily wants as Franklin said 100 years ago."

Brave language, alas, was not enough. Without money or the intervention of men or angels, Widstrand could not continue publishing, and with issue number 24 on December 18, 1877, *Truth Teller* expired. It was sad to think, commented the *Times*, "that the world will have no further information concerning the depredations of Nilson's bull." It was sad, too, to see how the *Times* ignored, as it had consistently, the nobler messages in Widstrand's paper. People who read such pronouncements in the *Times* had difficulty believing that Widstrand or his paper had any redeeming features.

The Monticello paper, particularly under the proprietorship of Perrine, had for years damned Widstrand with faint praise. A Republican meeting was harmonious when Widstrand was not there. When the Wright County Board of Commissioners was composed of an Irishman, a Swede, a Norwegian, a German, and a Yankee, the *Times* predicted that Widstrand would come around expecting to act as their interpreter. When Widstrand announced his candidacy for public office, the *Times* said that "with his accustomed modesty," a "remarkable fitness" for public office, and abilities "second to none," he was willing "to accept any office from U.S. Senator to pound keeper." When the *Times* reprinted Widstrand's poem, "Work Made Easy," it sarcastically called him "a majestic and herbivorous genius," who "above the scrub oaks and basswoods which environ his humble home . . . mounted upon the winged Pegasus, soars proudly through the empyrean." More than that, he was "philosopher, hermit, sage, editor and poet-laureate of Wright county." As the feud between Widstrand and his neighbors reached a feverish pitch, the *Times* said that he let go from "right and left with his rolling-pin, but nobody seems to mind the wild ravings of the poor lunatic." A lady who met Widstrand for the first time after reading much about him in the *Times* said, "How could I know but you was insane?"[59]

If Widstrand was misunderstood and his message ridiculed, it was not all the fault of the *Times*. The intemperate and outrageous language he used in *Truth Teller* shocked readers and conveyed an image of an irrational, blood-thirsty, bigoted, wrathful, unbalanced, or crazy man. "Evil inclined persons should in plain language kill themselves," wrote the editor. Those who let their animals and children annoy others "ought

47

to die immediately." Lawmakers were as little to be trusted as wolves. "A country where it is dangerous to tell the truth and live right, ought to be devoured by grasshoppers or the like." It would be better for the people of Wright County to strangle themselves or cut their throats than to vote either the Republican or Democratic ticket for candidates who were nothing more than "cattle, fools, knaves, imbeciles, slaves." He labeled Governor Cushman K. Davis an "ignorant, impudent and wicked whelp" and called a Monticello storekeeper-politician a "monster of verbosity, mean[n]ess, stupidity and cruelty." And if justice were truly done, both Nilson and Perrine, who had treated him so grievously, "should be in [*the state penitentiary at*] Stillwater, or still better, under water with a millstone or the like around their necks."[60]

All in all, men had a long way to go to achieve the *Truth Teller* ideal. "ZOOLOGICALLY," he wrote, "a human animal is named HOMO SAPIENS, which should be HOMO BRUTUS, Var. SAPIENS very rare." A man is not a man "simply because he has two legs and no feathers." And to those who said that Widstrand's standard of morality was "too dam'd high" or that he was ahead of his time, he answered, "Shame on the time!"[61]

Frustrated and discouraged as he was, and nearly submerged in a sea of mediocrity, it comforted the editor to know that his readers included thoughtful people who believed in many of his ideals. Among those who wrote him letters of approval and support were ten persons from St. Louis and many other "well-educated persons of both [sexes,] teachers, reformers, judges[,] bishops, professors, vegetarians" as well as "men and women who have not had the advantage of good education." A Granger took the *Agathocrat* to a meeting of Wisconsin state Grangers and urged the organization to buy copies for all subordinate Granges in the state. To a reader who could not understand why local Grangers did not rally in Widstrand's defense, Widstrand pointed out that Perrine, too, was a Granger and the master of the state Grange lived in Monticello. Another said surely the Good Templars (a temperance organization) would support Widstrand, to which the editor replied that it was too far to go to the society's meetings. Better yet, said another, a good lawyer should be able to help Widstrand protect himself from his neighbors' cattle and Perrine. No lawyer in Wright County would take on his case, Widstrand replied.[62]

Still another reader wrote to say that he stood shoulder to shoulder with Widstrand and would rather be the father of the *Agathocrat* than of the *New York Tribune*. The time was not far distant, he predicted, when Widstrand would be "most approved among editors." It was obvious, this reader noted, that Widstrand was being persecuted and called lunatic because others could not bear the truths he uttered. He wanted Widstrand to shake the dust of Minnesota from his feet and settle in Ohio "where there is more protection and more souls to benefit." When all else fails, "If they persecute you in one city, flee into another." Widstrand followed the advice to flee, but only after a final unhappy episode in his life at Lake Constance.[63]

Good letters were appreciated but more welcome were good neighbors. Widstrand yearned for good people to join him — good people who would live as at Fruitlands and abstain from bad food and bad habits. In *Truth Teller* he said: "The editor . . . has too much to do, and would be glad if some decent person, man or woman, young or old, would come here. Here is room for several."[64]

His farm at Lake Constance offered natural beauty, fertile land, and fewer difficulties to contend with than any other place he knew. Not more than half an acre of land, in his judgment, was enough to support one person in a Farist community, and "Having more is often injurious." His land was available, his house could accommodate several persons, "and when the house is full, it will be easy to get more." One who had good land "should ask good people (and bad also, if you can make them good) to come to you and carry out cooperation." The Lake Constance colony needed "men, women, children, who hunger and thirst after righteousness without humbugs."

In December, 1878, Widstrand placed a notice in a Chicago periodical, inviting persons who were of good habits and in need of work to come and live with him. Six of the letter writers who responded to his advertisement sounded like possible colonists. The letter of W. D. Sutton from Iowa interested him particularly — "if you read his letter you'd think he was an angel."[65]

Widstrand invited Sutton to Lake Constance, and the Iowan, with his wife and child, arrived in the spring of 1879. Shortly afterwards two others came; one was a man who appeared to be "whiskey bloated." More arrived and by June the colonists numbered five men and three women. All promised that they would not use liquor, tobacco, or obscene language, and that they would do no harm to others.

Together Widstrand and the men did the spring planting; each was to have a one-sixth share of the crops. After fields and garden were planted Widstrand found that he was not comfortable in his enlarged household. When it seemed impossible to concentrate on his writings and studies in the overcrowded house, he packed his satchel, entrusted house and farm to the Farist inhabitants, and went off to visit friends in Kansas. While he was away he expected that the colonists would take care of the farm duties and build themselves a house.

All did not go well in his absence. The colonists forgot their vows and smoked, drank, and quarreled among themselves. The men dug clay and made bricks, which they did not fire; they filled in Widstrand's good well and dug another that was not satisfactory. They did not build a house. Any work they did of lasting benefit amounted (in Widstrand's estimate) to less than $25. The colonists consumed or sold the crops, including hay, beans, and 200 bushels of potatoes, without reserving Widstrand's rightful share. Neglecting other farm work, the men hired out to neighbors and earned $200. All the while the colonists lived in Widstrand's house and used his wood and garden produce, free of any charge.

When Widstrand returned from Kansas, all of the colonists but the

Suttons had left Lake Constance. Sutton was drunk and had been drunk and disorderly many times, according to the reports of neighbors. He had quarreled with his wife, who threatened to drown herself. Sutton would not let Widstrand into his own house and threatened to shoot him if he tried to enter.

Taking temporary rooms at Buffalo, Widstrand tried without success to find a lawyer or law officer who would help him to regain his farm. Reluctantly, because he felt sorry for Sutton's family, he ordered Sutton to leave Lake Constance. Instead of leaving, Sutton presented Widstrand with a bill for $175 for work he said he had done on the farm. A friend of Widstrand's tried to explain the proceedings by which Sutton prevailed. "Because Widstrand neither was capable nor wanted to pay, Sutton took possession of the farm, encouraged by some of the county officials, and Widstrand, who had possibly forgotten to pay his land taxes on time, was forced to leave his possessions in the crook's hands. Several of Widstrand's friends in Kansas wrote to Sutton and threatened to sue him. He answered with coarse and slanderous letters about Widstrand and remained 'lord of the land.' "

Widstrand insisted that he had been wronged, that the land and house were legally his, but no one cared and the wrong was never righted. The title was cleared only after Widstrand was dead.

Driven out of his home and abandoning all that he owned, Widstrand left Wright County with only a satchel of worldly goods. He stopped for a time at Grove City in Meeker County where he exchanged work with the eccentric Dr. C. J. Erickson, editor and publisher of *Upplysningens Tidevarf* (The Age of Enlightenment), a radical publication that, under Widstrand's leadership, became "quite readable." According to an informal business arrangement between the two men, Widstrand would edit Erickson's paper and could use Erickson's press to publish *Rothuggaren* (The Root Chopper or Digger, or the Radical), a paper he started in 1880.[66]

Working conditions were not pleasant for Widstrand. He wrote about them to a Swedish-American journalist and friend, Ernst Skarstedt: "I received almost no payment, because he [*Erickson*] said that he had very little money. I slept on the floor in a draft, sat on a box and wrote on another box, worse than a missionary among other heathens and I saw myself like one." Widstrand claimed that he had written more articles for Erickson's paper than all other contributors combined, that he had translated much material and rewritten or improved Erickson's work, which was "worthless without rewriting." Erickson, too, complained to Skarstedt about Widstrand, and the journalist wrote that when he heard their tales of woe he did not know "whether one should cry or laugh." Another Swede likened the quarreling reformers to two fighting roosters.[67]

During the last years of his life Widstrand found a quieter, happier home at Litchfield. There he lived in rooms over a downtown store; kind friends supplied him with vegetables from their gardens and, under the protecting wing of the Litchfield *Independent*, he was able to continue publishing *Rothuggaren*. Ernst Skarstedt recalled how another Swedish journalist, Ernst Beckman, a liberal member of the Rikstag, found Widstrand, the "wise man of Litchfield" — the "blood-thirsty throne-toppler" reformer — in his attic room "chewing — on raw oatmeal." The aging Widstrand did not appear to Beckman to be a raving lunatic — far from it. "In writing[,] such a terrible rebel, but face to face a friendly, modest, helpful personality. In his outward appearance the publisher of Rothuggaren is a little, crippled old man with a peaceful face and a pair of kind eyes that blinked out from spectacles with broken lenses." Had he thought of visiting Europe again? asked Beckman. "I don't dare to do that," said Widstrand. "I might meet a king on the streets and that I could not stand, then I would get sick."[68]

Widstrand died in 1891, the same year that some of his free-thinking Swedish friends helped to organize the Emmanuel Independent Swedish Evangelical Church in Litchfield. Although there is no record of Widstrand joining them, he was buried from the town hall where the group met and the Rev. Olof A. Tofteen, their pastor, officiated at the funeral. Widstrand had no property in Litchfield, but friends collected money to buy a lot for him in the Litchfield cemetery where he lies in an unmarked grave.[69]

Skarstedt, his friend, wrote about Widstrand, the truth teller and reformer, in *Präirieblommen Kalendar, 1908*. He was in possession of many noble characteristics, said Skarstedt, but he was so impractical that it seemed he was not really sane. Yet, said the *News Ledger* (Litchfield): "Notwithstanding his communistic, anarchistic and other extremely strange teachings and practices probably a more inoffensive man never lived; he never willingly harmed an insect or any living thing. Peace to his ashes; May there never be a worse man in the world."

❧3❧

Elijah E. Edwards
Civil War Chaplain

*A Talented Man of the Cloth
Recounts Adventures
with the Seventh Minnesota Infantry
in the South*

O N JUNE 29, 1864, Elijah E. Edwards, 33, boarded the steamboat
"George H. Grey" at St. Paul for a journey down the Mississippi.
A professor, an artist of considerable talent, and a clergyman, he
had been appointed chaplain of the Seventh Minnesota Volunteer Infantry on June 11. Edwards was nearly six feet tall and spare of build, with
dark hair and eyes, a man of ready wit, natural warmth, and charity.
He looked forward to a new adventure; with a commission in his pocket
he was beginning the long, wearying journey from Minnesota to find his
regiment caught up in the Civil War somewhere in Tennessee. He carried with him notebooks in which he would sketch and describe his
experiences.

When low water and sandbars halted the "Grey" in midpassage,
Edwards transferred to the "Mankato" and then to the "Favorite" to get
to La Crosse, Wisconsin. From there the steamer "Northern Light"
transported him to Dubuque, Iowa, where he boarded a train that took
him south through flooding rain to the dust and almost intolerable heat
of Cairo, Illinois. Noting such evidence of war as soldiers patrolling the
debris-strewn border city and war refugees from Kentucky crowding the
levees, Edwards took to the river again at Cairo. He boarded the
"Commercial," bound for Memphis, Tennessee, and the war zone.[1]

Edwards slept in his clothes on the steamer's deck as the journey
wore on in stifling heat. The "Commercial" reached Memphis at midnight on July 3; five hours later the soon-to-be chaplain disembarked
and learned that the Seventh Minnesota was in camp near La Grange,
Tennessee, just north of the Mississippi border. Without stopping for
breakfast, he took a train for La Grange, an hour away. Asking further
directions, he then set out on foot for camp, a mile or so beyond the village, where he found the regiment.

Edwards' appointment papers were pronounced in order, and he was
mustered in without delay as the Seventh Minnesota's chaplain. During
the rest of his first day with the regiment he visited with a dozen or more
old friends from Minnesota and was assigned to a mess that included

three of them — Major William H. Burt of Stillwater, Captain Frank H. Pratt, and Lieutenant Henry (Frank) Folsom, both of Taylors Falls. Edwards' fourth messmate was Captain Theodore G. Carter of St. Peter, who was to become a fast friend and, later, a collaborator in telling the story of their wartime service with the regiment.[2]

The next morning at 7:00 Edwards began the first march of his military career "in the guise or disguise of a civilian." Lacking a horse, he walked with the regiment's enlisted men instead of riding in his rightful place with the staff officers. Thus he and his comrades set off to campaign in Mississippi as part of the Third Brigade, First Division, of the Union Army's Sixteenth Corps commanded by crusty General Andrew J. Smith. The Rebel-chasing of this corps in a number of states earned it such titles as "Smith's guerrillas" or "Smith's geography class."[3]

ELIJAH E. EDWARDS, CIVIL WAR CHAPLAIN

How Edwards was able to join the army, and, in fact, how he became a clergyman and chaplain, is a curious tale that begins with his early years in Ohio and Indiana.

Edwards was born in 1831 at Delaware, Ohio, to a Welsh father and a Dutch mother. He lived during his youth in Ohio and Indiana at places where his father, an itinerant Methodist minister, served small-town and rural parishes. Edwards was educated in country schools, served a short apprenticeship in a book bindery, and attended Indiana Asbury (now DePauw University) at Greencastle, Indiana. A bright but indifferent student in his earlier college years, Edwards nevertheless was graduated from Asbury with honors and became, in the words of a friend, "a true man full of gentleness and charity." He was not, however, interested at that time in preparing for the ministry, as his father hoped he would be. Neither solemn nor devout, even in revival meetings, "he could scarcely refrain from perpetrating a pun or drawing a caricature."[4]

Edwards was attracted to teaching instead. He became successively a rural schoolteacher, school principal, and professor and president of small church-related academies in Indiana. In 1858 he and his wife, also the child of a Methodist clergyman, followed another Indianian, the Reverend Benjamin F. Crary, to Minnesota. Crary became president of Hamline University, a fledgling college and preparatory school at Red Wing (it later moved to St. Paul), and Edwards taught Latin and Greek there for several terms. After leaving the state for a time to teach in a seminary near Chicago, Edwards returned to Minnesota in 1860 to accept a dual appointment at Taylors Falls as principal of Chisago Seminary, a year-old secondary and college preparatory school, and as pastor of a Methodist congregation then preparing to build a church. The Methodists had "licensed" Edwards to preach, but he had not been ordained. Yet he had no difficulty meeting the needs of his congregation, raised as he was in the shadow of a Methodist pulpit and educated as well as or better than most clergymen of the day. From the first he was popular among his parishioners and in the community.[5]

At Taylors Falls Edwards enjoyed the beautiful views of the dalles of the St. Croix River and sketched scenes in and around the little village. Fond of outdoor activities, he, his wife, and two small sons regularly

53

Elijah E. Edwards, ca. 1864. *MHS*

went picnicking, fishing, ice skating, or sledding — as the seasons allowed. Before long he also began submitting amusing poems to the local
newspaper and giving public lectures at home and across the river in
Wisconsin.

When war came Edwards actively supported Abraham Lincoln and
the Union and for a time held office in the local Republican party. When
a group of patriotic citizens arrived at Taylors Falls from nearby Stillwater and Marine to recruit soldiers for the northern army, Edwards
joined in their efforts. He and an Indiana friend and clergyman, Edward
Eggleston (future writer of *A Hoosier Schoolmaster* and other novels),
addressed a local crowd of 200 to 300 persons in a way "calculated to
warm up the coldest heart and fire it with patriotism for our country."
While the crowd sang "Red, White and Blue," 27 men signed the enlist-
ment roll. Some of them became members of the First Minnesota Volunteer Infantry, one of the earliest to join the Union cause. Edwards spoke
at another rally in St. Croix Falls, Wisconsin, where 53 men formed
what later became Company F of the First Wisconsin Infantry. Then he
traveled around Chisago County with his friend Burt on a recruiting
mission enlisting men for the Seventh Minnesota Infantry Regiment.[6]

Within a year most of the able-bodied men of Edwards' congregation
had volunteered for service and become members of Company C of the
Seventh Minnesota. Edwards, too, wanted to join up. He could see no
merit in remaining at home when one of the great dramas of human history was being played out on battlefields, when all around him friends,
neighbors, and students were shouldering knapsacks in the service of

their country. Edwards hoped to secure a commission as a lieutenant in recognition of his recruiting work for Company C. Unfortunately, he was rejected because he was suffering a recurrence of ague or malaria first contracted years before in Indiana. "His" company (59 of its men were from Taylors Falls) reported at Fort Snelling in mid-August, 1862. Soon after its mustering in, Company C served on the frontier during the Dakota War, or Sioux Uprising.

After a year in Minnesota and Dakota Territory, the Seventh went south. By the first of January, 1864, some of the men were on guard duty at St. Louis, Memphis, and Vicksburg. By then, too, William R. Marshall was the regiment's colonel, having replaced Stephen A. Miller who was promoted from colonel to brigadier general, then resigned to be elected governor of Minnesota. In the spring the Seventh was stationed near Paducah, Kentucky, and in June, 1864, it was assigned to the Sixteenth Corps under General Smith.

At about the same time a vacancy occurred among the Seventh's officers with the resignation of Chaplain Oliver P. Light, who evidently was not very popular. His departure left an opening in the regiment for Edwards, who had been living in a number of places. He moved from Taylors Falls to Hudson, Wisconsin, where he served the local Methodist church and took treatments for his illness from a Hudson doctor. For a few months he traveled every week by steamboat to Taylors Falls, where he edited the Taylors Falls paper after the editor went to war. Before the end of 1863 Edwards' health was much improved, and he and his family moved to the Lake Como area of St. Paul. He had been appointed librarian of the St. Paul Mercantile Library, forerunner of the St. Paul Public Library, and he studied photography and oil painting in his spare time in the studios of Danish-born artist Dr. Andrew Falkenshield.[7]

How Edwards learned that the Seventh needed a chaplain is not known; the news may have come from a man in the ranks, or from Governor Miller, or perhaps from his friend Dr. Benjamin Crary who, after leaving Hamline, had served as chaplain of the Third Minnesota Infantry. In any case, Edwards was ready to replace Light, and his friends helped him circumvent (in somewhat irregular fashion) several problems that stood in his way. The major obstacle was that Edwards had never been ordained. While it was true that other men had been called to chaplaincies with less impressive credentials — one was said to have been the only soldier in his regiment who could drive a mule team without swearing — Congress had decreed that, to become a chaplain, a man must have been ordained by a religious body. To make Edwards "legal" in this respect, he was ordained, apparently not by Methodists but by "Some St. Paul ministers — Congregationalists, and perhaps some others — [who] formed a council, synod, or some other ecclesiastical or extra-ecclesiastical body and ordained him after due examination."[8]

Edwards then faced another obstacle. It was customary for a regiment to recommend its choice for chaplain to the governor for approval. Captain Carter did not remember later that the men of the Seventh ever discussed Edwards' candidacy. Governor Miller, however, had only recently belonged to the regiment and may have known of Edwards' former relationship to it. For this appointment at least he seems to have anticipated the regiment's choice rather than waited to confirm it. He named Edwards chaplain on the same day that Light's resignation was officially accepted. Governor Miller then prudently supplied Edwards with the security of other credentials before the Seventh formally accepted him as chaplain. In a second official document addressed to "United States Officers and whom it may concern," Miller characterized Edwards as "a loyal Christian minister" and appointed him "at his own expense as a volunteer commissioner, to visit and attend to the wants of the wounded and afflicted soldiers of the 7th and 9th Minnesota Reg'ts now supposed to be in the vicinity of Memphis, Tenn. as well as all other of our State troops." The governor then commended him as a "Christian Commissioner to the courtesy of all transportation and Government officers." Shortly afterward, Edwards put his household goods in the care of a friend, sent his wife and little boys off to Indianapolis to live with her parents, and on June 29 left St. Paul for the war zone.[9]

The new chaplain had been with the Minnesota Seventh scarcely a day when the Sixteenth Corps of 10,000 to 12,000 men began a march toward Tupelo and Harrisburg, Mississippi. Putting together rumors and bits of firmer intelligence, the men concluded that their mission was to aid General William T. Sherman's Georgia campaign by destroying a railroad, thereby disrupting Confederate supply lines. They also were to keep the formidable General Nathan Bedford Forrest and his cavalry so busy that they could not interfere with the Union march on Atlanta far to the east. The mission was also one of retribution on behalf of some Union soldiers who had served with Brigadier General Samuel T. Sturgis only a month before at the June 11 battle of Brice's Cross Roads, Mississippi, an engagement on the Guntown road that had been disastrous for Union soldiers. On their retreat to Memphis southern civilians had shot at them. The northern men had noted the houses from which the shots were fired, and now both the houses and their inhabitants became special targets of vengeance as the corps traveled again in July through Mississippi. The flames of burning houses and thick black columns of smoke from stores of burning cotton marked the Tupelo campaign of July, 1864, as the corps marched through such Mississippi towns as Salem, Ripley, New Albany, and Pontotoc. Scattered bands of soldiers, separated from their command, ranged over rural areas burning, robbing, pillaging, and plundering — "gobbling" — despite strict orders against such outrageous practices.[10]

The cruelty and incivility of this "civil" war shocked and sickened Edwards. Lacking a uniform or any insignia of authority, he was powerless to prevent what he saw and unable to identify by regiment or company the gobblers of Smith's corps — the foraging counterparts of Sherman's "bummers." He deplored their acts but admitted looking on with "horrible fascination like that which an envenomed serpent exercises upon an unwilling spectator." Gobblers took food and supplies and much else, whether useful or not, and they frequently destroyed what

56

AREA IN WHICH
SMITH'S GUERILLAS OPERATED

they could not use. One soldier carted off a Webster's unabridged dictionary, remarking that his early education had been neglected and he was "going to begin over again and learn something." Others left schoolbooks strewn across the floor of a deserted schoolhouse. The new owner of a large mirror planned to have a good shave when he got to camp. Another gobbler took an empty barrel because "everything else had been stolen."

At war-torn Pontotoc Edwards' protests against the gobblers met with some results. He reported to Colonel Marshall the plight of an aged Methodist minister with a plundered house, his furniture hacked to splinters, food all gone, and horse and carriage stolen. Marshall became "furiously indignant" and ordered a posse to find and return the minister's horse and carriage. He also ordered that guards be stationed at many buildings in the area and that there be no more plundering. Marshall could do little more, for battle was imminent, "the horrors of which might prove greater than the pillaging of a poor little country town."

In fairness, Edwards noted that some soldiers meticulously spared, and even stood guard over, the homes of civilians who had cared for the Union wounded on the June retreat from Brice's Cross Roads. But when other soldiers found a human skull exposed on a fence post, and a southern woman remarked contemptuously that she fed her pigs on dead Yankees, vengeance was swift and predictable.

Each day Edwards found in these shocking events new revelations of human character. Beneath greed, lust, or revenge he sensed a grim humor. "The life of the soldier, or of the soldier who is a plunderer also, is not all diabolism. It reaches outward and upward toward the humorous. The humor of war rises in the concept that it is in itself a huge joke, and the roughest campaign is thereby turned into the wildest frolic." The chaplain sensed that, under their hilarity, the men knew a battle was coming and the enemy was about to descend.

One day the footsore chaplain met with good fortune in the blistering heat, when a man on horseback stopped him and asked for a drink from his canteen. Edwards recognized first the voice and then the person of Dr. Henry Murdock, a Taylors Falls friend and family doctor. Murdock offered him one of his two horses until the chaplain could get one of his own. That evening Edwards rode into camp "on a well caparisoned steed to the great astonishment of my messmates who knew of but one method of obtaining a horse while on the war path." But the horse was white, and as the corps drew closer to battle the chaplain had doubts about riding him. "I felt that the color of the horse might attract undue attention from the Rebel sharp shooters who were blazing away at us on our line of march." More often than not during the rest of the war Edwards found good uses for a succession of horses allotted him. He assigned one to the cook of his mess and others to men who were wounded and suffering but not judged so seriously injured as to rate a place in the ambulance. "It would have been heroic to ride that white horse into the thickest of the fight," Edwards acknowledged, but his place was not there prancing along the battlefront.[11]

The corps traveled rapidly and lightly with limited provisions, without tents or camp equipage, through intense heat interspersed with storms of drenching rain. Hot in heavy woolen uniforms under a blazing sun, or spattered and bedraggled by mud and rain, the troops moved over a devastated countryside. They passed the rudely marked graves of Confederate soldiers, the unburied bodies of Union soldiers killed in skirmishes on the Guntown retreat. At night they slept on the ground — "a clod for a pillow and the starry sky for a coverlet" — when the sky was not pouring rain.

In the valley of a beautiful winding stream they found the remains of what they supposed was a recent Rebel camp. The enemy was not far away. A minié ball "like the buzz of an infuriated hornet" whizzed close to the chaplain's ear. There was firing to the front and rear of the line of march. Six men were shot foraging too far from the road. A Confederate brigade was reported to be advancing toward the Union forces.

To Edwards the approach of battle felt like the onslaught of a violent thunderstorm. In camp at night the men slept uneasily on their weapons. Some, fearing they would be killed, gave the chaplain messages to send to their families. Dr. Lucius Smith, the regimental surgeon and another Taylors Falls friend who was "a man of great coolness and unquestioned bravery," confided in Edwards that he had a gloomy premonition of his own fate. Edwards wrote very little about what was told him in confidence, but he did note that "a large majority" of the men were thoughtful and grimly determined.[12]

On the morning of July 13, after drums beat tattoo and the bugle sounded, detachments of the Seventh were assigned to guard duty. Smith's corps marched south toward the railroad towns of Tupelo and Okolona. Confederates under Forrest were said to be poised along the line between them. At 2:00 the troops were halted and given an hour's rest. On foot again and somehow detached from the regiment, Edwards stopped at a farmhouse to fill his canteen, unaware of the Rebel forces hiding nearby in the woods on either side of the road. Suddenly volleys of bullets whistled through the trees. In the confusion wagons and men on horseback dashed forward furiously; foot soldiers scattered in all directions. Not sure where to find the Seventh, Edwards hurried forward and then back. Fortunately he found his way to the regiment, grateful to be alive but mortified at his carelessness in wandering away from his command.

Fourteen men were wounded in the encounter; Dr. Smith's death bore out his presentiment. Survivors hastily loaded dead and wounded in ambulances while the column plunged ahead through heavy fire from a battery hidden in a cornfield. Bursting shells ploughed furrows across the road as the column moved on in double-quick time to camp on the site of the nearly abandoned town of Harrisburg.

In camp Colonel Marshall, sparing the chaplain a reprimand for his carelessness, gave him detailed orders for the next day. Edwards was to organize the musicians of the regiment into an ambulance corps. They were to search for the wounded and take them to a field hospital, and they were to bury the dead.[13]

At 5:00 the next morning came the call to arms. At the end of a hasty breakfast, Edwards saw in the distance a long gray line of Confederates approaching over the hills. The thrilling scene held the chaplain spellbound, but only for a moment. He turned to the rear with a detail of three men to bury the body of his friend, Smith. While musket fire pattered like hail about him, Edwards chose a spot for the grave under three hickory trees, sheltered from bullets but still within range of enemy batteries. Exploding shells and grape and canister shot tore through the treetops a few rods away. During a lull in the firing the men dug the grave and buried Smith's body in a rude plank coffin. The chaplain read a brief burial service.

Edwards and the ambulance detail roamed the field that day in the bluish haze of battle to take up the Union dead and to carry the wounded of both sides to an improvised hospital. No spot was safe from the enemy's long-range artillery, and three times the hospital and its wounded had to be moved. After three hours of fighting, hundreds were injured and many died. The sweltering sun struck down officers and men on both sides. By evening the wounded were moved again to an improvised hospital in a farmhouse a short distance from the field of battle. Edwards had slept fitfully the night before and had eaten nothing since breakfast. He and Murdock, both on the verge of exhaustion, crawled under the overhanging bank of a dry stream and slept until morning, undisturbed by the continuing thunder of artillery.

Firing continued most of the night and more men were killed or wounded. In the morning the two armies watched each other warily, awaiting orders to attack. The orders that finally came were confusing, and Captain Carter of Company K complained about them to the colonel. Marshall agreed they were foolish but said that those were the orders he had been given. They came, it seemed, from General Joseph A. Mower, who had been drinking. Meanwhile, in passing between the hospital and the battlefield, Edwards saw the general and paused briefly to sketch him. Mower was on his horse, in heroic pose, rocking back and forth, waving his sword and shouting. An aide nearby told Edwards later that the general was "using the King's English in a very free and rather reprehensible manner." Carter heard that Mower said, "Give 'em hell, boys! Give 'em hell!" and, with much profanity, ordered the men to charge. Edwards and Carter agreed with the prevailing opinion that Mower was a good military man when sober, but that day "Old Joe was drunk." He was "drunk as a biled owl."[14]

Not all confusing incidents of the Tupelo-Harrisburg battle could be explained by Mower's condition. His order to charge was timed at noon under a blistering sun. The Union soldiers suffered from the heat as they marched forward on the double quick in their heavy uniforms. But the heat affected the Rebels, too. During the engagement some 80 southern soldiers were stricken and taken from the field, many of them unconscious. The enemy retreated over the crest of the hill, but, fearing an ambush, the Union troops did not pursue them. On the verge of victory the northern forces made quiet plans for a strategic withdrawal.[15]

Edwards was informed of these plans before they became general knowledge. The artillery was to remain in position to cover the withdrawal. In the midst of its firing the chaplain buried six of the dead and arranged for the seriously injured to remain behind in the hospital with officers and men detailed to care for them. The wounded who were able to travel were put in ambulances to go with the corps.

Then suddenly the Union forces were on the road back to Memphis, but few knew what was happening. While they had not destroyed a railroad, they had fought bravely in battle and had driven the enemy off the field — but not very far. As the Union men marched away from the Tupelo area, the enemy continued to harass their flank.

While the withdrawal proceeded Edwards waited on the battlefield with a mortally wounded officer. Regiment after regiment passed, their ambulances crowded with the injured. None would stop for the chaplain and his charge. Near the end of the long line General Smith came galloping by and reined his horse when he saw Edwards. Learning of the pre-

General Joseph A. Mower at Tupelo, by Edwards. *MHS*

dicament, Smith commanded the next artillery wagon coming by to pick up the chaplain and wounded officer — "no brave soldier of his . . . should be left living or dead on the field," said the general. Thus Edwards, his charge, and Smith were among the last to leave the Tupelo battlefield.[16]

Before long the wounded officer died, and the chaplain buried him late at night by the light of torches. Early the next morning the troops took up the hurried march toward their old quarters at La Grange. Why such haste when the men were pale and haggard, suffering from the heat? In one day from 3:00 A.M. to midnight they marched 25 miles on a single ration of spoiled hardtack and sowbelly (salt pork). Rations were short, and little food was available in a countryside "so war-wasted that a crow flying over it could not pick up a living." They marched back to La Grange in six days, half-famished most of the way, and under fire part of the time.[17]

At headquarters it was agreed that the expedition had diverted Forrest's troops. But to some of Smith's men, the Tupelo engagement did not seem noble or heroic, and military historians usually call it a skirmish rather than a battle. The hurried departure made the men feel they were in retreat, not celebrating a victory. Edwards tried to be philosophical about it all: "He that fights and runs away / May live to fight another day."

From La Grange the corps moved once more to a camp near Memphis, where the men rested until the end of the month. Edwards, like his fellows, looked the worse for the wear and tear of the expedition. A chaplain who had been a college friend was dismayed at Edwards' appearance: "His shoes were full of holes and would scarcely stay on his feet, his clothing almost rags, his hat well-nigh gone." The friend gave Edwards a coat, offered to lend him money to buy a hat, and "recommended him to the Quartermaster's department for shoes." Edwards then "buttoned up the coat and started down town to buy a hat holding up his head as though he could buy out all Memphis."[18]

What to wear as a chaplain was a problem Edwards had not yet solved. Some chaplains wore uniforms like those of captains of cavalry, with shoulder straps and cords, and some, although they were classified as noncombatants, wore a sash and sword. Custom varied from regiment to regiment, because army regulations in regard to chaplains' uniforms were almost universally ignored. It was clear to Edwards after a month in the field that anything very formal would be out of place among the bluff, hearty men of Smith's guerrillas. He finally settled on a black ministerial coat and a hat with an eagle emblem on it. Evidently his clothes were of minor concern, for he had become "a general favorite with both officers and men."

AFTER SERVING a month Edwards began to see his role in better perspective. He found his rank and pay equaled that of a captain of cavalry, just below the major and surgeon. He was the only member of the officer class who could move freely among both officers — including Colonel

62

Marshall — and enlisted men down to the lowliest private. A chaplain's position was unique in the army, but how effective he was in it depended much on his own personality. As another chaplain wrote, "it was his own fault if he did not avail himself of it [*his position*], and improve its advantages." It was said that "an officer of any grade was glad to meet in his army life one person to whom he could speak with entire freedom, if his chaplain had the qualities and experience to fit him for such fellowship. And the enlisted men could have no such communication with the supposed upper world of officerdom as was secured to them by a sympathetic and tactful chaplain.[19]

At the Memphis camp Edwards watched over the convalescents, and at the city hospitals he daily visited the more seriously ill or wounded. He was shocked at the number of men from Minnesota he found hospitalized — 180 from the Seventh Infantry alone. In the overcrowded hospitals "the sick, wounded, and dying lie in cots so closely crowded together that there is scarcely room for the nurses to pass between them." Given a choice, Edwards noted, men in a hospital would rather "take chances with their comrades in the field," and he quoted a regimental surgeon as saying that "in many cases it is equivalent to a death sentence to send them to the hospital." When word of these miserable conditions reached Minnesota, Governor Miller sent a representative to Memphis who with Edwards was able to arrange the transfer of sick and wounded men of the Seventh, Ninth, and Tenth Minnesota regiments to northern hospitals.[20]

Of all his duties, Edwards concluded, holding a formal Sunday service was of lesser importance. There had been, and would be, few opportunities on the march for such observances. When time and place did permit a sermon, it must be good. Edwards prepared them with care, wrote them out, and read them, as he had done for civilian congregations. For his first camp sermon he took for his text a verse from Matthew: "Think not that I am come to send peace on earth; I am not come to send peace, but a sword." Edwards thought it the most difficult he had ever delivered. His sanctuary was a clear space among the trees. He faced "an audience of soldiers in uniform under a profusion of American flag[s]." The men were "fresh from a hard fought battle and not yet rested from the fatigues of a forced march of six days duration." The congregation sang without musical accompaniment, and at the close of the service the chaplain could not say when they would worship together again, "for none of us knew in what part of that war-wasted land another Sunday should find us and whether on the march or on the battle field."[21]

The number of religious men in the Seventh was not large; not more than 200 or 300 could be so classified in Edwards' estimation. But they were zealous and warmhearted — a discriminating congregation from six or more different denominations and of many beliefs. Sermons for such a congregation, Edwards soon learned, must be "*the best in the barrel.*" In his view, "No audience is more severely critical than an audience of soldiers. There are men among them well posted on Bible topics who could themselves if need be preach sound argumentative discourses. . . . No men see more quickly through a sham than soldiers. A long face and solemn drawl go for nothing with them. They have no reverence for 'the cloth.' They hate cant, and are not moved by the 'glory hallelujah' style of oratory. Whatever they have been at home in the army they are not sectarian. They care not for Methodist or Baptist or Episcopalian . . . and seem to think doctrine of far less importance than conduct." Edwards noted that his observations applied to Catholics as well as Protestants.[22]

In carrying out his duties, Edwards worked closely with chaplains of two other regiments in the brigade, especially with Fred Humphrey of the Fifth Iowa Infantry. A staunch Episcopalian, Humphrey was cultured, refined, and deeply pious, and a man of fine appearance. His other close associate was a man of quite a different stamp — William Bagley of the Thirty-fifth Iowa Infantry. He was a member of the Newlight branch of Presbyterianism, zealous but uncultured, "an illiterate expounder" and "a sad jumbler of rhetoric and syntax." (It was he who, it was said, became a chaplain because he could drive a mule team without swearing.) Despite the irregularity of Bagley's views and credentials, Edwards and Humphrey treated him with great respect; he was a good man and in the army his influence was good.

Another duty Edwards took seriously was providing the regiment with reading matter. From the Christian Commission offices he gathered testaments, newspapers, and periodicals. But he rejected out of hand the small religious tracts offered to him calling them "unstimulating spiritual pabulum." The men of the Seventh, he insisted, were "generally capable of reading the very best material published. . . . The best newspapers are most read. They are literally worn out passing from hand to hand."

Once a month Edwards had to make a formal report on the "spiritual and moral condition of the men." His reports were frank but circumspect, suggesting his reluctance to make judgments and perhaps reflecting his conviction that the reports were ignored and probably consigned to the wastebasket before they reached division headquarters.[23]

During quiet moments, and sometimes even when under fire, Edwards acted as artist to the regiment. In his pocket diary he quickly sketched scenes and people, refining them later when time allowed. Some of his sketches, copied and given to others, were much treasured by the men. None of them, he insisted, was made "to the neglect of any of the duties devolving upon me as Chaplain."[24]

SMITH'S GUERRILLAS left their Memphis camp early Sunday morning, July 31, 1864, under orders to move south into Mississippi on another expedition against General Forrest. They were away for most of August on what became known as the Oxford raid.[25]

Edwards stayed behind in Memphis for a day or so to care for the sick and wounded. Those who could travel but were not strong enough for the early days of the march were put under Captain Carter's command and moved by train in boxcars with Carter, Edwards, and car-loads of equipment and supplies. The convalescents rejoined the regi-ment at Holly Springs, Mississippi, and moved with it to Waterford and to the Tallahatchie River. There they encamped while the pioneer corps built a bridge. They could not see the enemy, but the whistling of bullets overhead, the roar of artillery, and the bursting of shells proclaimed his presence not far away. In another camp on the Tallahatchie on August 13 they heard to the south the sound of a "considerable skirmish" which, Edwards thought, "would have been a battle in any other war than this." The Seventh rested while the sounds of the battle mingled with thunder and lightning and the wind swept a wall of water over their camp.[26]

In the midst of the general dreariness that continued for days, the men of the Seventh, no doubt encouraged by their chaplain, made the best of their lot. When the sun came out briefly they cheered. In fact, Edwards wrote, "they have an ingrained habit of cheering everything that comes under their notice from General Smith to a rabbit." Edwards commented with dry humor on the prevailing wetness and described the epidemic of punning that swept through the regiment. Standing around their campfires in vain attempts to dry out, they began to call themselves "Uncle Sam'[s] Wetter uns," and the soldiers spoke of the mud as a faith-ful friend who "sticks to us in adversity." Well plastered with mud on one day's march, Edwards observed that he was "glad to have escaped the usual preliminary lathing." But as the word-play proliferated, even the punning chaplain had had quite enough and wrote "[the one] who started this epidemic of punning [ought] to be taken out and shot."[27]

On the morning of August 22 the men marched toward Oxford, where they expected a battle. The Seventh halted in a field half a mile north of the city, over which hung dense smoke. Having no other duties Edwards mounted his horse and ventured into Oxford. "As the smoke grew denser the scene grew more weird and more like Hades," he wrote. Many houses were burning; others were being plundered by an unruly mob of soldiers carrying mirrors, rocking chairs, vases, wearing apparel, bedding, and books. A drunken man on horseback — said to be a sur-geon's assistant — came galloping through the smoke holding a grinning skeleton taken from a doctor's office.

The Union flag was flying over the courthouse, and as Edwards rode by he could see within General Smith and his officers, looking grim and determined because they had received unpleasant news. A detachment of Forrest's cavalry had been luring them on and obstructing their way to Oxford. As Smith's guerrillas marched into the city, Forrest's detach-ment slipped away, leaving Smith "in possession of a city he did not want, and for which he had no use." In the meantime, Forrest had skipped off with the rest of his force and for a short time at least had occupied Memphis. Although Oxford was in flames, Smith later insisted he had given no orders to burn it. In fact, he had at first posted guards around the city, but he withdrew them and planned to return to Memphis when he heard it was threatened. Smith, it was suggested, did not consider himself under pressing obligation to protect Oxford, a city which Forrest had so cavalierly abandoned. Edwards believed that frustration at the supposed failure of their mission sparked a temporary madness for destruction among the troops; others said that the news of the Confederate burning of Chambersburg, Pennsylvania, on July 30 had provoked revenge. Under the smoke of burning buildings, Smith's guerrillas began their march back to Memphis, harassed by a rear guard of Forrest's command. On August 29 the Seventh reached its old camp in the Memphis suburbs.

Three days later the regiment received orders to prepare to embark at any moment. No one said where they were to go, but the boats, it was reported, were chartered for a trip to De Valls Bluff, Arkansas. Memphis would remain the regiment's home base, and Major Burt, who was not well, was put in charge of a convalescent camp. Finally ordered to board the steamboats, the Sixteenth Corps endured a day of blistering heat at the Memphis landing before its departure. On the dock a mob of soldiers, unidentified by regiments, swarmed over the commissary stores, grabbed as many hams and other portable items as they could carry, and took off with them into the city. Edwards wrote of the scene: "They resembled most a vast army of black ants removing their stores from one locality to another. But for the criminality of the proceeding [it] would have been amusing." It was reported that "Two or three soldiers ate so much of the stolen goods that they died of surfeit." From the cabin deck of the steamboat "Patrick," General Mower "saw the whole transaction with the utmost indifference." Neither he nor any other officer attempted to stop or prevent the stealing — "it may be charitably supposed," wrote Edwards, "because the depredators did not belong to the 16th Army Corps."[29]

But, as Edwards learned later, since the First Division of the Sixteenth Corps was nearby at the time the crime was committed it was judged guilty of the theft. Its reputation was much damaged by the verdict. Edwards conceded that some of the division may have been guilty, but the men of the Seventh "stole less than the others, not because of superior integrity but [because] facilities were wanting." Unfortunately, every man of the division felt the consequences. The pay of all was stopped for months, and then in settlement the total value of the stolen goods was deducted from their pay, prorated according to rank. Edwards was later called to testify before a court of inquiry in the matter; he concluded privately that if anyone were to be held accountable it should have been General Mower.

When the flotilla of crowded boats passed down the Mississippi, the sun became fiercer by its reflection on the water. At Helena, Arkansas, the Seventh sounded a Dakota war whoop to greet men of the Sixth Minnesota Infantry on occupation duty there. Edwards later saw two emaciated officers of the Sixth, old Minnesota friends, who were walking evidence of the diseases that ravished their regiment and would also be visited on the Seventh during its sojourn in Arkansas.[30]

Beyond Helena the boats ascended the serpentine White River, whose stagnant waters and backwater swamps were a haven for mosquitoes and other biting insects. The men became sick from drinking the polluted river water and found little comfort for their misery on the crowded boats. During a stop at St. Charles many left the vessels for "elbow-room and breathing room and standing-room." They searched in vain for good drinking water, but did enjoy a refreshing bath. Edwards said "It was a sight to be seen and wondered at. There was a long, sloping beach with chrystal [sic] waters laving the beach, over which towered aloft and bent at various angles the most colossal willows I ever looked upon, the branches of some trailing in the water. Underneath these a long array of Smith's Guerillas, in nudis naturalibus standing in long glittering array upon the banks or splashing in the waters beneath." Edwards joined them, hanging his clothes "as Jewish captives did their harps on the bending branches of the willows." After his bath he found that his vest had been stolen, and with it thirty cents, at a time when he was nearly penniless. "Wherewithal was I to pay for my next letter home?" he asked. At Crockett's Bluff Landing, Arkansas, while some men of the Seventh were buying butter and other food for their mess, a few gobblers stole some chickens. Marshall had the offenders arrested and sent the confiscated chickens to the sick and convalescent mess. Every day more and more men became sick in Arkansas. Before the end of the month the men of the Seventh on active duty were said to number fewer than 300. Both Edwards and his tentmate, Captain Pratt, became ill near Brownsville, Arkansas, where the Seventh encamped on the edge of an odorous, coffee-colored cypress swamp covered with pea-green scum. Neither had a mirror, so each taunted the other about how he looked. The regimental surgeon diagnosed Pratt's red and swollen face to be the result of "jigger" bites and concluded that Edwards, with his "beaten gold" complexion, had a bad case of jaundice. He ordered both to the officers' hospital at Little Rock for treatment. Edwards objected, reminding Marshall that the chaplain of the Fifth Minnesota also had jaundice but was not being sent away. Marshall was not impressed and, said Edwards, "dryly [remarked] that it was perhaps well for me that I was in the 7th instead of the 5th Regiment."[31]

At this juncture able-bodied men of the Seventh joined the rest of Smith's corps on a lengthy, exhausting defense of Missouri against a raid by mobile Confederate forces under General Sterling Price. Separated several weeks from his regiment, Edwards kept busy. More than 300 of Smith's guerrillas, many of them unable to help themselves, were left on a depot platform at Little Rock awaiting transportation to hospitals. Though ill, Edwards helped care for them, sleeping on a plank until ambulances arrived the next day. Then he found his own way to the officers' hospital to battle "the worst case of jaundice" the surgeon in charge had ever witnessed.

Edwards spent nearly a month in the hospital. As he recuperated he rambled around Little Rock, sketching the churches, the capitol, and cemeteries. In his ward he was something of a curiosity because, unlike other patients, he could sleep without a net and not be bothered by mosquitoes. He concluded that his blood was too saturated with poison to appeal to the insects. By early October he was judged well enough to help transfer 600 enlisted men and a number of officers to hospitals at Memphis. There he found Major Burt and other men of the Seventh in the convalescent camp. Eventually he regained his health sufficiently to return to the Seventh with Burt.[32]

More adventure and other duties, however, awaited Edwards in Missouri before he was able to rejoin the regiment. At Warrensburg in the west-central part of the state, he came upon advance troops of the Sixteenth Corps who reported that the main body of Price's army was "practically annihilated." But the elusive Seventh was not with them; it had been sent off in pursuit of "bushwhackers."[33]

Forbidden to go after the regiment, since no one was sure where it was, Edwards struck out on his own. He chaperoned a party of convalescents traveling eastward to Sedalia where he saw the men of the Seventh marching by with the brigade, "wet, weary and muddy, bedraggled almost beyond recognition." Life on the march had been grim indeed, and the journey was not yet over. In rain and snow, without tents or blankets or winter clothing, the men were "saturated with slush which froze around their benumbed bodies as they slept." Edwards wanted to be with them, but he was given surprising new responsibilities. General John McArthur, who had just succeeded Mower in command of the First Division, sent an astonished Edwards a summons. The general's first special order instructed Edwards to collect and take charge of all enlisted men not able to march on foot and transport them by train to Jefferson City, Missouri. It was an assignment "quite out of line of my supposed regular duties," Edwards wrote, but he accepted it without complaint.

The chaplain's command grew almost daily. By November 7 it numbered 700 men. Some termed them stragglers, but Edwards preferred to call them a "Reserve Corps." They were "a somewhat motley horde," he admitted, and "made up of all sorts and conditions of men: the sick and the weary, the weak and the wavering, as well as sometimes the strong and the stalwart, for whom the way was too rough and the march was too long." But they were good men!

He explained: "It is not always the physically strong that best endure the strain of a long and arduous march or exposure to the storm and coldness of the winter; and often it is the well fed who feel most acutely the gnawings of hunger. Some of the weakest, hungriest looking men in the [corps] are best able to keep up when the march is most fatiguing and the rations most scant. That a man should be found in this body of so called stragglers is no evidence that he is a coward or shirk. There are as good men and true here as are many that are now wading in the freezing mud or lying down and we treat them accordingly."

Edwards guarded his charges all the way to Jefferson City, where he found quarters for them in the state capitol. He expected to relinquish his command there, but instead McArthur ordered him to stay with the men the rest of the way to St. Louis. Edwards located horses for those best able to travel and sent them off, but he also acquired new recruits, including some comrades of the Seventh.

Near Jefferson City a few days later Edwards was briefly reunited with the regiment for the first time since they had been separated at Brownsville. Marshall judged 100 men of the regiment to be unable to proceed and transferred them to Edwards' reserves. The rest of the Seventh trudged off in the rain toward St. Louis.

Edwards organized his Reserve Corps into squads by regiment and company, putting some able-bodied men in each group to care for those needing help, and he did battle with any who dared interfere with them. Aboard a steamer, for instance, when a number of sick men he had assigned to a cabin were evicted by a New Jersey cavalry captain, Edwards countermanded the officer's orders and put the sick in the cabin again with a guard posted at the door. The two officers finally compared the dates of their commissions; Edwards was discovered to outrank the New Jersey captain, and his men remained in the cabin.

The Reserve Corps traveled on the Missouri River by steamboat to Hermann, Missouri, and then boarded a train. Some 40 miles out from Hermann the corps overtook the tired, mud-covered Seventh. When the train stopped for a few minutes Edwards smuggled aboard some of the weariest of the foot soldiers. At last the train reached St. Louis, where on November 15 Edwards was relieved of his command.

The main body of the Seventh arrived at about the same time and moved out to Benton Barracks. The ragamuffin soldiers spent eight happy days in the St. Louis area. On November 17 the paymaster visited the regiment, and Colonel Marshall wrote to the *St. Paul Daily Press*: "What untold happiness did not that payment dispense! A good share was sent home to the dear ones there. . . . Then there was plenty left to buy gloves, comforters, and the innumerable little things that soldiers need, to say nothing of the pies and cakes, and apples, and oranges, and peanuts and chestnuts, and cider and beer, and everything that a man's fancy and appetite craves after he has been away from city shops and stands six months." Meanwhile the chaplain had time to visit libraries and art galleries in St. Louis, call on friends, and, on a four-day pass, slip off to Indianapolis to see his family.[34]

Since summer, Smith's guerrillas had marched more than 3,000 miles, mostly in Missouri, in what one officer called their "Raid Period" of military service. The sore feet were not all healed, but the men were well clothed and felt "human" once more when they marched again on November 23 from Benton Barracks to a fleet of steamboats heading for Tennessee. The Seventh Minnesota and the Twelfth Iowa regiments were assigned to the steamer "Silver Cloud." It was a shabby boat, with primitive accommodations and poor fare. Better suited to serving 250 passengers, it now carried 700 men who crowded into its cabins and packed its decks. With other well-seasoned veterans of Smith's guerrillas, the Seventh was on its way to Nashville by way of the Mississippi, Ohio, and Cumberland rivers.[35]

Military forces were hurrying toward Nashville, where one of the decisive battles of the Civil War would be fought. The boats seemed to be panting like racehorses. "Every soldier in this vast fleet," Edwards wrote, "is alive to the fact and the issues of this race." Union troops under General George H. Thomas were holding the city, a vital northern supply and transportation center. General John M. Schofield with troops of the Twenty-third Corps and two divisions of Smith's Sixteenth Corps raced toward the city, while Confederate troops under General John Hood were rushed toward it from the southeast. The soldiers of the Seventh "entered into the spirit of the race," cheering loudly and enthusiastically whenever the "Silver Cloud" passed another boat. When they heard cannonading to the south, which Colonel Marshall identified as the sound of battle between Hood's forces and those of Schofield in the vicinity of Franklin, Tennessee, "the excitement of our race rose to the highest pitch."

After the hurrying came two weeks of watchful waiting. On December 1 the Seventh arrived at Nashville, where it was joined by a group of its convalescents from Memphis. The regiment took its assigned position about a mile and a half from the Tennessee state capitol on the far west of the Union force's semicircular ring around the city. Union troops fortified the hills surrounding Nashville while General Hood's Confederate troops dug breastworks and completed redoubts along an outer ring of fortifications. The weather continued fair and mild for several days.[36]

Edwards and his messmates had pitched their tent on a hillside in the midst of a jungle of thorn trees and chaparral overgrown with mistletoe. In a strenuous effort to make the campsite more comfortable, Major Burt managed to build a stone chimney. Although he received no help from Edwards or Folsom, Burt generously shared it with them. "There was not such another cheerful fireplace in the camp," Edwards wrote. To make partial amends for not helping the major, Edwards drew sketches of the camp, the chimney, and Burt working on it. Much pleased, the major wrote a long letter describing his endeavors and sent it to his wife with Edwards' sketches.[37]

During the days of waiting at Nashville, Edwards explored the city. He visited the tomb of President James K. Polk and sketched General Smith in his "fighting hat" as he rode by on an inspection of the Union line. After searching for several days, Edwards found his own brother Wesley among Indiana troops of the Twenty-third Corps under Schofield. The brothers visited a photographic studio in Nashville to have ambrotypes made. At the Christian Commission offices Edwards selected reading materials for the soldiers and was welcomed at their campfires when he distributed them. The men of the Seventh had completed their entrenchments and made themselves as comfortable as possible in camp. They read, wrote letters, played cards, and some, like George Lea of Company C, made trinkets. Because Christmas would be the tenth anniversary of Edwards' marriage, he commissioned Lea to produce a special ring that he could send his wife as a present.[38]

Camp at Nashville; Edwards sketch. *DePauw University Archives, Greencastle, Indiana*

Meanwhile endless streams of refugees poured into the city. Edwards had time to sketch some of them. One fugitive named Jimmy was adopted by men of the Seventh, but they had no extra tent space for him. At first he was given a pork barrel to sleep in, his feet to the fire, his head and body inside. Then when Major Burt appropriated the barrel for his chimney project, Jimmy was resettled in a large cracker box.[39]

On December 7 and 8 a wintry storm blew in on Nashville. Rain, sleet, and snow froze into an icy crust on which neither men nor animals could keep their footing. A week of miserable weather followed. Headquarters in Washington clamored for action, but General Thomas refused to do battle until the cold abated and cavalry had found the additional horses it needed. Edwards and Marshall sought new mounts at a horse auction. There a beautiful mouse-colored Indian pony with soft, dark eyes and an affectionate whinny won Edwards' heart. Unfortunately she sometimes stumbled, was frightened by gunfire, and proved as useless to the chaplain as his other mounts.[40]

From one of the highest hills Edwards sketched the Nashville terrain — the Cumberland River, the city itself, the eight main roads leading out like spokes of a wheel, the camp of the Seventh, Fort Negley, and the gunboats in the distance. At night the scene was grand: "The amphi-

71

theater of hills about Nashville, [was] gemmed with a myriad [of] camp-fires. Firing from the batteries lit the sky like heat lightning."[41]

Then on December 14 flashes from the signal station at Fort Negley suggested action would soon come. At 4:00 A.M. on December 15, in dense fog, bugles sounded, music of unseen bands filled the air, and men groped their way about. Everyone knew what the bugles and drums and banners meant, and without delay the Seventh Regiment readied itself for a fight.[42]

The men were unusually boisterous, perhaps because of the excitement of battle preparations, perhaps to drive away sad thoughts. A few were pensive, many unusually courteous. "Handshaking," Edwards observed, "was common and cordial. Officers for once discarded the respectful but distant military salute and greeted each other and their men with a hearty handclasp." A few were not ready to fight a battle. Some of the loudest and bravest talkers discovered ailments. One man, convinced that he would die a noble death that day, and that his mother should be notified, instructed Edwards what to say to her. Alas, the soldier became violently sick and never took part in the fighting.

Long files of men disappeared into the woods and the fog. Mounted aides galloped along the line, and the Seventh moved out of camp with the Third Brigade, as a part of the First Division under General McArthur. Under cover of the fog they advanced along Charlotte Pike and through adjacent woods and fields. After a time the division halted to allow the Twenty-third Corps to pass by and take its position; Edwards watched in vain for a glimpse of his brother.

While the soldiers waited, Edwards and some other officers climbed a high hill on the left of Charlotte Pike. Below them lay "a scene almost Miltonic in its grandeur. At first was visible only a great silent sea of mist, reaching from our feet to the distant hills, where the rebels were entrenched and awaiting us. Underneath this silver sea our army was creeping noiselessly, stealthily forward."[43]

When the mist had melted away "as far as the eye could reach, the valley was filled with armed men, moving still silently, with their ranks of skirmishers in the advance, feeling their way to the . . . black hills that made our horizon." Below, the line moved across the pike, obliquely left toward the enemy lines, Company B of the Seventh skirmishing ahead. Edwards, on the hill, noted that "not a gun as yet had been fired, when suddenly a report came from the very base of the hill . . . and I noticed a little puff of white smoke that in an instant cleared away, and showed the prostrate form of a soldier in blue," dead from the accidental discharge of his own gun.

Thin bluish-white puffs of smoke rose from the skirmish lines; rifles sounded in the distance like the dull patter of hail and, nearer, "like the popping of innumerable champagne bottles." From the river came the roar of the guns on the ironclads and the answering discordant din of the Rebel batteries.

Edwards hurried down the hill to be with the medical staff and ambulance corps in an open field. Men of the Seventh were ordered to

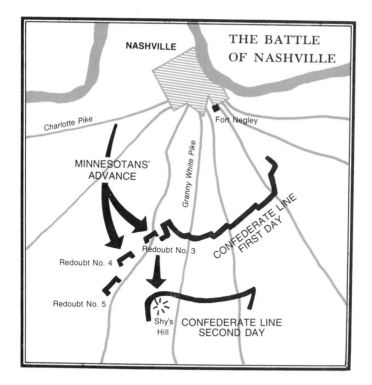

THE BATTLE
OF NASHVILLE

NASHVILLE

Charlotte Pike

Fort Negley

Granny White Pike

MINNESOTANS'
ADVANCE

CONFEDERATE LINE
FIRST DAY

Redoubt No. 3

Redoubt No. 4

Redoubt No. 5

Shy's
Hill

CONFEDERATE LINE
SECOND DAY

ELIJAH E.
EDWARDS,
CIVIL WAR
CHAPLAIN

lie down while the artillery fired on the enemy fortifications on the hills ahead and above them. In front of them lay a field of red vegetation with gnarled apple trees, a woods, another field, and another sparse growth of timber, the Union batteries, and a thin blue line slowly creeping forward and upward.

While the regiment and the ambulance corps waited, Edwards rode toward the front of the line where General McArthur and his staff sat quietly on their horses watching the progress of the battle. "McArthur looks the Highland chief in his tartan cap and plaid," Edwards wrote. "His staff wears Scotch caps[,] a bit of uniform that gives them a peculiarly dashing appearance." The general's party was in range of Confederate guns; shots tore up the ground at their feet. None of the other horses or men moved, but Edwards' horse "snorted wildly," and the chaplain allowed himself to be taken at an inglorious canter to a safer part of the field. As he rode away a shell passed over his head and burst ahead of him "with a deafening roar that shook the very hills."

Meanwhile he heard cheering as cavalry galloped along the pike. Expecting action, he hurried back to the ambulance corps in time to see the Seventh rushing forward. Abandoning knapsacks and blankets, the men moved across one field and then another on up into the hills west of Hillsboro Pike, disappearing into the smoke. The Third Brigade commanded by Colonel Sylvester G. Hill stormed Confederate Redoubt No. 3; Hill had barely gained the works when Confederate fire from another redoubt killed him. Before he was hit, Hill had given an order to charge a second redoubt; Major Burt of the Seventh heard and repeated the order. Colonel Marshall, next ranking officer of the brigade, assumed command and the charge was made, the men surging down a wall and crossing the pike to capture Redoubt No. 2. In the battlefield confusion men from another Union corps tried to claim credit for capturing it. But Captain Carter and others of the Third Brigade stood fast, reserving first rights and full glory for the victory.[44]

Edwards and the ambulance corps searched for the fallen and found Captain John P. Houston of the Fifth Minnesota, whose shoulder had been shattered. Three men of the Seventh were killed, and a few were injured, but the wounds of only one were serious. The general battle scene, however, was horrifying. Many injured lay among the torn and mangled bodies of the dead. Edwards cared for the wounded and saw them safely on the way to hospitals in Nashville. As the chaplain and corps searched, they saw hundreds of Rebel soldiers throw down their arms and rush forward to surrender. Six Union soldiers took charge of some 300 captives and marched them to the rear.

Meanwhile the regiment bivouacked for the night on the battlefield. Colonel Marshall had ordered Edwards to return to the regiment's Nashville camp with messages and instructions for those left there. Late at night in camp, while his memory was fresh, Edwards sat alone beside Burt's fireplace and wrote an account of what he had seen that day. The Union troops had driven back the enemy and doubled up the Confederate line; they had captured many prisoners and a number of fortified positions — all with the loss of comparatively few men. At the end of the day there was a promise of ultimate victory, but the struggle was far from over.[45]

At daybreak on December 16 Edwards returned to the regiment,

Storming the battery at Hillsboro Pike, December 15, 1864; Edwards sketch. *DePauw University Archives, Greencastle, Indiana*

74

now drawn up in a long double row and waiting for orders. The Seventh was at the far left of McArthur's Third Brigade; to its right was the Twelfth Iowa, its right resting on Granny White Pike, a road leading to the city. While the men waited, the postmaster came with letters from home, but few had time to read them before the bugles sounded and shooting began in the distance. Skirmishers were ordered forward, and the men lay prone while the batteries behind them shot over their heads toward the enemy.[46]

The new Confederate battle line, farther south than that of the previous day, extended some two and a half miles from a steep hill (later named for Confederate Colonel William Shy, who was killed there that day) to another on the right known as Overton or Peach Orchard Hill. Union forces covered three sides of Shy's Hill, and facing it about 600 yards from its base lay the Seventh Minnesota. The enemy fortifications were protected by a high stone wall and large rails slanting from the wall to the ground. Confederates fired cannon from pits within the fortifications on top of the hill, and their sharpshooters kept blazing away from barricades somewhat in advance of the wall.

In early afternoon the shooting stopped as a cold rain began to fall. Edwards took advantage of the lull in the fighting to sketch the battle scene from his vantage point to the rear of the regiment. With the idea of later reproducing his sketch on a larger scale, he explained the view: "The sketch represents in the foreground our battery. . . . The hostile lines are in the middle ground, our right resting upon the base of a high hill on the summit of which rested the enemy's left. In the distance was the broken hill country. On the left was the Bradford mansion, afterwards our field hospital. . . . Between the house and foreground of the picture meandered gracefully a small creek, and under the shelter of its right bank soldiers were filling their canteens, or idly sitting and discussing the events of the day, and some of them . . . [were] playing cards."[47]

So the regiment lay until late afternoon, when it was handed shovels and ordered to dig entrenchments. It seemed as though there would be no attack that day. Yet someone in authority was not content to rest any longer. No sooner had the men of the Seventh taken up their shovels than they saw soldiers in motion on their right. The First Brigade had started forward across the cornfields to the west, the Second followed in echelon, and Marshall, seeing that they needed support, ordered an advance of the Third. The men dropped their shovels and took up their guns. Against fierce fire from the redoubt above, the assault on Shy's Hill — the entire battle's key action — had begun.[48]

Edwards returned from caring for some wounded just in time to see the Union forces press forward over muddy ground, fields, and hedges and then push up the slope. "There was no regular line. Some were far in advance[,] others seemed to lag in the rear, but all were moving, all save those [who] would never rise up at sound of trumpet or tap of drum." In a few minutes a cheer echoed across the valley, and the Union flag waved over the crest of the hill.[49]

75

Colonel Marshall on horseback led the Third Brigade to the top of the hill, leaped over the barricades, and plunged into the fight, urging the Confederates to surrender. A bullet hit him in the breast, but his life was saved by his heavy gauntlets stuffed in his coat.[50]

Close behind the colonel was Captain Carter at the head of Company K. Carter's men boosted him through a notch in the stone wall and quickly followed him. They captured the Louisiana Point Coupee Battery and its "four fine brass Napoleon 12-pounders." At Carter's order his lieutenant stayed with the guns, which Colonel Lucius Hubbard of the Fifth Minnesota, commanding the Second Brigade, soon demanded as spoils of war. Carter's man refused to give them up, so Hubbard then proposed to Marshall that they divide the guns between the two brigades. After some discussion Marshall agreed.

It was all very well for Marshall to appear so magnanimous, but Carter saw no need to share the guns with Hubbard's brigade or anyone else. Right or wrong, Carter concluded that Marshall's behavior was politically motivated: the colonel planned to run for governor when the war was over, and by sharing guns with fellow Minnesotan Hubbard he put the rival colonel in a position to support his candidacy.[51]

Edwards, other chaplains, and the men of the ambulance corps searched the hillside for the dead and wounded. After the injured had been taken to the emergency hospital in the Bradford mansion, Marshall ordered Edwards to return to Nashville to notify the people at home. He was to telegraph to the St. Paul newspapers the details of the battle and the names of the dead and wounded. He also was to send an account to Mrs. Marshall. It was late when he completed his mission and found his way back to the regiment.[52]

Edwards was exhausted when he returned to the Bradford house. He tied his horse outside, went in, found a blanket, and fell asleep on the kitchen floor. In a few hours he awakened and saw "The wounded and dying . . . around me, ranged in rows upon the floor and upon cots and stretchers. . . . [F]ew of them seemed to realize that their last battle was being fought." The chaplain wrote letters for some; for others he read from the Bible and prayed. A young soldier dictated a letter for Edwards to send to his elderly parents; he wanted them to know that he had been wounded but that he hoped to recover. Edwards added a postscript warning the parents that their son's condition was critical and perhaps he would not survive. The chaplain addressed another letter to a young wife whose husband told her "He had fought bravely, had fallen, but did not fear to die. He had loved her, he loved her still. This was the last letter he would ever write—would she meet him in heaven?"

In the afternoon Edwards buried the regiment's dead "in a single wide grave side by side in the field where they fell. There were seven Minnesotans and a nameless man found dead among them." He also placed a wooden grave marker on the site for each one.

In addition to the Fifth and Seventh, two other Minnesota regiments

— the Ninth and Tenth — fought at Nashville. All four regiments served under General John McArthur of the First Division and General Andrew J. Smith, whose detachment was part of the Army of the Tennessee. The Seventh was in the Third Brigade commanded after December 15 by Marshall, the Fifth and Ninth were in the Second Brigade under Hubbard, and the Tenth was in the First Brigade under Colonel William McMillen of Indiana. At Nashville 63 Minnesota men were killed, 237 wounded, and one was missing in action. On the casualty list for the Seventh were 62 men. Minnesota's two brigade leaders were fortunate. Marshall was hit but not injured; Hubbard was unscathed although he had one, two, or three (reports varied) horses shot from under him.[53]

After the Nashville rout, the remnants of Hood's army retreated toward Franklin and eventually crossed the Tennessee River into Mississippi. The Minnesota Seventh was among the Union troops that chased in vain after the Confederates. The pursuit was impeded not only by abominable weather but by skillful rear-guard action by Forrest's cavalry.[54]

Edwards stayed behind with other chaplains and regimental surgeons to move the wounded to Nashville hospitals. On one of his last hospital rounds, he found Captain Houston of the Fifth Minnesota whom he had helped carry from the battlefield on December 15. A hospital surgeon had decided to amputate the captain's arm, but Houston refused to allow it. Edwards helped him locate the Fifth's surgeon, Dr. Vincent Kennedy, who agreed to try to save the arm. The doctor removed part of the bone and socket, leaving the arm several inches shorter but sufficient for handshaking, writing, or other light work.[55]

On Christmas Day Edwards joined a party of ten men that left Nashville for Franklin to rejoin their regiments. It was a dreary journey, wrote Edwards, "over the path of the retreating and pursuing armies. The marks of carnage were everywhere visible. . . . Carrion birds flew in circles above the field. The graves of the hastily buried dead met the glance in almost every direction. How quiet their slumber after the storm of battle!"[56]

Would the brave men be forgotten when the temporary wooden headboards were gone, Edwards wondered, "Or will a grateful nation take them into remembrance, as heroes and saviors of their country?" The chaplain hoped that the nation would remember the families of its veteran dead with useful rewards like homesteads, stocks, or greenbacks, not just with huge monuments.

Edwards and his companions traveled southward through a number of ravaged towns and soon caught up with their regiments in southwestern Tennessee. During an idle day in camp, men of the Seventh discussed, among other things, news reports they read of the Nashville battle. They agreed that Chaplain Humphrey's account gave more credit to the Twelfth Iowa than it deserved and that Ohio newspapers glorified General Schofield and the Twenty-third Corps at the expense of the First

Division under General Smith. "Soldiers, in the main," Edwards commented, "are fair to themselves and the command to which they belong."[57]

As the army moved on, Edwards found the ruined towns less distressing than glimpses of poor white people living along the line of march. He wrote: "Never have I been more convinced of the justice of our cause than when I have looked upon the poor whites of the South. But at one blow the shackles shall fall from black and white. This double emancipation will be worth all the toil and tears and blood that we have given for it."

On New Year's Eve the Seventh camped in a cornfield during a snow-storm. "The old year could not well avoid dying [on] such a night as this," wrote the chaplain. When they guessed their destination the men kept asking local people, "How far to the [Tennessee] river?" Edwards sketched one old man, "a thorough loyalist, [who] took his stand on a stump by the roadside, and without waiting for the question continued shouting till he was hoarse: 'Only seven miles to the river! Only seven miles to the river! . . . Glad to see you boys! . . . Seven miles to the river.' " Finally reaching the stream, the marchers greeted it as joyously as Xenophon's Greek army greeted the sea, but, Edwards slyly noted, for this army it was the "Tennes-see"! From Clifton, Tennessee, they traveled by gunboats to Eastport and made camp amid magnificent pine trees on high land a few miles from the river.

A city of 15,000 rose almost overnight as its soldier invaders felled trees in every direction and built small, mud-daubed, bark-covered log cabins. After months in constant motion the men welcomed a site rumored to be their winter quarters. Edwards and his messmates took what comfort they could in their little lean-to shelter, built on a hillside under Major Burt's direction. Burt "bantered" the chaplain in theological discussions, and while disbelieving, nevertheless conversed "respectfully." Edwards and Burt played a nightly game of chess while the major's adopted tailless rooster, "A. J. Smith," sat disconsolate on the end of the bed.[58]

On January 26 in the rude shelter amid "all that makes discomfort picturesque," Edwards celebrated his thirty-fourth birthday. A feeling of melancholy came over him with the thought that he had completed almost "half of the allotted pilgrimage of man." He imagined a future home on Lake Como, a home with roses and honeysuckle about the porch and a studio with good light for painting.

On January 31 Edwards penned his monthly report on the moral condition of the regiment. "With but few, if any[,] exceptions," he wrote, the men are "temperate, orderly, and soldierly in the best sense of the term, in these respects comparing favorably with the men of other regiments." Chaplain Humphrey of the Twelfth Iowa found more to criticize in his report. Edwards observed that Humphrey "thinks . . . it is his duty to expose the sins of the army of men and officers and in his report denounced certain men (commissioned) for gambling and swearing and

78

other vices." Humphrey's statements on these matters, Edwards reported, "created a profound sensation."[59]

Despite differing views of their mission, Edwards and his fellow chaplains of the Third Brigade worked together in brotherly harmony most of the time. When weather permitted they held joint Sunday worship and prayer services at Eastport. Thinking that the troops would stay in camp for the rest of the winter, some of them proposed to build a house of worship. Edwards did not believe they would and opposed the plan, but he was outvoted. The marching orders came, as Edwards had predicted, and the reorganized Sixteenth Corps, still commanded by General Smith and including McArthur's brigade of which the Seventh was part, was sent to the Army of the Gulf to help besiege Mobile, Alabama.[60]

On February 8 the men sailed on the steamer "Magenta" down the Tennessee. Eventually they also went down the Ohio and the Mississippi to New Orleans, stopping several days on the way at Cairo and Vicksburg, where Edwards gathered a store of literature and stationery for the regiment.

On the "Magenta" the brigade's officers were quartered in a 60-by-80-foot cabin where they occupied themselves reading, writing, playing cards and chess, or making out payrolls. Chaplain Humphrey wanted to take over the cabin for a series of prayer meetings, but Edwards and others opposed the plan, so it was dropped. To make amends Edwards agreed that Humphrey should be in charge of the united Sunday worship services.

Humphrey did not suffer defeat for long. A few days later he reported that some brigade officers were gambling. He told Edwards they used colored beans, each bean representing a unit of money, and privately exchanged the beans for money when their game was over. No matter how circumspect their behavior, they *were* gambling and gambling was illegal. So it was, said Edwards, that the heroic Episcopal chaplain did battle with the "gigantic windmill" of the army. Wrote Edwards: "He first button-holed the Officer of the day, but obtaining no help from that quarter called upon the Col. commanding, and then upon the officers themselves, who swarmed around him angry and threatening, like bees or hornets. In vain they stormed and abused. He smiled blandly, but was immovable. Gambling was a sin and prohibited by law. . . . He threatened them each with court-martial and all the publicity that he could give the matter in the papers. They saw that arguments were useless as threats, and gambled no more, at least when the chaplain was around."

On their southward journey the troops passed Natchez, Baton Rouge, and Plaquemine, Louisiana, sailing by mansions of the rich, neatly whitewashed quarters of slaves, and homes of poor whites. After moving through the bustling city of New Orleans with its crescent-shaped wharf, the men disembarked near a moldy old-fashioned mansion just south of town. It had been General Andrew Jackson's headquarters in January, 1815, when his American troops routed the British in a famous battle of the War of 1812. The soldiers filled the air with golden flying missiles plucked from bitter orange trees, and they feasted on oysters in a camp on the edge of a cypress swamp, near an unfinished monument to Jackson's victory. A Minnesota soldier was bitten by one of the snakes infesting the coffee-colored water. He was treated with a full quart of whisky to neutralize the venom.

It was a miserable place for a camp, but rumor had it that Smith's guerrillas were not to be trusted close to the city. Nevertheless, after numerous complaints, the Seventh was relocated nearer the city in a brickyard between a potter's field and a hospital. There, said the chaplain, the mud was only six inches deep. His blankets and clothing had been wet since the New Orleans landing, and in the new camp Edwards was taken sick and hospitalized with violent cramping and other symptoms similar to those of cholera and malaria. Once again he was left behind while the regiment moved on.[61]

Looking out his hospital window he caught glimpses of the New Orleans Mardi Gras paraders in their grotesque masks. When he felt stronger he walked with one of the doctors to visit churches, a cemetery, and the theater. In spite of such diversions, Edwards felt depressed because he was not with his regiment.[62]

He learned from newspaper reports and officers who visited the hospital that the Seventh had moved across the Gulf of Mexico to Dauphin Island, at the mouth of Mobile Bay. Encamped on a sandy beach and living on an oyster diet that had begun to pall, Smith's corps was getting ready to join other troops under the over-all command of General Edward R. S. Canby in a late-in-the-war campaign against Mobile.

When they learned that hospital patients were to be sent north to Natchez, Edwards and another Minnesota officer slipped out of the hospital and started for the front. The other officer was scarcely able to walk but determined to go, and Edwards was ready to help him. "There is something dreadful and yet fascinating about a great battle and I for one cannot keep away," he said.[63]

By March 30 they had reached their Minnesota regiments, which by now were helping to besiege Spanish Fort, an important post some twelve miles east across the bay from Mobile. The fort, on the outer line of the city's defense, had to be captured before Mobile would fall. Two other chaplains gave Edwards particulars of the action, and he took up his duties in the division hospital. A hundred soldiers already were casualties, among them Colonel Marshall, who was wounded by a bullet that grazed his neck while he rode at the head of his brigade toward the fort. Another "wounded" officer, Edwards' messmate Lieutenant Folsom, got little sympathy. He was hit in the seat of his trousers and became the butt of many good-natured jests.[64]

Although Smith's men were scattered over rolling forestland in an exposed position in front of Spanish Fort, the Seventh Minnesota suffered

Battlefield at Old Spanish Fort, April 3, 1865; Edwards sketch. *DePauw University Archives, Greencastle, Indiana.*

few casualties. Some of the soldiers fired their guns now and then in a desultory manner; others reclined or slept in grassy dugout shelters in the midst of the din, played cards, read, and smoked. "Their coolness is refreshing," Edwards noted.[65]

Among the grim machines of war that proved influential in the siege of the fort was a platoon of wooden mortars resembling old-fashioned ironbound buckets. Fashioned of gumwood, they were lightweight, were easily transported, and fired four-inch shells with one ounce of powder. Installed in ditches close to the Rebel works, they were pointed nearly vertically and fired almost without noise into the fort.[66]

Late at night on April 8, 1865, the Confederate guns ceased firing from Spanish Fort. In the sudden stillness the men of the Seventh cheered when they heard Major Burt's rooster crowing from a pine stump. Whenever the rooster crowed, the enthusiastic soldiers cheered again. In the morning 600 prisoners marched out of the fort through rows of wooden cannon, "at the sight of which their curses were not loud but deep." And the regimental bands played "Yankee Doodle."[67]

After surrender of the fort, Edwards walked beyond the regiment's campground to make a sketch from a hillside. The spires of Mobile lay in the distance across the silvery bay. In the foreground stood pine trees festooned with Spanish moss, and underfoot grew white, purple, and yellow flowers and the crimson buckeye. Edwards sketched until shells from guns out in the bay started bursting all around him; then he made haste back to camp. Excitement reigned there: men threw their hats in the air, shouted, hugged each other, and cheered. They had just learned that Lee had evacuated Richmond! Surely the war would soon be over.[68]

Cannonading continued for several days, however. The Third Brigade marched forward toward another work, Fort Blakely, but it was taken by the Second Brigade before the Third reached the front lines. From across the bay came the great roar of an exploding powder magazine — and more news. Union troops had entered Mobile. In the welcome silence the chaplain gathered the religious men of the regiment for prayer and praise to God.

On the quiet Sabbath-like day that followed, the men lay in camp, hoping to be sent home. Instead, their new orders sent them on the march again with fifteen days' rations, this time northward toward Montgomery, Alabama.

On April 13 the men struck their tents and started marching through desolate pine barrens and past rude log homes of poor people in an impoverished frontier countryside of Alabama. Smith's guerrillas behaved well — there was little or nothing to plunder.

The men had not traveled far when a messenger came galloping by shouting the news of Lee's surrender. This precipitated two hours of celebrating not only by the troops but by some southerners who, wrote Edwards, "came from their lurking places into our lines, weeping, cheering, handshaking with our men. Tongue cannot describe the enthusiasm that prevailed."

As the troops passed along, they were greeted by houses displaying white flags, some carrying such mottoes as "the Union forever" or "the United States forever." Poor people hung out white towels or tablecloths, and one woman waved a white undergarment "that being recognized received cheer after cheer as the Corps passed by." But it was clear that many wealthy residents tended to discredit the news of surrender, and they sullenly refrained from gaiety.

On April 21, the men marched nonstop for 18 miles in chilling rain and "unfathomable" mud. Edwards recognized symptoms of malaria and dosed himself hourly with quinine. They camped that night at Greenville, Alabama, a quaint and beautiful place with many fine residences embowered in trees and roses in full bloom. The city had three churches and a cemetery of "rare beauty" where Edwards wandered the next day and copied some of the gravestone inscriptions.

The Union forces announced Lee's surrender to the townspeople with a 200-gun salute. The band played "The Girl I Left Behind Me," and some of the Minnesota soldiers took over the local printing office to put out an issue of the Greenville newspaper filled with official dispatches on the surrender. On the march again the troops announced the surrender at each community along the road to Montgomery.

As they neared Montgomery the roads improved and the farms appeared more prosperous, so a few bummers slipped away to gobble. Some from Minnesota were attacked by Rebels, "Who saw no good reason why they should be robbed in time of peace." Among the prowlers were musicians who ran off when fired upon, leaving their horns in possession of the enemy. Back in camp "a Scripture text was hurled at them[,] 'The horns of the wicked shall be cut off.' "

Union cavalry had captured Montgomery only shortly before Smith's troops arrived in the city. The Union flag fluttered over the statehouse, and poorer white people and blacks offered the men cakes and pies, drinks of fresh water, and quantities of Confederate scrip. The soldiers camped that night about three miles north of the city on the banks of the Alabama River and near a small brook with an old mill. Millers in the ranks put the mill in running order and ground corn and wheat for their rations.

Rumors had spread among the Confederates for some ten days that President Lincoln was dead, but his assassination was not confirmed at Montgomery until the boats arrived on May 1. It was fortunate that the news dawned on the army only slowly, Edwards thought. "If the soldiers had been at first convinced of its truth it is probable that no power could have prevented scenes of violence." Union services were held in the state-house to honor the martyred president, and the chaplain conducted services for the regiment in camp.[69]

Edwards had few other duties in Montgomery and found time to walk about the city and visit the cemetery. The men amused themselves playing ball or marbles, firing the wooden mortars they had brought along from Spanish Fort, gambling with Confederate money, or playing in the brook — anything to kill time "since other killing has become murder." Now that their fighting days were over, the men wondered what kind of work they would find at home.[70]

Fighting may have officially ended, but among the regimental chaplains belligerency was still alive. The 24 chaplains who met at the state-house to discuss "matters and things" included a Minnesotan "brim full of loyalty which was right enough." He wanted the chaplains to take over all the pulpits in Montgomery and give the rebellious citizens an opportunity to hear "a loyal and star-spangled gospel." Although the others appeared to favor the idea, Edwards again voiced opposition. "I am sorry to say that the lot fell upon me the Jonah of the company to rebuke the high handed measures proposed," he wrote. There were indeed 24 chaplains who could fill Montgomery pulpits, "but there were also 24 regiments to whom their services were first due," Edwards reminded them. "Let us attend to our own regimental business, and leave the city pulpits in the hands of those who have hitherto held them. War confers upon us no right of the kind suggested." It was clear that Edwards' words were not popular, yet no one spoke against him. Subsequently some of the chaplains accepted invitations to speak from local pulpits, but their tenure as ministers of the gospel in Montgomery was short-lived. On May 10 came orders to move on, this time to Selma, Alabama.[71]

A short journey westward down the Alabama River on the steamboat "Peerless" took the men on May 12 to Selma, a city in smoking ruins. Union cavalry under General James H. Wilson had just taken the city, plundered it, and destroyed its factories, which had long produced cannon and other military supplies for the Confederate army.[72]

Bitterness and hatred ran rampant in Selma. Many local citizens refused to believe that Lee had surrendered and did not disguise their contempt for the Yankee occupiers. Edwards spoke for many of the Union troops in deploring the barbarism visited on Selma, but he also commented that Rebels were "fiends" at Andersonville and Fort Pillow, and that widespread atrocities committed by southern owners against their slaves were equally deplorable. There were other hostilities. Middle-class and poor whites resented aristocratic southerners and blamed them for the war. Whites feared the blacks, who were fleeing by the hundreds from the outlying rural areas to Selma for the protection of the Union army, to escape death and starvation and to find freedom.[73]

The troops settled down in camp in a grove west of the city. There the men fashioned shelters roofed with canvas or with window shutters, lattice work, and boards stolen from ruined buildings. Several companies of the Seventh were sent off for duty in other cities, but the rest remained encamped near Selma in relative idleness through much of a hot summer. The Seventh Minnesota and the Third Brigade were to spend more than three months in occupation duty among freed slaves and unreconstructed Confederates at Selma.

Their "raiding, roystering" days were over. It was a time of weary waiting "in a land of whipped Tigers, when the air of noon day is like the breath of an oven." Their camp looked out on an abandoned battle-field, ruined houses, few living things — stray, snarling curs, forlorn turkeys and cows, happy freedmen, dejected whites. There was no reading matter, no mail, no "pleasant objects of contemplation."[74]

Many of the men tried to make the best of things. The more industrious mended watches, made rings and trinkets, tailored, made shoes, and dickered. Company C was the most industrious. Its row of tents became a place of shops with every man busily engaged. One had a bellows and a small smelting furnace. "The whole camp resounds with hammering, sawing and filing," wrote Edwards. "Some have gone into the mocking bird business and the trees are hung full of cages, and the camp is vocal with the melody of the captive songsters. The birds are native and are brought into camp and disposed of by country rustics.[75]

Edwards improved his morale with some new clothes — black pants, a shirt, a white vest. Dressed in his newly acquired finery, he walked under the myrtles and mulberry trees of Selma's Broad Street, pleased with his improved appearance. But his new plumage made no favorable impression on one Selma resident: "A rather handsome young lady met me, made a wry face as she brushed past and muttered with clenched teeth and white lips 'tyrant.' I wonder if she means me?" Many southern ladies displayed bitterness and spite toward the Union troops; Edwards especially noted that women would walk out in mud ankle deep to avoid passing under the Union flags hanging outside army headquarters. Yet there were people of all classes who were friendly and conciliatory. Indeed Edwards performed a number of marriages between southern women and northern soldiers.

The chaplain kept busy in other ways. Usually he conducted religious services in camp on Sunday afternoons, and on Sunday mornings after inspection he attended one or more of the Selma Protestant churches. At one he met a venerable Methodist bishop his father had known. When a Bible study class was organized by men of the Third

Sketching at Selma, May 24, 1865. *DePauw University Archives, Greencastle, Indiana*

Brigade, Edwards was invited to teach it at the Presbyterian church. Other times he attended the Baptist church to hear a talented young girl sing.[76]

Some of the clergy of Selma were unreconstructed Rebels and in fact were prepared to close their churches for the duration of the military occupation. But Marshall, now commanding the brigade, took note of their threat and issued one of his own. He ordered that the churches, if closed, should be opened by military authority for use by the chaplains of the various regiments. Said Edwards: "Thus nearly did we become installed as pastors of Southern churches. The situation was a grave one, but the idea of a Northern Gospel proclaimed in Southern sanctuaries was a little too much, and the preachers reconsidered . . . closing the churches."[77]

Edwards performed several weddings for blacks and a number of times attended their services in the basement of the Methodist church. He was invited to preach there, and the black Methodists asked him whether they should leave the southern branch of the church to join the northern Methodists. In their pride as freedmen they did not want to worship in the Methodist church basement while the white folks worshiped upstairs. Edwards advised them to consider carefully before taking such a step, in particular because they would forfeit their right to any part of the church property.

Prejudice and the abuse of blacks, covert and blatant, were all around in Selma. One of the worst cases involved a light-skinned mulatto who had run away from her master after he stripped her naked and burned her with red hot tongs. Unfortunately Union soldiers were not guiltless either. Edwards told of the black man who came to camp bringing with him his only treasure, a fiddle: "A soldier begged it away from him. The grateful darkie had no sooner given it away than the receiver smashed the piece on his woolly pate. I do not think that I am particularly barbarous or unfeeling," the chaplain wrote, "but there are some men at whose funeral I should be glad to officiate."[78]

Edwards' monthly reports to the adjutant general charted the state of affairs in the regiment during the Selma occupation. At the end of May he wrote: "The men although relieved by the general cessation of hostilities from their more arduous and dangerous military duties, have not deteriorated, either in the observance of laws, in courtesy and good feeling toward each other, or the respect due their officers."[79]

A month later he was less pleased with them and with conditions in camp: "While the conduct and deportment of the men are as heretofore orderly and commendable, there still exist sources of demoralization that must in time tell upon their character. There is an intimate relation [between] good rations and good behavior. The rations furnished to the regiment during the past month have been both scant and unwholesome, and the result must necessarily be impaired digestion and soured temper." Furthermore, good reading matter was very much needed. Without it, "resort is too frequently had to games of chance, to frivolous pursuits and amusements, or to more hurtful dissipation." The chaplain's report concluded: "There exists a widespread feeling of discontent at not being mustered out of the service and returned home, which is aggravated by the heat of the climate, a great amount of sickness in camp, and the impression, just, or unfounded, that a pressing demand for their services no longer exists."[80]

The hot weather continued, as many as half of the regiment were on the sick list at one time, and the hospital was overflowing. And there was far too much drinking. At last in exasperation Edwards spoke directly to the men. He preached a Sunday sermon on drunkenness, and his July chaplain's report treated the subject "in full and unsparing [way]."[81]

The chaplain visited the ill in the hospital, conducted funeral services for the dead (five of the regiment died at Selma), and, at the request of friends of one of the deceased, carved a special headstone for the soldier's grave. He copied architectural drawings for a local hotel company, and he spent many spare hours at the office of the provost marshal, sketching the faces of blacks who came there on business. There, too, he met again Captain (now Major) Houston, whose arm was sufficiently healed for him to greet the chaplain with a firm clasp of his right hand.[82]

Near the end of July army red tape unwound enough for the Selma veterans to start for home and be mustered out. On July 20, with trumpets sounding, drums beating, and ragged banners waving, they marched for the last time through Selma, bearing their cages of mocking birds as well as goats and dogs of all kinds. Ambulances carried the sick who were able to travel; only a few were left behind in the hospital. On both sides of the soldiers' route followed long files of blacks, many of whom wanted to go north with the troops. Long before the men of the

Seventh reached Minnesota they were parted from their black friends and forced to abandon most of their Selma treasures.[83]

On the last leg of its journey home the Seventh sailed up the Mississippi on the steamboat "Savannah," pausing for ceremonies at Winona, Red Wing, and Hastings. The returning heroes were cheered and fed, and tears filled many an eye for the local boys who were gone forever. At St. Paul a reception committee met the boat at the levee and escorted those who could march to the capitol. The mayor, the governor, and Marshall all gave speeches. The colonel concluded his with a tribute: "The men who have carried muskets and knapsacks for thirteen dollars a month are the true heroes of the war." After the speeches the women of St. Paul served the heroes a bountiful repast, and some took food and comforting words to those who lay ill on the steamboat. The regiment then moved out in formation on its last march to the levee for the trip to Fort Snelling, where the men laid down their arms and were mustered out of the service.[84]

ELIJAH E. EDWARDS, CIVIL WAR CHAPLAIN

With the ceremonies and official functions in St. Paul over, Edwards spent time with old friends, preached two sermons, and officiated at the funeral of a relative of one of the Seventh's officers. Tired, depressed, and suffering from another "aguish" attack, he nevertheless took the steamboat "Enterprise" for Taylors Falls to join in one last celebration, this one honoring the return of Company C. In a grove of trees the ladies of the town had spread a picnic feast. The tables were "laid out in the most tempting manner, loaded with viands that buried 'hard tack' in oblivion," said the *Taylors Falls Reporter*. Edwards' regimental comrades and their families wanted to entertain him, but he was too ill to accept any invitations, and he became more depressed when he tried to comfort Mrs. Smith, widow of his doctor friend who was killed at Tupelo.[85]

By early September, 1865, Edwards had returned to St. Paul, where he arranged for the shipment of his household goods to St. Louis and made plans to accept Dr. Crary's offer of a position on the *Central Christian Advocate*. Fifty years of Edwards' life remained. He spent them as editor, clergyman, and educator in Illinois, Missouri, Colorado, Minnesota, Indiana, North Carolina, and Wisconsin. Wherever he lived he continued to sketch and paint. As a popular Memorial Day speaker and chalk-talk lecturer, he delighted old comrades, and he treasured the memory of his experiences with them until his last, feeble days.

Dr. Thomas Foster
Indian Historiographer

*A Minnesota Editor Wrestles
with Washington Bureaucrats to Establish What Would Become
the Bureau of American Ethnology*

I N THE SUMMER OF 1872 Thomas Foster of Duluth left his home on the shore of Lake Superior in pursuit of an idea whose time, he thought, had come. The 54-year-old newspaper editor, medical doctor, and Republican party worker had decided to follow a star he had glimpsed 20 years earlier. He wished to become a historiographer of the American Indian and he wanted the United States government to support his efforts. At a time when no university in the country offered courses in anthropology or ethnology and the notion still prevailed in the West that the only good Indian was a dead one, Foster dreamed of creating a federal bureau that would collect and study data on the native peoples of North America. Eventually his dream was to become reality as the Smithsonian Institution's Bureau of Ethnology, but Thomas Foster would not be on its payroll.[1]

A stocky man, five feet, six inches tall, Foster was looked upon with affectionate benevolence by some Minnesotans as a patriarch with a heart "bigger than his house." To his detractors and political enemies he was a "blatherskite" and "a walking beer barrel" with a "red nose and bad eyes." The doctor, who relished such verbal attacks, did indeed have weak eyes, having suffered from trachoma, and he was far from temperate in most matters although he drank liquor only in moderation. An equalitarian Whig in philosophy, Foster was generally a main-line Republican in politics. He was unpredictable and outspoken, venting editorial wrath without fear or favor on sacred cows, specious arguments, greedy politicians, and stupidity in all its branches.[2]

Foster became interested in Indians after moving to Minnesota Territory from Pennsylvania in 1849. He came as private secretary to Alexander Ramsey, the new territorial governor, and as the territory's first librarian "ex-officio." Born in Philadelphia and educated in a private school and a classical academy, Foster had edited newspapers since he was 18; in his spare time he studied and then practiced medicine. A political activist from his earliest years, he became acquainted with Alexander Ramsey in the 1840s. In 1848 the two worked together in a remarkable grass-roots organization that, conquering Pennsylvania for the Whigs, helped elect Zachary Taylor to the presidency. In the spring of 1849 President Taylor appointed Ramsey to the positions of governor and superintendent of Indian affairs for Minnesota, and Ramsey invited Foster to accompany him to the new territory. Although the jobs of secretary and librarian were temporary and poorly paid, Foster accepted them as an opportunity for an expense-paid adventure and a chance to look over prospects for a home in the West.[3]

DR. THOMAS FOSTER, INDIAN HISTORI-OGRAPHER

One of Foster's duties that summer was to compile background information for Ramsey's first report on Indian affairs in Minnesota. By the time the doctor had completed detailed research on Minnesota's Dakota (or Sioux), Ojibway (or Chippewa), and Winnebago tribes, he decided that he wanted to continue the study of American Indians. He began seeking a government position that would nurture his plan. Since the Democratic Indian agent to the Winnebago in Minnesota was due for replacement by a Whig, Foster recommended himself for the post to friends in the Taylor administration. He returned to Pennsylvania at the end of the summer of 1849, and while awaiting the results of his campaign for office, he began the "study [of] Ethnology, the science of races[,] and Philology, that of languages."[4]

Still without an appointment in August, 1850, Foster traveled to Washington, D.C., to lobby in his own behalf. With Henry H. Sibley, the fur trader who was Minnesota Territory's first delegate in Congress, he promoted legislation authorizing the negotiation of treaties to acquire Indian lands within the Territory. Foster reasoned that if Ramsey were appointed a treaty commissioner, he would be willing to give Foster

Dr. Thomas Foster, sketched by an anonymous artist. MHS

89

some position under him. To be associated with Indian treaty-making would give Foster valuable experience in Indian matters and thus perhaps help him to find some more permanent way of continuing his Indian studies.

In October Congress provided funds for negotiating with the Dakota and Ojibway Indians of Minnesota, but the treaty commission was not appointed for some months. Zachary Taylor's death and the succession of Millard Fillmore to the presidency ended Foster's hope for the Winnebago agency post. The position went to a friend of the new president and Foster was offered a meager clerkship in the treasury department in Washington. "To such a collapse of all *sound, intellectual* and *political* position as follows the acceptance of a $1,000 clerkship, there I will not subject myself!" commented the outraged Foster.[5]

Instead he returned to Minnesota early in November. With no employment, Foster accepted Ramsey's offer to name him superintendent of schools at the Long Prairie Winnebago Agency in present Todd County. The salary was only $600 a year, and at first the place seemed to Foster "an infernal hole" inhabited by "a damned devillish set of intractable savages." Still the job offered an opportunity to study the Winnebago, and the new superintendent set out to meet its challenges with his usual zest.[6]

In his first seven months at Long Prairie, Foster developed some firm principles for running the school. All students, from orphans to the children of chiefs, would be treated equally; tribal leaders were not to be bribed to keep their children in school; discipline would be tightened. Nor did the doctor intend to tolerate any meddling in school affairs either by Indian leaders or by Abram M. Fridley, the newly appointed agent. Foster drew up plans for new buildings to replace the agency's inadequate school facilities, and he brought his wife and two of her relatives to Long Prairie as instructors to ease the teacher shortage. This move aroused Fridley's disapproval. Before long he and Foster were at loggerheads, having "failed to agree on anything," as one observer put it.[7]

In his spare time Foster took advantage of the exceptional opportunity for firsthand research on the Long Prairie Indians. He began compiling a Winnebago dictionary, a valuable exercise for his later, more ambitious plans. In preparation for the forthcoming treaty negotiations, he expanded his earlier studies of the Dakota and Ojibway people as best he could and requested from Ramsey numerous reference works for his research.[8]

In June, 1851, the summons came to join Ramsey and Luke Lea, United States commissioner of Indian affairs, on the treaty-making expeditions. Foster willingly laid aside his research and left the Winnebago school in the charge of assistants. The official party negotiated treaties with the Upper and Lower Sioux for lands in southern Minnesota and with the Pembina and Red Lake Ojibway bands for the broad acres of the Red River Valley. Foster helped draft all three treaties, copied them for signing, kept a journal of the proceedings, and wrote

Signing the Treaty of Traverse des Sioux, oil by Frank B. Mayer. Foster sits at table. *MHS*

the commission's report. He also acted as physician and surgeon when needed. In Frank B. Mayer's painting of the Upper Sioux treaty negotiations at Traverse des Sioux, Foster sits under a bower and presides over the treaty signing. For the would-be scholar the experience was undoubtedly valuable to his study of Indian affairs. Between the feasts and official sessions, he was able to talk with missionaries, traders, and members of various other Indian tribes.[9]

When the negotiations were concluded in November, the doctor returned to Long Prairie determined to work on a book. He gave it a long, tentative title indicating that its contents would cover the three treaties, a description of the Minnesota and Red River valleys, and "original Ethnological and Philological notes upon the Chippeway, Sioux, Winnebago, Cree, Assiniboin, Shienne, and Blackfeet Tribes of Indians." He made little progress on this undertaking and abandoned it in 1853 when John W. Bond published a book on a somewhat similar subject entitled *Minnesota and Its Resources*.[10]

Foster's continuing disagreements with Fridley soon led him to seek other employment. He moved his family to a new house in Hastings, where he had staked a claim within the Dakota cession. Late in the fall of 1852 he assisted Ramsey at treaty payments to the Lower Sioux Indians and obtained a temporary appointment as physician to them.[11]

For the next few years, Foster was no more content than he had been at Long Prairie; he worked at jobs as diverse as operating a drugstore, building a flour mill, and editing the *Minnesotian* (St. Paul). In 1859 a rival newspaper, the *Minnesota Statesman* (St. Peter), said that while Foster held the appointment as doctor to the Dakota he had attempted to seduce an Indian woman with gifts that included a barrel of flour, blankets, calico, and other items procured from a trader on credit to the amount of $47. Foster had been unsuccessful in his suit; according to the account the woman bit him on the shoulder, and subsequently the trader threatened to sue him for nonpayment of the $47.[12]

In the late 1850s Foster helped establish the Republican party in Minnesota. When the party came to power in 1859 with Ramsey's election as second governor of the state, Foster again served his old friend as secretary and as state librarian. In 1861, at the outbreak of the Civil War, he helped organize and outfit the First Minnesota Infantry Regiment. Shortly afterward he took a commission as captain and commissary officer in the Union army, serving on the general staff, Department of Ohio, throughout the war. There followed a brief clerkship in Washington, short stints as editor of the *Minneapolis Chronicle* and the *St. Paul Dispatch*, and nearly four years of promoting the fledgling city of Duluth and editing its newspaper.

In the summer of 1872 Foster traveled in the East and supported the re-election of President Ulysses S. Grant. After the victory, Foster decided that it was an auspicious time for a Republican to go to Washington. Learning that the commissioner of Indian affairs planned to resign, he launched a campaign for his own appointment. The eager candidate wrote to Senator William Windom for support, asserting that it was not a "baseless egotistical claim" to say that he was "probably better fitted for this position than any man in the United States."[13]

Foster reviewed his experience with the Winnebago, the Upper Sioux, and the treaty commission, and pointed out that he had "made Indian matters[,] their history, ethnology and tribal relations generally, my study for years." He admitted that he really wanted the opportunity to complete his Indian project, which he now described as an "Encyclopaedia of Indian Affairs and of the Race in the U[nited] States." If he were commissioner he would use the "valuable data" in the files of the Indian office, including materials collected by author, explorer, and ethnologist Henry Rowe Schoolcraft, who under government auspices in the 1850s had produced "the first general compendium on the American Indian." Foster and his clerks could in their "official leisure" prepare a work that would redound to the credit of the administration and "receive the approval of men of Science at home and abroad."

Windom and the other three members of Minnesota's congressional delegation, which at the time included Foster's old friend Ramsey, gave the would-be scholar their approval, and all signed a supporting letter that was sent with Foster's application to President Grant. The doctor, while waiting for the wheels of government to turn, took the next step in his campaign. He wrote and published at his own expense an anonymous circular entitled *Hints by an "American Citizen," as to the TRUE METHOD of Managing and Civilizing the Indian Race of the United States*. Copies went to the president, selected congressmen, and probably to members of a conference of religious groups then meeting in Washington. Only after Foster was assured that the *Hints* had been favorably received did he publicly acknowledge his authorship and send copies to all other members of Congress. On January 21, 1873, the circular, with a covering letter from Foster, was referred to the Senate Committee on Indian Affairs and, much to its author's satisfaction, printed as an official government document.[14]

In the *Hints* and its accompanying letter, Foster clarified his views of Indians and Indian matters. "In ruling any people," he wrote, "it is statesmanship to take them as they are, and not as we would have them." Experience had taught him that Indians did not have "a wild nature," but, like other people, varied in disposition, temperament, and aptitude. He believed that "Education from generation to generation elevates" as certainly as "Degradation and Ignorance . . . depresses and brutifies a Race." In the last analysis, "the civilization of the Indians *by means of Law and the enforcement of Law*, must come, measurably *from within themselves*." Until that day came, Foster favored a policy that would control them "yet preserve them from extermination." The United States should make treaties with them for their land, which was destined by God, not for deer or buffalo parks, but to be "tilled by millions." In addition, the government should "aid the Christian denominations in civilizing them, affording them special opportunities for doing so, alike by judicious appropriations for the Indians' material welfare, and by well-considered Laws, from time to time to protect them *from each other*."

Foster, doubtless recalling his experiences with the treaty commission in 1851–52, went on to urge reform of the traders' licensing system, revision of the methods used in treaty making, and simplification of Indian-office management so that fewer and more qualified people could carry out its program.

Then he came to the topic nearest his heart. To dispel widespread ignorance about Indians Foster recommended that the Indian office sponsor a handy encyclopedia of the Indian race. "Indeed, there is no subject upon which the common and even the more cultivated minds of the country err so greatly or so constantly as in their comprehension of Indians, of their nature, their manners and customs, their separate and aggregate histories; even their names; their relationships to each other and to the whites, past and present are misunderstood," he complained. The public either "elevates them into heroes of romance, or unjustly classes them all with devils, assigning them the attributes of fiends incarnate." The seed was planted, and Foster hoped it would take root.

Early in February, 1873, he realized that he had no chance of becoming commissioner of Indian affairs. The job went to Edward P. Smith, a man Foster respected, who had once been Indian agent to the Ojibway in northern Minnesota. But while Foster had lost the commissioner's post, his Indian project was far from abandoned. He reworked the section of *Hints* about the need for an encyclopedia, adding practical suggestions and cost figures. Then he had the statement reprinted and sent it with a letter to members of each of the congressional committees on appropriations and Indian affairs.[15]

In his statement he proposed appropriations of $3,000 for the annual

93

salary of a "Historiographer and Librarian" of the Indian office; $1,000 for expenses "incidental to the preparation by the Historiographer, of an ENCYCLOPAEDIA OF INDIAN AFFAIRS on the plan proposed by Dr. Thomas Foster of Minnesota"; and $2,000 for the launching of an "Ethnological and Historical Library, and an Archaeological Museum of the Indian Race" to be supervised by the historiographer. It would be to the nation's credit, he said, to preserve for future generations "the relics which show the manners, customs, domestic and warlike habits of the widely extended wild tribes who once possessed or roved through our country." This library-museum would require only a small portion of an annual Indian office budget of $5,000,000 or $6,000,000. In fact it would be so useful to bureaucrats and perhaps even legislators that it "would probably save ten times" its cost.

By February 18 Foster's proposal had been approved by officials of both the Indian office and the interior department, but it clearly had no high priority in the view of the secretary of the interior. "Without entering into the details . . . I have to say that I approve of the general idea," the secretary wrote, "but I do not desire to make any distinct recommendation in regard to it." The miscellaneous appropriations bill, which included Foster's proposals, came before the full Senate on March 3, 1873. As Foster waited out the last hours of debate in a nearby committee room, he penned a letter to his Minnesota friend, Ignatius Donnelly. A postscript carried the news that "my Historiographer matter failed."[16]

Again Foster called on the Minnesota delegation for help. As though no setback had occurred, Ramsey, Windom, and Representative John T. Averill all wrote to the Indian office supporting Foster's appointment as historiographer. Commissioner Smith, a creative administrator, then saw a way to please everyone. While no money was appropriated for the position of historiographer, Smith found funds for appointing Foster a special agent, with the same duties, for six months beginning June 1, 1873. And so it was accomplished. Foster had slipped into the Indian office tent, to remain there for nearly four years.[17]

Smith notified Foster of his appointment, describing the position in terms that Foster could well have written. The new special agent was to "Collect Statistics and Historical Data respecting the Indians of the United States, comprehending the manners and customs, religion, government, language, tribal relations, country, emigrations, removals, vital statistics, rights acquired by treaty, present condition and prospects, and whatever else may be found of interest concerning them in the past and at present." As if that were not sufficient work for six months, Foster was also asked to prepare "a complete special history of at least one of the tribes," to be submitted to Congress "as an illustration of the effort to be undertaken for all the different tribes in the United States."[18]

One of Foster's first letters written on a letterhead from the "Historiographer's Desk" went to an old Minnesota friend, the Reverend Edward D. Neill. "You will perceive," wrote the new bureaucrat, "that

I have entered upon the threshold of the favorite enterprise of my life —
the writing in an Encyclopaedia form the History of the Indian Race."
He hoped to write 25 comparatively short articles on "minor" subjects
within five months. The twenty-sixth would be a history of the Winnebago tribe. The ambitious author intended to prepare his "reliable
and ready Dictionary of reference" so that "when anything is desired to
be Known on any Indian subject," it could be located easily. He wanted
to improve on Schoolcraft's compendium. Foster projected a more comprehensive work with superior organization of his data so that one would
not be "obliged to wander" as one did in using Schoolcraft's six volumes
"only to find, perhaps, that all is barren." It would not have been possible to accomplish all that he had agreed to do before the end of December, 1873, he admitted, had he not "piled up some accumulations of
Knowledge" over the past 20 years.[19]

Because Foster's preliminary research in the Library of Congress
revealed the inadequacy of that institution's source materials about
Indians, he asked permission to spend $200 or $300 on general scholarly
works as the nucleus of an Indian-office reference library and to acquire
for it two full sets of the office's annual reports. Another project occurred
to him for which no funds were needed — an idea half a century ahead
of its time. "Scattered through the different rooms of the Indian Department, or packed away in inaccessible darkness . . . ," Foster reported, "are Manuscript books and Reports of Treaty and other Councils
with the Indians." Were these "carefully preserved where they could be
accessible," he suggested, they would be "a mine of reference for the
historian. I would recommend that these manuscripts be collected and
handed over for proper preservation in the [Ethnological and Historical]
Library when organized and established."[20]

The commissioner approved Foster's suggestions for acquiring books
and authorized the requested expenditure. Thus by mid-July, 1873, the
historiographer had received generous encouragement and limited funding for most of the proposals Congress had turned down in March. Only
one project had been ignored, that of the Indian museum. Perhaps
because Foster began to recognize the magnitude of his other duties, he
did not speak of it again.[21]

By the end of August Foster found it "absolutely necessary" to make
a field trip. He requested and received funds to travel to Wisconsin,
Minnesota, Nebraska, and Dakota Territory to "perfect parts of the work
which I have already under advanced preparation" and to "verify on the
spot" notes he had made. September 18 found him in Duluth, where he
spent several weeks.[22]

His next stop was St. Paul. There he asked Ramsey's help in arrang-
ing extensions of his appointment and of the deadline for presenting his
report to Congress. Ramsey obligingly wrote the secretary of the interior
that Foster had been "zealously engaged during the period discharging
the duties imposed on him" but that he needed more time. Ramsey requested the secretary to "direct the Commissioner" to extend Foster's
appointment for another six months. Looking to the future, the senator

observed, "I think we can get the necessary legislation providing for a permanent office and the extended preparation of an Encyclopaedia." In a list of Foster's proposed topics for investigation, Ramsey included a new one — a Winnebago vocabulary and grammar — which from that time apparently became an integral part of the project.[23]

From St. Paul the doctor traveled on by train to Mankato. There he hired a wagon and a driver to take him 12 miles south in Blue Earth County to where the Winnebago Indians had gone after their removal from Long Prairie in 1855. Following the Dakota War of 1862 the Winnebago were moved once more to a new reservation in Dakota Territory, but Foster found acquaintances of his Long Prairie days who still lived in the county. Indians, mixed-bloods, and former traders worked with Foster on the Winnebago vocabulary and told him a number of old tribal tales, including a version of the "fall of man" and an account of a traditional midwinter "Feast to the Spirits of the Night." When Foster went on to the Winnebago reservation, a government interpreter there helped him record another legend, "The Story of the Giants." In Nebraska, he visited a mission for the Omaha Indians, where he borrowed a letter book and a grammar of the Omaha language, both of which he took to Washington.[24]

Back at the capital in December, he submitted accounts to the interior department covering his expenses since August. He had been gone 105 days — 12 days traveling and 93 "stationary." He was entitled to 10 cents per mile while journeying and $4.00 a day when "stationary." Although he had been given travel funds, he had not been paid his salary, and he requested it. He received nothing, however, until February, 1874. In March, 1874, in belated response to Ramsey's November letter, the department extended Foster's appointment, retroactive to December 1, 1873. As for the $1,000 he had been allowed to draw for travel and the purchase of books, the auditors noted that only about $800 was properly accounted for and that $200 was to be deducted from his overdue salary payment. If Foster had bought books with funds allowed for that purpose, he should have supplied vouchers for his purchases.[25]

In the spring of 1874, as the last days of the congressional session drew near, Foster felt he should get at least a part of his manuscript into print. On May 18 he recklessly promised the commissioner that a large part of his report would be ready for the printer in June, but he failed to meet this self-imposed deadline. Congress, before adjourning on June 23, appropriated $3,500 to continue Foster's project for another year. With funds assured, Foster saw no point in hurrying the report.[26]

In this new, financially promising climate, Foster became expansive. He moved from crowded quarters in the department to rented rooms at 326 Pennsylvania Avenue, across the Mall from the red, turreted Smithsonian castle. The rooms very likely served Foster for both office and living accommodations. He seems to have had no plans for his wife to join him, and their three sons were grown. Apparently feeling confident that his position was secure, he asked the Smithsonian for a set of its publications for the Indian-office library he was beginning. In return Foster promised to send the Smithsonian a copy of his book when it was published.[27]

But the wheels of government moved more slowly than Foster did. Not only was his precipitous move to rented quarters unauthorized, but he had not yet been officially appointed for another year. Moreover, he had ordered "a font of peculiar type for Indian vocabularies." Apparently without consulting other scholars or his Indian-office superiors, Foster had designed special characters to represent Indian sounds and words and had ordered a font of the type cast in New York.[28]

To further complicate matters, when he received seven months' back salary at the end of June, 1874, he hired a clerk to begin "copying" for him. He also started taking meals at the National Hotel at one dollar per day (an expense the government auditors later disallowed), hired a servant at one dollar a week to clean his office, and arranged for the delivery of ice at five cents a day. In yet another unauthorized action, he subscribed for three newspapers and billed the government. On July 5 he complained to the commissioner that he had received no letter of appointment; that he needed to buy books, stamps, and envelopes; and that he had no money to pay for the type font, which was expected to arrive within ten days.[29]

Finally on July 17, 1874, he was informed by the commissioner that he had been reappointed and that most of his plans for increased expenditures were approved. An exception was the special type, which was not to be purchased until Foster's work was ready for publication. Possibly, however, the type could be paid for from another fund. At the commissioner's suggestion Foster attempted to persuade A. M. Clapp, the government printer, to purchase the type, but Clapp "was not very favorably disposed" to the idea. Clapp did say, however, that "when the Requisition came from the Secretary of the Interior" for printing Foster's book, "any special type . . . which he had to procure for it would be charged to the Interior Department Printing Appropriation as part of the expenses of printing." In other words, if a manuscript were ready for printing Foster might not have to pay for the type from his own budget.[30]

The next 12 months saw steady progress on the historiography project. Foster hired copyists, bought books, and in September spent nine days in Philadelphia libraries researching Indian matters. In October he moved to new rooms for the winter. To increase the tempo of work, he asked for more money: to acquire a gaslight so that he could work longer days; to buy more reference works; to pay additional copyists; and to travel. Although he assured the commissioner on October 5 that the "First Report on the subject assigned to me, will of course, be made in time for the next session of Congress," he submitted no manuscript in 1874 or 1875.

Foster and his clerks continued to labor while the work "widened" in his hands. Early in October, 1875, the commissioner asked for a "full, complete, and comprehensive history" of the project. The historiographer, in his response, promised not one or two books but a series of volumes. The manuscript for the first was to be delivered to the printer on or before January 1, 1876. In encyclopedic form with a few woodcuts for illustration, the book would contain elaborate articles and brief notices on the existing Indian tribes and some extinct ones, Indian terminology, and the history of the Indian office. In addition a complete history of the Winnebago would include a 3,000-word vocabulary presented in a special type "with the proper diacritical marks and accents." Material for a second book would be "partly prepared" by June 30, 1876, and Foster envisioned the completion of other volumes "from time to time."[31]

The bill for special type that Foster had ordered so hastily in 1874 was now long overdue, as the commissioner reminded him on several occasions. Clapp, the government printer, "manifesting some unfriendly personal feeling, declined to pay." Foster had approximately $1,500 to carry his program through the fiscal year 1875–76. If he paid the type bill, he would have about $1,100. Then, deducting his salary for half a year, only about $100 would remain to cover expenses. By the end of December, 1875, the commissioner was inquiring not who would pay for the type but, returning to first principles, why Foster needed the type at all. In that extremity, Foster paid the bill.[32]

During the new quarter beginning January 1, 1876, financial stringency was only one of Foster's problems. He reduced expenses by moving to cheaper rooms, but he retained one copyist until mid-May. There were other changes. The old guard of Minnesotans who had supported him so handsomely was dwindling. Representative Averill and Senator Ramsey had been retired from Congress, and Commissioner Edward Smith had resigned. John Q. Smith, the new commissioner, was not acquainted with Foster or his work. His office queried Clapp as to whether Foster had submitted any manuscript for "historical or statistical matter relating to the Indians." Clapp answered that Foster had "talked of it but no copy has been furnished." In May Foster was ordered to report in person to the commissioner's office. There, pressed for results, he agreed to have a volume ready for printing by the end of June.[33]

He soon regretted the promise. In June he informed the commissioner that he had been ill and that the "jointing-together" of the data he had collected was a "work of greater proportions and slower progress than either of us anticipated at our last interview." Like many another author before and since his day, he shrank from the final task of writing up his information while any question was unanswered, any stone unturned. Since his encyclopedia would be "in a certain sense a scientific work," its facts must be "thorough" and "reliable" and carefully examined, a process requiring "time and deliberation." And as John Gilmary Shea, the translator of Charlevoix, advised him, "to hurry the work is to spoil it."[34]

He needed to spend some time, he said, on additional research in Philadelphia libraries and to make two field trips to visit a remnant of the Catawba and Yuchi Indians in North and South Carolina and the

Quappawas (Arkansas) and Natchez in Mississippi. Uncertainty about funding for his project continued until the last days of the 1876 congressional session; but it was clear that, with or without a new appropriation, the historiographer's first manuscript was far from ready to go to press.

Nevertheless, Foster could no longer ignore the pressure to get something into print. Thus while he continued to temporize, he maintained that some of his materials were in an "advanced state towards completion." Yet he was exceedingly reluctant to submit them to the government printing office, where Clapp retained authority and where in Foster's imagination typesetters were "groping in the dark amidst the Indian languages."[35]

In this dilemma Foster devised a plan that would permit him to control the printing while he continued collecting, verifying, and revising. The procedure he outlined, stripped of its recital of justifications, was a simple one. He proposed to borrow from the government printing office the type, supplies, and workmen needed to operate a small temporary shop in his own rooms.

To anyone but an old newspaper editor the prospect of working in the multiple roles of author, editor, proofreader, and printing foreman could have been unnerving. But Foster was more than willing to assume the extra duties without any supplementary pay in return for the satisfaction of having full charge of the operation in his own office. The plan, which would allow him to begin printing even though he had not yet completed enough material for a volume, inspired him to certify parts of his collected work as ready for typesetting. If the commissioner approved and funds were made available, he would commence the printing at once — in fact, within a week.

In August, 1876, he learned that Congress had at last passed a bill authorizing $3,500 for him to continue his work for another fiscal year. The legislation also contained a clause requiring that "when sufficient matter to make a volume" had been prepared by the historiographer, it was to be referred to the Smithsonian Institution for written approval before publication. The full impact of the new provision did not become clear to Foster for some months. At first he chose to regard it as a strong justification for his printing plan. Thereafter when he referred to this proposal, he spoke of "print-copying" or "type-copying" with emphasis on *copying*. He reasoned that this form of reproduction did not constitute *publishing*; therefore it could proceed without the approval of the Smithsonian. In fact, it would provide accurate, easy-to-read copy for submitting to Smithsonian scrutiny, and, like galley-proof sheets, it would be subject to corrections and revisions before final publication in book form.[36]

By this time, it was perhaps not surprising that the commissioner was confused about Foster's intentions. On August 19 he summoned the historiographer for an interview during which, said Foster, "a full explanation was had of all matters and misunderstandings in the past, and everything in reference to the future progress of the work . . . com-

pletely and satisfactorily arranged."[37] The commissioner seemed to have
given his approval to the print-copying plan, but week after week went
by and still no funds came down to Foster from the upper levels of the
bureaucracy. Instead the secretary of the interior requested the Indian
office to provide a full review of the historiographer program.[38]

The commissioner's office replied, enclosing a letter from Foster. On
his "progress and prospects" he reported that during three years in office
he had compiled 20 Indian vocabularies, ranging from 300 to more than
3,000 words each. His collections embraced a large mass of manuscripts
in detached sections which needed to be "jointed together." He was
proceeding with this work "as fast as possible," but it went very slowly.
"History was not made in a day, nor can it be written safely in a hurried
manner," he stated. As for "this Indian subject . . . the nearer you get
to it, the broader it is — and new matter and 'data' continually crowd
upon you." His original concept of preparing a useful, one-volume handbook had grown to a plan for multiple volumes. Moreover, in his search
for truth he had found scholars guilty of egregious errors; published
sources contradicted each other and were proved wrong by living Indians or unpublished sources. "My work," he insisted, "is not merely a
Compilation from published data of doubtful validity, but it is one of
original research, aiming to correct previous data by direct reference to
the fountain-source of all correct knowledge in regard to the Indians —
the Tribes themselves. Closet Indianology or Philology is not often reliable." Undoubtedly the purpose of the Smithsonian proviso, Foster
observed, was to obtain the "imprimateur or stamp of approval of 'experts' in Indian ethnology and Indian philology (if any such exist) upon
my labors before they should be given to the world with the imprint of
the Government Printing Office upon them." Old editor and politician
Foster was no more impressed by scholars than he was by a variety of
other categories of the human race. If he had, indeed, asked scholars
other than John Gilmary Shea to advise him, he left no record of their
counsel.

Yet he seemed to be supremely confident that his work would survive
scholarly scrutiny. He now said that he would put the type-copied proof
sheets in scrapbooks, making volumes convenient for examination by the
Smithsonian regents. By this process Foster would produce a *printed*
volume, if not a *published* one, and the scrapbook volumes would then
provide copy of the best sort for the government printers to use in preparing the formal books.

Foster reduced his printing plan to its barest essentials. To proceed
he would need only the Indian type font, funds, and the approval of the
interior department. By print-copying in his own office he would avoid
problems with the government printing office. He would find workmen,
regular type fonts, and materials, and pay for the contracted goods and
services out of his budget or, if necessary, out of his own salary.

On October 24, 1876, the secretary of the interior finally came to a
decision about Foster. If the commissioner "should deem it best," wrote
the secretary, he was authorized to advance the sum requested by the

historiographer "for reducing his memoranda to printer's proof" before submitting them to the Smithsonian. More than four months had gone by since the beginning of the fiscal year. With the released funds Foster could now pay his bills and proceed with his printing. He moved to rooms on a corner at 902 G Street Northwest that were to be his last refuge as historiographer.[39]

Throughout November, 1876, the doctor and two assistants print-copied four, four-columned newsprint pages of *Foster's Indian Record and Historical Data*, volume 1, number 1. Costs amounted to just under $124, including setting up the office, "laying" (arranging) the Indian type, typesetting, taking proofs, buying paper, and renting other type. Foster said that these costs were "partly borne by the editor from his private means." How much he absorbed cannot be determined, but it was, of course, to his advantage to have the cost of print-copying appear to be as reasonable as possible in comparison with the expense of hand-copying. At this point work came to a halt, because Foster was again out of funds. He received no more money until the last working day of the calendar year.[40]

But the department had not forgotten him. A message from the secretary of the interior on December 14, 1876, reached Foster's office five days later. The secretary wanted from the historiographer "a full printed copy of his work so far as he had progressed with it." Foster replied immediately, noting that he was out of money and as a result, he was able to send only one number of the *Record* and one more proof sheet of a single column of type.[41]

The secretary, without informing Foster of his intentions, forwarded Foster's print copies to Professor Joseph Henry, secretary of the Smithsonian Institution, for an opinion on "whether in view of the sum expended, the time occupied and the work accomplished, the result is at all commensurate with the outlay, or that the present work will ever be made of any practical value to the government." Henry, in turn, sent Foster's materials to William D. Whitney of Yale College and J. Hammond Trumbull of Hartford, Connecticut, "two of the most distinguished linguists in the United States." He told them that the secretary of the interior wished to know "whether from what Dr. Foster has done . . . the Government will be justified in continuing his services." The two scholars were instructed to base their answers on the printed materials enclosed.[42]

The four newsprint pages of the *Record* probably comprised a fair sample of the data Foster had been collecting. The *Record* quoted at length from scholarly sources, but in format, style, and general content it seemed designed for nonscholarly readers. It contained an explanation of the special Indian alphabet Foster had developed, short pieces on the Apache, the "Avoyelles" and "Attacapas" Indians that once lived in the Louisiana area, a remnant of the Attacapas language collected by Albert Gallatin, and the beginning of a longer article on the Iowa.

By far the larger part of the space was devoted to the Winnebago — a history of the tribe from its earliest known contact with whites near

Green Bay, Wisconsin; an etymology of the name Winnebago, which concluded that it meant marsh or muddy-water people; stories about Winnebagos Foster had known; and a section of nearly 300 family names, based largely on his own research among tribal members, describing the four-clan family organization and the significance of fours in Winnebago culture.

Foster's investigations led him to two views that varied from those held by many scholars of his day. In his opinion the Winnebago were not a dying race, but a tribe decimated in prewhite times by constant warfare and now (in the 1870s) much more numerous. In his research, too, he thought he had found indications that these so-called primitive and savage people once had a high degree of social, political, and cultural life. The Winnebago he knew were a "remnant," a social and political "wreck" of a once highly developed culture.

In the second number of the *Record*, which Foster issued on January 13, 1877, he continued the Iowa monograph, provided a long discourse on the origin of the word Kentucky, a short note on the Arapaho, and a three-column article on the word "sachem," a meaningless, bastard term, Foster said, which was neither Indian, Dutch, French, nor English. In his research on the matter, the old editor had found various so-called authorities in flagrant error, and he concluded that the word was a "Dutch abbreviation with a Yankee sound . . . the approximate meaning of which is, probably, the Land-Father."

Again the Winnebago filled the greater part of the content. The "Feast to the Spirits of the Night" was printed, along with tales of other feasts, celebrations, and magic. In this issue, too, Foster began to print his English-Winnebago vocabulary. Noting that because the amount of special Indian type was limited he could print no more than two columns of words in each issue, he estimated that ten issues of the *Record* would be needed to finish it. The compilation was, he said, the "result of a very great amount of painstaking [work] which only those who have attempted reducing a savage language to a written form can appreciate. It has passed through the alembic, so to speak, of five distinct interpreters, under the one notation of the Indian Historiographer in person."

Number 3 of the *Record* was printed sometime between mid-January and February 21, 1877, while Foster awaited approval of a requisition for $750 for the quarter beginning January 1. It offered articles on the etymology of Indian words for "half-king," Connecticut, Cincinnati, Housatonic, opossum, and 'possum language; brief gleanings from research on the Erie, Mohegan (Mohican), Osage, and Oneida Indians; a comment on the Iroquois designation of George Washington as "town Eater or Town Destroyer"; a continuation of the Winnebago vocabulary; Winnebago myths, legends, and medical and astronomical knowledge; and anecdotes about more Winnebago individuals Foster had known. Intermingled in the text were provocative remarks and sly barbs at so-called experts who were obviously misled, and a letter of good wishes from "friendly critic" Edward Neill of Minnesota. Neill had mentioned a few errors in numbers 1 and 2 of the *Record* and cheerfully admitted his own responsibility for some that he had made in a passage quoted by Foster.

The historiographer hoped to continue print-copying as soon as funds were released for his use, but not until February 20, 1877, did he receive any word from his superiors. Then he learned to his dismay that number 1 of the *Record*, with the additional column he had supplied in December, had been sent to the Smithsonian and that no more funds would be authorized for his work until its report was received.[43]

Foster protested. The interior department's action was based on a misapprehension of the purposes of print-copying and the law requiring submission of his materials to the Smithsonian. *Record* number 1 did not comprise a volume; and numbers 2 and 3 had not been submitted. Taken together they were only specimens of the print-copying process. Foster insisted that "there is yet nothing before the 'Regents' upon which, *legally*, they can be called upon to express an opinion; not any more than they would be to comment on a few loose sheets of my MSS." Funds were needed to continue the work. In his view, only when the Smithsonian regents had in hand a full volume of material could they render a verdict.

Joseph Henry of the Smithsonian was largely responsible for the two months' delay in deciding Foster's fate. Whitney and Trumbull had answered promptly on January 6, saying that neither in Foster's plan nor in the "method of its prosecution" did they find "any evidence that it will be made of practical value to the Government or of benefit to science." The two critics then spoke of Foster's special alphabet, which they found "singularly ill-adapted to the purpose for which it is employed. The alphabetic scheme is unscientific and defective. The introduction of new characters and numerous diacritical marks put[s] difficulties in the way of general readers, without gaining any compensating advantage in increased accuracy of notation, and the cost of printing must be greatly increased by the use of the new letters. . . . We are confident that those who are interested in the study of American languages, or of language in general, will agree, almost without exception, in this opinion that this alphabet should not be employed in any publication made by the government of the United States."[44]

Joseph Henry held the scholars' verdict until February 20. Then he wrote to the secretary of the interior, quoting from their joint letter. The view of these distinguished linguists, Henry asserted, "may be accepted as that of the most competent authority in the United States for deciding the question propounded in the letter of the Department."[45]

The secretary of the interior, on receiving Henry's letter, acted promptly. On February 21, he told the commissioner that "the most eminent authority" had not found any merit in Foster's Indian linguistics. "In view of the opinion cited, I do not feel justified in further continuing this work: you are, therefore, hereby instructed to inform Doctor Foster that his services are no longer required; directing him at once to close his labors and render his accounts to your office as speedily as possible."[46]

103

Five days later the commissioner terminated the services of his Indian historiographer in accordance with instructions from the secretary of the interior. Foster was informed that he would be required to turn over the government property in his possession and render his accounts by March 1 — two days later.[47]

Foster did not protest his summary dismissal; such a move would have been fruitless under the uncertain conditions prevailing in Washington. The presidential election had been held in November, 1876, but it was not until the end of February, 1877, that the electoral college decided whether Republican Rutherford B. Hayes or Democrat Samuel J. Tilden would take office on March 4. The Republicans remained in power, but Foster had few strong ties to the new Hayes administration. Carl Schurz, newly appointed secretary of the interior, had in fact stumped the Midwest for Horace Greeley four years earlier when Foster supported Grant. Despite instructions Foster was in no hurry to file his accounts. After he did so, another four years elapsed before the government succeeded in collecting $200 that it claimed Foster owed.[48]

THERE IS REASON to suspect that Joseph Henry and the two scholars he consulted had more than academic considerations in mind when they rendered their verdict against Foster's work. Perhaps half of the historiographer's appropriation remained unspent — just how much would be discovered when Foster settled his accounts. A bid to take over what remained of his funds and the materials he had collected came from within the department. It was made by John Wesley Powell, who had close ties to Henry as well as to the two linguists. Powell may not have been responsible for the requirement that the Smithsonian approve Foster's work before its publication, but he must have known about it, and he surely knew how to make the most of the conditions the proviso created.

Powell, as the man in charge of the United States Geological and Geographical Survey of the Rocky Mountain Region, had a special interest in Indian matters. His fascination with the West and its native inhabitants had begun ten years before. His daring expedition down the Colorado River in 1869 made him a public hero. He remained in the public eye when he conducted a second exploration of the river in 1871–72, wrote articles on his experiences for *Scribner's Magazine*, lectured, and in 1875 published a book on his expeditions.[49]

By degrees Powell was able to gain government support for his work, with the help of such influential friends as Ulysses S. Grant, under whom he had served in the Civil War, and James A. Garfield. By 1874 Powell's surveys were fully sponsored by the interior department, and as geologist he was drawing a government salary of $3,000 a year. About Foster's height and 16 years younger, bearded and slight of build, Powell found his way among Washington bureaucrats as surely and skillfully as he had through the plains and mountains of the West.

His connections in the academic community were good. He had been professor of geology at the University of Illinois at Normal when he made his first field trip to the West in 1867. Since 1868 Joseph Henry had provided scientific instruments from the Smithsonian for the use of Powell's expeditions. And it was Henry who had alerted Powell to the importance of collecting data on Indians and Indian languages.

As a result of Powell's interest in native Americans, the geologist was also well known to the Indian office. For example, he claimed that during the course of his western surveys, he had provided the office with information on 88 tribes. In 1873, when Foster was lobbying for his historiography project, Powell arranged to be appointed one of two special commissioners who were to visit Indians in Utah and Nevada. His report of this undertaking appeared in the Indian office annual report for that year.[50]

The study of Indians and the gathering of vocabularies became to Powell second only to geology in the work of his western surveys, and he saw the need for systematizing and organizing Indian data more effectively. In January, 1875, he interested Commissioner Smith and the secretary of the interior in a proposed Indian classification system, which he hoped would be of great value not only to science but also to the administration of Indian affairs. Powell was instructed to provide a report on the subject. His response was a classification of the Indians of Alaska, a bare beginning for an extensive task, but one that further established his credentials in the realm of Indian studies.[51]

By 1876, when Foster reported that he had gathered 20 Indian vocabularies, Powell said that with the aid of his survey team he had amassed more than 100. He had also collected a large amount of other material which he planned to include in his geological survey reports as a series on North American ethnology. Friends connected with the Smithsonian encouraged him, and he had established good working relationships with scholars in the field of linguistics, to whom he could turn for assistance. Among them were Whitney in New Haven and Trumbull in Hartford. Powell was influenced by Trumbull's paper, "On the Best Method of Studying the North American Languages," and he had asked Whitney to devise a special alphabet for use by his survey teams in transcribing Indian languages.[52]

In October, 1876, while Foster waited for funds, Powell asked Secretary Henry to send him all the Indian vocabularies in the Smithsonian collections for study and publication. The Smithsonian had offered the materials to Trumbull, but he had declined the enormous task of preparing them for publication. Now he willingly endorsed Henry's suggestion that they be turned over to Powell. In the same month another official in the Indian office transmitted, not to Foster, but to Powell, a paper on the Indians of western Washington and northwestern Oregon, saying that he would be grateful if Powell could "secure its publication."[53]

So it happened that in December, 1876, when Joseph Henry accepted the responsibility for passing judgment on Foster's work, he had been associated with Powell for at least eight years and was willing to give him substantial assistance with his work. As for Professor Whitney, he had devised, or was devising, a special alphabet for Powell's use, and Professor Trumbull had within the month supported the transfer of the full Smithsonian Indian language collection to Powell. Thus perhaps only Foster was surprised when the scholars found no merit in his work. Nor should anyone have been surprised that, when Foster was dismissed, it was the astute John Wesley Powell, himself intensely interested in the collection and publication of historical data on the Indians, who sought not only what remained of Foster's appropriation but also the materials Foster had collected.

Powell made his request in a letter on May 3, 1877. He reminded the commissioner that he had been asked to prepare an ethnological classi- fication of the Indians of the United States. The task, "one of great magnitude," required the study of an immense amount of manuscript material, "embracing vocabularies and grammar of various Indian stocks." He now had in his possession, said Powell, about 900 vocabu- laries, including those transferred from the Smithsonian. Although he had the assistance of many scholars such as Whitney and Trumbull, said Powell, the task was "much too great for one person." Moreover, there were tribes whose "ethnographic relations" were still unknown. In an attempt to fill some gaps, he wanted to send a competent person to in- vestigate Indians in Oregon and make an accurate census of them.[54]

His candidate for this field work was Albert S. Gatschet, a Swiss immigrant who had been recommended by Whitney and employed on Powell's surveys. A talented man, Gatschet was one of the first trained philologists to study Indian languages. Powell wanted the Indian office to hire Gatschet for one year with the funds left by Foster. He believed that the sum was $2,500 and recommended that from it Gatschet be paid $175 a month, with no other allowances. In the hands of such "a thor- oughly trained man," wrote Powell, even this small expenditure could accomplish much.[55]

The department of the interior consulted Henry about the appoint- ment and then approved the hiring of Gatschet, but for only six months. Meanwhile, a competing proposal for spending Foster's funds had come to the secretary's attention. As part of the nation's centennial celebra- tion, the department had authorized the preparation of a history of the progress of Indian education and civilization. The centennial was over and funds for the project were exhausted, but the history was not yet complete. By limiting Gatschet's appointment to six months, the depart- ment was able to allocate "not more than" $500 for the completion of the centennial history.[56]

The well-informed Powell, also mindful of the books and manu- scripts Foster had assembled, wrote to the commissioner: "Dr. Foster lately the Indian Historiographer of the Indian Bureau left a small library of documents relating to the history of North American Indians in the hands of Mr. Randall, a clerk in your bureau. As I am now, with a number of assistants, engaged in this work, under the direction of the Hon the Secretary of the Interior, I would respectfully request that this library be temporarily turned over to me. Most of the papers are such as I wish to consult almost daily and it would save my appropriation to the amount of their value." The transfer was approved.[57]

Thus at the end of 1877 Powell had in the newly combined historiographer-survey office Indian ethnological information from his own surveys, augmented by the Smithsonian's vocabulary collection and by Foster's materials, which if Foster had turned them over to the Indian office should have included 20 additional vocabularies. Gatschet was in the field gathering additional data on western Indians; somewhat more than $1,000 of his salary came from Foster's funds. No less needed than when Foster first talked of it in 1849 was an "Encyclopaedia" of the Indians of the United States, but that was not to become a reality until both Foster and Powell were dead. Not until 1905 did Powell's assistants at last complete the enormous task.[58]

Print-copying, too, survived Foster's tenure on the Indian project. The idea of producing printed copies of a manuscript preliminary to its perfection in a book found favor in Powell's ethnological domain. In 1885 the Bureau of Ethnology produced the "Proof-Sheets" of Powell's assistant, James C. Pilling. Pilling's research, like that of Foster, "grew on his hands" from year to year and led to a "preliminary, tentative, and incomplete catalogue" of works on Indian languages. Produced in a limited edition of 100, the "Proof-Sheets" were to be circulated among knowledgeable persons who would offer suggestions for correcting, revising, and editing the text before its final and formal publication. And among the scholars whose works were listed was Thomas Foster; his *Indian Record* was said to contain "many notes of value and interest to philologists and a few vocabularies."[59]

The end of the historiographer project can be traced one step farther. In the sundry appropriations of Congress for 1879–80 another mysterious Smithsonian proviso made its appearance. This time $20,000 was to be made available for completing and preparing for publication contributions to North American ethnology, "Provided that all the archives, records and materials relating to the Indians of North America, collected by the Geographical and Geological Survey of the Rocky Mountain Region, shall be turned over to the Smithsonian Institution that the work may be completed and prepared for publication under its direction," if the transfer met with the approval of the secretaries of the interior and of the Smithsonian. Powell did not wait. Writing to the secretary of the interior on July 8, he said that he had already given the Smithsonian a large portion of the materials and was prepared to transfer what remained.[60]

Spencer F. Baird, Henry's successor as secretary of the Smithsonian, agreed to the transfer but disavowed any complicity in the legislative scheme. He wrote that although the Smithsonian did not take part in having the provision inserted in the bill, "we are quite willing to accept the responsibility of receiving and taking charge of the archives, records & material relating to the Indians of North America." To do so the institution created a new department — the Bureau of Ethnology — with Powell as its director. In consequence, the Indian materials were transferred from the custody of Powell, geologist in charge of surveys in the interior department, to Powell, director of the new Smithsonian bureau. He held the two positions concurrently until 1894 and retained the bureau post until his death in 1902.[61]

Foster, too, remained in the Washington area. Only after he was threatened with legal action did he relinquish, in May, 1877, the government property that he still held. In the same month Mrs. Hannah C. Foster, his wife of 35 years, obtained a divorce, alleging that her husband had deserted her and had failed to contribute to her support since December, 1873. Their second son had drowned in Lake Superior in August, 1875, and Foster seems to have had little communication with his family after that time. Foster did not contest the divorce action and Mrs. Foster was awarded the family property in Duluth. Very shortly thereafter the doctor married again, and in January, 1878, a son was born of this second union.[62]

By that time the old editor was up to his elbows in another enterprise that allowed him to continue printing his Indian data. In January and February, 1878, he published four issues of the *Old Whig*, a newspaper devoted to a potpourri of politics, agriculture, household hints, puzzles, jokes, and genealogy. Each issue carried two columns of "Indianology," which Foster described as his "specialty" and a continuation of the *Record*. There were articles on "Alleghens," Algonquin tribes, the meanings of the words Niagara, Minnehaha, Mississippi, and Missouri; there was more information than had appeared in the *Record* on the origins of George Washington's Indian name; and there were some slighting remarks about Schoolcraft's six ponderous volumes of "much theory, scant facts and dogmatical guesses." Foster was gratified to report kind words from Colonel Garrick Mallery, a fellow "Indianologist" and author of a study of Indian sign language published by Powell.[63]

Another quarter century of Foster's life remained. At times during those years he worked for the government in the war, treasury, and auditor's departments, and was associated with the publication of *The Liberal*, a newspaper in Alexandria, Virginia, and with three papers in Tennessee. He retained his interests in politics and in Indian history. For a time he worked as a storekeeper in the internal revenue service at a distillery near Greenbrier, Tennessee. After the death of his second wife, Foster was married a third time, to Carrie Fell, the daughter of an old Minnesota acquaintance.[64]

Foster's last position in government service was a modest clerkship in the sixth auditor's office under the direction of Henry A. Castle of Minnesota. He resigned in 1902, but before leaving Washington he was interviewed by author-journalist William A. Croffut, a former Minnesotan. Croffut, who had previously worked for John Wesley Powell as an editor and popularizer of geological survey reports, wrote about Foster's eventful life for the *Minneapolis Journal*. Foster had continued his research in Indian languages, history, and ethnology, according to Croffut, and had "tabulated whole newspaper pages, tracing the Indian names of all the states and many of the rivers." The old editor's "mental clarity and energy were unabated," Croffut wrote, and he showed "continual anxiety that the result of his investigations might be put in permanent form." More of Foster's Indian historiography, it seemed, awaited print-copying.

In the fall of 1902 Foster crossed the continent to live in California with the son of his second marriage. He died the following March, two months short of his eighty-fifth birthday, and was buried in the army cemetery at the Presidio in San Francisco. The papers he took with him on his last westward journey were lost in the San Francisco earthquake and fire of 1906.

DR. THOMAS FOSTER, INDIAN HISTORI-OGRAPHER

5

A Circus
Gone Up

*The Great Australian Circus
is Stranded in North Branch, Minnesota
and its Employees Sue
to Recover Lost Wages*

T HE NEW GREAT AUSTRALIAN CIRCUS lay in camp in February,
1877, at Mount Clemens, Michigan, a city of mineral springs soon
to become a winter haven for circus people. The Great Australian
had two round-top canvases, 65 horses, and 21 wagons; it had "the finest
ring-horses, the finest band-chariot, the finest wagons, paraphernalia
and trappings of any circus in the West." The wagons were painted red,
green, and gold, and the most elegant was the expensive, new, imported
"Golden Chariot of Cleopatra."[1]

There is reason to believe that the circus was "New" and "Australian"
in name only. Owned by three men of Jackson, Michigan, the Great
Australian Circus had emerged from the Great Pacific Show, an enterprise closed in Illinois the previous year by poor attendance and four
weeks of rain. It then was moved to Mount Clemens, placed under the
management of William H. Dwyer, and renamed — apparently to evoke
the glamour of far-off places. The "Great" in its name was no measure
of its size; rather it was merely an ordinary circus-language superlative.[2]

On February 17 Dwyer announced in the *New York Clipper*, a show-
business publication, that the Great Australian was ready to hire in "all
branches of circus business." Personnel required were agents; masters of
canvas, wardrobe, transportation, and stables; music and equestrian
directors; a chief of the brigade to distribute posters; a "layer out" who
assigned employees to hotel rooms; ushers, various assistants, and officials; and such performers as riders, leapers, vaulters, jugglers, gymnasts, clowns, and side-show artists. Lest anyone interested in joining
the company harbor inflated notions about prospective earnings, Dwyer
warned that salaries "must be low." He promised, however, that pay
would be "sure" — an important consideration to any performer who had
been stranded, hungry and penniless, when a circus had closed, or "gone
up," on the sawdust trail. Indeed, another unrelated Great Australian
Circus, one of four by that name known to have existed during this
period, had been disbanded in New England in 1870 after a dispute between its proprietors.[3]

"The Circus of the Period," from the *New York Clipper*, April 19, 1873.

By the middle of April, 1877, Dwyer's company was fairly well organized for the tenting season. More than 40 officers, workers, and performers were named in a roster published in the *Clipper* on April 14. The entire company was said to include 80 persons, 14 of whom were band musicians. Not all those listed on the roster had actually signed contracts, and some never did. David Castello, for example, a 17-year-old bareback rider later to achieve fame in the circus world, joined P. T. Barnum instead. Dwyer explained that he had been dealing with Castello's agent and, fully expecting the young man to sign, had billed him as a star performer. Now, said Dwyer, he needed another male equestrian.[4]

All who had agreed to join the Great Australian were asked to report at Mount Clemens on May 9. A day or so later the circus performed there and then began its summer tour. It was scheduled to "show" around the Great Lakes, traveling on the company's propeller boat. Billed to tour lumbering and mining towns on Lake Superior and in Michigan, the circus proceeded by boat as far west as Duluth, Minnesota. From there it turned southward, traveling by rail, if advance billing may be trusted, in a train composed of ten flatcars, five boxcars, two passenger coaches, and a Pullman palace drawing-room car. Hopes were high for a profitable season.[5]

Bills posted in Duluth a few days before the Great Australian Circus arrived announced that it would give one performance on Monday, July

111

16. Three days before the big event, the *Duluth Daily Tribune* observed that local boys eagerly looked forward to the show. "Almost any of them are just now willing to do chores, if by so doing, they can earn the necessary 'quarter.' " The *Duluth Minnesotian-Herald* predicted on the same day that the circus would "please the children both great and small" and "take the small change out of town." Neither paper had more to say about the circus or its performance, perhaps because the management failed to buy advertising space. After the performance in Duluth the entire circus outfit — performers, wagons, horses, musical instruments, jacks, ladders, stake pullers, tents, banners, flagstaffs, and much, much more — was loaded onto cars of the St. Paul and Duluth Railroad, and the whole shebang headed south to Rush City in Chisago County.

The *Rush City Post* carried advance word (but no advertising) that the circus was coming and would show in that city on July 17. As a community service, editor and publisher Hial P. Robie gave the coming event a respectable amount of publicity in his paper of July 13. On page one Robie called the Great Australian one of the best circuses traveling, remarking that it was the first ever to stop between St. Paul and Duluth.

Twenty-six-year-old Robie, a man with an "in-born capacity to see the fitness of things," wore two hats, which makes his testimony about the Great Australian Circus worth repeating. Under one hat he was a fighting editor with an independent mind, bright and contentious, eloquent and opinionated. In his desk drawer he kept a cheese knife and "one of Colt's best" in case he had to defend himself against an irate reader. Wearing his second hat, Robie was a justice of the peace. By day or night, as the need arose, he dropped his editorial and publishing duties to convene the local justice court. In his twin capacities Robie was to learn much about the Great Australian Circus.[6]

On July 13, 1877, Robie said that the circus was good, clean fun for the whole family and that attendance at a performance would provide "the pleasantest time for the money ever spent in Rush City." He reported that the company was "composed of 30 talented artists and 25 beautiful horses and ponies, everything new and in its splendor." Although in numbers of people and horses the circus seemed considerably smaller than it had been described in the April *Clipper*, its quality was impressive still.

Eight lady performers included women of undoubted talent. The Leopold sisters, for example, were "without peers" in the new specialty of performing "upon the swing trapeze, bars, and rings, executing the most terrific leaps from bar to bar, of sixty feet." More superlatives described Eva Albertina, who made a "perilous leap for life in mid air, from the extreme top of the tent to a perpendicular rope hanging at a distance of 50 feet." Equally marvelous were the "surprising accomplishments" of Mademoiselle Lavina Brockway on her "famous educated horse," and Mademoiselle Christine, whose forte was parlor gymnastics. "Madame Gosh," who was not mentioned by the *Post*, was a tightrope dancer who achieved fleeting fame outside the ring a short time later.[7]

Most remarkable of all the women athletes, and one of the best known, was Mademoiselle Annie (Annette) Worland. This "young and beautiful" lady, who performed "graceful feats" of what Robie called "exquestrianism," was expected to appear in a "wonderful performance of walking forward and backward blindfolded on the tight rope without the aid of a balance pole." This feat had never been attempted by any other lady, Robie stated. At 1:00 P.M. on Tuesday, July 17, before the regular circus performance, Miss Worland would give a free exhibition. She would make "a startling ascension from the ground, to the top of the tent, on a small wire rope."

Although Robie believed the Royal Imperial Brass Band of 14 pieces was alone worth a trip to town, he named only a handful of men performers. No one had bothered to tell him that David Castello "late of Russia" (he was actually a native of North Carolina), the "champion somersa[u]lt bareback rider," was not present. Ed Holland of the famous Wisconsin circus family was expected to entertain viewers by "packing himself into a 24 x 30 inch box." Professor Sands and his son would perform acts of "posturing, tumbling and leaping." Clown Joseph Fields was billed as the "joker and fun maker of the world." The *Post* admitted that it did not mention "many other performers of remarkable note."[8]

Among those overlooked and soon to be known in Chisago County was lithe, red-haired Lemuel A. Quillin, a "First Clown." Quillin, who was 28 in 1877, was not a newcomer to the circus profession. He had been advertising his talents as "the great American Clown and Shakespearean Jester" for at least three years. After traveling with J. W. Couch & Company's "Colossal Museum, Menagerie and Globe Circus" in 1873, he proclaimed that he was also a "Tumbler, Leaper and Champion Gymnast." By the spring of 1874 he was billing himself as one of the "funniest and happiest clowns"; at the end of 1875, as he looked toward a new season, he advertised again. "Here I am," he trumpeted, "Comic Clown and Vocalist, also Leaper and Champion Gymnast." Just before joining the Great Australian in 1877, Quillin called himself a "Great American Jester, Comic Clown and Vocalist."[9]

Quillin came from Syracuse in Meigs County, Ohio, a river town frequently visited by circuses. It is not known when he first became a performer or how he learned the trade. Lem and his younger brother Lauren, or Lorenzo as he became known, were both men of many talents. Lauren's grandnephew remembered him "standing still jumping up in the air and flip flop[p]ing backwards and landing on his feet straight up with his body." Lauren could also "throw his neck out of joint" and make his head "flop like a dead chicken." Of Lemuel, the younger brother would only say, "He was a dusey."

Answering the *Clipper* call, Lemuel left brothers, sisters, parents, wife Anna, and baby daughter Lulu to sign a contract on March 31, 1877, with the Great Australian Circus Company. By its terms he agreed to make himself "generealy [sic] useful in the capacity of Clown &

Player in Concert" for the sum of $25 "payable Weekly at the Expiration of each and every Week." Two months later, when the Great Australian Circus reached Minnesota, Quillin had received little of his salary.[10]

Not another word appeared in the *Post* about the circus performance. No eyewitness described the daring deeds under the tent, or the acrobatic clown in his gay red, orange, pink, and yellow costume with black buttons. No one memorialized in print the joys of consuming peanuts, popcorn, gingerbread, or pink lemonade. No one remembered what tunes the band discoursed in sweet harmony, or recalled the raucous cries of the candy butcher and side-show barker, the popping of balloons, the squeaking of whistles. The day was soon over, the tents struck, the wagons loaded. The Great Australian company then proceeded southward to the north branch of the Sunrise River. To the audience, all had seemed normal bustle and order. Behind the curtains and inside the wagons, however, trouble was brewing.

Some 18 miles south of Rush City at North Branch, A. A. Beckett, assistant manager of the circus, had made arrangements for the company to stop a week or so to "recruit up" both animals and employees in the small railroad town. He reserved accommodations at several places, among them John J. F. Swenson's hotel and Benjamin Wilkes's boardinghouse. Wilkes also agreed to keep some of the circus horses at a stable across the road from his house. Beckett's financial arrangements with Wilkes are not known, but he contracted with Swenson to feed from 9 to 19 circus people for a week at 13½ cents a meal. If the company stayed longer than a week, the rate would go up to 16 cents.[11]

"JJF" Swenson, one of the first businessmen of North Branch, also kept a saloon and a general store, which in the next few weeks met other needs of the circus people. At 29, Swenson was successful and well traveled. Born in Östergötland, Sweden, he had come to America with his parents in 1850. After landing in New Orleans, the family, with three children, including two-year-old John, became stranded without funds in St. Louis, where a boy and a baby girl died of cholera. Pastor Gustaf Unonius, touched by the family's plight, persuaded Jenny Lind, the Swedish singer, to help pay the Swensons' way to Minnesota. Anders F. Swenson, John's father, was among the earliest of the many Swedes who settled in the Chisago Lakes area. He became the proprietor of Center City, which in 1876 was named the seat of Chisago County.[12]

Until John reached the age of 19, he worked on nearby farms. Then he left Minnesota and traveled to New York, Panama, and the West Coast. During the two years of his absence, he accumulated enough money to launch a business career when he returned to Chisago County. First he ran a general store in Center City, but he soon moved to the new railroad town of North Branch. By 1877 he was married, the father of two children, and the second largest taxpayer in Branch Township.

Benjamin Wilkes, like Swenson, reached North Branch almost immediately after the town was established in 1870. A New Yorker, Wilkes was a canny, hard-working man with an enterprising wife. The two lived in a comfortable house where Chloe Wilkes took in boarders; Wilkes

Lemuel A. Quillin, about
1889. *MHS*

A CIRCUS
GONE UP

Quillin's contract. *MHS*

kept a stable and blacksmith shop across the road. Mrs. Wilkes later expanded her business into a full-scale hotel, but in 1877 it was still an unpretentious boardinghouse.[13]

When the circus came to town, Swenson and the Wilkeses thought they could make an honest penny or so, but they were not prepared for what happened. Well into the second week of the Great Australian occupation, the *Post* of August 3, 1877, reported that the ravenous boarders threatened to eat North Branch residents "out of house and home." In that rustic environment there was little to do but eat. Opportunities for amusement were available in St. Paul about 40 miles away, but few circus employees had money for the train fare. They had not been paid for weeks. Soon they became restive, pestering manager Dwyer with requests for money.

Dwyer stalled for a few days and then told his employees that he was going to St. Paul to get some cash so he could pay them. The trusting souls let him go off aboard the train. Madame Gosh, his favorite among the tightrope ladies, quietly slipped away after him. Together they vamoosed; and that was the last seen of the two in North Branch and Chisago County.

Some facts about Dwyer then became public knowledge. It was reported that when he started the season with the circus company, his wife was traveling with him, but he did not pay much attention to her. Thrown as he was in constant contact with women of "distinguished proportions and marked physique," Dwyer had been unable to resist their charms. He was fascinated in particular by Madame Gosh. Somewhere on the trail between Mount Clemens and North Branch, Dwyer's behavior became unendurable to his wife, a "high spirited lady who knew her rights." Deciding that her husband's case was hopeless, she left him and went home to Mount Clemens. Thus the traveling Dwyer was free to dally undisturbed with the tightrope dancer.[14]

At the same time, Dwyer had furthered his long-range plans by putting aside a substantial amount of money from the circus receipts. When he left North Branch before the end of July, he took with him $7,000 — a sum gathered probably not only from admission fees but also from the management's share of the profits from candy and other concession sales. (At 25 cents a ticket that amount would have represented the income from the sale of 28,000 tickets!) The *St. Paul Pioneer Press* of August 17 later inferred that Dwyer did not see how he could pay his employees without giving up a large part of the $7,000. So, "thinking a bird in the hand was worth two in the bush," he took the money and the dancer and, said the *Post* of August 10, headed "for the sunny south."

When it dawned on the citizenry of North Branch and the circus members that Dwyer and the tightrope dancer were not coming back, trouble erupted "all along the line." Some of the circus people remembered that the previous year, the Great Pacific Show had collapsed in Illinois and its employees were forced to settle for wages of 37 cents on the dollar. The Great Australian Company members wanted more than 37 per cent of what was due them.[15]

Swenson and Wilkes wanted more too, and they were the first to enter claims against the company. Eight performers followed suit. The complainants enlisted the help of Lewis D. Dent, a Rush City lawyer, and his associate B. C. Newport. Dent, who happened to be in North Branch on other business, took them all to Rush City to Robie, the justice of the peace, who put their cases on the court calendar. Robie also gave County Sheriff John Shaleen writs of attachment enabling him to hold circus property to cover delinquent wages and other debts incurred by the company.

Sheriff Shaleen, in his often thankless job as a public servant, was at times underestimated even by his constituents. Some said he had not gone to college, that his penmanship was "wre[t]ched," his spelling errors "gross and frequent," and his knowledge of mathematics "limited." It was true that he had only a grammar-school education and that in drawing up inventories of the circus property he misspelled the word wagon as "waggan." But English was, after all, his second language. A bilingual Swede, Shaleen was a member of a talented immigrant family. Robie and others defended him; they contended that he was an able man, that he knew the law, and that he was a "perfectly competent" public official.

During the last days of July and the first part of August, the sheriff listed and attached enough circus property to cover the claims of the suing employees and the bills of the two businessmen. The employees claimed amounts based on wages due at a weekly rate of $15 for tumblers and leapers, $18 for the aerialist, and $25 for Quillin, the first clown. None had received half, some much less, of what was owed them.[16]

For the benefit of tumblers Arthur Buckles and W. L. Merrick, the sheriff attached the "Band Waggan" and three sets of jacks (the supports placed under tiers of seats) — 42 each of small, medium, and large jacks. Shaleen listed 15 items in the writ of attachment filed for leaper and tumbler S. R. Romer. Included were band coats, caps and plumes, flagstaffs, saddles, a bass drum, banners, wagon lights, and the "Ticket Waggan." For Joseph Bignon, another tumbler and leaper, a third wagon was attached, as well as a "water-tank heater," an iron plane, a stake puller, and a ladder. Two gray horses were held for assistant manager Beckett and for "Signor Montanio," the "arial trapheaze" artist, one spotted stallion, and one sorrel horse. A dark horse, a bay, and two saddles were attached for the claim of J. J. F. Swenson. The water wagon was claimed for Lem Quillin's overdue wages, but R. L. (Gus) Warner, a representative and agent of J. E. Warner, said that the wagon was owned by the latter and asked that it be released to him. The sheriff complied. Shaleen then called on some of the circus men to help him guard the attached property until their cases were heard in court.

So there they were and there they stayed, the whole of the Great Australian Circus Company — less two — stranded, penniless, and more or less hungry, among the pastures, oak trees, prairie chickens, and other occupants of North Branch. As the circus boys waited for justice to be

117

done, some of them took an additional precaution to protect the property from vandalism and other dangers. They removed and secreted all the nuts and bolts from the wagons.[17]

After someone notified the proprietors of the circus at Jackson, Michigan, that they were being sued, John S. Hurd, one owner, hastened to St. Paul, where he engaged the firm of Davis, O'Brien and Wilson to defend the company. Two attorneys, Christopher Dillon O'Brien and E. Stone Gorman, took on the owners' cases. They in turn hired a county lawyer, Alexander Young of North Branch, to assist them.

Friday, August 3, was a day of activity in circus affairs. The "high-toned dignitaries," Hurd and Gorman, had taken the train to Rush City. Joined by Alexander Young, they climbed the stairs to justice court in Robie's office on the second floor of the Emigrant Building. The *Post* had gone to press for the week, and Robie was free to give his undivided attention to the matters before the court. After Shaleen served Hurd with the necessary papers, Robie heard the first circus case.

Early the following day, Saturday, St. Paul lawyer O'Brien, accompanied by a Ramsey County deputy sheriff, stepped off the train at North Branch bent on urgent business, to be described later. Sheriff Shaleen had also gone to North Branch and was at or near the circus corral. At the same time, plaintiffs and defendants gathered in court in Rush City for the second day of the trials. Robie's docket was so crowded that he was forced to schedule cases into the evening.

The Wilkes case had been heard when attorney Gorman began to feel thirsty. Fishing around in his pocket, he pulled out a 50-cent piece, turned to Lem Quillin, who was not busy at the moment, and asked him to go to a nearby saloon and bring back 50 cents' worth of lager beer. While Quillin was gone, Gorman handed a bundle of papers to attorney

John Shaleen, about 1883. *MHS*

Christopher D. O'Brien, about 1885. *MHS*

Young and told him to take them into the adjoining room and prepare an answer to the next case on the docket, because he (Gorman) was "busy."

Editor Robie described what happened next. About the time the beer arrived, Gorman took advantage of the lull in the proceedings to go downstairs. Robie, too, stepped out for a short time. When the latter returned, he made the startling discovery that some of the court's papers were not where they had been when he left. Where were they? Lawyer Dent remarked helpfully that Young must have them. Young, who was about to leave the room, denied that he had any papers except Gorman's. Robie was not impressed; he ordered that Young, who had reached the hall, be surrounded and searched. When Young's "old fur cap" and long-tailed, 16-year-old overcoat were "investigated and shook," pleadings, attachment papers, affidavits, bonds, and writs tumbled out "thick and fast." In fact, the county lawyer had "stolen everything" relating to the Great Australian Circus Company lawsuits except the docket and the court itself.

After the papers were retrieved, order was somehow restored, and one after another the cases came to trial. The last of the day, that of aerial artist Montanio, was heard at 8:00 Saturday evening. By then Hurd and his attorneys were well aware of the temper of the court. Sometime over the weekend Hurd and Gorman returned to St. Paul and Young to North Branch.

None of them appeared on Monday, August 6, when Robie reconvened court at 9:00 A.M. The plaintiffs, their attorney, and the justice waited an hour for the defendants to appear. When they had not arrived on the morning train, Robie concluded that they would not come and carried on without them. He heard the cases of Beckett, Buckles, Merrick, Bignon, and Quillin. Words were not minced. Robie found that facts supported the claims of the local businessmen and the circus personnel. Accordingly he ordered the proprietors of the Great Australian Company to pay what the plaintiffs wanted, plus costs. Before the night was over, local events tended to support Robie's conclusion that the circus employees were honorable people who deserved favorable verdicts.

Frank Johnson, a circus member who had been a witness in some of the court cases, although he did not himself sue the company, stayed in Rush City the night of August 6. About 12:30 A.M. he heard the cry, "Fire!" Hastily getting up, he followed the sound and saw flames at the home of S. C. Norton, the station agent. When Norton discovered the fire, he quickly "seized" his wife and child from bed and helped them through a window to safety. He himself went out, only to return immediately to rescue a vest in which he kept a watch, a pocketbook, some money, and some railroad papers. Only after leaving the burning house a second time did he remember his sleeping sister Cora, alone upstairs.[18]

By then others had gathered, and before Norton could return for his sister, he saw a strange man carrying her downstairs. When she awakened to find the room and hallway full of smoke, she had "presence of

119

mind enough to put a bed quilt around her head." Starting for the stairs, "she was met by a man who was going up to assist her down. She was nearly suffocated and exhausted and ready to fall, when she was caught up in the strong arms of her rescuer and carried down." The young hero was Frank Johnson of the Great Australian Circus Company, who had been "one of the first at the fire."

Meanwhile on Saturday, August 4, lawyer O'Brien and the Ramsey County deputy sheriff had arrived at North Branch with one purpose in mind. While O'Brien's colleagues were doing battle in court in Rush City, he and the deputy prepared to claim the circus property and take it to St. Paul for safekeeping. For a time Sheriff Shaleen, who was on guard at the corral with the well-muscled circus employees, thwarted O'Brien. Shaleen knew that O'Brien had no right to take the attached property without proper bonds, accepted and approved by the court, and he stood firm. Besides, the resourceful circus men had removed "all the nuts, bolts and screws" so that none of the rolling stock could roll.[19]

O'Brien, confronted with this frustrating situation, fell back to talk over strategy with the St. Paul deputy. As a result, the deputy retraced his steps to the depot and took the next train south. O'Brien stayed around to keep an eye on the company property and to argue, parley, reason, and try in various other ways to soften the resistance of the sheriff and the circus boys. Shaleen remained unmoved. The circus men were belligerent, "browbeating" and "blackguarding" poor O'Brien almost to exhaustion. They threatened to send whoever touched the circus property on a long and unrewarding journey to "where the brimstone was deep."

The deputy, back in St. Paul, soon rounded up a *posse comitatus*. In other words, the *St. Paul Pioneer Press* explained, he got together "enough men to capture, overwhelm and defeat the circus men who appeared to be a desperate crowd." The posse of 20 good men and true included a formidable Irishman named Pat O'Regan and "other warriors of like prowess." The deputy and the posse piled onto a chartered train and steamed northward to North Branch.

As the day wore on and O'Brien's patience evaporated, he detected the puffing smoke of an engine heralding the arrival of the train bringing his deliverance. At once he began to breathe more freely, according to the *Pioneer Press* version of events. When the train stopped at the North Branch depot, the St. Paul task force scrambled out and hurried to the circus corral. At once the *posse comitatus* spread out and "each one stood up by the side of a circus man, ready if the circus man made a movement to drop him."

Against this force, the St. Paul newspaper reported, the Chisago County sheriff and the circus men saw that they were outnumbered and overpowered. Resistance was useless and "they wilted." Without further interference O'Brien, the deputy, and the Irish tough boys searched out the nuts, bolts, and screws and put the wagons in running order. They took all the equipment and loaded it on the train. No one revealed how or where they found the hardware. The deed was done, however, and the train steamed and chugged south again taking circus property, O'Brien, the Ramsey County delegation, and perhaps some members of the company who had not filed suits to St. Paul in triumph. All was over but the complaining — the complaining of the posse, unhappy because its members had wanted a good fight. That there had been none "was what hurt," said the *Pioneer Press*.

The civil confrontation between circus employees and circus owners now began to assume a broader dimension. Back and forth the *St. Paul Pioneer Press* and the *Rush City Post* traded insults, arraying high-toned city slickers from Ramsey County against Chisago County hicks. The *Pioneer Press* championed Irishmen, city lawyers learned in the law, rich property owners, property rights, and public officials who kept regular office hours. The *Post* supported Swedes and New Yorkers, rural lawyers learned in the law (with the exception of Alex Young), downtrodden wage earners, and public officials who had a comparatively relaxed attitude toward office hours. Virtue, intelligence, and good horse sense, the *Post* expounded, lay at the northern end of a 60-mile train ride from St. Paul to Rush City.

Editor-justice Robie righteously put the opposition in its place. Whom was the *Pioneer Press* trying to fool? Did it think for one minute that millionaires from Jackson, Michigan, and a rowdy bunch of Irishmen from St. Paul could put anything over on a Swedish sheriff, a Yankee justice, and a handful of talented and wronged circus performers? Fearlessly he offered his readers his version of the truth. The circus employees had not been paid; they had appropriately and legally sued the company for back pay. In the employees' behalf the court had issued legal writs of attachment on company property. Sheriff Shaleen, with the kind assistance of the circus people, was guarding the property under attachment when O'Brien and his posse tried illegally with threats and Irish shillelaghs to take it away. They were properly repulsed. Shaleen "did not scare worth a cent," and his cause was just. In order to obtain the release of the property, O'Brien was forced to give bond for the Great Australian Circus Company in the amount of $4,000 — twice the sum of the suits pending in court. Then only, after the bonds had been signed and delivered to Justice Robie and accepted by him, was the circus property released by the sheriff. Whereupon editor Robie, who was not a "wilter," sarcastically offered three cheers for O'Brien and his fighting men.

When circus proprietor Hurd learned in St. Paul that Justice Robie's decisions had all gone against the circus company, he and his attorneys made plans to appeal to the district court, which was to meet in October. The company would try to bring in Dwyer, the manager, as a witness; perhaps there would also be time to attempt out-of-court settlements with the suing employees. The company and its attorneys, in order to appeal, had to file notices with the justice at Rush City. Robie was in his office on August 4, 5, 6, 7, and 8, but he had no inkling that the

121

company wished to appeal, he said later. On Thursday, August 9, after he had put the *Post* well on the way to publication, he took the morning train to Duluth on business, returning on Saturday.

While he was gone the circus company representatives arrived at Rush City and went to Robie's office. The doors were closed, the records not accessible. No knowledgeable person could be found to help them file their appeals. To the company people only one explanation was possible. Robie had "run away" to keep them from filing. Since they were not without other legal remedies, they returned to St. Paul and went as soon as possible to the Ramsey County Courthouse. Doors were open *there* and accommodating people were on duty, ready to help them, crowed the *Pioneer Press*.

The superior court of Ramsey County issued a writ of mandamus ordering Robie to appear in his office so John S. Hurd could file the company's appeals. It was alleged in the writ that Robie had "absconded" and "conspired" with the employees' attorneys to cheat and defraud Hurd of his rights and had "hidden" the court records so Hurd could not discover the dates of the judgments or the amounts of money the circus company was required to pay. Of course the *Pioneer Press* did not mention that if the company officials had attended the court sessions held in Rush City on Monday, they would have had that information.

The writ of mandamus was mailed to Rush City, where Robie found it August 11 when he returned from Duluth. Now it was his turn to speak — through the columns of the *Post*. The allegations in the mandamus were a lot of nonsense, he wrote on August 17. The "allegator" (Hurd), although he came from Michigan, "was a (blank) [*sic*] little mistaken." The Ramsey County newspaper apparently took its law from "last year's almanac or Blackberries commentary." Point by point, the editor-justice expounded the law pertaining to the circus cases, concluding that the judgments against Hurd and his company were all lawfully rendered. Next time, Robie suggested, the *Pioneer Press* and the "allegators" should mix a little truth with their mandamus.

Robie admitted that he was not in his office when the "allegators" came to call and asked whether a justice of the peace was required to stay in his office 365 days a year. If called out of town, should he leave his docket on the sidewalk or in his office with the door unlocked for "anybody and everybody to erase[,] change, mutilate or steal?" He had once favored such an open administration of justice, but his recent experience with Gorman and Young in the circus cases had been disillusioning. The sight of those pleadings, attachments, affidavits, bonds, and writs tumbling from Young's coat and hat, as though he were a country post office, had persuaded the justice to be less trusting. He was now keeping court records under lock and key. "But if we ever play lawyer," he concluded, "and want to appeal from a judgment where the justice resides 60 miles from us, we will write or telegraph to the justice that we will be at his office on such a day, to appeal certain cases, and if this had been done in this case they would have found us in our office."

By this time the circus affair was generating even more traffic on the St. Paul and Duluth line between Rush City, North Branch, and St. Paul. Soon, Robie and the circus employees' lawyers boarded the train for St. Paul with the court docket and other papers relating to the claims cases. They went to the Ramsey County Courthouse to answer the questions raised by the mandamus. They explained why Robie had not been in his office, why he had gone to Duluth, and why he had put the court records in a safe place while he was away. It was further pointed out, in simple English, that the circus company had until August 17 to file its appeals. Robie and friends were unable to find Hurd or his attorneys in St. Paul. Nevertheless they went home rejoicing, having billed the circus company $100 for travel costs. Of the trip Robie wrote, "we have not fully made up our mind as to whether the joke was on Mr. Hurd or the mandamus."

Robie, back at his editorial desk, urged the *Pioneer Press* to please "give us a rest," and to "sing the forty-eleventh hymn, and Pat O'Regan pass around the saucer, to be followed by music by the Rush City band." Enough was enough! The legal sparring ended for awhile. Robie allowed the company to file its appeals in the eight cases, and the matter passed out of the jurisdiction of his court.

Nevertheless Robie continued reporting on the stranded circus people. A number of them found part-time work on farms and in the wheat fields. Harvesting had just begun, the crop was immense, and the *Post* reported on August 3 that hired hands were "worth from $1.50 to $2.00 per day, and the demand for labor is good." Some performers, under the direction of Signor Montanio, traveled about the county giving entertainments, while others went to St. Paul in search of more interesting activities.

Little Kilkenny, the youngest clown, found free board and room 14 miles northwest of North Branch at Cambridge in nearby Isanti County. There he stole a watch; he was arrested, tried, and given 30 days in jail. Pleading for mercy, Kilkenny said, "You know how it 'tis yourself Mr. Justice. I was dead broke and the old watch was only worth $1, anyhow. Make it ten days Mr. Justice." The justice was unsympathetic, but the rest of Cambridge tried to atone for his cruelty. "Just now," Robie wrote in the *Post* of August 17, "the jail is the most inviting place in Cambridge, and crowds go there daily, the ladies with loads of flowers, cakes, pies and nick nacks [sic] for the little fellow, while he shows his appreciation of their kindness by singing songs[,] turning sommersalts [sic] standing on his head &c."

When the summer was over, Little Kilkenny disappeared from public notice, and most of the other circus people seem to have left the area. Bignon, Montanio, Merrick, Meyett, Buckles, Romer, and Beckett — all but one of those who had brought suit — apparently settled their claims out of court. Robie thought "that Mr. Hurd, the principal defendant bought off the balance of the boys, for a small part of their indebtedness to prevent them from appearing against him." It is presumed that many

123

of the employees who had not sued went on with the owners, returned to their homes, or found other employment.[20]

Of the original complainants only Quillin and Swenson refused to settle. They retained additional legal counsel, hiring James and Ira Castle of Stillwater to aid their defense. Three other circus men remained in Chisago County to see what luck Quillin would have when the appeal was heard. Wilkes made some mutually satisfactory agreement with the company and dropped his suit.[21]

District court met in the middle of October at Center City. The new, two-story frame Chisago County Courthouse was situated near the end of Main Street on a peninsula in a jewel-like setting of green grass and trees then in autumn colors, surrounded on three sides by a lake. The *Taylors Falls Journal* remarked on October 19: "This is court week at Center City. That burg is lively, lively as a cricket. We never saw so many people assembled there. They came from all parts of the County, and are from all walks of life. The well dressed and stylish St. Paul and Stillwater Lawyers, and the Chisago county farmers met together to gull and be gulled. Judge [Francis M.] Crosby looked his best, and rules with becoming dignity." The *Journal* editor did not believe in quarreling and did not like lawsuits, but he concluded, "We still hold . . . that if one smites you on the right cheek, it is your duty to 'give it to him' on the left."

Some brief details of the arguments in the Swenson and Quillin cases were reported in the *Post*, but only the sketchiest of notes in the court records indicate the company's defense. Hurd and R. E. Emmons, the two circus owners who appeared in court, tried to convince the judge and jury that they were not responsible for the actual operation of the circus, having turned over the management to Dwyer. Their attorneys argued that it was necessary to have Dwyer's testimony. Emmons said he had heard that the ex-manager was in Detroit, but a search failed to locate him there. Just before leaving Jackson to attend the trial, Emmons had learned that Dwyer was traveling with the Fair Brothers circus; there had not been time to trace him further. Hurd and Emmons then requested and were granted a continuance of the cases until the next term of district court, to allow them time to find Dwyer.[22]

Now came a new development. Lem Quillin decided that the limited amount of money he would receive from the company was not enough, particularly if a settlement were delayed and more legal fees incurred. He therefore began a new suit for a larger sum. The three other circus men who had been looking on — Thomas J. Whelan, Charles Wagner, and Edwin (or Edward) J. Downs — all decided to sue for their back wages. The lawyers, Castle and Dent, were suddenly so busy making up new sets of papers to serve on the company that Robie, who was present to report the proceedings and to participate in a suit of his own, gave them a hand.[23]

When Hurd and Emmons realized that they were about to be sued again, they hurriedly "buttoned their coats" and left the courthouse. Not pausing to enjoy the beautiful view, they began walking toward Wyoming, the nearest station on the St. Paul and Duluth railroad line. O'Brien and Gorman, observing that the company men had gone, also hastily departed, hitched up their team of horses, and went after their clients to give them a lift.

While the lawyers and Robie worked on the papers, Lem Quillin, who had been sworn in as a deputy sheriff, prepared his horse for travel. As soon as some of the papers were readied and thrust into his hands, he leaped on the horse and galloped down the road toward Wyoming. Two miles out of Center City, Quillin stopped the "Jackson millionaires" and served the papers.

Back at the courthouse, the last papers were finished and given to a waiting constable. He in turn mounted a horse and set out. So it was that on a mid-October Indian-summer afternoon, an unusual number of travelers plodded, ran, galloped, or otherwise proceeded from Center City toward Wyoming. Like Quillin, the fast-riding constable overtook Hurd and Emmons and served the remaining papers before they and their attorneys reached the railroad station. The train then took the men from Jackson, Michigan, out of the lives of Chisago County residents.

Neither returned to Minnesota when the Great Australian Circus suit was continued a year later in district court at Stillwater. Instead Darlin B. Lincoln, the third of the circus owners, represented the company. In that court session, the jury's decision favored Quillin and his friends, but for some reason, not clearly stated in the transcripts of the case, Lincoln was not considered liable for the company's debts and there were more delays in the final settlement. At last the bonds posted by attorneys O'Brien and Gorman were forfeited to pay for court costs; goods and merchandise were sold; and services rendered long before were in some measure recompensed.

The Great Australian Circus Company had "gone up" and its eventful encounter with the people of Minnesota soon faded from local memory. No record has been found of what finally happened to the circus. Some of its performers who rose to greater professional heights were named in later issues of the *Clipper*, but the Great Australian Circus of 1877 was not mentioned there again. In all probability it underwent another metamorphosis, to emerge under new owners with a new name, another manager, and certainly another first clown.

In Chisago County, Sheriff John Shaleen was elected to the first of two terms as state senator. He also served twelve years as probate judge. Hial Robie later moved to Yankton, South Dakota, where he edited and published a newspaper. J. J. F. Swenson built and operated a sawmill at Almelund, nine miles east of North Branch. The Wilkes family prospered in their joint blacksmithing and hotel businesses, but Mrs. Wilkes eventually divorced her husband.[24]

Clown Quillin stayed in North Branch, but for years the circus fever remained in his blood. On January 19, 1878, he again advertised in the *Clipper*, seeking an engagement as a "Musical Clown, Trick Tumbler, Gymnast, Leaper and Champion Double Somersault thrower over nine horses." A month later his advertisement was altered to read simply

125

"Champion Double Somersault Thrower of the World over nine horses."
In the spring Quillin's wife and their little Lulu arrived in North Branch
from Syracuse. They became active members of the local Episcopal
church and Lem joined two fraternal orders, the North Star Lodge of
the Ancient Order of United Woodmen and the Knights of Pythias. He
went into a short-lived business arrangement with a local storekeeper
dealing in dry and liquid goods. "For a good square drink of corn or
grape juice," the *Post* said, "go to Quillan's [*sic*]. He keeps also a fine line
of cigars and is very obliging."[25]

Three years later the *Clipper* reported that Lem had given a Fourth
of July oration followed by a comedy entertainment to "several thousand
people" at a celebration sponsored by the Lake Elizabeth, Minnesota,
boating club. His ability as a clown and his skill as a "negro comedian"
were highly praised. In May, 1882, a week after Quillin's son Leon was
born, the *Post* reported that "Lem Quillan [*sic*], the double-jointed
clown and comedian has left the mercantile business here, and accepted
a position in a first-class circus traveling from Chicago to New Mexico.
We wish him success and a safe return to gaze upon the young clown
he left behind." A year later, calling himself a "Comic Clown and
Vocalist" and "the Great American Shakespearian Clown and Comic
Singer," Quillin advertised that he was open for engagements for the
tenting season.[26]

When no tempting offers came his way, the former clown purchased
most of a block in downtown North Branch and expanded into several
lines of business. He was postmaster of North Branch during the first
Cleveland administration, he operated a grocery and dry-goods store,
and he became the proprietor of a hotel. In leisure moments he wrote
poetry, umpired baseball games, and hunted deer and bear with other
North Branch sportsmen. Although he had said good-bye to the circus
world, he was not ready to abandon show business, for in the 1890s he
built and managed an opera house.[27]

The ground floor of Quillin's two-story, 26-by-80-foot Opera Hall in
North Branch had a storage room, Lem's office, and a "sample room" or
bar which sported a nickel slot machine. Upstairs the hall was "finished
complete with stage and curtains and all the paraphernalia of a theatre."
It had a seating capacity of 600, curtains with scenes painted by
"Sasman & Lands of Chicago," and a $900 piano from the Nathan Ford
music store in St. Paul. The *Post* predicted that the "fun loving" Lem
would "no doubt give the people many an opportunity of enjoying
Shakespeare on his own boards." Notices in the Rush City and North
Branch newspapers suggested that the fare tended to light comedy
rather than to Shakespeare, but there is no doubt that in its heyday the
opera house was a popular place.

Quillin advertised that he would "play all traveling troupes on per-
centage, or rent the house by the night." Among the groups to appear
were the St. Paul Comedy Company, the Kickapoo Indian Medicine
Company, Professor W. F. Whittier of Minneapolis, who gave exhibitions of mind reading, and Rush City amateurs performing the comic

drama "Broken Fetters." A variety of musical and dancing programs in the Opera Hall provided additional entertainment for North Branch residents of the gay nineties. Local citizens engaged the hall for birthday dances; there were "social" and "soda" hops and fancy balls on St. Patrick's Day, Washington's Birthday, and Thanksgiving Day, as well as a Promenade Concert on Christmas Eve.[28]

Following Opera Hall entertainments Lem often arranged special suppers at his "repaired and newly furnished" Arlington Hotel, where the dining room could serve 100 guests at a time. On one occasion more than 200 "lovers of terpsichore" from nearby towns arrived by special trains to attend a ball and supper at this "popular hostelry." On another evening the Quillins entertained 14 tables of progressive euchre, and Lem, a gracious host, won the booby prize. The hotel, which was said to be the best-equipped house on the St. Paul and Duluth line, catered especially to traveling salesmen, 14 of whom stayed there on one banner night in April, 1895.[29]

Always the showman, Quillin not only sold dry goods and groceries at his "Old Reliable Store" but offered entertainment, too. Someone has recalled that Lem would juggle balls to entertain children. Effie Klicker, who lived near the Quillin home as a small girl in the 1890s, remembered him as a "short, heavy-set" man with red hair and a stomach that "shook when he laughed" who "loved to play with kids." In a typical gesture, he put old wooden "circus horses . . . in the backyard of the store for kids to play on."[30]

The Quillins had four children of their own, two boys and two girls. Lulu became a teacher, then married a Northern Pacific Railway Company employee; the other daughter, Myrtis, was a department store clerk in St. Paul. A son, Lemuel (Mac), also worked for the Northern Pacific. The other son, Leon, a talented athlete, played baseball for Stillwater, Duluth, Minneapolis, and the Chicago White Sox.

Overextended credit and general hard times forced Quillin out of business at North Branch. For a time he managed a hotel in Hibbing, but by 1906 he and his family had moved to St. Paul, where he became a traveling salesman. During the next 20 years he worked for a number of companies "on the road"; he was still employed, by the McFadden Company of Dubuque, Iowa, selling tea, coffee, and spices when he died in 1925 at age 76. In North Branch his Opera Hall and hotel are gone, but his old house still stands on Sixth Street near Elm, the only tangible reminder of Lem Quillin, first clown of the Great Australian Circus, the first circus to show on the railroad line between St. Paul and Duluth.[31]

6

Ski-Sport Heroes
from
Norway

*Norwegian Immigrants
Introduce the Fine Points
of Skiing as a Sport
to Admiring Midwesterners*

SKIING AS A SPORT began in the Upper Midwest in the 1880s when some of the first American ski clubs were organized. Conditions in Minnesota, Michigan, and Wisconsin favored the sport, which required, in order to thrive, "a climate where snow abounds during the winter months, plenty of steep long hills and the Scandinavian," according to Jens K. Grondahl, a Red Wing skier of the time. In addition, the annual St. Paul Winter Carnival sponsored ski competitions among its earliest activities, which also helped the sport. And midwestern railroads encouraged skiers to organize and travel to other communities for competitions by offering them special fares.[1]

It was the Scandinavian connection, however, that was crucial to the development of the sport. Finns, Lapps, Norwegians, and Swedes from the northern districts of Sweden all had skill and experience on skis. But the Norwegian immigrants of the 1880s were the most able and influential, bringing from the old country their special skis and techniques for using them. And among the Midwest's Norwegian immigrants none were more skilled in skiing than Mikkel and Torjus Hemmestvedt from Telemark. In Minnesota, Wisconsin, and Michigan, as in their native country, they became the heroes of the slopes.

The Hemmestvedts and their Scandinavian associates who pioneered in the midwestern ski-sport followed a tradition extending back to prehistoric times. No one knows how far back or where in arctic lands northern people first fastened boards on their feet to slide over the surface of the snow. A stone-age rock carving at Rødøy, Norway, possibly 4,000 years old, shows a hunter on skis surrounded by moose, reindeer, and other animals. He wears a cap with ear flaps and carries in his hands an object much like a stick or an ax; his knees are bent. His skis resemble those of today, but their turned-up tips are carved in the shape of serpent heads. Ancient skis, preserved for a thousand or more years in bogs and now housed in Scandinavian museums, vary in size and shape. They are short, long, broad, thin, bare, or covered with skins; they have been fashioned with or without bottom grooves, bindings, or decorative designs; they are made of ash, pine, birch, and other woods. Tales of the past, mingling fact and legend, tell of hunters, reindeer herders, soldiers, and even gods and goddesses who traveled on skis. Annual races in Norway and Sweden today commemorate the deeds of those illustrious skiers.[2]

Scandinavians in the United States, particularly Norwegians who immigrated before the 1880s and had grown up on skis, found them useful when the snow lay deep in the northern latitudes. In 1853 a Norwegian skier using so-called Lapland snow skates, which were "strips of smooth wood, about six feet long and three inches wide and turning up like sleigh runners before [in front]," traveled from Lake Superior to St. Paul at the rate of 80 miles or so a day. In Wisconsin a Norwegian clergyman took to skis to visit his parishioners, who hunted deer on skis. In the mining regions of Colorado and California at mid-century, men held informal ski races with gold dust for prizes.[3]

In central Minnesota Norwegians carried the mail on skis during the week and on Sunday afternoons skied into the next county to visit friends. At Fergus Falls in 1881 a county official made a 150-mile ski journey to collect taxes. On his return he carried a burden of 50 pounds — his records and a bag of silver tax money. An athletic skier traveled 65 miles from Glenwood to St. Cloud for groceries, returning with a bag of provisions under one arm and a 100-pound sack of flour strapped to his back. Pallbearers on skis at Reno, Minnesota, carried a woman in her coffin to her last resting place. Residents of many American states and territories — Scandinavian pastors, miners, mail carriers, farmers, hunters, and the neighbors who learned from them — found skiing a practical way to travel and, at times, a skill vital to survival in snowbound, pioneer days. It was said, in fact, that in the 1880s "the first thing that a Norwegian-American does as soon as he realizes that he is on earth to stay, is to look about and order his skis ready for use as soon as he can walk."

Meanwhile in Norway skiing had become a popular competitive sport. Local contests offering substantial prizes were held in the 1850s and 1860s and the first ski club in the world is said to have been organized there in 1861. New techniques and refinements in style and equipment were perfected and demonstrated by skiers in Christiania (Oslo) before admiring throngs. One of the best skiers was Sondre Norheim of Morgedal in the Telemark district of south-central Norway. An extraordinary athlete, he was a daredevil so graceful that skiing seemed the natural way for him to move. Energetic and highly competitive, Norheim entered many contests and won numerous prizes. He pioneered in new ways of skiing while he instructed and inspired countless young skiers. A kind man with a "nice smile," he was the hero of the young people of Morgedal.[4]

Mikkel Hemmestvedt remembered how little boys peered out from farmhouse windows hoping to see Sondre approach the ski hill. "If they saw him coming from his home in his characteristic rocking style, then they came to life behind the window panes," and their mothers could not restrain them. "The skis must go on . . . and soon there was a swarm of life" on the hill. Norheim showed the children how to jump, and he made "featherlight landings" even when he was nearly 50 years old. He encouraged both boys and girls to ski, and in 1878 Mikkel's sister, Aasne, won a prize in one of the first girls' races in Morgedal.[5]

Like other Telemark men, Norheim made skis and sold them at competitions. His innovative design was adapted from that of the shorter, traditional Telemark mountain skis, which were made of pine, narrow in the middle and wider in front with longer tips "rather like a swan's neck." To hold the foot more securely on the ski, for both downhill travel and jumping, Norheim developed a simple but effective birch withy fastened from the toe band around the heel.

While jumping and cross-country travel were considered equally important in competition, the jump was more daring and dramatic. The young people of Telemark, who followed Norheim to the capital and to Husebybakken (Huseby Hill near Christiania) for tournaments, became skilled in both jumping and cross-country running through woods and mountains. They traveled easily and jumped with astonishing grace, standing upright without poles; they held a small twig in one hand as "more or less a club badge." They landed with one leg bent slightly, one foot in front of the other. They halted abruptly with a rounded-off "Telemark" turn of the outer ski to face the hill they had descended. This maneuver, along with the Christiania turn, the slalom course, the long jump, and the Telemark skis with Norheim's bindings set a new style in the sport. Modern skiing is said to date from 1868, when Norheim first demonstrated his skis and these techniques in Christiania.[6]

Among Norheim's most able pupils were Mikkel, Aasne, and Torjus Hemmestvedt, whose parents encouraged them in the sport. Their father, Torjus Bjørgulvson, was a traveling teacher before he settled on a small farm in Morgedal in the 1860s. He and his wife Birgit raised eight children there and took the family name "Hemmestveit" (in America it became Hemmestvedt) from an earlier owner of their farm. The elder Torjus, at best a halfhearted farmer, took up the more congenial occupation of ski-making when his children became talented skiers. In skill and grace on skis few surpassed his sons Torjus and Mikkel. A ski historian wrote that "it is hard to say which of them was the better skier, for they were both extremely able, almost equally good in cross-country racing and in jumping."[7]

And they made it look so easy! One contest judge considered Torjus among the best distance runners on skis Norway had ever produced. He recalled a 35-mile championship race in which Torjus, "in his easy way, smiling and hardly sweating, cleared the hill beautifully and was the undisputed winner of the first prize of 400 kroner in gold." First one then the other of the brothers won top honors at Husebybakken contests in the 1880s. After a contest in 1881 they and other good Telemark skiers stayed on at the capital to give lessons. Instructing young men and women as Norheim had instructed them, they are said to have started the world's first ski school.[8]

When hard times came to Norway in the 1880s, many of Telemark's most talented skiers emigrated to America, "the golden land in the west." Among them was Norheim, who took his family to Minnesota in 1884 and settled at Oslo, Marshall County, in the Red River Valley. Four years later he homesteaded in what is now North Dakota. But the Norheims found hard times in America, too; when Sondre died in 1897, he had not been able to prove up his land claim. His family moved away, and his grave in a churchyard near Denbigh remained unmarked until the Norwegian Society for the Promotion of Skiing and the State Historical Society of North Dakota placed a monument there on the 150th anniversary of his birth.[9]

Norheim's days of ski competition were over before he settled at Oslo, but his pupils, Mikkel and Torjus Hemmestvedt, were at the height of their skiing careers when they followed him to Minnesota. Mikkel arrived first and remained in America from 1886 to 1893. Torjus, who immigrated in 1888, settled permanently in Minnesota. Both initially resided at Ada, Norman County, in the Red River Valley. For nearly a decade the brothers demonstrated their Telemark skills before thousands of admiring spectators and other skiers who learned from them in contests and exhibitions at St. Paul, Minneapolis, Red Wing, and Stillwater in Minnesota, at St. Croix Falls, Eau Claire, La Crosse, and Stoughton in Wisconsin, and at Ishpeming, Michigan.

Like other Norwegians who settled in Minnesota, the Hemmestvedts immigrated to join relatives who had already arrived. Many of these earlier immigrants had lived for a time in the Norwegian-dominated southeastern region before moving on to the more sparsely settled, but even more emphatically Norwegian, Red River Valley. Anund K. Strand, the brothers' first cousin, left Norway for Mower County, Minnesota, before 1880; in that year he moved his family to Norman County. Mikkel joined his cousin in Lake Ida Township in the summer of 1886, after he had won the King's Cup for competition in long-distance skiing and jumping at Husebybakken near Christiania. At the end of October, he and Norwegian-born Bergit (Briget) M. Tveitane were married, and the following winter they lived with the Strands.[10]

Although the prairies of Norman County were "not the best place for ski practice" Mikkel's arrival stirred local interest in the sport that was gaining popularity throughout the Upper Midwest. Soon he was making skis for himself and other Norwegians in the community. And within a few months, Mikkel, the seasoned competitor, would have an opportunity to match his skill against skiers from other parts of Minnesota as well as from Wisconsin and Michigan where ski clubs were being organized.[11]

The ski clubs that developed in the Upper Midwest were similar in many ways. Members wore colorful blanket-cloth uniforms; to keep fit they took part in gymnastic exercises, cross-country excursions, or practice jumps and runs; they visited neighboring towns to demonstrate their skills. Men and boys of all ages and, in some clubs, women, too, participated in activities on and off the ski hills. Although skiers competed in

131

"Down a St. Paul Hill on Ski," from *Northwest Magazine*, Winter
Carnival issue, 1887.

tournaments as individuals and won prizes of money or goods for individual performances, club affiliation was important. Reduced fare on
trains was usually available only to members of an organization traveling
as a group. Sometimes a club further subsidized members' expenses from
its treasury. Those fortunate enough to win were even known to share
prize money with less successful fellow members.

When a club sponsored a tournament, local businessmen in the host
community often subsidized its costs. The press covered its activities,
and politicians and public officials often appeared at the festive events.
An all-day tournament included races for different classes of skiers who
were judged on form, style, length of jump, and time for cross-country
runs. Indispensable to a successful tournament were a downtown parade, a banquet, and speeches stressing patriotism, notable events in
Scandinavian history and literature, and the manifold virtues of the
noble sport. Music and dancing ended the festivities in the early morning hours.

As the popularity of the ski-sport flourished, clubs began to compete
for the membership of the stars of the slopes. Offers of employment in
a local community, as well as the advantages of belonging to an active
ski club, induced some skiers — the Hemmestvedts among them — to
move from place to place. In some places, ski-making became a source
of income, and here, too, the Hemmestvedts pioneered.

One of the earliest and most effective promoters of skiing as a competitive sport was the St. Paul Winter Carnival, established in 1886 as
Minnesota's first organized winter extravaganza. Through the participation of the Scandinavian Ski Club of St. Paul, organized shortly before
the first carnival, a multitude of non-Scandinavians became acquainted
with "the most tremendous and exciting sport peculiar to winter." Sixty

strong, the colorfully costumed club members shouldered their "long and curious shoes" for a grand parade and later raced like the wind in exhibitions of downhill runs on Robert Street. Although a sudden February thaw aborted the ski tournament that year, a bigger and better carnival competition was scheduled for 1887.[12]

When Mikkel Hemmestvedt and his Norman County friends learned that a top prize of $100 would be awarded in the ski tournament planned for the second winter carnival and that only members of clubs would be eligible for the prize, they decided to organize and send Mikkel to represent their club. The *Norman County Index*, supporting the move, reasoned that if Mikkel carried away the prize, "Ada and Norman County will get a share of the honor." So on January 20, 1887, 25 charter members founded the Norman County Ski Club in the office of the register of deeds, Norwegian-born Joris C. Norby, who was named secretary. Within a few days, club president A. H. Myram led a contingent to St. Paul to see Mikkel compete in his first American ski tournament.[13]

Hemmestvedt and his Ada friends were among 80 skiers entered in the first Midwest ski tournament on January 25, 1887. It promised to be a contest in which "experts would exhibit the novel manner of traveling and coasting in vogue in their native land" — one of the "greatest novelties" of the winter carnival. Snow and weather conditions were good; the St. Paul club had laid out a mile run and built a "chute" 20 feet high on Halsted Avenue (later part of the city's airport). Below it was a jump or 'precipice' that, without any personal effort, sent the runner at least forty feet out in mid-air." Skiers from Ada, Minneapolis, Stillwater, and Red Wing, and from Eau Claire, St. Croix Falls, and Altoona, Wisconsin, chose two members from each of their delegations to act as judges; all agreed to contest rules.[14]

Twenty-three skiers participated in the first-class competition; each was allowed three jumps and after the third he was timed on the mile run. Mikkel jumped more than 60 feet on his third leap and ran the mile in four and a half minutes, beating his closest rival by more than a minute. He had not topped his record, set in Norway, but he had "scooped" all American competitors. Next to Hemmestvedt, the *Pioneer Press* ranked as outstanding Oscar Arntson of Red Wing, a youth of 14 and first-place winner in the second class competition.[15]

After the races the skiers dined at Grote's Tivoli, a popular restaurant, and then indulged in the favorite carnival custom of "bouncing" (or tossing) the prize winners in a blanket. Speeches and toasts prolonged the festivities, until participants joined in the glorious ritual of storming the ice palace to unseat King Boreas and shorten winter's reign.

Mikkel Hemmestvedt emerged from the second St. Paul Winter Carnival an unqualified success. After the formal contests were over he bowed to his admirers' request and gave a special skiing exhibition near the present state capitol. There he so impressed St. Paul skiers that they urged him to join their club and make St. Paul his home. Other skiers and businessmen wanted him to live and work at St. Croix Falls. For the moment he accepted an invitation from the Aurora Ski Club of Red Wing to participate in its first tournament, planned for February 8, 1887.[16]

The Aurora Club was a year old. Its organization had followed close on the heels of a visit by members of the St. Paul club, who had gone to Red Wing in 1886 to demonstrate skiing and promote winter carnival attendance. From the first, the Red Wing club was committed "to foster outdoor winter sport and especially the sport of running on 'skis.'" It was largely Scandinavian and all male in membership; its officers were limited to Scandinavians by either birth or descent. Its first president was Christian H. Boxrud, one of four brothers who had immigrated from Eidsvold, Norway. Although club business was conducted and minutes were kept in Norwegian, it was necessary at one early date to remind the secretary, who had lapsed into English, that some members did not understand the new language. Applicants for club membership had to be sponsored by current members; boys under 18 could join at half price.[17]

Other activities of the Aurora Club indicate that it was an ethnic as well as an athletic organization. After the 1886 carnival, members practiced singing Norwegian patriotic songs and in May journeyed to Faribault to take part in a *Syttende Mai* (May 17) celebration to commemorate the adoption of Norway's constitution. References in the minutes to a Scandinavian mutual benefit association suggest that members considered, too, the practical merits of club membership in obtaining insurance. Yet unlike some other ski clubs of the 1880s, the Red Wing group seems never to have lost sight of its primary objective. The club held practice runs each week and cross-country excursions of 30 to 40 miles when snow and weather permitted. A consistent record of success in tournaments brought the Aurora men an enviable reputation among midwestern skiers.[18]

After 15 members took part in the second St. Paul Winter Carnival in 1887, the Aurora Club, numbering more than 50, went home to prepare for its own first tournament. In addition to building a jump that could be raised or lowered for different classes of contestants, members solicited money and merchandise for prizes. The "ladies of the club" (who were not members) prepared food for a banquet and decorated the halls where the indoor festivities would be held. Aware of political niceties, the men voted to make newly elected State Senator Peter Nelson of Goodhue County an honorary club member and invited him to attend.[19]

Aurora members were worried that warm, wet weather would spoil prospects for a successful tournament, but they rejoiced when February 8 dawned clear and cold. On hand to race were 9 skiers from Stillwater, 23 from St. Paul, 22 from Eau Claire, Wisconsin, and Mikkel Hemmestvedt from Ada. A grand procession formed at Armory Hall; led by a platoon of police and the Red Wing cornet band, the skiers marched through the downtown district and then tramped out to McSorley's Hill. There, 100 feet up the bluff, the running course began.

The jump, six feet high for first-class skiers, was lowered to four for the less experienced who competed in second class, and to two feet for boys competing in third class. Mikkel Hemmestvedt easily carried off the honors in first class, making the jump standing three times and winning the first prize of $35 in gold. He also received a special purse for an exhibition run from 50 feet above the top of the track which he made "with an ease and grace unsurpassed."

After the races all trooped down to the halls gaily decorated with banners and flags of the United States and the Scandinavian nations for a "delicious and bountiful repast." President Boxrud welcomed the guests in Norwegian and awarded the prizes, the band played "enlivening" music, and various speakers recalled Norway and the sport that had originated in the rigorous northern climate. F. A. Husher, editor of the Minneapolis paper *Fædrelandet og Emigranten* (The Homeland and the Emigrant), "a genuine Norwegian . . . large of build, hale, and fleshy standing straight and firm," was greeted with cheer after cheer as he spoke of the native sports of Norway, recalled how he learned to fall on skis, praised Red Wing for holding "the first genuine ski tournament," and led three cheers for its hosts. Then the band struck up again and, the *Red Wing Advance Sun* reported, "the dance went merrily, and the healthy, rosy cheeked young men and young ladies whiled the hours away in the hearty, cordial manner characteristic of the nationalities represented."[20]

The Aurora skiers, competent as they were, had not known of the remarkable Telemark innovations in the ski-sport until they saw Mikkel Hemmestvedt in action in St. Paul and Red Wing in 1887. Instructed by Mikkel and later by Torjus, they proved to be apt and diligent pupils. In the next few years they perfected the Telemark way of skiing, which became known as "Red Wing style." The characteristic Telemark skis, fashioned in Red Wing, also became identified with the town.[21]

When the 1887 Red Wing tournament was over, Mikkel Hemmestvedt returned to Ada, where the *Norman County Index* proposed that he be sent to the state senate in the next election, "as he appears to be the only man in the Red River Valley that can attract the attention of that august body." The *Index* said, "Hurrah for Mikkel!" and predicted a great future for him, the county, and Ada, which would make neighboring towns "turn green with envy."[22]

Although Norman County continued for a time to claim Mikkel as its own, his loyalties were divided. His wife apparently remained there, but Mikkel left for Wisconsin in the fall of 1887 to begin a ski manufacturing business and to ski for another club. At St. Croix Falls, Wisconsin, he joined fellow Norwegians H. U. Hetting and his son Ole in forming the Excelsior Ski Company, the first known firm to manufacture skis in the St. Croix Valley and perhaps in the United States. The design of the Excelsior skis was undoubtedly Hemmestvedt's and he supervised their production; the senior Hetting, a railroad contractor, and his son, who was an active skier, provided quarters for the business.[23]

The company was soon rushed with orders, and subcontracted with the St. Croix Falls planing mill of John Elmquist and Isaac Weinhardt to help meet the demand. The skis manufactured for the Excelsior Company were said to be of pine, "light and trim in style." Soon a local market developed among members of the St. Croix Falls Ski Club, organized in January, 1888. The *St. Croix Valley Standard* credited the "excellent Excelsior Ski" for arousing village interest in the sport. Both Mikkel and Ole Hetting were officers of the new club, which from the first admitted women and counted most of the town's business and society leaders among its members.[24]

For practice the club chose the west slope of the bluff fronting on Adams Street, locally known as Mount Pisgah. There "champion skiest" Hemmestvedt presented a public exhibition in mid-January. The *Standard*, in a booster spirit like that of Norman County, boasted that with Hemmestvedt as a member, "the St. Croix Falls Club will stand at the head of all northwestern organizations."[25]

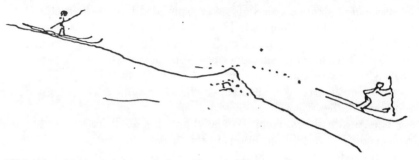

Elijah Edwards' view of skiing. *DePauw University Archives, Greencastle, Indiana*

From a vantage point across the river in Taylors Falls the Reverend Elijah E. Edwards mused on the new sport. Edwards, the local Methodist pastor, was a winter sports enthusiast who enjoyed sleighing, tobogganing, and ice skating. In his journal he described the "peculiarly Scandinavian sport" in words illustrated with small drawings. "The ski-runner," he wrote, "is mounted upon two long skate like runners formed of thin elastic planks four or 5 inches wide and 14 feet long turned up like skates at the toe." He likened the skier's passage on the slopes to the "down and oblique swoop of a bird, only swifter and more terrible." Skis are worn like skates, he wrote, "but bend to the inequalities of the surface, and will bear the wearer safely over snow that is in the least compacted on the surface; and down long slopes acquire a fearful velocity." Edwards sketched two skiers traversing a hill broken by a hump and explained: "A favorite sport with ski runners is to arrange midway down the slope an artificial break or rise, reaching which the ski-runner, with all his accelerated velocity springs into the air and sometimes clears a span from 60 to 100 feet before he touches the snow again." For his part, Edwards was content merely to watch the skiers, preferring for his own active enjoyment the "compact, *concentrated* fun of the toboggans."[26]

Early in 1888 Hemmestvedt, the Hettings, and other St. Croix Falls club members went on demonstration tours to nearby Osceola, Wisconsin, and Franconia, Minnesota. At Franconia prizes were offered for the best runs down the steep St. Croix river bluff and St. Croix Falls "carried away the boodle." St. Croix Falls and Mikkel collected bigger "boodle" that season on ski hills at Eau Claire, La Crosse, St. Paul, and Minneapolis.

A tournament at Eau Claire was the first of the big four. Sponsored by the Dovre Ski Club on January 17 it drew 175 skiers from Red Wing, Stillwater, St. Paul, La Crosse, Minneapolis, St. Croix Falls, and Stoughton. Only 60 of them were brave enough to take the plunge down the breath-taking course south of the city called "Dovrefjell," said to be "the steepest and longest in the world" in both ways outranking the royal hill at Christiania. Sufficient snow and brilliant, mild weather helped to make the tournament "a glorious success." In the throng of 4,000 spectators were many to whom ski running was a "startling" novelty. Mikkel Hemmestvedt took first place with a "splendid hop" of 70 feet, sailing through the air "like an eagle . . . so powerful and elegant are his movements." When the contests on the slopes were over, a banquet, a reception, an awards ceremony, speeches, and a ball filled out the long day.[27]

The next morning skiers from St. Croix Falls, Eau Claire, and Red Wing took the train for a second tournament at La Crosse. There they were guests of the Norske Ski Club, which had been organized in November, 1887, and was notable for a number of reasons. Its Scandinavian officers invited young men of all nationalities to join, and several non-Scandinavians, referred to as an "American faction," did so. At its first regular meeting the club decided to accept women members, although it gave them separate status. Like the men, women were required to wear the club uniform, but they were not asked to pay the dues or other fees assessed the male members. Women took part in the ski runs and played a leading role in the club's social events, but they were seldom mentioned in reports of competitions. In January the club numbered 58 members, 15 of them women. The principal attraction at the tournament was Mikkel Hemmestvedt; second only to him was Mary Davidson, a recent immigrant from Norway who was billed as the "champion lady ski runner of the world." First prize in the competition, a gold watch and chain, was awarded to Mikkel, and a second-prize gold medal was taken by Olof Lee of Eau Claire. Davidson, who apparently did not enter the competition, won "the delight of the crowded and jubilant multitude" for her exhibition of skill.[28]

The St. Paul Winter Carnival tournament on January 27 was next on the St. Croix Club schedule. Mikkel and 26 club members took the train for St. Paul, now attired in handsome new uniforms of "light brown Mackinaw goods with blue and white trimmings; knee pants with leggins; blue sash and blue and brown caps." The 60 competitors and the spectators were mostly Norwegians; Mikkel Hemmestvedt later remembered hearing a variety of Norwegian dialects spoken in the crowd.

Mikkel won first prize but his jump was far below his record — one report said it was 24 feet, another said 50. In second and third class, Red Wing skiers excelled, winning six of eight prizes. While skiing gained more extensive press attention than in other years, it was a poor second to curling in popularity.[29]

Before the skiers from St. Croix Falls joined their fellow sportsmen in the storming of the ice palace, they traveled to Minneapolis to take part in a last memorable day of competition for the season.

The Minneapolis tournament was sponsored by two local ski clubs on January 30, 1888. Early in the 1880s the city's Norwegians organized Den Norske Turn og Skiforening, a club that combined the healthful pleasures of skiing with vigorous gymnastic exercises like those of the German Turners. Another club (or perhaps a branch of the Turners' group) calling itself the Norwegian Snowshoe Club, was said to be in existence early in 1885, but no record of its organization has been found. By the end of 1887 the two active skiing groups in Minneapolis were known as Den Norske Turn og Skiforening and the Viking Ski Club. Both took part in the Minneapolis tournament.[30]

On a Sunday before the contest the Turners' group built a slide and jump on Kenwood Hills, west of the Minneapolis and St. Louis railroad shops on Lyndale and Western (later Glenwood) avenues. The tournament began with a parade down Washington Avenue from Dania Hall near Seven Corners to the Union Depot at Nicollet Avenue. Led by a drum corps, bearers of American and Scandinavian flags, and a platoon of police, skiers from the Minneapolis clubs and others from St. Paul, Eau Claire, Stillwater, Red Wing, St. Croix Falls, and Albert Lea trudged along in their bright-colored flannel shirts and tasseled toques with long, curved skis strapped to their backs. Occasionally a skier would shout, "Tuch-hey-son-son-son," which the *Minneapolis Tribune* labeled a Viking war cry. At the depot the skiers boarded an 11-car train for the short ride to Kenwood Hills.[31]

The *Tribune* reported that 3,000 persons witnessed the contests. "All along on either side of the course from the top of the hill to the bottom was one line of expectant faces." People clambered up on freight cars to get a better view. In trees near the course spectators clung to the branches and "occasionally in their ardor they would forget what a precarious foothold they had and tumble off up to their necks in a 20 foot snow bank." After the judges mounted a stand part way up the hill, the bugler took his place to sound the beginning of the contest. The starter called "Number One!" and the call was taken up all down the hill. Number One arranged his skis, grasped a small balancing stick in his hand, bent slightly forward, "and in a moment he was dashing down the course like a rocket. On nearing the 'hop' he would crouch slightly, like a [lion] about to spring, and then he was sailing through the air over the hop, landing from 60 to 80 feet from where he took the leap. After striking the ground again he would gradually straighten himself up and finish the rest of the hill amid the plaudits of the spectators." When some less skilled runners fell after jumping and rolled down the hill "hurly-burly" fashion, everyone laughed. The successful jumpers were greeted with an admiring call which the *Tribune* interpreted as "ak heverapper (beautiful)!"

One of the most graceful performances, said the paper, was that of Mikkel Hemmestvedt of St. Croix Falls, "champion of the world." Mikkel was a short, sturdy man, who "in going down the course stands as erect as an arrow. He made the largest jump, 72 feet, for which he received the prize." Another noteworthy performance was that of the Aurora Club's Oscar Arntson. "The young boy from Red Wing was the favorite of everybody," said the *Tribune*, and he "passed down the course, and over the hop three successive times without losing his balance or falling. The only thing he failed to defeat the champion in was the jump."

When the contest ended judges and skiers returned by train to the city, where a "bountiful banquet" for 180 persons was served in Turner Hall. Upstairs after dinner there were speeches, the Turners performed gymnastics, and Nicolai Grevstad of the *Tribune* presented the prizes. Hemmestvedt received a parlor clock (said to be worth $40) and extra prizes of a silver cake dish and $5. After the ceremonies, a grand ball concluded the tournament festivities and the round of ski competitions for the season.[32]

Back at St. Croix Falls the *Standard* was moved to say that no competitor questioned Hemmestvedt's right "to the championship of the world and golden medals of both hemispheres." Mingled with pride in the club and Hemmestvedt's success was perhaps some local frustration that other members had not done so well. For this and possibly for other reasons, the club soon announced that it had broadened its objectives to embrace social activities and to promote indoor as well as outdoor sports. Plans for a euchre party and a dance and supper as well as a Washington's Birthday ball suggested at least some of the indoor sports that found favor.[33]

By November, 1888, Mikkel had moved his wife to St. Croix Falls. With the Hettings he fitted out new quarters for the Excelsior Ski Company in a shop owned by Nels Strandberg. While the factory was modest, its product was of the highest quality. Its "skis stand without a rival, both as to workmanship and material," proclaimed the *Taylors Falls Journal*. Soon the little factory had a large stockpile of materials and had installed steam boxes for bending skis. The company shipped skis to St. Paul and by mid-November advertised 50 pairs for local sale; it also offered clubs quantity discounts on prices of its "A No. 1" skis. Competition reared its head when former subcontractors Elmquist and Weinhardt started their own ski factory and began to make skis of locally grown hickory and rock elm at their planing mill. Like the Excelsior skis, these were steamed, with the tips notched and "bowed up" in the manufacturing process.[34]

The winter of 1888–89 was too warm for good skiing and sales apparently declined. Although tournaments had to be canceled at some places, Mikkel went to Stillwater to give advice and to ski in a competition there. The Norwegian club at Stillwater, like that in Red Wing, had been organized in 1886 after a special excursion train brought uniformed winter carnival promoters from St. Paul. The rowdy visitors were not well received by the local press. Their practice of bouncing was not very funny, said the *Stillwater Messenger*. In fact the popular carnival custom had "some elements of danger and brutality." As for the visitors' costumes, the *Messenger* sniffed, "The mackinaw blanket 'uniforms' worn were no novelty in this lumbering center and were no more attractive or picturesque than are those of our own boys of the woods when they slick up in the dandy attire of new clothes preparatory to a winter's hard and honest work in the pineries."[35]

Nonetheless Stillwater had decided to participate in the St. Paul Winter Carnival hoping to advertise itself as a city of push and enterprise. Skiers would help promote the town, and under the impetus of the carnival three clubs were organized in 1886. Little is known of the one that the *Messenger* called the "Scandinavian ski club of snow-shoers." Of unusual interest was the short-lived "Little Crow Ski Club," the first known midwestern ski club for children, composed of 37 boys between the ages of 10 and 15. By February 4, 1886, the boys were in uniform and had accompanied the Stillwater delegation to the first carnival. The third and most enduring organization was the Norwegian Ski Club, probably founded after the others and sometime before January, 1887. It was to remain active for a decade and originally included "Three expert skiers from the old country" who hoped to win prizes and glory for Stillwater in the second carnival.[36]

The *Messenger* advised those who wished to avoid "scandalizing" the local Scandinavians to pronounce the unfamiliar word "skee" and *not* "sky." Discussing the sport, it said that the "ordinary" ski was "about ten feet long, three to four inches wide, turned up at the front and made, preferably of 'fat' Norway pine. Some [skis] said to be the swiftest, have bottoms with deer hide, the hairy side out." Skiers, it advised readers, ascended hills by " 'tacking' like a ship sailing before the wind," and they descended at incredible speeds.

Before the 1888–89 season, when champion ski runner Mikkel Hemmestvedt visited the Norwegian Club to give them pointers, members had done poorly in competition. Infused with the new ideas and encouragement from Hemmestvedt the group was ready, the *Messenger* reported, "to do itself and the city proud in contests with any ambitious organization of any kind." Contributing to its cheerful aspect were new uniforms of blue jackets and trousers with "Astrakhan trimming, brown leggings with leather fastenings and blue caps adorned with variegated tassels."[38]

But the weather did not co-operate. The St. Paul Winter Carnival was canceled when the warm sun melted the ice palace. Undaunted, the Stillwater club persevered with plans to hold a tournament on the Mulberry Street Hill. On March 1, 1889, the appointed day, "soft" warm weather prevailed, but the tournament went ahead on schedule. Mikkel Hemmestvedt won the first prize of $15.[39]

Stillwater's Norwegian Ski Club, 1888; Mikkel Hemmestvedt seated far right. *MHS*

Because of unseasonably warm weather, the ski circuit that year was short in both duration and financial rewards. A tempting offer from Christian Boxrud at Red Wing, where the hills were good and the skiers more active and successful, persuaded Mikkel Hemmestvedt to leave the Excelsior Ski Company and move with his wife to a new home and a job in the furniture factory at Red Wing.[40]

Another 1888 event of importance to the future of the ski-sport in the Midwest went largely unnoticed. Torjus Hemmestvedt, a new champion, arrived at Ada. Sometime that year, after he had won the King's Cup and the cross-country race at Huseby, Torjus, his wife, his young son, and his brother Summond immigrated to the United States.[41]

At the beginning of the 1889–90 season, the Aurora Club of Red Wing made two momentous decisions. It would admit Mikkel Hemmestvedt to membership and sponsor a tournament in January, 1890 — provided, of course, there was enough snow. Weekly practice runs were scheduled and new restrictive rules were adopted for scoring runs and jumps.[42]

By mid-January a sufficient fall of snow encouraged the club to make definite plans for the tournament. A "spirited" communication to the Minneapolis weekly *The North* invited every club in the Northwest to take part.[43]

Aurora members solicited contributions of money and a variety of merchandise for prizes and made mighty efforts to renovate the club uniforms. Members had for some time been dissatisfied with the original club uniform of white blanket-cloth coat, blue knee breeches, red stocking cap, and blue belt. In December, 1888, they agreed to have the uniforms dyed a dark color and trimmed with yellow bands. Finally, more than a year later, it was reported that 20 suits would be ready for the tournament. Everything else was in order — except the weather. The sun was shining and temperatures were mild, prompting some clubs to cancel plans to attend. Yet a good number arrived from the Twin Cities, as well as from La Crosse, Eau Claire, Ada, and Ishpeming.[44]

The event made skiing history for the Hemmestvedt brothers. Mikkel competed for the first time as a member of the Aurora Club, while Torjus made his first American appearance, representing Ada. The course ran down Sorin's Bluff and Bush Street. In trial runs the jump proved to be poorly positioned and had to be altered before the contest began. A crowd estimated at 3,000 to 5,000 persons stood "on the tiptoe of expectation." Torjus cleared the jump in great shape and was cheered all along the line. Mikkel made an elegant jump, "sailing through the air in such a way as only he can," but below the jump he fell into the sticky snow and broke one of his skis. There was "something wonderfully fascinating about him on skis, something inimitably graceful," and he was clearly the crowd's favorite. When it came to jumping, said a report of the event, the Hemmestvedt brothers "both showed how far superior to any one else they really are."

Other Red Wing contestants, however, were also outstanding. In the

From left: Paul Honningstad, Mikkel and Torjus Hemmestvedt, and B. L. Hjermstad, members of Aurora Ski Club, 1890. *Goodhue County Historical Society, Red Wing*

contest for the longest jump, Torjus had attained 68 feet, but "amidst the wildest cheering," Halvor Olson won, the second time around, with 78 feet. Seven of the ten prizes awarded in the boys' contest went to Red Wing youths.

The ladies of the Aurora Club took charge of the "simply perfect" banquet that followed the contest. At the Opera House after the dinner (for which a local Norwegian American recalled her mother baking "thin bread" to accompany other Norwegian and Swedish foods on the overladen table) came speeches in Norwegian and English and then the awarding of prizes. Mikkel received $40 in gold; Torjus was awarded $25 in silver. Other handsome prizes for the men included a silver watch, silver goblets, an album, toilet case, shaving set, gold-headed umbrella, smoking set, and silk muffler; and for the boys a watch, clock, lamp, album, sled, pair of skis, cap, skates, silk muffler, and pocket knife.[45]

DEVELOPMENTS at the end of 1890 promised to bring new excitement to the ski-sport. Members of the Dovre Club of Eau Claire had for some time been considering the benefits of organizing a league or association of ski clubs. In November they proposed that two delegates from each organization meet to form such a group. As a result, representatives of the Eau Claire, St. Paul, Minneapolis, Red Wing, Stillwater, and Ishpeming ski clubs gathered in St. Paul in late December and founded the Central Ski Association of the Northwest, the forerunner of the National Ski Association and probably the first such group in the United States. A major responsibility of the association was to set and adopt standards for the sport. Carl Ilstrup of Minneapolis was chosen as president, Christian Boxrud of Red Wing, vice-president, and Dr. C. L. Opsal, also of Red Wing, secretary. The delegates decided to hold the annual meetings of the association in the last week of November each year and authorized three tournaments for the 1890–91 season.[46]

Ishpeming, in upper Michigan, was selected as the site of the Central Ski Association's first tournament on January 23, 1891. There a bountiful supply of snow with brisk cold weather promised well for the sport. The Norden Ski Club, host for the tournament, was a lively group that had organized in 1887 and held its first public contests in the next year at the Lake Angeline Mine. The club's two captains were Carl Tellefsen and Ole Sundlie, the latter one of its best skiers. In Norway Tellefsen had been an organizer and president of the Trondheim Ski Club; in the United States he was one of the foremost early promoters of the sport.[47]

On tournament day in 1891 the various clubs took their positions on Cleveland Avenue in Ishpeming to begin a two-mile march to the ski slide on Lake Superior Hill west of the Excelsior Furnace. A detachment of police in uniform led the parade, followed by an 18-piece Scandinavian band, a standard-bearer carrying the American flag, and the members of the Norden Club. Snowshoe clubs from Marquette and Ishpeming and skiers from Red Wing and Eau Claire were among the more than 200 persons who marched in the procession. According to one reporter, "the hills and valleys were crowded with spectators, and the streets and fields thronged with vehicles of every description." Five thousand people, said to be the largest open-air crowd gathered in Ishpeming up to that time, watched the contest with "breathless interest."[48]

Three new members added strength to an already impressive Aurora team that starred Mikkel Hemmestvedt. One of them was Torjus Hemmestvedt, who, like his brother, had moved to Red Wing before the end of 1890 and began working at the Red Wing Furniture Company. After hours both men made skis at the company's factory; the two of them also made bobsleds for some "rich Norwegians." In November Torjus had become a member of the Aurora Club, and in January, just in time for the trip to Ishpeming, Bengt Ludwig Hjermstad and Paul Honningstad, two able skiers recently arrived from Norway, had been admitted.[49]

On the ski hills at Ishpeming the Aurora men were obviously the masters. Each contestant in the first class made four runs. In the first runs some of the nine competitors fell on landing, but the Red Wing skiers "carried themselves without a fall and were roundly cheered."[50]

Torjus won first place with the best record of runs, but Mikkel, who won second and an additional prize for the longest jump, was the sensation of the afternoon. "Hemmestvedt is a small man, not weighing over 135 pounds," the *Ishpeming Daily Press* reported, "but the amount of nerve and muscle in his firmly built body would suffice to make two average men. Hemmestvedt's longest jump was 78 feet, and the sight was one that will never be forgotten by those who witnessed the leap. Standing with one foot slightly advanced, his skis close together, and leaning forward he sped down the steep hill. At the jump he gathered himself for the leap, and with a mighty bound sailed into the air. Twice he gathered himself together and leaped while in mid-air, raising himself apparently as a bird would raise. It was a revelation to the vast concourse of people whose eyes were focused on him, and the cheers that arose when he came safely to the ground . . . seemed to rend the firmament."[51]

The next day Fred Braastad entertained the skiers at his farm, where many of them demonstrated again informally. The *Daily Press* said that their "fancy work" was better than it had been the day before. Mikkel, who may have been somewhat nervous before the huge crowd at the contest, made another jump that "fairly held his audience spell bound." After the jump Braastad "placed a gold piece in the champion's hand, and it is said of no small denomination." Even without the extra gold piece, the Red Wing men took home with them that night over two-thirds of the more than $350 in prize money from the first tournament of the new Central Ski Association.

The Aurora Club members returned in triumph to a victory celebration, but Stillwater skiers suffered great chagrin, for they had not been represented at Ishpeming. And why not? One report said that the Norwegian Ski Club lacked funds to send skiers so far. Another blamed *The North* for not publishing details of the tournament early enough. The members, said the secretary, "were thrown off our guard, or out of our reckoning as it were, and failed to make arrangements, in time, for our men to get away." The club, making amends, invited skiers to attend what became the season's second major tournament at Stillwater.[52]

That event on February 17, 1891, followed the well-established ritual — a parade, two races (one for adults and another for boys under 16), competitions with participants from Stillwater, Red Wing, Minneapolis, St. Paul, Eau Claire, La Crosse, and Hudson, and a banquet with the awarding of prizes. The course near Lily Lake was 350 feet long with an "average incline of forty-five degrees," and the winners were predictable. The first skier to stand erect when his skis struck the snow at the bottom of the hill was Torjus Hemmestvedt, who was greeted with a round of applause. Other Red Wing skiers followed, "almost all of them standing." Mikkel, although handicapped by a sprained ankle, made the longest jump — 87 feet — and Torjus cleared 86. But first prize, for the three best standing jumps, each of 74 feet, was won by Oscar Arntson of Red Wing. Arntson, then 17 and competing in the adult race, was slight, weighing scarcely 115 pounds, and as graceful as he had been in Twin Cities competitions in 1888. With Arntson, the Hemmestvedts, Hjermstad, and Honningstad, Red Wing won the first five prizes.[53]

Again the Aurora Club returned home in triumph. Its secretary, mindful of the obligation of guests who had carried off most of the awards, sent a "graceful" letter of thanks to the host club. Published in the *Stillwater Daily Gazette* of March 6, the letter spoke of the city's hospitality, kind and courteous treatment, liberal prizes, and the "impartial way in which they were awarded." It said that the Aurora Club would "take the first opportunity offered to in a measure reciprocate."

Although Red Wing was not ready to put on another full-scale tournament, the Aurora Club ended the 1890–91 ski season in a spectacular way. Its annual medal run early in March was a "real stunner," and again the hero was Mikkel. The weather was favorable and the snow in good condition, although a strong northwest wind made it difficult for contestants to control their skis in the air. As for the incredible outcome of the competition, Opsal, secretary of the Central Ski Association and of the Red Wing club, sent *The North* a copy of the score card for the races and explained how they were judged to satisfy skeptics who might say that "such things are impossible."[54]

Eight skiers competed and each was graded from one to ten points for "character" (style). Any mark below five represented a fall; any mark between five and ten indicated a standing jump. Each contestant was allowed three runs and was scored both in total number of feet jumped and in character points. Fifteen points were deducted from the skier's total score for one fall, an additional 25 points for a second, and a third fall eliminated him entirely from competition.

Four contestants — among them Torjus — were eliminated in this way, despite having made remarkable jumps. Mikkel stood for two out of three runs. On his extraordinary third run he jumped 102 feet, setting a new world's record, but he fell on landing. Spectators held their breath while he was in the air and then "indulged in the regulation Comanche yell that stands for the American way of cheering" when he landed far down on almost level ground. Opsal said that if the hill had been steeper and Mikkel had landed on a slope, "I would have been willing to bet a pair of Red Wing skis, as our Ishpeming friends dubbed them, that he would have made it standing." Mikkel's total score was 279 points. Next in rank was young Arntson with 259, third was Opsal scoring 230, and fourth was Faber Hanson with 213. "This, I dare say," wrote Opsal, "shows the most remarkable ski jumping ever done in any contest on skis."

How far the Red Wing skiers had come in four years! At the first Red Wing tournament Mikkel was the only expert who knew anything about ski running. Skiers in America, like those in Norway, had learned from the Hemmestvedts. "There are now a good many both here and in other places," wrote Opsal, "who have adopted their way of standing, and who can go as far in a jump perhaps as they can, but their gracefulness, their elegance — that is something beyond imitation almost."[55]

It was known in Red Wing that Mikkel planned, after the ski season was over, to go back to Norway on a visit, in part because his pregnant wife wanted their child to be born there. But it was not to be. On March 23, only a few weeks after Mikkel's triumph, his wife died in childbirth at Red Wing and their infant son lived only a few minutes. Mother and baby were buried in the same coffin.[56]

It was a year of double tragedy for the brothers. Torjus' wife, Tone (Hylland), mother of Torjus, aged five, and Emma, not yet two years old, died of tuberculosis. Mikkel did not go to Norway that year but a sister, Bergit (Bertha), and a younger brother, Halvor, immigrated to Red Wing. Halvor became the third Hemmestvedt skier to compete in midwestern tournaments.[57]

The three brothers participated at Eau Claire in a hundred-foot jump on Mount Washington at the major ski event of the next season, a Central Ski Association tournament on February 19, 1892. Between 50 and 60 runners took part in the contests, which were witnessed by at least 5,000 persons, according to the *Eau Claire Times*. There were ten entries in first class, in which John Hauge of Eau Claire won first place, Torjus Hemmestvedt second, Mikkel third, Arntson of Red Wing fourth, and Hans Olson of Stillwater fifth. Mikkel fell in one run but remained world's champion. He received the special prize for the longest jump. His brother Halvor made the second longest.[58]

In the second-class competition 25 skiers took part and Red Wing won four of the five prizes. The winner was young A. E. Johnson, who almost missed the contest. Years later Johnson remembered that Christian Boxrud, discovering that Johnson did not have money enough for the trip to Eau Claire, paid the boy's expenses. But Johnson had no skis and when it came time for the second-class races, Mikkel Hemmestvedt loaned the youth his own skis. With Mikkel's skis Johnson won first place in the boys' class and $10 in gold.[59]

In the early weeks of the 1892–93 season, according to the *Red Wing Advance Sun*, the ski-sport had "fallen somewhat into disuse" because of a lack of snow. Nevertheless the Aurora Club began weekly runs on South Bush Street, where members again made history. A new, light snow and below-zero temperatures were conducive to good sport. On January 12 one skier made five standing jumps of 59, 64, 78, 81, and 90 feet. Arntson jumped 93 feet, and Torjus Hemmestvedt broke the world's record. The run was over 300 feet long and very steep. Halfway down was a wooden platform covered with snow. Torjus came down "as gracefully as if he had been a statue placed on a stationary pedestal. He held a little switch in one hand (a custom always observed by himself and his brother), and the other hand rested at his side. His skis were evenly balanced and parallel. He remained in the air about 2½ seconds, and presented to the spectators a beautiful and thrilling sight." Torjus' jump, marred only by a fall at the end, measured 103 feet, one foot more than Mikkel's record set in 1891.[60]

The Aurora skiers, cheered by their triumphs, acted as hosts for the fourth Central Ski Association tournament on February 9, 1893. Three classes of skiers competed in a blinding snowstorm for prize money totaling over $200. In spite of the weather an estimated crowd of 3,500 came and stayed. People stood in the storm 10 to 20 deep, "packed together as closely as if welded in one mass." Below the bluff, the flat land was black "with a mass of humanity huddled together in companies of a score or more — all standing in snow in some places almost knee deep."[61]

The Red Wing skiers took many of the prizes and again the Hemmestvedts distinguished themselves. Mikkel won first place, Torjus fourth, and Halvor fifth in total scores for three runs. Torjus won the special prize for the longest jump, but it was only 86 feet, far short of his record. Then, Torjus and Mikkel together made a memorable demonstration run, descending the hill gracefully hand in hand, jumping, and landing on their feet.

A report of the tournament in *The North* of February 15 suggested that the presence of such excellent teachers as the Hemmestvedts and the "fortunate topography of the city and surrounding country" were responsible for the attainments of the Aurora team. Another correspondent noted the popularity of ski jumping but observed, "If the ski-sport in this country is to be developed to what it ought to be viz. one of the grandest and most healthy sports on earth, the 'ski boys' must go to work and show what they can do in the way of a distance run." Such a run, the writer believed, should not be less than 15 or 20 miles for men over 20 years old. The steady practice of distance running, in his view, was "absolutely necessary" for "a good development of the body." He recommended that clubs get together for practice, "each man carrying his own grub, and stay out all day, returning at night." With such training boys would become good ski runners, "and on a day's exploring you are sure to find all the hills and all the jumping you wish for."[62]

147

Ski hill on South Bush Street, about 1905. *Goodhue County Historical Society*

Another tournament at Stoughton, Wisconsin, south of Madison, took Torjus and Halvor Hemmestvedt farther from home that season to compete on February 25. It was the second of the season's Stoughton contests and it was expected to decide the championship of Wisconsin, with the winner to receive $50 and a gold medal. The local ski club charged a ten-cent admission fee and provided seats for the spectators. The club shared the profits with the local ladies' benevolent society.[63]

The large number of spectators saw six first-class and 13 second-class skiers compete; each was allowed to make three runs, but ten feet were subtracted from the total score for each fall. When scores were calculated in the first-class competition, Torjus and a local skier, H. Loftus, tied for first place, each with 183½ points. How the tie was decided — whether with an additional run or visitor courtesy — was not revealed, but Hemmestvedt was declared the winner and became, in Stoughton eyes at least, the champion skier of Wisconsin. Loftus was awarded second place, and third prize went to Halvor Hemmestvedt, who scored 176½ points. Total receipts of the tournament were $150 and it was estimated that after expenses were paid, $70 would remain to divide between the two sponsors.

The year 1893 marked the end of the Hemmestvedts' dominance of the sport of jumping. During the year Halvor moved to western Minnesota and Mikkel returned to Norway. Only Torjus remained at Red Wing in American ski competition and in the business of making skis. In September, 1893, he married again, this time to his first wife's youn-

148

ger sister, Mary Hylland. At the year's end, according to the *Red Wing Advance Sun*, he was "devoting himself to the making of skis of the same kind which he himself uses. The orders thus far have been far in excess of the output."[64]

When the fourth annual meeting of the Central Ski Association was held in Stillwater at the end of 1893, a major economic depression was under way. No club offered to hold a tournament, but the sport was far from dead. Two new clubs organized in the Twin Cities held local cross-country races and jumping contests. In St. Paul members of the new and handsomely uniformed Birkebeiner Ski Club hoped, as had their predecessors in the Scandinavian Ski Club, to be the nucleus of an organization for the promotion of skiing in the Midwest. Secretary of the short-lived group was Aksel Holter. He later moved to Ishpeming, where he became the first secretary and a moving force in the National Ski Association, organized in 1904. Another new Minneapolis group called itself the Fritjof Nansen Ski Club in honor of the arctic explorer who so effectively dramatized the pleasures and advantages of skiing in his book, *The First Crossing of Greenland.*[65]

In the 1890s ski groups were reported at Hudson and Ellsworth, Wisconsin; Devils Lake, North Dakota; and Winona, Northfield, Glenwood, Starbuck, Cannon Falls, Grand Marais, and Duluth. At Ellsworth women schoolteachers took to the slopes, while at Northfield women as well as men students at St. Olaf College practiced the sport on Manitou Heights.[66]

Yet in the 1890s Red Wing with its steep hills and its talented runners was generally recognized as the Midwest center of the noble sport. By 1894 people of all ages were skiing at Red Wing. Boys who were given skis for Christmas organized their own youth club and held weekly runs on Kingman Hill. Lads five or six years old jumped with as much or more courage than their elders. The county sheriff, an Aurora Club member, and his deputy made their rounds on skis to summon jurors for the next term of county court. Hemmestvedt and other ski-makers did a thriving business and in a practice run on icy slopes Torjus is said to have jumped 120 feet.[67]

In Red Wing's ski-happy environment a visitor from Indiana learned about the sport, saw skis for the first time, and met the Hemmestvedts. Charmed, he found his way to their small shop and bought skis for himself and for his Yankee host. How to put them on? Why, he was instructed by the Norwegian ski-maker, "yust put mine [*your*] feet in the strap and leave 'em loose." Not to be fooled by a Norwegian, the Hoosier slipped his feet into the bindings, tied them securely, and suffered the consequences. Careening down the slope in his host's back yard, he crashed into an apple tree and came to rest, skis still secure on his feet and entangled in the branches of the tree, his head buried in snow "up to the third button of his coat."[68]

Undaunted, he climbed the hill for another, and yet another, wild descent. Somehow he and his reluctant host survived their first day on skis. Scratched, bruised, lamed, and repaired with sticking plaster, the

Hoosier waited impatiently for the next ski adventure while his host prayed fervently for a thaw.

Other warm winters and consequent ski doldrums may have encouraged Torjus Hemmestvedt to abandon Red Wing and the ski business. In 1896 he and his family moved back to Norman County, settling on a farm in McDonaldsville Township east of Ada. Halvor and Summond Hemmestvedt farmed near by and Aasne (Mrs. Peder Ramstad) lived south of town. In the next few years Torjus farmed and did carpentry and wood carving. His projects included the steeple of the Scandia Lutheran Church southeast of Ada, a church his brother Summond helped to organize. Tragedy came to the family again in 1898 when fire destroyed their house. Torjus lost many wood carvings, his carpenter tools, and most of the mementos of his skiing career.[69]

He won no more trophies although he competed in tournaments at Ishpeming and at Red Wing. On February 27, 1904, he was one of 28 skiers who participated in the first competition of the newly organized National Ski Association at Ishpeming. Twelve skiers jumped 70 feet or more; the longest standing jump was 77 feet; Torjus' best jump was 69. In 1905 his record was better at Red Wing, but there, although his longest jump was 90 feet, he fell on landing.[70]

In the spring of 1905 he and his family traveled from Ada by horse and wagon to a new homestead in Kratka Township, Pennington County, Minnesota, farther west but still in the flatlands of the Red River Valley, where other immigrants from Telemark had settled. Torjus and his older children built a small house and a barn. They raised cattle, wheat, oats, and flax, and Torjus worked at carpentry. A monument to his skill, the Telemark Church near their home is still in use today.[71]

Many years later a granddaughter recalled that all the Hemmestvedt children learned skiing skills from their father. They made their own skis of oak, steaming the boards over a boiler in the kitchen. They used them in hunting coyotes and rabbits, and "When the snowdrifts were high they would ski down the roof of their barn, while snow-covered straw piles provided a good jump for the younger children . . . and as soon as the children were old enough to walk they were out skiing cross-country without the aid of poles."[72]

In 1928 when Torjus was 66, two honors came to him. In Norway, where Mikkel was still living, the brothers were awarded medals for their contributions to the ski sport at Holmenkollen, the ski tournament center that had superseded Husebybakken. That same year Torjus was an honored guest at the Red Wing tournament of the National Ski Association, now numbering 175 clubs.[73]

It was a gala affair featuring a carnival, an ice palace, a queen, glittering lights, parades, dog races, skating by Eddie Shipstad and Oscar Johnson, and radio broadcasts on WCCO. Trucks and privately owned autos transported the 250 ski contestants and thousands of spectators to Charlson Hill for the competitions. A total of 15,000 people bought tickets for the races; 3,000 more pressed against the fences outside the ski area. The American Legion sold nearly a ton of weiners to hungry spectators. An airplane equipped with ski runners landed on Mississippi River ice with a journalist to cover the tournament for the national press. A photographer aloft took aerial views of the races.

Yet the ethnic flavor of the sporting event persisted. Swedish and Norwegian national anthems shared honors with "America," and all roads leading to Red Wing were marked with "snus box" signs for the event. On duty at the ski hill to give first aid to any skier who needed help was Dr. A. E. Johnson, the youthful champion who wore Mikkel Hemmestvedt's skis at Eau Claire in 1892.

It was a time for remembering the early days of the sport, for reliving the triumphs of the glorious days when the Hemmestvedts showed the Red Wing boys how to handle their skis. Old photos of the young Torjus and Mikkel and the eager champions who followed them shared newspaper space with a picture of Torjus, now an elderly man, talking to an eager nine-year-old boy clutching modern skis.[74]

Torjus died two years later. He was buried in the cemetery of the Telemark Church he helped to build. Mikkel died in Morgedal, Norway, in 1957. A nephew, Thorleif (Tollef) Hemmestvedt, became well known on the ski circuits of the Midwest in the early years of the century as "the man with the iron legs." Other Hemmestvedt family members skied in Norway, and Olof, Mikkel's son by his second marriage, carried the torch for the 1952 winter Olympic games from Sondre Norheim's hearth at Morgedal to Holmenkollen. Yet in the United States, where the Hemmestvedts contributed so much to the early development of the sport of skiing, their name is nearly forgotten. The National Ski Hall of Fame at Ishpeming has yet to enroll the names of Mikkel and Torjus Hemmestvedt.[75]

7

The Tale
of a Comet
Including
DONNELLY AND *RAGNAROK*
and
1883

T HE YEARS OF *1882 and 1883 were remarkable ones on the Earth, in the sky, and in the life of Ignatius Donnelly, Minnesota author and man of distinction. In 1882 Donnelly's first two books,* Atlantis: The Antediluvian World *and* Ragnarok: The Age of Fire and Gravel, *were published. The author's fascinating tales of popular science described cataclysmic events in the Earth's history; they were based on a mixture of ancient myths and scientific theories of the day. Although the books were disdained by many members of the scientific community and rejected by some conservative churchmen, they were widely reviewed and successful in the years of their launching. In those years, too, nature conspired to keep the books in the public eye. A series of disasters on the Earth and spectacular events in the sky seemed to bear witness that such extraordinary occurrences as Donnelly described were indeed possible in a so-called orderly world.*

Donnelly
and *Ragnarok*
Ignatius Donnelly Argues
that the Earth Suffered
Terrifying Catastrophes
in a Close Encounter with a Comet

I GNATIUS LOYOLA DONNELLY, a lawyer, politician, lieutenant governor, congressman, legislator, and orator of exceptional ability, was born November 3, 1831, in Moyamensing, a suburb of Philadelphia. He was the third of seven children of Philip Carroll Donnelly, an emigrant from Fintona, County Tyrone, Ireland, and Catharine Gavin Donnelly, a second-generation Irish American. Donnelly's father died when Ignatius was nine years old; his mother supported her children by operating a pawnshop.[1]

Ignatius Donnelly, photo-
graphed sometime between
1873 and 1886. *MHS*

Donnelly attended a neighborhood elementary school and then en-
rolled in Central High School, taking a classical course of study equal
to that of many colleges of the day. Between 1849 and 1852 he studied
law in the offices of Benjamin H. Brewster (later United States attorney
general) and in 1853 he was admitted to the Pennyslvania bar. During
the next four years he supplemented his small legal practice by acting
as a consultant for a number of land and building associations. He began
his political career in 1855 as an Independence Day orator at a Democratic gathering in Philadelphia. In that year too he married Katherine
McCaffrey, an elementary school principal and a talented singer. The
McCaffreys, like the Donnellys, were a devoutly Roman Catholic family
of small tradesmen. Donnelly did not remain a practicing Catholic (he
dropped his middle name), but he was deeply interested in religious
matters all of his life. His wife and children — Ignatius C., Mary, and
Stanislaus J. — remained in the Catholic church.

Shortly after his marriage Donnelly visited Minnesota. Convinced
that his future lay in the West, he helped to locate the townsite of
Nininger on the Mississippi River some 17 miles south of St. Paul and to
organize an emigrant aid association, composed largely of Philadelphia
friends and associates, for its settlement. Donnelly, his wife, and their
infant son Ignatius left Philadelphia for Minnesota in May, 1857. At

153

Nininger he built the fine house that was to be his home until his death in 1901.

In Minnesota he soon entered politics, beginning a long career as officeholder and crusader for liberal, third party, and agrarian causes. He was elected lieutenant governor in 1859 and representative to the United States Congress for three terms, from 1863 to 1869. Donnelly tried several times to regain his congressional seat; then, after a defeat in 1878, he began a new career as a lecturer and author of books.

Donnelly read widely and shared the enthusiasm of his day for the new frontiers of science and for the study of ancient civilizations. In his first book, *Atlantis: The Antediluvian World*, he tied together much of science, religion, and prehistory to argue that Plato's fabled Atlantis was once a real island in the Atlantic Ocean. He maintained that Atlantis had long supported a rich and powerful civilization until suddenly, in a terrible convulsion of nature, it had sunk beneath the sea.[2]

In *Atlantis* Donnelly supported the theory of catastrophism, which held that such violent and cataclysmic events had at times destroyed life and altered the face of the planet. After each destruction, catastrophists argued, higher forms of life developed to repopulate the Earth. But by the 1880s, when Donnelly wrote, catastrophism was not in vogue among American scientists. They had discarded the theory in favor of uniformitarianism and the conviction that the Earth's development had occurred by gradual changes over eons of time. So, too, living creatures had developed to higher forms in slow, evolutionary steps, the more adaptable and stronger surviving and multiplying. Catastrophes, they argued, were minor events in isolated places and did not seriously disturb the deliberate, orderly, and predictable uniformitarian universe. Donnelly's *Atlantis* did not find favor with uniformitarian scientists.[3]

Church people were either disturbed or inspired by the religious

Donnelly's home at Nininger, 1893. *MHS*

implications of *Atlantis*. Some were pleased to compare Atlantis with the Garden of Eden and to liken the Atlantis flood to Noah's flood. Liberal churchmen, flexible in their interpretation of scripture and already willing to think of a Biblical day as a geological age, found Donnelly's ideas to support, rather than threaten, Biblical truth. The more funda- mentalist theologians needed no support, scientific or otherwise, for the truth of Biblical events; the chronology of Bishop Usher, who dated the events of the Old Testament, was sufficient to describe their universe. *Atlantis* shocked and distressed them.

Controversies, both scientific and religious, served to encourage the sale of *Atlantis*. The book was a popular and financial success from the first. Seven editions were published in 1882; 23 editions appeared in the United States and 26 in England by 1890. A century later, *Atlantis* is still a popular book, and Donnelly is considered "the father of the modern science of Atlantology."[4]

The success of *Atlantis* encouraged its author to write a second book, also dealing with catastrophes. At a time when "the air and people's heads . . . [were] full of comets," Donnelly's new tale theorized that once, and probably more than once, with vast and catastrophic results, a comet encountered the Earth.[5]

The comet was at the heart of the story, but Donnelly did not begin chapter one with this visitor from space. Instead, he started the book on solid ground, with something more familiar to readers. He discussed the origins of "drift," also known as till or hardpan, the layer of mixed clay, sand, gravel, and rocks that lies under topsoil and over bedrock. Drift, Donnelly noted, is largely devoid of traces of life, although artifacts and the remains of men and animals can be found at its bottom. "It covers whole continents," he wrote. "It is our earth. It makes the basis of our soils; our railroads cut their way through it; our carriages drive over it . . . on it we live, love, marry, raise children, think, dream, and die, and in the bosom of it we will be buried."[6]

Where did it come from? Donnelly discussed some of the views generally accepted by scientists of his day, drawing ideas from, among other sources, Louis Figuier, a French naturalist and popularizer of science, and geologists James Geikie, a professor of geology at Edin-burgh University and member of the British Geological Survey; James Croll, a resident geologist in the Edinburgh office of the British Geo-logical Survey; John W. Dawson, a professor of geology and principal of McGill College (later University), Montreal; and James Dana, a pro-fessor of natural history at Yale University and author of a popular text-book and a manual of geology. The geologists Donnelly cited, like most scientists of the day, struggled to reconcile their religious beliefs with the new scientific theories of evolution and uniformitarianism, but they were not united in any one answer.[7]

Donnelly found flaws in all of the 19th-century hypotheses of the origin of the drift. He first examined a theory, popular early in the century, that the drift (or "Diluvium," as it was then called) originated at the time of the Biblical deluge. Gigantic "waves of translation" swept madly over the Earth, leaving the drift behind when they retreated. This theory was well out of fashion before the 1880s, and Donnelly, too, rejected it. The absence of marine fossils in the drift and the fact that drift rocks had marks or striations not found on seashore rocks convinced him that the drift was not associated with the ocean.

Next he considered the "iceberg" theory. It asserted that the drift was caused by icebergs that, scraping over the surface of the Earth, ground up and dragged debris with them in their migration from arctic regions. As the icebergs melted, they dropped their holdings on sunken lands that later rose above the waters. Donnelly recognized a number of objections to this theory; he quoted James Croll's *Climate and Time*, which argued that "the icebergs nowadays usually sail down into the oceans without a scrap of *debris* of any kind upon them." The iceberg theory, too, had lost favor among many scientists.

The "glacier" theory was very popular, but it did not satisfy Donnelly. One could imagine a glacier, he wrote, "taking in its giant paw a mass of rock, and using it as a graver to carve deep grooves in the rocks below it; and we can see in it a great agency for breaking up rocks and carrying the *detritus* down upon the plains." Agreeing with Geikie, Donnelly found glaciers alone to be an unsatisfactory agent to explain the origin and nature of thousands of miles of drift enfolding the world.

Donnelly also rejected the theory most popular with scientists of his own and later times. This held that continental ice sheets, once covering an area from the poles to 30° or 40° of north and south latitude, had ground the drift from surface rocks over long periods of time and moved it from place to place as they retreated and advanced. Critics asked questions about the extent of the ice. Could it have covered the tops of mountains? Could the ice sheet have covered equatorial regions where scientists said they found drift? Why were some cold regions ice-free? While not denying that ice had moved some of the drift around, Donnelly maintained that "the Drift is *not* found where ice must have been, and *is* found where ice could not have been; the conclusion, therefore, is that the Drift is not due to ice." Ice could not have deposited drift in beds of uniform thickness over thousands of square miles of the Earth.[8]

Returning to first principles, Donnelly asked: What *caused* the ice? In *The World Before the Deluge*, Figuier observed that the ice came to an Earth that enjoyed a mild and agreeable climate. The cold came so suddenly that mammoths in Siberia perished and, "*enveloped in ice at the moment of their death*," were preserved — hair, skin, bones, and flesh. Scientists could not then explain — and have not since explained — what caused the sudden change in temperature. Donnelly reasoned that heat must have come first. Before sudden cold and ice could envelop the Earth, tremendous heat must have evaporated water from the oceans into the clouds. The clouds would shut off the sun's rays; the Earth would become cold; the moisture from the clouds would condense and fall again in rain or snow to form ice.

What was the source of the heat that achieved the stupendous results necessary for this cold? Donnelly maintained that nothing on Earth could have created it. Noting other geologists' descriptions of the forests and rocks under the drift, he asserted that "There was something, (whatever it was,) that fell upon them with awful force and literally *smashed* them, pounding, beating, pulverizing them, and turning one layer of mighty rock over upon another, and scattering them in the wildest confusion." He concluded that the drift must be the result of a sudden and "world-convulsing" catastrophe. At this point in his story he was ready to introduce the comet — the source of the heat, the source of the drift, the cause of a world-shaking cataclysm of which ice became a secondary result.[9]

Once, perhaps more than once, a comet, "a blazing nucleus and a mass of ponderable, separated matter, such as stones, gravel, clay-dust, and gas," came rushing out of space and struck the Earth. The marvel, wrote Donnelly, was not that a comet struck the Earth in the remote past, but that the Earth had escaped a collision with a comet "for a single century . . . a single year." The astronomer Johannes Kepler, he noted, said that "comets are scattered through the heavens with as much profusion as fishes in the ocean." And comets, said Donnelly, are "celestial immigrants whom no anti-Chinese legislation can keep away." Primitive people had watched them with dread, likening them to dra-

The comet sweeping past the Earth, as illustrated in *Ragnarok*.

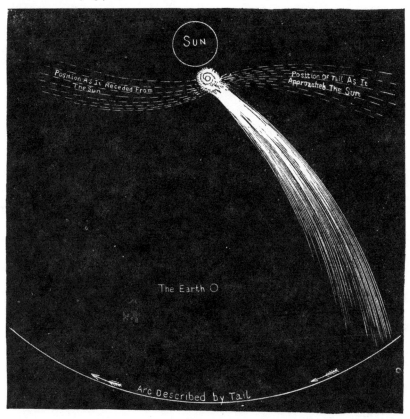

gons, snakes, serpents, boars, bulls, wolves, dogs, tigers, or lions. Donnelly was amused to think of the Earth as "a lost child in the midst of a forest of wild beasts."[10]

Donnelly's investigation of the nature of comets took him to Alexander von Humboldt's *Cosmos*. Humboldt's work, an extremely popular 19th-century treatise on the physical world, described comets as "the most wonderful class of bodies that belong to our solar system." The author noted the general fear of comets and acknowledged that scientific discoveries about their nature had only increased that fear. He listed ominous facts: "a certainty of there being several periodical comets within the known planetary orbits, visiting us at short intervals; the considerable perturbations which Jupiter and Saturn cause in their paths, whereby apparently harmless wanderers of the sky may be converted into peril-fraught bodies; the orbit of Biela's comet passing through that of the earth," and the probability that "our atmosphere was mingled with the vapour of the comets' tails of the years 1819 and 1823.[11]

Donnelly read about comets in Humboldt's work and in the books of Amédée Guillemin, H. Schellen, and Daniel Kirkwood, as well as an article on comets and meteors in the *Edinburgh Review*. Meanwhile, astronomers were watching and writing about other remarkable comets in the skies of the 1880s. Seven comets were observed in 1880, eight in 1881, and five in 1882.[12]

March, 1882, marked the inauguration at Carleton College in Northfield, Minnesota, of the *Sidereal Messenger*, a periodical edited by Professor William Payne and designed to publish popularly written scientific articles on astronomical subjects. Its first issue featured an article entitled "Comets — Their Composition, Purpose and Effect upon the Earth," by Lewis Boss, director of the Dudley Observatory in Albany, New York. While there is no proof that Donnelly saw Boss's article, it is likely, considering Nininger's proximity to Northfield and the interests of its resident, that he did. Boss undertook to describe what in 1882 were the generally accepted theories about comets and their smaller companions in the sky; Donnelly's other sources agreed in many particulars with what Boss said.[13]

The professor confessed that, although modern science had taught much about the physical nature of comets, "no one has yet been able to construct a theory which is either complete or free from objection." Boss favored the supposition that comets originated outside our solar system, perhaps in some "primeval nebula from which a solar system has been evolved." Comets traveled in elliptical orbits around the sun. They were made of the same elements as planets, including carbon and hydrogen; a comet's nucleus consisted of either solid or liquid matter. It glowed, probably in part by its own light and in part with the reflected light of the sun. The cometic tail was an elongated collection of loosely adhering particles, probably electrically or magnetically charged and self-luminous. Boss did not believe that the tail of the comet contained gases in any appreciable amounts. Meteorites (shooting stars), meteors, and aerolites (large meteors) traveled in the orbits of well-known comets; they were the scattered remains of disintegrated comets.

Comets were small in mass in comparison to planets, and it was generally believed that when they came near, they were influenced in some ways by the larger bodies. On the other hand, Boss believed that the effect of a comet on a larger heavenly body such as Earth was "quite insignificant." He conceded that comets could perhaps "affect the earth's magnetic condition, and thus to some extent, possibly its meteorology," but "No such effect has ever been perceived." He discredited ancient superstitions regarding effects of comets on the Earth. "In spite of some chance coincidences between the apparitions of great comets and remarkable public events," he wrote, "no well-informed person now believes that there is any real connection between them. By a liberal and credulous interpretation of any frequently occurring celestial phenomenon, similar coincidences could be shown."

"It may be said," the professor prophetically concluded, "with all due respect to scientific decorum, that the appearance of a great comet does exert one most happy influence on the earth, in that it stimulates the curiosity of mankind and directs their thoughts to the more particular contemplation of the glorious universe which surrounds them." In the two years after Boss's article was published, astronomers in 46 observatories in the United States and many others around the world were busy studying remarkable events in the sky. Widespread public interest in astronomical events early in 1882 may, in part, have inspired Donnelly to write *Ragnarok*.[14]

Donnelly did not accept three of Boss's general premises: that comets all originated in outer space; that they did not have gases in their tails; that they were no threat to the Earth. He thought that not only were comets composed of the same material as planets, they were in fact blown-off fragments of planets, and some of them came from our solar system. Comets, he believed, had appreciable amounts of gas in their nuclei, and in, or associated with, their tails. They had come close to the Earth in the past. Because of their heat, their gases, their speed of travel, and their erratic behavior in orbit around the sun and close to planets, they represented a very real threat to the Earth. Evidence of their encounters with the Earth, Donnelly maintained, lay in the drift.[15]

He described the consequences of a collision between a comet and the Earth. Debris fell on the side of the Earth facing the comet. The comet's great heat enveloped the Earth, causing its surface to melt or become softened to such a plastic state that it retained the scratches of rocks hurled against it and the footprints of living creatures who stepped on its surface; the impact may have created "those mighty excavations," the Great Lakes. In other places the heat degraded the surface rocks and freed their minerals. The first fall of fine clay debris sifted into the scratches and footprints and then baked hard on the hot Earth, preserving indentations and forming the hardest part of the till or hardpan clay.[16]

159

The intense heat brought the Earth's waters to a boil. Moisture from rivers, lakes, and oceans was drawn into the sky to form dense clouds which, with fine comet debris suspended in the air, blocked out the sun and caused darkness over the land. Gas from the extended tail of the comet, combining with oxygen in the atmosphere, exploded with appalling sounds; as it fell in drifts and patches on the Earth, it fed raging fires, poisoned the air and water, and killed living creatures.

Volcanic eruptions, earthquakes, tidal waves, great heat, fires, and electrical, magnetic, and cyclonic storms were the consequences of the wrenching collision. Dense clouds blocked the Earth from the sun; moisture fell from the clouds in torrential rains, or in snow, hail, and ice, bringing a period of bitter cold.

And what of the human race? Donnelly imagined the terror, the horror, the immense destructiveness of the experience. "And this human ant-hill, the world, how insignificant would it be in the grasp of such a catastrophe! Its laws, its temples, its libraries, its religions, its armies, its mighty nations, would be but as the veriest stubble — dried grass, leaves, rubbish — crushed, smashed, buried, under this heaven-rain of horrors."

Only small numbers of people would survive. "And poor humanity! Burned, bruised, wild, crazed, stumbling, blown about like feathers in the hurricanes, smitten by mighty rocks, they perish by the million; a few only reach the shelter of the caverns; and thence, glaring backward, look out over the ruins of a destroyed world."

Both savage and highly civilized beings had existed together on the Earth long before the comet, Donnelly asserted. He pointed to the testimony of those who had found the remains of human beings in various stages of development far beneath the surface in Britain, France, Germany, California, and Kansas. From those who lived through the cataclysm came legends about the terrible experience. Donnelly ranged through the folk literature of China, Persia, India, Egypt, Saxon England, Cornwall, Assyria, Russia, Rome, and Scandinavia for evidence; he also used stories from the native tribes of the western hemisphere and the Old Testament books of Genesis and Job. The legends differed in many details, but they agreed on certain facts: "the monster in the air; the heat; the fire; the cave-life; the darkness; the return of the light." Donnelly saw the need to put all of their testimony together "to make a consistent whole."[17]

The legend of Phaëton, the son of the sun god Phoebus-Apollo, as told by Ovid in *Metamorphoses*, presented Donnelly with vivid and suggestive details. Phaëton begged for and finally received his father's permission to drive his chariot, the sun, for a day. When the boy mounted the chariot, he was unable to control its mighty horses. The luckless charioteer, his steeds racing madly out of control, followed an erratic course among the stars, passing the Serpent and the Scorpion (thus following, said Donnelly, the orbit of Donati's comet of 1858 and coming from the same direction the drift must have followed). As he approached the Earth, flames from his chariot destroyed trees, crops, great cities, and whole nations. Terrible heat dried up the Rhine, Rhone, Nile, Po, and Tiber rivers; it depleted the ocean; it melted gold in the earth. The ground burst asunder and people took refuge in caves or in water. Then Jupiter sent a thunderbolt that shattered the chariot. Its debris fell and Phaëton, his body smoking, flames consuming his yellow hair, plunged headlong from the sky. His father the sun god hid his face in grief, and darkness covered the Earth. Black days followed until Phoebus-Apollo could be persuaded to travel again on his daily journey across the heavens.[18]

Donnelly found further evidence in one of Plato's *Dialogues*, in which an Egyptian priest tells Solon that the Phaëton story "has the form of a myth, but *really signifies a declination of the bodies moving around the earth and in the heavens, and a great conflagration of things upon the earth* recurring at long intervals of time."

A Toltec legend from Central America gave intimations that catastrophes on the Earth were related to the movement of such heavenly bodies. The story described a "third era" of the world when rains of gravel and fire fell on the Earth and "*all which existed burned*." While rocks "*boiled with great tumult*, there also rose the rocks of vermilion color."

In the Old Testament Book of Job Donnelly found much to support his comet theory. He could not believe that this ancient book was "simply a record of the sufferings of some obscure Arab chief from a loathsome disease." Job's recital of woes, Donnelly said, was "comprehensible as a description of a great disaster of nature, but it is extravagant language to apply to a mere case of boils." The sun does not rise, the Earth is shaken, mountains are removed, people perish of heat, the waters dry up, earth is overturned, and people grope in darkness. In the sky is a "crooked serpent" whose "sneezing is like the shining of fire." Job's lament, said Donnelly, "sounds like the cry not of man but of a race, a great, religious, civilized race, who could not understand how God could so cruelly visit the world." Verse by verse, Donnelly interpreted the Book of Job in the light of the comet.[19]

At the risk of seeming irreverent, he shone that light on Genesis as well. Concluding that the story of creation had been confused by human error through the ages, and that it was actually two stories, he rearranged verses accordingly. One part was an account of the original creation; the other, he suggested, was the story of the rebirth and resurrection of life after the visitation of the comet.[20]

In the Scandinavian *Eddas* he found other lore of compelling interest. Fenris-wolf and the Midgard serpent (two comets, said Donnelly) were loose in the sky. Fenris devoured the sun, and the Midgard serpent vomited forth venom, defiling the air and water. It was a time of great fire and heat, the stars were hurled from the heavens, the Earth shook violently, trees were torn up by their roots. Smoke, dust, and gravel fell from the sky. It was a day of judgment; mountains were dashed together, men abandoned their homes, the sun became dark. Then "snow drives from all quarters. The frosts are so severe, the winds so keen, there is no joy in the sun." The Fenris-wolf fed on men's bodies and stained the seats of the gods with blood, which, said Donnelly, probably referred to the red clay cast over the Earth by the comet. It was the Fimbul winter, the "Ragnarok." Donnelly offered alternate translations of the word. It could mean either the darkness of the gods, "from *regin*, gods, and *rökr*, darkness," or the rain of dust, from "*regn*, a rain, and *rök*, smoke, or dust."[21]

Donnelly had originally intended to name his book *Phaëton*, but as he studied the Norse legends, he decided to change the title to *Ragnarok*. It was appropriate for a Minnesota author from the north country to give his book a Scandinavian name. "Every snow-storm, every chilling blast that blows out from the frozen lips of the icy North, is but a reminiscence of Ragnarok," Donnelly wrote. Although he was an Irishmen, he also identified himself with the Norsemen (did not Vikings settle in Ireland?) and he spoke eloquently of the Ragnarok version of the comet story. "What history, what poetry, what beauty, what inestimable pictures of an infinite past have lain hidden away in these Sagas — the despised heritage of all the blue-eyed, light haired races of the world!" No tale of ancient Greece or Rome could "parallel this marvelous story."

Donnelly had given his readers evidence from astronomy and geology, and legends from around the world. In a fourth section of seven miscellaneous chapters he reminded his readers that men were civilized before the drift and concluded that the comet catastrophe was indeed the Biblical fall of man, "From comfort to misery; from plowed fields to the thistles and the stones; from sunny and glorious days in a stormless land to the awful trials of the Drift Age; the rains, the cold, the snow, the ice, the incessant tempests, the darkness, the poverty, the coats of hides, the cave-life, the cannibalism, the Stone Age." Man had been driven from the Garden of Eden, but he survived the cometary catastrophe and returned to the garden to live until the great flood. The Garden, said Donnelly, returning to the subject of his first book, was Atlantis, the island-home of the race.[22]

In two chapters Donnelly established the connecting links between *Ragnarok* and *Atlantis*. He speculated that a "bridge" or mountainous ridge between Atlantis and Britain was destroyed by a cometary catastrophe, but perhaps the tops of the mountains remained as small island stepping stones between Atlantis and surrounding continents. Some 20,000 years after the drift, by Donnelly's estimate, came the great deluge in which Atlantis sank. In Atlantis originated the myths that told of the great catastrophes. Altered over time by each small group of survivors and their descendants, the variant tales were true stories of what had happened to mankind.

Donnelly then added to his manuscript a curiously informal chapter of questions and answers, such as might have followed a lecture. He strengthened some of his arguments; on other points he equivocated. He told one imaginary questioner that just because deep scratches were found under glaciers there was no reason to conclude that the glaciers did the scratching, for "A porcelain nest-egg found under a hen is no

162

proof that the hen laid it." Furthermore, scratches were found on rocks far from where glaciers were thought to be. To another imaginary critic who called Donnelly's explanation "out of the usual course of nature," Donnelly said, "If you reject my theory, you do not get clear of the phenomena. . . . Go out and look at the first Drift deposit; dig into it a hundred feet or more; follow it for a few hundred miles or more; then come back, and scratch your head, and tell me where it came from!" Donnelly explained that drift materials in the comet's tail would not burn up in the Earth's atmosphere as meteorites did because they had "parental attraction" to restrain them until the moment of impact. If, contrary to his theory, drift were found on more than one side of the Earth, the discovery would mean simply that the drift fell over a longer time and therefore covered more of the Earth. When another imaginary critic asked by "what right" had Donnelly expressed views so much at variance with the prevailing opinions of mankind, the audacious author replied, "All recognized truths once rested, solitary and alone, in some one brain." He swore allegiance to both science and religion. "If God has led life from the rudest beginnings, where fossils are engraved, (blurred and obscured,) on the many pages of the vast geological volume, up to this intellectual, charitable, merciful, powerful world of to-day," he wrote in his most optimistic mood, "who can doubt that the same hand will guide our posterity to even higher levels of development?"[23]

The question-and-answer period ended, Donnelly was not yet ready to adjourn the meeting. He sought to bring the subject of comets to his readers in a more immediate way. While the encounter with a comet may have occurred in a remote time, say 30,000 years ago, danger still threatened in the sky. In the "celestial game of ten-pins, with the solar system for a bowling-alley, . . . the earth [is] waiting for a ten-strike."[24]

The Earth may indeed have been grazed by a ball in recent times, Donnelly asserted. He agreed with Humboldt that "It is probable that the vapor of the tails of comets mingled with our atmosphere in the years 1819 and 1823." Moreover he and Humboldt believed that Biela's comet had come close to the Earth in 1832 and perhaps on later orbits. In one reappearance it was seen with two tails; it disappeared mysteriously and was discovered again by telescope in November, 1872, without any tail. Astronomers conjectured that a magnificent display of meteorites seen in Europe at that time was a part of the "demoralized" tail. And where were the other "assets of this bankrupt comet?" Could they have been hanging around in Biela's orbit where the comet abandoned them?[25]

Donnelly suggested that perhaps the Earth had passed through gases of Biela's tail on October 8, 1871, a day he and thousands of other midwesterners would never forget. "There was a parched, combustible, inflammable, furnace-like feeling in the air. . . . It was weird and unnatural." At the same hour in the evening, hundreds of miles apart in Wisconsin, Michigan, and Illinois, "fires of the most peculiar and devastating kind broke out, so far as we know, by spontaneous combustion." The great Chicago fire, accompanied by fierce winds and electrical disturbances, left 125,000 people homeless. In Brown County, Wisconsin, 400 square miles and the town of Peshtigo burned under flames swept by raging winds; 1,500 people died. Fires in Michigan destroyed the homes of 15,000 people. And on the same day, Donnelly noted, "the States of Iowa, Minnesota, Indiana, and Illinois were severely devastated by prairie-fires; while terrible fires raged on the Alleghenies, the Sierras of the Pacific coast, and the Rocky Mountains, and in the region of the Red River of the North."[26]

The lesson, he noted, was that "All this brings before our eyes vividly the condition of things when the comet struck the earth; when conflagrations spread over wide areas; when human beings were consumed by the million; when their works were obliterated, and the remnants of the multitude fled before the rushing flames, filled with unutterable consternation."

Who was to say, Donnelly asked, how often extraterrestrial sources had caused fire and pestilence, crop failures, and famines on Earth? Who was to say how many times a comet, an "erratic, unusual, anarchical, monstrous" creature, loose in the heavens, had damaged our planet? In the view of some, said Donnelly, comets may be impalpable or insignificant, but in the universal belief of mankind as expressed in ancient tales, they are "loaded with death and ruin" and "man can not contemplate them without terror."

Unwilling to end his book on this bleak, hopeless note, Donnelly the writer on science abandoned "scientific decorum" and Donnelly the reformer added a homiletic "After-Word." He sought to dispel any impression that God, in allowing such a catastrophe as he had described to come to Earth, did not care for his people. It was not possible for man to understand God's plan; good could come out of disaster. Man survived the cataclysm, the world rose again to higher levels of creative development. In fact, some of the world's richest soil was drift from the comet. Perhaps, too, under the stress of catastrophe, the human brain had been forced to higher development.[27]

Donnelly the reformer took the opportunity to warn the Biblical Dives, the rich man in the parable of Lazarus who valued his property and worldly possessions, that it was time to consider greater spiritual values and to attend, in compassion, to the health and happiness of other humbler temporal creatures. At any moment, from Aldebaran or Arcturus or some other point in space, another comet "of glowing countenance and horrid hair" could be raging through the heavens with millions of tons of debris in its tail to overwhelm Dives and his possessions. If Dives would "widen" his heart and put his intellect to work to "readjust the values of labor, and increase the productive capacity of Nature, that plenty and happiness, light and hope, may dwell in every heart," then, Donnelly promised, "from such a world God will fend off the comets with his great right arm." In the face of Donnelly's contention that in the past merciless heat, bitter cold, drift, and death had overwhelmed the just and unjust alike without discrimination, the suggestion that God would intervene next time was not reassuring.

Donnelly finished writing *Ragnarok* on July 8, 1882. Five days later he started east with his only copy of the manuscript in search of a publisher. Harper and Brothers, who had been delighted with the success of *Atlantis*, declined to publish the new book, saying that it would be denounced or ignored by scientists. Charles Scribner's Sons rejected the manuscript after sending it for review to a New Haven scientist who dismissed it as "scientifically ridiculous." Not yet ready to abandon his newest child, Donnelly submitted the manuscript to O. B. Bunce, an editor at D. Appleton and Company.[28]

The author had returned to Minnesota when Bunce sent the glad news on August 4 that Appleton was "disposed to undertake the publication" of *Ragnarok*. In subsequent negotiations the author and publisher agreed to terms. The retail price was set at $2. Donnelly would receive no royalties on the first thousand copies sold, 10 per cent on the second thousand, 15 per cent on the third, and 20 per cent on all additional sales. The author told the publisher that he was confident that if the book were "properly urged" it could sell from 20,000 to 30,000 copies, "as it is so novel and curious and touches so many interesting and important questions." Donnelly would prepare an index, and Appleton agreed to supply him as many as 100 copies of the book at half the wholesale price. Donnelly would distribute them judiciously where they would do the most good. And, in a decision Appleton must soon have rued, the firm agreed to let the author add some new matter to the text.[29]

In September, October, and November, 1882, Donnelly read proof and sent sections of the galley sheets to friends for their comments. He revised industriously and added new material until Appleton, complaining of the cost and trouble of making so many changes, begged him to cease.

In the meantime, nature obligingly set the stage for the appearance of the new book with a series of remarkable events in the sky. Observers at Lebanon, Connecticut, reported seeing curious triangular, luminous "appearances" on the moon. An astronomer at Jersey City saw an unidentified object in the sky that remained stationary for the extraordinary period of three-quarters of a minute. At Davenport, Iowa, a piece of ice eight inches long and one and a half inches thick was said to have fallen in a hailstorm. A mass of ice weighing about 80 pounds was reported to have fallen at Salina, Kansas. In September the year's last comet, the Great Comet of 1882, appeared in the heavens. One astronomer maintained that not for a quarter of a century had "so splendid an object" been seen in the sky. During October came what one observer called "perhaps the most wonderful display of northern lights that the continent of North America has ever witnessed. . . . The ignorant were frightened, the wise were puzzled, poetic souls uplifted, fanatics convinced that the world was coming to an end, and the whole nation of the United States profoundly stirred." From Maine to Florida, Alaska to Minnesota to Mexico, the phenomenon was noted and described. In November astronomers observed unusual turbulence on the sun, auroral displays with a brightness greater than that of the full moon, and violent magnetic storms both in Europe and America. All these activities, reported an Illinois astronomer, "seem to indicate a bond of union between solar and terrestrial energy, the secret of which yet eludes research." At the Royal Observatory in Greenwich, England, an astronomer saw a body "very definite in form, like a torpedo," traveling across the sky. Other people in England, Holland, and Belgium described it as shaped like a fish, a cigar, a spindle, or a shuttle.[30]

Before the end of November all of *Ragnarok* had been set in type except the index, which Donnelly soon finished. Appleton issued a show bill advertising the book and D. D. Merrill's St. Paul Book and Stationery Company ordered 500 copies. Bunce expected the book to do well and wrote Donnelly that it was "a puzzle with us all here, how it is that Harpers came not to accept it." Complimentary and review copies were distributed around the country well before December 7, when *Ragnarok* was officially published.[31]

And so, under a sky filled with comets, meteors, auroral displays, and unidentified objects, *Ragnarok* was launched on its career. The *St. Paul Dispatch* thought it was "destined to hew a new channel for human thought, and open up fresh fields for scientific controversy. Its converts will be fewer than its readers and admirers. But all will join in praise of the ingenuity, the learning and the literary skill of its author." The reviewer for the *Hartford* (Connecticut) *Times* thought that Donnelly had found "abundant cause" in the comet "to explain all existing phenomena." An early review in the *St. Paul Pioneer Press* called *Ragnarok* "an interesting work of the imagination, a well constructed and well carried out burlesque," and a "quasi-scientific" diversion opposed to modern science, "which rejects, in the main, the old line of cataclysms."[32]

Worse was yet to come. A flippant and condescending review entitled "Mr. Donnelly's Comets" in the *Philadelphia Bulletin* said that Donnelly had picked up "the grand idea . . . that comets are the cause of almost everything extraordinary that takes place on earth and in the realms of space." Donnelly had searched diligently and "squeezed out" his proof from "all the books that may be found in a Minnesota collection," and he was to be applauded for diligence if for nothing else. But the *Boston Evening Traveller* confessed that whatever the scientific verdict on *Ragnarok*, "the book has a primeval sensationalism" and "no one can read it without a thrill of excited interest." Others likened its author to Jules Verne, the "great French Romancer" who "applied modern science to the wild machinery of fiction and adventure."

Ragnarok, ridiculed or ignored by scientists, continued nevertheless to be read by the public. In 1887 Donnelly paid Appleton $400 for the plates and reprinted the book himself. By 1899 it had been published in 19 American editions. The text was not revised; Donnelly, who was daring in his thesis but timid in following where his comet led, seems

By IGNATIUS DONNELLY,
Author of "ATLANTIS."

RAGNAROK
The Age of Fire and Gravel.

12mo, cloth, illustrated.   Price, $2.00.   **D. APPLETON & CO., New York.**

Advertisement for the new book. *MHS*

not to have considered incorporating into his book new material that related to one or another aspect of his theory.[33]

In the century since *Ragnarok* appeared others have explored the idea that sizable heavenly bodies have either come close to the Earth or collided with it. Hanns Hoerbiger, a Viennese engineer, theorized in 1913 that six such heavenly bodies had approached the Earth, each causing catastrophes and each successively becoming the Earth's moon. In 1950 Immanuel Velikovsky's *Worlds in Collision* advanced the theory that one of the comets that had a close encounter with Earth became the planet Venus. Velikovsky appears to have used *Ragnarok* in a German edition and to have drawn on some of the same sources.[34]

Scientists have hypothesized that a fragment of a comet exploded with enormous power above the Earth in the Tunguska region of Siberia in 1908. Its blast wave killed herds of reindeer and flattened forests over thousands of square kilometers. The flash was seen 400 kilometers away, the shock waves were felt 60 kilometers from the point of explosion; it is estimated that several million tons of comet debris were dissipated in the atmosphere. Lubor Kresak of the Slovak Academy of Scientists has argued that what hit Siberia was a fragment of Encke's comet, which reappears every three and a half years.[35]

Since the 1950s other scientific speculation recalled Donnelly's ideas. Harold C. Urey, a chemistry professor and Nobel laureate from San Diego, theorized in 1957 that tektites (glassy bodies of unknown origin found in certain areas of the world) were debris from collisions of comets with the Earth. He subsequently suggested that such encounters could have caused great variations in climate, violent physical effects, and the termination of geological periods. Frederic B. Jueneman, analytical chemist and author of *Limits of Uncertainty*, wrote in 1973 of Donnelly's idea that the 1871 fires at Chicago and elsewhere could have been fueled by gases from Biela's comet. Jueneman wondered whether anomalous peaks of carbon dioxide in the atmosphere since the 14th century — revealed in the rings of Bristlecone pine trees — could not better be related to the burning debris of a comet than to the increased burning of fossil fuels.[36]

More recently, interest in the cometary thesis came from other quarters. A team of scientists at the University of California, Berkeley, hypothesized in 1980 that some 65 million years ago an encounter between the Earth and an asteroid could have caused the extinction of many forms of life. Examining clay beds in Italy, Denmark, Spain, and New Zealand, they discovered unusually high quantities of iridium, an element rarely found in the Earth's rocks but abundant in meteorites. After studying a number of possible explanations, they favored the hypothesis that the clay was the fallout of a close encounter or collision with an asteroid that spread some 500 billion tons of extraterrestrial matter on the Earth. Both in the shock of the encounter and in its aftermath, when tons of dust in the stratosphere screened the sun's rays from the Earth and diminished photosynthesis, forests were destroyed, tidal waves swept over the land, and many species of plants and animals were exterminated. Such an encounter at the end of the Mesozoic Era could have caused the disappearance of as many as 75 per cent of the previously existing species. Scientist Dale Russell, like Donnelly, perceived some good in this hypothetical reconstruction of events. The destruction of the brainier dinosaurs, he suggested, could have opened the way for the development of man.[37]

Still more recently, other evidence recalled Donnelly's discussion of the origin of the Great Lakes. Three American scientists announced at St. Louis in 1982 that they had identified a 1,700-mile-wide buried crater basin stretching from the mouth of Hudson Bay to an area south of the Great Lakes. They conjectured, from data gathered on land and by satellites, that a meteoroid some 60 to 90 miles in diameter struck the region and created a ring basin. The collision could have set off volcanic eruptions and the heat-generated melting of granitic materials could have formed the great granite shield that now stretches across the continent.

Donnelly's description of a comet's structure is similar to the later "gravel bank" model, in which a swarm of rocks, gravel, and dust travel independent but similar paths around the sun. According to the "dirty snowball" model, favored by present-day astronomers, the comet's nucleus of water, ice, and dust is surrounded by a spherical coma of gas and dust; the tail, also composed of gases and dust, is believed to be far too rarefied to affect the Earth's atmosphere or set fires on the Earth. Scientists agree, however, that the results of a collision or near-collision with the nucleus of a comet could be catastrophic, as Donnelly envisioned. If modern theories are correct, such an encounter is likely to occur at 30- to 100-million-year intervals.[38]

Yet the results of a cometary encounter would depend on the size of the nucleus as well as whether or where (on land or in ocean) it landed. Even a small hunk of Encke's comet exploding above the Earth caused a vast amount of damage in Siberia. Perhaps, with the ancient ones, we should regard with awe the brilliant comet, its glowing tail streaming behind as it careens madly across the heavens. Who really knows what the next celestial immigrant will do?

1883

Events of a Remarkable Year
Recall Donnelly's Ideas
and Help Sell
his Books

THE YEAR was chiefly remarkable for extraordinary natural calamities. A volcanic outburst devastated one of the most populous and productive regions of the world, the cholera mowed down the population of another, earthquakes demolished whole towns, freshets ravaged the valleys of Central Europe, and tornadoes spread desolation in the United States. The minor catastrophes and accidents by land and sea, when aggregated, present an appalling sum of destruction, suffering, and death.
— *Appletons' Annual Cyclopaedia*, 8:321 (1883)

I GNATIUS DONNELLY's *Ragnarok* was published at a time of great progress in the United States: the Civil War was well over, the economy had finally started to boom after the recession of 1873, and promising opportunities for advancement beckoned. People of Minnesota and the Midwest, in particular, saw enormous population growth and economic expansion all around them. In a St. Patrick's Day address at Faribault in 1882, Ignatius Donnelly characterized the era as "the most earnest, practical and progressive age the world has ever known . . . an age that looks forward, and moves eagerly forward, towards opportunities and a destiny so vast as to dwindle into insignificance all the doings of mankind in the past."[39]

Many people living in this optimistic era were made uncomfortable by Donnelly's suggestion that a comet could strike the Earth and de-

molish its population. Some of the devout saw in the comet tale a denial
of their religious faith: a God who cared for his creatures would stay the
comet in its course and not permit them to be destroyed. Scientifically
minded persons, comfortable with the idea that they stood at the head
of an evolutionary procession on an Earth weathered through eons of
slow change, rejected the thought that a disruptive comet could cause
any appreciable damage to this predictable universe. They admitted
that man did not yet know all the answers about his world, but they did
not expect their lives to be disrupted by unpredictable or inexplicable
events.

Ignatius Donnelly spent much of 1883 at home in Nininger tending
to family and business affairs. Occasionally he ventured away from
home for lecture engagements at Winona, Fergus Falls, Minneapolis,
and Brown's Valley, and he took care of business matters for his farms
at Nininger and in Stevens County. He corresponded with many people
about his books; he collected reviews, noted events in the world at large,
and defended his views to those who would listen. At times he was
oblivious to all else in research for a third book. His year was a happy
one.

For many other people 1883 was a year filled with extraordinary
events, some of them catastrophic enough to shake the faith of the
complacent. A series of disasters brought death and destruction to tens
of thousands of people on Earth. Extremes of temperature, from blasting
heat to bitter, bone-chilling cold took their toll of life. Tornadoes,
cyclones, hurricanes, mudslides, avalanches, earthquakes, volcanic eruptions, floods, tsunamis (tidal waves), raging fires, and epidemics of
disease wiped out thousands more and left survivors scarred, battered,
and homeless. And in the sky, sometimes over the afflicted areas, appeared comets, fireballs, meteors, meteorites, aerolites, and other identified and unidentified flying objects.

Of course, 1883 may not have held the most disasters of the century
or even of the decade. Yet many who lived through the year thought so.
Bewildered survivors asked who or what was responsible for the year's
enormous tragedy. Had sinful men somehow brought the wrath of an
angry God on themselves? Or was it a normal manifestation of elemental
power — capricious, godless, unpredictable, imperfectly understood?

In Minnesota as elsewhere people searched the debris and ashes for
victims — and scapegoats. Some blamed agencies of government, such as
fire or water departments, street commissioners, weather forecasters,
building inspectors, legislators. Others assigned culpability for particular events to newspaper reporters, architects, engineers, contractors,
schoolteachers, arsonists, or tramps — or to ignorance, shoddy work,
greed, dishonesty, or filth. Even some of the victims were blamed when,
surrendering to panic at real or imagined danger, they trampled other
people to death in their haste to save themselves.[40]

There were other responses to the terrible events. Many of Earth's
inhabitants went about their daily rounds untouched by personal tragedy and oblivious to the plight of victims. Others sent money, food,

clothing, tools, and medical assistance to aid the stricken. Clergymen preached sermons about faith, compassion, guilt. Patent-medicine salesmen offered panaceas.

Some scientists attempted to quiet public anxiety by describing phenomena in less threatening terms: an earthquake, for example, was not really an earthquake, it was simply a subsidence of the earth; the many fires burning around the world were isolated, coincidental events and therefore did not constitute a major disaster or catastrophe.[41]

As a beneficent result of disastrous events, public officials promulgated new laws, ordinances, and regulations for the protection of the public. New water systems, dams to withstand 100-year floods, and forest conservation practices were developed; buildings were redesigned, and compassionate individuals, deeply touched by tragic events, chose careers dedicated to the public good.

Throughout 1883 writers for newspapers and periodicals continued to comment on *Ragnarok*. The book sold steadily in bookstores as the daily press, month after month, confronted the thoughtful reader with evidence that unpredictable, titanic forces of nature did cause sudden wholesale destruction all around the world, and men were helpless against them. And as men and women devised new and creative ways to protect themselves and survive, *Ragnarok* reminded its readers that out of tragedy perhaps some good could come.

In the Midwest, 1883 began with bitingly cold weather that, Donnelly observed, "dwarfs and shrivels the bodily strength and the mental

Donnelly's library at Nininger, ca. 1925. *MHS*

171

energies." People seeking warmth could only sit around a stove, "like devotees around a black idol — a *kaba* stone," and be thankful for an adequate supply of wood. Those who could read their newspapers found more reason to be thankful. In January alone, fires took buildings and lives in Milwaukee, Des Moines, Minneapolis, Brainerd, and Moorhead; earthquakes shook southern Illinois, Kentucky, and Ohio; thousands starved in a drouth in Mexico; torrential rains brought floods and landslides to the West Coast. Widespread and disastrous floods in Europe drove thousands of people from their homes in the Rhine, Danube, and Moselle valleys. Two ocean liners sank with many casualties, and a smallpox epidemic raged in Minnesota logging camps.[42]

Midwesterners who watched the night sky were more directly reminded of Donnelly's book. On January 3 residents of southern Wisconsin, northern Illinois, and Indiana saw a meteor "resembling an electric light in brilliancy and color, lighting the entire heavens." A group of people in Duluth watched a burning meteor come "sailing up" Lake Superior, traveling "about as fast as a man could run" at an estimated elevation of several hundred feet. It looked like a ball of fire, about four feet in diameter, and gave off shooting sparks in its course; it finally "anchored near the extremity of Rice's Point," which juts into the Duluth-Superior harbor from the Minnesota side.[43]

By the end of January, some newspaper editors began to comment on these events in a way soon to become familiar. The *Winona Republican* described the "Appalling instances" of the month's wholesale destruction and noted that the timid and sensitive almost dreaded opening the morning paper. The *Duluth Daily Tribune* observed that "A season of most appalling disasters has sent shudder after shudder of abject horror throughout the civilized world, disasters that might have been averted had the ordinary precautions against danger been taken. . . . Whether at home or in travel the general public are in momentary danger of being pitched headlong into eternity without warning."[44]

Newspapers also printed reviews of *Ragnarok*, but their reviewers did not agree. The *San Francisco Evening Bulletin* said that Jules Verne in his most imaginative moments never thought of anything so irrational as *Ragnarok*, which "scornfully laughs at demonstrated and theoretical science, setting up against it the imagery of the ancients in perverted form." The *San Francisco Chronicle* called the book an "imaginative bit of science." The *Hastings Gazette* said that *Ragnarok* was written in Donnelly's "best style, and there is not a dull line in it." The reviewer wondered if Washington Irving (writing as Diedrick Knickerbocker, in his *History of New York*) had Donnelly in mind when he suggested, "Should one of our modern sages in his theoretical flights among the stars, ever find himself lost in the clouds, and in danger of tumbling into the abyss of nonsense and absurdity, he has but to seize a comet by the beard, mount astride of his tail, and away he gallops in triumph."[45]

Of greater moment to Donnelly was Alexander Winchell's review in the January *Dial*, a literary publication in Chicago. Winchell, professor of geology at the University of Michigan, felt that the book was "A

Scientistic Romance," not science, not pure romance, but Jules Vernean "science romanticized." He gave faint praise to the work as a literary production, noting with amusement the way "myth is made to confirm the hypothesis and the hypothesis is summoned to interpret the myth." Was Donnelly really in earnest, he asked, or was it all a grand joke? On the chance that Donnelly was serious, the reviewer used his own scientifically orthodox views to attack Donnelly's "questionable" facts, "strained" analogies, and "protrusive" credulity.[46]

Donnelly, furious at what he considered the insolence and arrogance of Winchell's critique, believed that he was being "pooh-poohed out of the court of argument" because he was not a teacher or professor, because he had mingled in public affairs, and because Winchell (who needed "a sheet of ice . . . to cover the nakedness of his intellect") made "genius geographical," having the idea that neither learning nor wisdom "could possibly pass the eastern shore of Lake Michigan."

In the following months other reviewers echoed Winchell's tone. *Popular Science Monthly*, edited by Professor Edward L. Youmans, called *Ragnarok* a peculiar kind of science that "escapes all perplexing and stupid inquiry about its truth." The *Pall Mall Gazette* of London answered challenges to the book's truth with: "What a childish question to ask at the conclusion of a spirited and delightful romance!" The *London Daily News* noted that there was an "agreeable fascination to unscientific minds" in the conglomeration of Genesis, preglacial civilization, and Atlantean myths, like "Walt Whitman's nightmare after an indigestion of popular geologies and astronomies, and a 'big drink' of Victor Hugo." *The Churchman* (New York), saying that one could not answer Donnelly with a sneer, found his theories entirely compatible with scripture. "The catastrophe, which both Christ and St. Peter predict — the shaking of 'the powers of heaven' and the 'melting of the elements with fervent heat' — and the subsequent appearance of a 'new earth,' instead of being incredible, will only be a repetition of something like what happened ages ago."[47]

As a consequence of the debate on Donnelly's theories in the press both of his books were selling well. Throughout the rest of the winter and into spring, a steady sale cheered the author, and Stan made monthly trips to St. Paul Book and Stationery to count his father's books on the shelf. New Orleans chose Atlantis for the theme of its annual Mardi Gras celebration, and a correspondent sent Donnelly programs and other mementos of the event. Readers from across the United States and Great Britain wrote Donnelly to comment on *Atlantis* and *Ragnarok*. Several reported on strange objects they had found well preserved beneath the drift: a pile of carpenter's chips, petrified trees, a copper coin. Scandinavians offered encouraging words about *Ragnarok*, reviewing it in their publications and moving to translate it into Swedish; a Norwegian signed his letter, "Yours faithfully in Odin." A Jesuit priest in Madrid, Spain, wrote that he would put a notice of *Atlantis* in the second edition of his own book, *Harmony Between Science and Religion*.[48]

Even as these readers corresponded with Donnelly, more disasters occurred around them. An early thaw and heavy rains in the Ohio and Mississippi valleys sent down higher and more destructive floods than white settlers had ever seen. The settlers were, in part, responsible: lumbermen had denuded the steep mountain valleys of the Ohio watershed, removing beaver dams and forest cover, so that swift yellow torrents washed away the land. The Braidwood mine in southern Illinois flooded, killing 69 men. The earth shook in Illinois, Michigan, New Hampshire, and Connecticut, and an especially severe quake brought great destruction to Agra, India. Fires burned buildings in St. Paul and Minneapolis; when a conflagration destroyed 13 buildings in downtown Duluth, the city voted to construct a waterworks to guard against a recurrence. The Standard Oil Company's refinery in Jersey City, New Jersey, hit by a shaft of lightning of "unequalled brilliance," was destroyed by fire. Mount Etna on the island of Sicily began erupting on March 20 with earthquake convulsions and "loud roarings"; it belched forth rock, ash, and smoke. Violent storms pushed through the Midwest and the South, and after unprecedented torrents of rain fell on Rush City, Minnesota, a "small army" of frogs appeared on the streets and sidewalks. Fourteen people were trampled to death in New York on Memorial Day when crowds who came to see the new Brooklyn Bridge were "panic-stricken at nothing whatever." Two weeks later 200 children were victims of a mysterious panic at Sunderland, England. And on May 20 Krakatoa, a dormant volcano on an island in the Sunda Straits between Java and Sumatra, began to erupt, sending columns of fine ash and steam miles into the sky and spewing out streams of lava.[49]

In the sky over all these disasters appeared meteors and comets. Every month brought reports from the American East and Midwest, from Italy, from France. Meteors were sighted at the times of earthquakes in Connecticut and Rhode Island. Reports from Marseilles, France, told of objects irregular in form that crossed the sun, some of them moving as if in alignment. A mysterious object with hieroglyphics was reported to have fallen near Round Out Creek, New York. Astronomers spotted spectacular meteors, studied a total eclipse of the sun, and found a new asteroid. On May 18, in Hillsboro, Illinois, "a number of stones of peculiar formation and shape" unknown to the neighborhood fell during a tornado.

THE SUMMER of 1883 was to prove especially active for Donnelly and the world around him. While strange objects traversed the sky, winds blew hot and cold, and the Earth shivered and shook in preparation for more calamitous events, at Nininger family considerations were foremost in Donnelly's life in June. Ignatius, newly graduated from medical school in Philadelphia, opened his practice over a drugstore at the corner of Seventh and Wabasha streets in St. Paul. His parents spent $78 for his office furniture; soon after, Kate Donnelly bought an upright piano at a bargain price of $242 as a wedding gift for Mary. The Donnellys entertained a hundred guests in honor of Mary and her fiancé, George Giltinan, a transplanted Philadelphian; dinner and dancing (the music

174

provided by a group brought by train from St. Paul) graced the evening. A festive family dinner for the young couple followed their wedding on June 28.[50]

Although Donnelly had just won a case in court at Hastings, neither his earnings from his law practice nor the income from his farms met the expenses of the month. To balance his budget, he persuaded the protesting Appleton's agent to send him an advance on royalties — the publisher had, after all, printed more than 3,000 copies. Donnelly put off a creditor with an optimistic note about his books' sales and his current project, a work proposing that Francis Bacon was the real author of Shakespeare's plays. It would be called *The Great Cryptogram*.

Readers commented on both *Atlantis* and *Ragnarok* in letters to Donnelly during June. An English bookseller noted that Sir Anthony Carlisle had some years before propounded the idea of a comet striking the Earth, and "thus accounted for the sudden alteration of the axis of the Earth & the submerging of all low lands[,] change of climate at the poles & all other phenomena — among others the presence of animals in Australia non existent in any other parts of the globe." Donnelly also received, at second hand, some comments from Professor Youmans of *Popular Science Monthly*. When he was asked whether any attempts had been made to refute Donnelly's views, Youmans wrote that it was unlikely an attempt would be made "because the minds that are taken with that work are in a very unpromising condition to reason with. . . . Don[n]elly is ingenious enough, but his performance is ridiculous."[51]

Donnelly's life was peaceful compared to the lives of many in the world around him. Destruction by fire and water was widespread in North America during June. Extensive fires raged in the Adirondacks and the Michigan pineries; eight fires started at once in Toronto; explosions and fires struck Duluth, Barnesville, and Chaska in Minnesota, a distillery in Pennsylvania, a factory in New Orleans, and Barnum's Circus in Chicago — the latter consuming the entire canvas, costumes, and paraphernalia "like a flash." Torrential rains and cyclonic winds visited a broad area of the continent, hitting West Virginia, Ohio, Illinois, Michigan, Iowa, Wisconsin, Nebraska, Kansas, and Missouri. Rising waters inundated the Thames Valley in Ontario, Canada; on the Mississippi they broke through a levee at Alton, Illinois, surrounded St. Louis, and covered large areas of Kansas. The floods ruined crops, undermined buildings and mine timbers, and washed out bridges and railroad lines. Chippewa Falls, Wisconsin, reported hailstones six inches across.[52]

Extremes of temperature marked the onset of July. A blistering heat wave that originated in the Rocky Mountains brought "phenomenal" temperatures: 110° Fahrenheit at Glendive, Montana Territory, 107° at Fort Buford, Dakota Territory, and 100° at St. Paul, the highest ever recorded there on that date, according to the United States Army Signal Service. Then in the middle of the month, while New York sweltered and mortality was "frightfully on the increase, either owing to the great heat, the dirty conditions of the streets," or a higher death rate in an increased

175

population, temperatures dropped to nearly freezing at Fort Garry, Manitoba, and North Platte, Nebraska. It was uncomfortably cool at Nininger, and the over-all average for the region was the coldest on record for July.[53]

These temperature differences brought a violent tornado season to the Midwest. Especially fierce storms struck Wisconsin, at Manitowoc, Green Bay, Milwaukee, Madison, and Fond du Lac. Wind, rain, and hail cut a swath 18 miles wide across two states, destroying Clarinda, Iowa, and Burlington Junction, Missouri. On July 20 and 21, a storm slashed across southern Minnesota to Wisconsin and Iowa, destroying buildings, trees, crops, bridges, and railroad tracks, and derailing cars near Owatonna and near Red Wing.

Reports of an earthquake in Lima, Peru, and a volcanic eruption in Lake Nicaragua were followed by a more fatal tragedy in Italy. Ischia, a beautiful volcanic island off the southern Italian coast, was a favorite resort for tourists. Authorities "hushed up" news of a small earthquake on July 23, fearing that "if the report was sent abroad visitors would be deterred from visiting the island"; five days later, a violent earthquake leveled the city and opened large crevices in the ground. Some 3,000 people were reported to have died in the catastrophe.[54]

The *St. Paul Pioneer Press* reported these events and finished the month's sad burden of news with accounts of train wrecks in Iowa, Ohio, and New York; floods in Michigan; fire in Minneapolis; deaths of 1,500 people a day in a cholera epidemic in Egypt; the drowning of 65 people when a wharf collapsed in Baltimore. The newspaper ran two editorials in the month of July discussing the disasters. On July 7 it assessed the record of the previous "Half a Year's Horrors," each "bound up with the sacrifice of scores of human lives." Human carelessness and "human liability to panic," together with the "wrath of elemental forces," had combined to produce in six months disasters enough for any full year. "Never since it has been possible to keep a record of the work of storms over a wide area, was there such a succession of aerial conflicts at this early period of the year, attended by such loss of property and life." On July 31, after the list of disasters had grown, the paper noted that readers had come to expect a daily report of some new calamity by which "scores of thousands" of people had been "hurried out of existence."

The editorials answered the objections of those who would say that "the increase of telegraphic facilities and the greater activity of news-gathering enterprise" accounted for the larger number of reported accidents. But while that argument might account for the thousands of minor accidents covered in the papers, the *Pioneer Press* stoutly insisted that it did not adequately explain the succession of extraordinary events that "would have required and received investigation and notoriety any time for many years past." The editor insisted that no activities of the collectors or distributors of news, nor any "appetite for the horrible," could account for the "grisly procession" of disasters. Nor could any epidemic of carelessness or terror among men account for the frightful wrath of earth and air.

The July 31 editorial theorized that the Ischia quake, following so closely the great storms in North America, suggested some connection between those events and could revive a currently discredited theory that earthquakes and storms were caused by an "electrical impulse." This current passed through the Earth's crust and "threw the assumed fluid center into storm waves, which beating upon the outer rind, were felt upon the surface as the dreaded shock." Since scientists' attempts to explain these phenomena amounted to little more than a "confession of profound ignorance," the old theory was perhaps worth resurrecting. "The great lesson of the year," the paper summarized, "seems to be the humbling of human pride by the piling up of horrors from causes which man, so far from controlling, cannot even understand."

There were more reports of remarkable events in the sky. At Reading, England, "lumps of earthy matter" dropped during a rainstorm; on the slopes of the Appenines rain brought down twigs, leaves, and tiny toads; large chunks of ice fell on Chicago. Meteors over New Zealand, England, Quebec, Montana, Florida, Massachusetts, and Maine awed observers; astronomers reported "very marked activity" on the sun, including solar flares and sun spots.[55]

In August the usual meteor showers almost "totally failed," but an astronomer in Mexico photographed "bodies" that crossed the disk of the sun on a west-east course; he counted 283 in two hours. They appeared to be similar to those seen earlier in the year in Marseilles.

Hailstorms and tornadoes continued, bringing great destruction. An editorial in the *London Standard* noted the "horrible" cyclones in the American Midwest and observed that cutting down forests disturbed the rainfall patterns, causing drouths and floods. Could Americans, in time, learn to subdue or at least ameliorate the harmful effects of these storms? Perhaps, for example, they could take a lesson from the Swiss (who had developed a style of architecture designed to withstand avalanches) and "adopt a mode of building suited to the necessities of the case."[56]

A patent medicine company turned the widespread concern about storms to its own advantage. Dr. Horace Hamilton, in a lecture published on August 10 in the *Rush City Post*, noted that although scientists had long investigated tornadoes, storm after storm continued to sweep across the land "carrying destruction to scientists as well as to the innocent dwellers in its track." Dr. Hamilton pointed out that dark spots on the sun invariably seemed to cause great commotion on the Earth. The cause was far away — even as the cause of a headache may be found far away from the head in the liver or kidneys. While Dr. Hamilton had no specific remedy for tornadoes, he recommended for headaches a treatment by "the wonderful power of Warner's Safe Cure."

Learned scientists arrived in Minneapolis to deliberate on tornadoes and other phenomena in mid-August, convening for the thirty-second annual meeting of the American Association for the Advancement of Science (AAAS). The Donnellys were invited to attend the opening reception, and Ignatius was asked to speak at one of the social events scheduled for the distinguished visitors.[57]

The well-turned phrases of the state's dignitaries on opening day were soon followed by discussions of the burning scientific issues of the time. William Watts Folwell, president of the University of Minnesota, noted that the doctrine of evolution had "quietly taken possession of the modern mind." It was a most useful working hypothesis of the *mode* of creation, but the mystery of that creation would, he predicted, "forever mock the powers of man." The supposed conflict between science and religion over evolution, he said, was no more than crude theories on the part of science and cruder superstitions on the religious side. Science and religion should work together in the search for truth.[58]

Professor John W. Dawson, outgoing president of the association, gave a less conciliatory response. Nature may advance by leaps and bounds, he insisted, as well as by long, slow change. In fact, his own investigations indicated that an environment of expansion, not one of struggle, furnished more satisfactory conditions for developing new forms of life. Evolution was a theory, not proven, and not science, and was "not only fatal to the Bible, but to science as well, for in giving up the divine ancestry of man we give up all science."

Professor Edward D. Cope of Pennsylvania, representing those who opposed Dawson's views, pointed out that biologists considered evolution a fact, not a theory; he had no doubt that the link between man and the higher forms of apes was not a large one and would be found. It was in the organism's mental response to impact and strain, he insisted, that the "true origin of the fittest" would be found.

Among the presentations were many of interest to Donnelly, especially those on geology. Scientists carried on a lively and sometimes bitterly contentious debate on ice and glaciers. Professor Dawson argued that "perpetual snow" was only local, not continental in extent; he did not think glaciers could have moved huge granite boulders 4,000 feet above sea level along the line of the Canadian Pacific Railway. Professor J. S. Newberry of New York, arguing for the continental ice theory, branded opposing views heresies held out of either ignorance or error. The Great Lakes owed their origin to the erosive effects of ice, said Newberry. Others, including Professor T. Sterry Hunt of Montreal, argued that there was no reason to believe that glaciers had created the lakes; one scientist called this hypothesis "sheer nonsense" and "arrant folly."[59]

Among the boulders and other debris of the scientific debate Donnelly found a choice nugget in Professor Newberry's admission that geologists could not explain the cause or causes of the ice age. Newberry said that no earthly agency could have brought about such widespread and stupendous results. A variation in the heat of the sun, changes in the Earth's orbit, or some other all-powerful "extraneous and cosmical" influence must have been responsible. For an explanation of the cause of the ice age, the geologist looked to the astronomer.[60]

The outspoken divisions of opinion among the geologists encouraged Donnelly to hope that some of the savants were ready to take *Ragnarok* more seriously. Not waiting for that moment, he turned the ice-age debate to his own advantage, summarizing the arguments from the point of view of *Ragnarok* for Edgar L. Wakeman, a correspondent of the *Louisville Courier Journal*. A column appearing in that paper, which seems to be part Donnelly's and part Wakeman's, asserted that the intelligent public had accepted the theory of *Ragnarok* and scientists had been "set to thinking," as the ice-age debate at the meeting showed. "We are gradually learning," the authors argued, "that we are part of the universe; one of a family — not a cosmic orphan; and that a storm can not occur on the face of the sun, 90,000,000 of miles distant, but that the face of this little orb responds in cyclones and earthquakes."[61]

Meanwhile the storms on Earth continued, with winds that leveled buildings in Montana and Dakota followed by unseasonable cold. Ice was reported to be an inch thick in Yellowstone Park.[62]

But the most widely publicized of the season's storms to hit Minnesota struck on August 21. It did the greatest damage to Rochester, a town of 6,000 on the Zumbro River, the seat of Olmsted County, and a wheat marketing center. Rochester had six churches, two weekly newspapers, five flour mills, a grain elevator, a creamery, a carriage factory, an iron foundry, the state hospital for the insane, a convent of the Sisters of St. Francis, and a number of doctors, but no hospital.[63]

All day on August 21 the weather was unsettled and a high southeast wind tossed clouds about the sky. It was nearly 3:00 in the afternoon when a black cloud appeared in the west, but a furious wind drove it away. Two hours later low black clouds approached from the southeast, assuming a "horrible appearance" as they neared the city. The sky glowed with "a ghastly sort of lurid light, indescribably awful, and referred to by many as inducive of strange mental disturbances." The clouds swept around in gigantic circles. It grew dark and a whirling, swaying funnel west and south of the city moved to the northeast, down the valley of Cascade Creek, in a track a mile wide.

The storm struck Rochester at 7:00 and lasted from 12 to 15 minutes. The greenish sky changed to a copper color and the monster wind drew into its whirling mass trees, stones, animals, and debris of every description. Trees snapped like a "cat o' nine tails" or were "twisted like corkscrews . . . and lifted bodily into the air with tons of earth clinging to their roots. Animals were dashed against stone walls, and their backs and bones crushed to powder. The roar of the wind was like nothing ever heard before," and the atmosphere was charged with electricity. Pellets of rain and hail were driven as if shot from a rifle.

The elevator crashed onto the railroad tracks. Two bridges over the Zumbro were destroyed; the Methodist church lay in ruins; other churches and the insane asylum were damaged. North of the railroad

179

line not one whole structure was left standing and every public building in the rest of the city was damaged. All telegraph lines into the city were down.

Some buildings simply disappeared. Others collapsed into cellars, crushing those who had taken refuge there. A "cyclonic bite" was taken from a big flour mill; its owner was hurled against a wall, his body crushed. Familiar landmarks were gone and it was almost impossible to identify the site of any home in the area.

Just as the storm struck, Doctors Will and Charlie Mayo drove across the Zumbro River in their buggy. After they had crossed the bridge, it was smashed to bits. A cornice of the Cook House Hotel crashed onto the dashboard of their buggy and broke its shaft and wheels. The two young men at once found their father, Dr. William W. Mayo, who with other doctors set up temporary emergency hospital stations. All night long, by the fitful light of lanterns, men searched for the wounded and dead. The Sisters of St. Francis joined the doctors and many other volunteers in caring for the hurt and homeless.[64]

Many of the injured were cut and bruised about the upper parts of their bodies with dirt and powdered stone ground into their wounds. Mothers and fathers searched frantically in the darkness for lost children, some of whom were so disfigured by dirt, blood, and wounds as to be unrecognizable to their own parents. Survivors wandered around the sites of demolished houses, crying bitterly and "almost bereft of reason."

The storm cut a swath of destruction from three-quarters to two and a half miles wide across parts of Olmsted, Dodge, Wabasha, and Winona counties in Minnesota before raging on into Iowa and Wisconsin.

After the storm, aid from other communities poured into the area. There were 110 homes to be rebuilt, 253 families to clothe, nearly 100 injured to care for, and 35 dead to be buried. Donnelly's son Iggy wrote his father, "I thought of Ragnarok where the account says that even the earth was carried in places away." But as Donnelly had noted in *Ragnarok*, out of great tragedy some good could come. The Sisters of St. Francis decided to build a hospital; from the collaboration of the sisters and the Doctors Mayo came the foundation of the medical center known throughout the world as the Mayo Clinic.[65]

In a reaction that had become habitual by August of that memorable year, the *St. Paul Pioneer Press* reported the tragic events and then attempted to discern causes, assign responsibilities, and advocate preventive measures. It was generally believed that the sudden throwing together of air strata of different temperatures and densities gave birth to cyclones. The original cause of the pressure was a mystery. Since the breeding ground for tornadoes appeared to be in the unbroken plains and prairies of the West, perhaps building houses and barns, or planting trees alternated with fields of grain, could prevent or ameliorate the effects of cyclonic winds. The paper did not join the many others who blamed the Signal Service for not giving proper warning of storms. It had reported a high pressure area in the west but it would have needed the gift of prophecy to foretell the probable course of the tornado. Considering what was known about cyclones, the whole state could be kept in "perpetual alarm" to no purpose.[66]

The *New York Times*, from an East Coast vantage point, viewed the matter somewhat differently. Meteorologists, it said, should study storms and their warning signs. "Whether or not this be an exceptional year, it would seem to be a legitimate task for the Signal Bureau to analyze the observations that have been or may be made, and instruct the people of the portions of the country subject to such storms as to the means of recognizing their approach. Life and limb at least could be rendered more secure in this way." But in the last analysis, the *Times* put the burden of responsibility on the public. "It will probably, however, require numerous such experiences to change the habits of people sufficiently to obtain any serious gain in safety."[67]

In the ten days between August 15 and 25, while newspaper editors moralized, the old Earth shivered, shook, and burned in numerous places, and many strange things occurred in the sky. Fires "apparently caused by spontaneous combustion" swept over the cities of Rock Island and Moline, Illinois, and Davenport, Iowa. In Chicago blazes destroyed the U.S. Rolling Stock Company car shops and the Western Union Telegraph Company offices. On New York's Long Island a huge oil tank exploded and burned. On Rainy Lake at Rat Portage, Ontario, a new lumber mill was totally destroyed by fire; arson was suspected. At Williamsport, Pennsylvania, 30 million board feet of lumber went up in flames. Fierce winds and rainstorms hit Winnipeg. Seas were running heavy in the Atlantic; a meteor considerably brighter than Venus shone over England; "afterglow" was reported in the sky over California and in South Africa; San Francisco felt an earthquake shock. In Australia ashes dropped from the sky and snow fell for the first time in 25 years at Victoria.[68]

Eruptions began again on the quaking island of Krakatoa on August 21, the day of the Rochester tornado. Avalanches of ash and stone spilled down the mountainsides, bridges were down, roads sank into the ground, and the waters of the strait were 60 degrees hotter than usual. Mountainous waves lashed the coast 500 miles away. Waterspouts leaped from the sea. Almost all of the volcanoes on Java and Sumatra began vomiting enormous streams of mud and lava. The rumbling on the night of August 25 kept people awake a hundred miles away, and in the midst of the upheaval spectacular showers of meteors or "volcanic bombs" were visible in the sky.[69]

Nothing in modern history equaled the force of the volcanic explosions on August 27. Krakatoa erupted four times, tearing itself apart; its third explosion was so violent that it was heard more than 3,000 miles away. The entire Malayan archipelago, 65 miles of volcanoes, exploded and sank into the sea. Debris darkened the sky for hundreds of miles around. The explosions generated colossal tidal waves that engulfed thousands of helpless people and hundreds of villages. The shock waves raced around the world at an estimated 350 miles an hour; sound waves circled the globe more than seven times; whirlwinds swept into the air what soil remained above the ocean in the afflicted area. Fourteen new volcanic mountain peaks rose in the Sunda Straits, each bursting lava, steam, and stones.

There was no way to blame human beings for the Krakatoa catastrophe. Said the *Pioneer Press* on August 30: "In all the chronicles of casualties known to the human race nothing has occurred to picture so completely to the imagination the pitiable helplessness of man in the face of natural forces. A human being is as much out of place in such an eruption as he would have been in chaos endeavoring to walk on gaseous and nebulous matter." The paper saw no "earthly utility" in the catastrophe — unless it could perhaps assist "certain good people who are in need of symbols to describe a future state consequent on certain transgressions of the moral law."

The *New York Times* on the same day noted a possible meaning for science. "Anti-cataclysmists in geology have for a long time had so much the better of the controversy that there can now scarcely be said to be a controversy. But the changes that have been wrought in Java within a few minutes must give rise to doubts whether many geological problems may not fairly be referred to the hypothesis of cataclysmic changes."

Readers of *Atlantis* and *Ragnarok* could see verification of some of Ignatius Donnelly's theories. In a single day, in a great convulsion triggered by an unknown cause, a huge area of land had, like Atlantis, sunk into the sea. The drift of Krakatoa settled seven feet thick in some places; like that of *Ragnarok* it needed no glacier or eons of time to grind its particles fine.

Day by day, as the world gathered more details of the terrible catastrophe in Java, people saw more comparisons with the Atlantis story. The *St. Louis Spectator* said, "Mr. Donnelly foreshadowed to almost the minutest particular, exactly what has happened at Java." *Harpers Weekly* stated that the explosion showed Donnelly's theory to be "highly probable." The *Philadelphia Evening Star* offered evidence from the eruption of Krakatoa "to substantiate and confirm the theory of the lost Atlantis."[70]

Donnelly, meanwhile, was enjoying himself as one of the guests of honor at the festivities celebrating the completion of the Northern Pacific rail line to the Pacific. As one of the congressmen who had sponsored the land grant legislation for railroads, he mingled with such other dignitaries as former President Ulysses S. Grant (who looked "older and puffy about the face . . . [with a] grim, saturnine countenance"), President Chester A. Arthur, Northern Pacific president Henry Villard, and Carter Harrison, the mayor of Chicago, who was enthusiastic about *Ragnarok*. "You are a genius, Donnelly," he told Ignatius, "but as crazy as a loon — all original thinkers are crazy." Some of the visiting British dukes and earls told him they had read *Atlantis*, but Bishop John Ireland was far better company. He was "⁹⁄₁₀ths of a convert to the 'Ragnarok' theory," noted Donnelly in his diary, and the two had a long conversation after the festivities.[71]

On September 6 Baltimore's annual Oriole parade and pageant took Atlantis as its theme and boosted sales of the book. But Donnelly was not yet satisfied with the public and private acclaim coming his way. He had hoped vainly for some serious consideration of *Ragnarok* by the scientific community. The fact that some geologists were dissatisfied with the the ice theories, and had said so at the AAAS meetings, was not enough. Donnelly wanted *Popular Science Monthly*, Appleton's own publication, to give *Ragnarok* more friendly notice than it had carried in its February issue.[72]

In February *Popular Science* had called the book's theories "absurd"; in June Professor Youmans had labeled Donnelly's performance "ridiculous." Donnelly had not protested. Now, in September, he was ready to do battle. He began corresponding with O. B. Bunce, his editor at Appleton, arguing that the publisher should insist on a more favorable notice of a book it had published in a magazine it owned.

Bunce did not agree. One had to accept the fact that a "scientific" publication could not publish views on scientific subjects unless they came from an "authoritative" source. An article on *Ragnarok* would be appropriate in a popular magazine, Bunce said, "but a science magazine having a reputation as a scientific authority to maintain is another thing."

Donnelly fumed. On such grounds Darwin would have been denied a hearing a generation earlier. On such a principle "the Pope imprisoned Galileo." He quoted to Bunce the words of Professor Newberry at the AAAS meeting: "for the causes of the Drift we must turn to the astronomer for there is no merely earthly cause that could have produced such results." He chided Bunce for allowing *Popular Science Monthly* to print an article that called the theories in *Ragnarok* absurd.

Bunce replied that Appleton did not tell the *Popular Science* editors what to print. If a geologist of good repute would speak out in favor of *Ragnarok* the pages of the magazine would be open to him. Donnelly argued that the so-called authorities in geology could be counted on the fingers of one hand. He did not know any of them, and futhermore, all had probably committed themselves in lectures or in books to the ice theory of the origin of the drift. Bunce, ignoring all possibilities of appeal to scholars, terminated the discussion: "It is impossible for scientific men to consider the book as serious science, and we never supposed it would be so considered."

Curiously enough, Donnelly made no effort to enlist the support of astronomers. But he called Bunce's attention to no less an authority than the astronomer C. A. Young, who wrote in the *North American Review* (Boston) that a cometary collision with Earth or the sun was "practically certain" some time, and such an encounter would devastate wide areas of the globe.[73]

Donnelly was to receive one response from a geologist of stature who

183

seriously addressed his theories of the drift. In November he sent a copy of *Ragnarok*, with a request for an opinion, to the brilliant, charming, and iconoclastic Dr. T. Sterry Hunt of Montreal, whom he had met at the AAAS meeting in Minneapolis. Hunt, called by some egotistical, scintillating, strident, and obsessive, was a talented nonconformist who had been a chemist and mineralogist on the Canadian Geological Survey, a professor of geology at both Massachusetts Institute of Technology and McGill College in Montreal; he had been a prime mover in the organization of the American Chemical Society and of the First International Congress of Geologists.[74]

Hunt, often on the "skirmish lines" of scientific controversy, had retired from teaching and was devoting his time to writing. He wrote Donnelly a long thoughtful letter about *Ragnarok*, saying that he believed water, ice, and the uplifting of continents accounted for the drift, but the "previous question" was how rock decayed to form the clay of the drift. Hunt considered Donnelly's assumption that drift was composed of disintegrated granite a "fatal defect" in his theory. He said the drift was no more disintegrated granite than alcohol was disintegrated wheat, and it was possible to explain it without invoking a comet. While he branded some of the ideas of glaciologist James Dana as the "wildest nonsense imaginable," Hunt had kinder words for *Atlantis*: "I think your former book . . . accounts sufficiently for the legends which you have brought together & render[s] unnecessary the second [cometary] hypothesis which I cannot regard as in any way tenable." The Canadian trusted that Donnelly would pardon his frankness, "as I know you, like myself, are a seeker after truth," and he encouraged Donnelly to prepare a revised edition of *Atlantis*.

Donnelly's autumn was otherwise a pleasant one. In delightful fall weather — the corn yellow, the leaves turning bright — he took the train for Brown's Valley, stopping on the way to see his daughter and her husband at Morris. He was met at the Brown's Valley depot by a band of musicians and several leading citizens, including Gabriel Renville, a Dakota Indian leader. Renville and others of his band of Indian farmers joined local white residents in attending Donnelly's speeches at the county fair and at the schoolhouse. The lecturer spoke of Atlantis and the flood, the Bible and Indian legends, Krakatoa and the brotherhood of man. A reporter said that Donnelly was "the most interesting and instructive speaker who has ever visited Brown's Valley."[75]

Near the end of the month Donnelly attended a fair at the Roman Catholic Church of the Guardian Angels in Hastings. Before the festivities he chatted with several Catholic priests about *Atlantis* and *Ragnarok*. He found them "all believers in the Ragnarokian theory & ready to regard much of Genesis as a collection of ancient legends." Such views in years past, Donnelly thought, would have sent them to the stake, but now the priests assured him that "similar views are expressed in Europe by clergymen without any condemnation by the Pope." Donnelly's lecture on "The Growth and Prosperity of Our Country" discussed the progress of agriculture, the need for farmers to treat land as something sacred, and the grandeur of farm life, with every house having a cupola, or if not a cupola, at least a mortgage. After 45 minutes of sparkling Donnelly wit the audience applauded and they all sat down together to an oyster supper.

But for many other people around the world, the remaining months of 1883 carried on the patterns of destruction and disaster. High seas and violent storms on the oceans followed the explosions of Krakatoa, causing worldwide damage to shipping. Buildings in cities across the United States burned; because of the large numbers of local fires, insurance companies announced a 25 per cent increase in their rates for Minneapolis. Earthquakes killed 2,000 in Smyrna, Turkey, and shook Algeria, southern Spain, Malta, and Bermuda. A volcano erupted near Cook Inlet, Alaska, spreading ashes five inches deep on the water; shock waves were felt in San Francisco and a new island, a mile and a half long, rose out of the ocean.[76]

On November 9 at Madison, Wisconsin, a young university student named Frank Lloyd Wright watched the south wing of the Wisconsin state capitol suddenly collapse into a pile of rubble. Wright clung to a fence watching the rescue of men caught in the wreckage and the recovery of the bodies of the dead. The horror of the scene remained in his memory to "prompt" him during his long and illustrious career as an architect. An inquiry into the cause of the disaster showed the contractor at fault for carelessness; the architect was ruined.

A tremendous mid-November gale swept across the continent from British Columbia to New England and Newfoundland, causing vast damage to forests and Great Lakes shipping. Among the ships lost or wrecked was the steamer "Manistee" of the Lake Superior and South Shore Line. Sailing with a heavy cargo, it vanished in the storm between Ashland, Wisconsin, and Ontonagon, Michigan, with 19 crew members and four passengers. Across New England and particularly in northern Maine, the storm mowed over thousands of acres of pine timber. The *New York Times* reported that the blast, following years of reckless cutting and wanton burning, had crippled the lumber industry for years and destroyed millions of acres that could not recover in less than a century. President Arthur noted this damage and that of the earlier floods in his annual message to Congress. These "irregularities," he said, were in great measure caused by the removal of the timber that protected the sources of the water; he recommended the establishment of forest preserves as a matter of highest consequence.

Continued reports of brilliant meteors and sightings of comets prompted the *New York Times* to comment on September 26: "This has been an extraordinary year for disturbances, celestial and terrestrial. The startling behavior of Brook's comet as described by the astronomers, and recent earthquakes in this vicinity have led anxious persons to inquire if the *Sun* is not likely to suffer some injury and whether these strange phenomena do not foreshadow the end of the *World*."

But it was the appearance of the sky toward the end of 1883 that impressed all observers. As early as the end of August reports came from

Brazil, Trinidad, and India of a sun that appeared blue or green. An old sea captain later described the moon over Chinese seas as "blue as a hedge sparrow's egg."[77]

On December 9 Donnelly noted in his diary, "For a week or more a strange red light has preceded sunrise and followed sunset." It appeared almost as though there were a fire southwest of Nininger. "This phenomenon has attracted great attention in the east & it has, very reasonably been suggested that it might be due to a great mass of meteoric matter around the sun or between the sun & earth, which lighted by the sun's rays, shone by reflected light while the sun is below the horizon. At the same time we are having exceptionally warm weather — every day the thermometer is above the freezing point. The same dust or gravel that reflects light must reflect increased heat to the earth. Now if it would drop upon the earth . . ."

On the day that Donnelly made those notes, hundreds of people in Philadelphia stood gazing at an extraordinary two-hour spectacle in the sky. A reporter for the *Philadelphia Star* wrote, "The red globe of the sun descended below the house tops about half-past four o'clock, and a fantastic transformation of the sky began about fifteen minutes later. The air became suffused with a yellowish haze, and through it the sky around and just above the sun, shone with a brilliant pale green, which as it stretched toward the zenith, gradually changed to pale pink." A glittering metallic moon appeared as the sun set. Dark clouds spreading across the sky turned to a pea-green, "the beauty of which was greatly enhanced by the rosy background of the sky." As the green coloring gradually disappeared, the western sky filled with a "blood red blaze" like flames and smoke. "It was after six o'clock before the weird colors in the sky had died out and the stars appeared in the darkened dome."

Although scientists agreed that the red glow and other unusual hues in the sky did not appear to be "aural" or "electrical," and that they persisted through a variety of atmospheric conditions, they could not agree on the reasons for the phenomena. Some theorized that they were produced by the diffusion through the atmosphere of ashes and cinders from Krakatoa. Those who argued against that theory thought that this debris could not have so quickly reached the enormous heights necessary for it to be visible around the world as early as August. There was also, said *Appletons' Cyclopaedia*, "the difficulty of its remaining suspended so long." With Donnelly, they believed that the Earth had passed through a cloud of "cosmic dust," noting that persons in England and Switzerland had collected unusual amounts of fine matter, like that of meteoric stones, in fresh-fallen snow. One astronomer calculated that the glow originated about 61 miles above the Earth's surface and that it was a reflection from meteoric dust.[78]

The irrepressible purveyor of Warner's Kidney and Liver Cure was "pretty certain" that the Earth was "enveloped in the misty substance of the tail of some unseen comet or a surrounding stratum of world dust or very small meteors." The threat to health was grave, but a man who kept his liver and kidneys in good shape could expect to gain "immunity from the destructive influences which seek his ruin."[79]

On Christmas Day a bobsled full of Donnellys went to church at Hastings, heard a good sermon, and returned home to enjoy a "royal dinner." On New Year's Eve Donnelly looked back on the year. His daughter was happily married, one son was established in his profession, and the second son was well on the way to being a "great lawyer." He was in good health; his wife's health had improved; and he had been able to meet all his financial demands. Although the public reception of his two books had brought him national attention during the year, he did not dwell on his literary success, noting only that he had "practically solved the great cipher of Francis Bacon in the Shakespeare plays." The year of 1883, so tragic for so many, gave Donnelly many blessings to count. "I may therefore," he concluded, "write down 1883 as a golden year in my calendar."[80]

8

Reindeer People
Including
THE ALASKAN REINDEER SERVICE
and
THE CHRISTMAS REINDEER SHOWS

FAR BACK *in history, perhaps even in prehistoric times, the reindeer (cervidae, species Rangifer tarandus) was hunted, captured, herded, and harnessed by man in the arctic and subarctic regions of Norway, Sweden, Finland, Russia, and Siberia. The reindeer was admirably suited to arctic life. Its soft brown-gray coat, with each hair shaped like a hollow tube, provided the animal with the finest of natural insulation against the cold. Arctic mosses, lichens, grasses, and shrubs furnished the reindeer's food which its keen sense of smell enabled it to detect beneath the snow. With padded and deeply cloven hoofs it could walk easily on the snow and dig beneath it for food.[1]*

Full grown, the reindeer was not a large animal; it stood less than five feet tall and measured, on an average, some seven feet from nose to tip of tail. Yet, trained by man, it carried burdens on its back and pulled heavily loaded sleds. Man provided the deer a supply of salt and some protection against its predator, the wolf. Man's campfire smoke kept mosquitoes away from the deer, and when man played a musical instrument or sang, the deer stood and listened "as children would with a music teacher."

The semidomesticated deer provided man with friendship, transportation, food, clothing, and most other basic needs for life in the arctic regions. This antlered creature, an "herbivorous, graminivorous, gregarious, semi-migratory, ruminant and ungulate mammal," dependable, docile, and intelligent, became "among the earliest and best friends man has ever had."[2]

One man more than all others deserves credit for introducing this remarkable animal to North America. Sheldon Jackson, once a Presbyterian minister in southern Minnesota, was not the first person to say that the reindeer, like its North American cousin the caribou (Rangifer stonei and other related species) could thrive in the American Arctic. Nor was he first to suggest that reindeer culture could provide a significant addition to the economy of the Eskimo and of all Alaska. But Jackson saw the possibilities and he had the vision, the energy and

*enthusiasm, the fund-raising and political skills to make the experiment
and see the project through. During his tenure as agent for education
in Alaska for the United States Bureau of Education, reindeer were
brought to North America, were nurtured, throve, and multiplied.
Jackson carried out his reindeer projects with the help of other midwesterners, including Hedley E. Redmyer of Cook County, Minnesota.*

*Reindeer for food, clothing, and fun! The Minnesota reindeer con-
nection begins with Jackson and Redmyer in Alaska, and moves on to
the Lomens of St. Paul and Nome. It continues into the 1930s with other
reindeer people — Nicholas Dimond, his wife, and his northeastern
Minnesota associates from Duluth, Grand Portage, Clearwater Lake,
and Ray — Charlie and Alec Boostrom, Clifford Samuelson, Hermund
Melheim — and others yet unidentified beneath parkas, grease paint,
and Santa Claus whiskers.*³

The Alaskan Reindeer Service

A Presbyterian Minister and his Midwestern Associates
Introduce Reindeer to North America

SHELDON JACKSON (1834–1909) was born in Minaville, in upstate
New York, the son of strongly religious Presbyterian parents. He
attended Union College, Schenectady, New York, and after
graduating entered Princeton Theological Seminary to prepare for a
career in the foreign mission field. When the Presbyterian mission board
concluded that he was not physically strong enough for a foreign assignment, he was sent to teach in a Choctaw mission school in Oklahoma.⁴

Jackson and his wife, Mary Voorhees Jackson, went to Oklahoma
shortly after their marriage in 1858 but stayed only a year. Jackson discovered that he did not like teaching; in addition he contracted malaria,
and he found the southern climate debilitating.

In 1859 Jackson and his wife were transferred to the more invigo-
rating climate of Minnesota, where he became a home missionary with
headquarters at La Crescent on the Mississippi River in Houston
County. Under his diligent cultivation, his mission field soon extended
from Chippewa Falls, Wisconsin, to Jackson, Minnesota, over an area of
13,000 square miles. For ten years, in all seasons, he looked after his
broad parish.

During his Minnesota years Jackson developed a special talent for
raising money. In 1860 he organized a "Raven Fund," named for the Old
Testament story of Elijah and the ravens, to solicit from friends and
churches in the East contributions that would help the struggling young
congregations in his home mission parish. The funds were used to build
church structures, to supplement salaries of pastors until the local congregations were large enough to pay them adequately, and to meet other
needs not provided for in the denominations' budgets. According to

Sheldon Jackson, 1834–1909.
*Presbyterian Historical Society,
Philadelphia*

Arthur Lazell, a Jackson biographer, the Raven Fund was evidence that "Sheldon Jackson refused to sit and wait for manna to fall from heaven if he had any way of plucking it from the skies."

By 1869, the year the first railroad to the Pacific Coast was completed, Jackson saw a greater field of service beckoning in the West. He and friends who shared his concerns convinced a regional Presbyterian Conference at Sioux City, Iowa, that the church should follow the people. As a result, the conference, which lacked funds to offer Jackson a salary, appointed him its missionary superintendent for seven Rocky Mountain states — a parish covering 571,000 square miles. Belatedly, the Presbyterian mission board in New York recognized the importance of what he was doing and gave him an official appointment that carried with it a salary of $1,500 a year, but no travel funds.[5]

In the Rocky Mountain region Jackson refined the skills he had developed in Minnesota. Far from the seat of church power, he often took action in "an aggressive spirit" to carry out projects before they had received official approval. Somehow he was able to justify and finance them. Sometimes it seemed to his superiors on the mission board that he was traveling too far and too fast. They suggested that instead of looking for new projects he should settle down and cultivate his fields more deeply. But all attempts to control Jackson were useless.

In the first year of his work in the Rocky Mountain region Jackson traveled 29,000 miles, through mountains and blizzards, by stage, on horseback, and on foot, to organize 22 churches. When money was slow in coming from the mission board, he dusted off his "Raven" hat to raise funds. In addition to his regular duties he received an appointment with the Board of Indian Commissioners to escort Indian children from the Southwest to government schools in the East. In 1872 he launched the *Rocky Mountain Presbyterian*, a four-page monthly that both provided "an excellent picture of the people, places and problems of the west" and encouraged readers to contribute money to Jackson's projects — some under way, and others not yet begun.

In 1877 Jackson heard of a new mission field that was to occupy him the rest of his life. He learned about it in a letter from an army private stationed at Wrangell, Alaska. As many as a thousand Indians lived in the vicinity and, the writer said, a school and mission could "reclaim a mighty flock." Jackson visited Wrangell, encouraged another missionary to start a school there, and traveled to New York to tell the Presbyterian mission board what he had done. The board, presented with a newly organized school and a teacher in residence, as well as a fund of $12,000 that Jackson had raised from private sources, accepted his commitment to the first Presbyterian mission in Alaska.[6]

In the more than ten years since Alaska had been purchased from Russia, prevailing public opinion regarded the territory as practically worthless. Congress was not far behind in this view. Jackson, in his zeal to educate everyone about "Uncle Sam's Icebox," delivered some 900 speeches to church and nonchurch groups between 1878 and 1884. He moved to Washington in 1883 and became a virtual one-man Alaska lobby. The need for schools in the territory was his primary concern; he worked with the National Education Association and other organizations to persuade Congress to establish the system of public education promised the territory when it was purchased.[7]

In 1884 Congress passed legislation that provided for a civilian administration in Alaska. The new law established a public school system under the U.S. Bureau of Education in the Department of the Interior; in 1885 Jackson was appointed the bureau's first agent for education in Alaska. He held the position for more than twenty years.

In the minds of many his name was already synonymous with Alaska. He was fifty years old — not young, but vigorous, fervent, and resourceful. Well connected in the Washington bureaucracy and on Capitol Hill, he had friends on both sides of the political aisle and his superiors in the department were warmly supportive. Jackson was, moreover, well known throughout the country, he had easy access to the news media, and he was highly regarded by educators and church people of many persuasions. He was backed, in short, by a formidable constituency.

On the other hand, he was at times opinionated, stubborn, shortsighted, and at odds with colleagues in Alaska on trivial matters as well as substantial issues. He was constantly criticized, even ridiculed, by persons whom he had irritated and by others who were equally critical of any champion of a region that seemed so far removed from the nation's vital interests. He struggled constantly with problems of inadequate funding and the need, with each change of political administration, to solicit, cajole, and educate new sets of public officials.

There were other obstacles. Travel was difficult both to Alaska and over the vast distances and rugged terrain within the territory, and it was nearly impossible during much of the year when rivers and seas were frozen. Alaska had few roads and, until the end of the century, no railroads. Civil government, as well as the school system, was woefully underfunded. With little or no government presence in many areas, white men introduced liquor to the natives and operated uncontrolled commercial enterprises that were rapidly depleting game and fish resources. In many places the worst elements of white culture already threatened the native ways of life.[8]

Jackson had seen at first hand in Minnesota and in the Rocky Mountain West what happened when government vacillated and whites were allowed to prey on the American Indians — and how, when the Indians' own economy was destroyed, they became public wards. He saw in Alaska the same threatening circumstances and hoped, as did many enlightened Americans of his day, that an adequate system of education would prepare the natives for citizenship and help them to meet in self-reliant ways the problems that arrived with the whites' technology and culture.

The impatient Jackson, in pursuing his educational programs for Alaska, was not prepared to wait for manna either from heaven or from the federal government. When budgets were inadequate, or when money was not appropriated, he dramatized needs and called on the public to help him meet them. With such a mix of public and private support he was able to launch one of his most ambitious programs, that of introducing reindeer culture to the American Arctic.

While at first glance there may have seemed no logical reason for making reindeer culture a staple of the educational system in Alaska, Jackson saw ample precedent. Since the 1860s the federal government had provided financial support for colleges and their associated experiment stations to foster educational and vocational training in agriculture. In a region where the raising of crops and animals from temperate climates was impractical, reindeer culture could be a valuable substitute. Furthermore, since the federal government had spent much money promoting agriculture among the Indians in the western territories, why should it not make a similar investment in the promotion of reindeer culture among the Alaskan natives?[9]

But why reindeer? The idea was not original, and to Jackson and his supporters the argument was simple. Reindeer flourished on arctic vegetation; in Asia and northern Europe they were successfully herded and contributed materially to the economic well-being of arctic people. They could, therefore, likewise be herded, flourish, and contribute to the well-being of natives of the American Arctic. Some critics said the natives of Alaska would not want to herd reindeer. Natives who were traditionally hunters and fishermen could not be expected to change their life style. The proponents of reindeer culture argued that the native life style was already changing because of the encroachments of the whites, and it was now a question of *what* changes to make. Reindeer culture offered an environmentally and economically sound way to meet basic needs of Alaskan natives for food and clothing.[10]

Jackson wasted no time in taking action once the idea was fixed in his mind. When Congress refused to support a reindeer experiment, he appealed through the press for contributions. Appreciative readers sent him more than $2,000. The Raven Fund had become a Reindeer Fund![11]

In the next two years, with a creative mix of public and private support, Jackson was able to overcome the doubts of many. The Revenue Cutter Service of the U.S. Treasury Department took Jackson to Siberia, where he bought deer and hired herdsmen to care for them. Religious groups with schools in Alaska accepted loans of deer to start herds and reindeer herding became part of the schools' curricula. Eskimo students became apprentices supervised by Siberian herders. The government budget paid for teachers; the mission budget covered school supplies. It was not always clear to the public who, other than the ubiquitous Dr. Jackson, was responsible for the innovations.[12]

The first herd, with herdsmen, landed on the Alaskan mainland at Port Clarence in July, 1892. The station established there was named for Jackson's friend, Senator and former Secretary of the Interior Henry Teller, who in 1893 helped persuade Congress to make its first direct appropriation for Jackson's reindeer experiment. By September, 1893, the herd had grown, through births and purchases, from its original 171 to 346 animals. But the Siberians proved to be unsatisfactory as herders or teachers; they were careless with the deer and not well liked by the Eskimos. Jackson decided to send the Siberians home and to hire Lapps, reputedly the most highly skilled in reindeer culture, to replace them. Jackson's later reports to Congress argued that the Lapps had much to recommend them. For them, the deer substituted for the horse, cow, sheep, and goat; their way of life depended on the animal. Lapps were "civilized and Christianized," thrifty, affluent, moral, expert on skis, and "perfectly cool and self-possessed in the midst of every danger."[13]

In December, 1893, Jackson sent an announcement to Scandinavian-language publications in the United States and Canada headlined "Men Wanted to Take Care of Reindeer in Alaska." Across the continent more than 250 Scandinavians, including several from Minnesota, responded to the notice, most agreeing that men from Lapland and Lapp dogs could best do the work.[14]

From the letter writers Jackson chose 32-year-old William A. Kjell-mann of Madison, Wisconsin, a Norwegian "of robust health and excellent habits" who had herded deer in his native Finmarken, in the Lapp district of Norway, until he was 22. He had then spent six years buying and selling reindeer products in Lapland before immigrating to Madison, where he ran a fish-marketing business.[15]

Jackson made Kjellmann his reindeer superintendent and sent him to Norway to recruit Norwegian-speaking Lapps to replace the Siberians as teachers and herders. Jackson meanwhile searched for a pastor for the

Jackson (second man standing from right) landing the first reindeer at Port Clarence, July 4, 1892. *Presbyterian Historical Society, Philadelphia*

Lapps who could also teach in the government school. He found a man eminently qualified for both duties in Tollef L. Brevig of Crookston, Minnesota. Brevig, a graduate of Luther College in Decorah, Iowa, and Luther Seminary, had taught for twelve years before studying for the ministry of the Norwegian Synod. With manifold duties as a government teacher, reindeer manager and superintendent, minister, missionary, and postmaster, Brevig was to serve in Alaska until 1917.[16]

In Madison, Wisconsin, Brevig and his family joined Kjellmann and his Lapp party of seven men, five women, and four children on their journey across the United States. The train stopped briefly in St. Paul, where the group's exotic appearance brought out the press. Early in the morning of May 22, 1894, while the travelers were sleeping in their special car left on a siding, a curious and impertinent *Pioneer Press* reporter boarded with the connivance of a conductor. As the conductor shone his lantern on the sleeping faces of the immigrants, the reporter took note of their "swarthy" faces, "queer costumes and headgear," and the "pungent odor" in the car. A continuous procession of curious St. Paulites visited Union Station during the day. Some were able to enter the car and "inspect the visitors at close quarters," but soon after breakfast several of the Lapps donned their brightly colored clothes and ventured out to the streets. Followed by "a hundred or more idlers," they wandered about the city, sampling American liquors and laying in a supply of port and blackberry wine, rye and cognac, for their journey west. As they strolled through the state capitol, they met Norwegian-American Governor Knute Nelson, whom they later referred to as "the king of Minnesota." Nelson joined a group at the station wishing the Lapps farewell.[17]

During the three years of the Laplanders' service with the Bureau of Education, Jackson and his reindeer project weathered much misunderstanding and antagonism. Conflicts were perhaps not surprising when one considers the ethnic, national, religious, and bureaucratic amalgam of persons concerned — Eskimos, Laplanders, Norwegians, Swedes, and Siberians, as well as stateside Americans; Lutherans, Catholics, Mission Covenanters, Quakers, Congregationalists, Presbyterians, and federal employees of the United States Navy and the Treasury and Interior departments. People came and went in the reindeer service, and as time passed they learned to understand or to tolerate one another. The reindeer multiplied under careful management in a hospitable environment. In all, through 1897, 538 deer were imported from Siberia. Some 600 were sold, some were butchered or died of other causes, but at the end of that year, despite losses, there were in Alaska 1,132 deer in four herds. Through 1897 Congress had appropriated $33,000 for the reindeer project; this figure does not represent the full cost of the program, as it does not include direct and indirect financial support from private sources and from mission groups.[18]

Jackson described the growth of the program in a series of reports to his superiors in the Department of the Interior. But the 16 reindeer reports published between 1890 and 1906 were, in typical Jackson style, designed for a wider audience. They were lavishly illustrated with maps, photographs, and drawings by native school children, and carried excerpts from the works of popular writers and translations of items from foreign publications. This was the sort of educational resource teachers prized. Journalists, mission groups, and members of Congress turned to them for interesting background information on scenes, events, and inhabitants of the American Arctic. Jackson, who felt the white man's burden resting heavily on his shoulders, explained the objectives of the program in simple terms the average person could understand: "To convert the nomadic tribes of fishers and hunters in northwestern and central Alaska into raisers of reindeer; to change their occupation from the precarious pursuits of hunting wild animals and of taking fish from the waters of inland rivers to that of herders and teamsters; to elevate a people who in their wild, uncivilized state are the prey of unscrupulous transient immigrants into a self-supporting race, not enemies but friendly allies and auxiliaries of the white man."[19]

Jackson's plans for the program reflected these goals in 1897, for example, when four of the Lapp families prepared to return home at the end of their three-year tour of duty. Jackson, well pleased with their service, decided to import more Lapp herders to continue their work. He wanted the department to expand the apprentice program, establish new stations, and train more Siberian reindeer, which he hoped to put to use carrying mail and freight. He and Kjellmann wanted to establish a new station near the fine beds of moss that lay between the mouth of the Tanana River and Circle City, where the Yukon makes a broad loop in its course near the placer gold mines of Birch Creek.[20]

But changes in Jackson's status and in that of Alaska were to shape the next chapter of the reindeer story. In the summer of 1897 Jackson was elected moderator of the general assembly, the highest office of the Presbyterian church. The position gave him greater prestige in Washington and around the country, but it did not silence his critics. Some of them were convinced that the Presbyterians were running affairs in Washington and that Jackson periodically manufactured crises (such as reports of starving natives) to serve his own special interests.[21]

Events of 1897 were cases in point. When a fleet of whaling ships was caught by a sudden arctic winter, 300 sailors were stranded at the government refuge station at Point Barrow. Food supplies were low; no rescue ship could approach through the ice; starvation threatened. Jackson was invited to attend a meeting of President McKinley's cabinet called to discuss the situation. At Jackson's suggestion, a herd of some 400 reindeer at Cape Prince of Wales was driven overland to Barrow. There the would-be rescuers found that the sailors had salvaged some food from the ships' stores and trapped wild game, so that only a part of the herd was needed for food. Jackson decided to use the remaining animals as the nucleus of a new, permanent herd at Barrow for the benefit of Eskimos and as insurance against another such emergency in the Far North.[22]

A second arctic crisis resulted from the mad rush to the gold fields of the Yukon. Word of strikes in the Klondike region of Canada reached the outside world early in 1897, and "Klondicitis" gripped the United States. Military officers sent in August and September to investigate reports of lawlessness reported a mental attitude that "savors strongly of insanity" among those bound for the Klondike. Few of the gold seekers had enough provisions to last more than four months; supplies could not be carried far up the Yukon, as it was unusually low and would soon be frozen; Dawson, in the heart of the Klondike, was overcrowded and already short of food.[23]

The secretary of war, impelled by these and other reports and undoubtedly by suggestions from Jackson and the commissioner of education, recommended that food be taken by reindeer teams to the gold region; that "reindeer be purchased in Lapland to the number of 500 and permission be granted to bring reindeer drivers from that country; this upon the information that it requires much skill to manage these animals."

The uproar over the plight of the miners, the news that growing numbers of Americans were preparing to go to the Klondike in the spring, and the information provided by the secretary of war helped persuade Congress to pass emergency legislation. In late December the secretary, authorized to spend $200,000 for relief, sent Jackson and his helpers to Norway to purchase 500 reindeer broken to harness, gather hundreds of tons of moss to feed them, and recruit drivers — all to be delivered to the United States by February 15.[24]

Kjellmann, who had gone ahead to Norway accompanying the returning Lapps, now heard of his new task from Jackson. In an astounding feat, hampered by a driving blizzard that raged over Lapland,

Kjellmann and his assistants, including two of the returned Lapps, traveled 3,000 miles "through long reaches of unsettled forests, over storm-swept mountains, and along the edges of dizzy precipices in the darkness of night." They purchased 547 reindeer and persuaded 113 Lapps, Finns, and Norwegians to "be ready in two weeks to start for the end of the earth." While Kjellmann searched for Lapp drivers, Jackson and a representative of the U.S. Army dealt with all other diplomatic and fiscal difficulties. The rendezvous on February 1 in Alta, Norway, was "all bustle and excitement," wrote Jackson. "The hundreds of Lapps, in their bright-colored, picturesque national dress, those that were going away and those that had come to see them off, greeting old friends and meeting new ones, the unpacking of sleds and preparations for embarkation, all made a picture never to be forgotten."

The voyage to the United States on the "Manitoban" was no less memorable. The ship sailed for nine days through storms of increasing violence, buffeted by snow, sleet, hail, and winds of hurricane force that smashed a lifeboat and tore away the ship's figurehead. The captain claimed that never in 42 years at sea had he seen a worse storm; Jackson waded through ankle-deep water in his cabin; many of the immigrants were miserably seasick and five people came down with measles. But the reindeer adjusted to the motion of the sea and lay on deck "as if they had been on their native pasture."[25]

Some of the immigrants aboard the "Manitoban" had achieved fame; others were to become famous in the new land. Samuel Balto, a Lapp, had crossed Greenland with Fridtjof Nansen and was decorated for the feat by King Oscar II of Sweden and Norway. Olai Paulsen, a Norwegian, had won three awards from King Oscar for his skill as a rifleman. Johan Stalogargo, a Finn, had for eight years carried mail on the world's northernmost postal route; twelve of the other immigrants had carried mail with reindeer. In later years, Jafet Lindeberg, a Norwegian, would become rich as one of the discoverers of gold at Nome, Alaska, and Andrew Bahr would become the best known of the Laplanders as the hero of another remarkable reindeer trek in the 1930s.

When on February 27 the "Manitoban" tied up next to a cattle barge at the Jersey City stockyards, about a thousand curious people of many nationalities stood on the dock to give the travelers an uproarious welcome. The reindeer and the immigrants boarded two trains of 19 cars each, including sleeping cars for the immigrants, stockcars for the deer, and boxcars for the moss, sleds, and other baggage. Although the expedition did not stop in St. Paul, the *Pioneer Press* of March 4 published a creditable and interesting account of its travels, describing Jackson's plans for the reindeer project and the appearance and habits of the deer. The Laplanders received special notice: "Notwithstanding the general condition of their lives and their nomadic ways, the reindeer drivers and herders are fairly bright men and remarkably domestic in their habits." Most were "Lutherans in church belief and observance," and nearly all could read and write — a prerequisite for confirmation in the Lutheran church. As if to make amends for the amused condescension with which

Lapp men and woman, waiting in Seattle for transportation to Alaska. *Washington State
Historical Society*

the paper had viewed the Lapp expedition in 1894, the *Press* reporter
spoke respectfully of William Kjellmann as the United States government's "expert in the care and exportation of reindeer."[27]

When the trains arrived in Seattle on March 7, 1898, no ship was
ready for the trip to Alaska. It was not surprising that the army's effi-
ciently managed reindeer operation failed at this point. Just three weeks
earlier the battleship "Maine" had been sunk in Havana harbor, and the
army was in the midst of mobilizing for the Spanish-American War. The
immigrants were housed temporarily at Fort Lawton and, to save moss,
the deer were put to pasture in Woodland Park.[28]

But while the expedition had made its way across the country, other
events in Alaska and in Washington, D.C., had caused a drastic alteration in plans. The secretary of war had received news from Alaska that
the miners were not starving and that food sufficient to last until spring
had already reached the mining region. The Lapp-reindeer expedition

198

was not needed and would therefore be canceled. What then should be done with the Lapps and the reindeer?[29]

Dr. Jackson, called upon for suggestions in Washington, was at no loss for ideas. In a proposal submitted to the secretary of war on March 3, Jackson contended that military officials in Alaska would find the deer valuable for transporting supplies, that postal contractors could use them and the Laplanders to carry the mail, and that these animal and human resources would be a happy addition to Jackson's educational program among the Eskimos. The secretary of war, persuaded by these arguments and by the absence of other proposals, transferred custody of the deer and the immigrants to the Department of the Interior and Sheldon Jackson. This contingency, of course, had been in Jackson's mind from the beginning of the Lapp-reindeer expedition.[30]

Jackson drove a good bargain for the reindeer service. The immigrants were to remain on the War Department's payroll for the first year of their two-year contract — or until the deer were delivered to the Yukon. The Department of the Interior, which had paid none of the transportation costs, would then receive a fortuitous and valuable asset for its reindeer service.[31]

Jackson's proposal also arranged for a tidy end to the expedition. Women, children, and men not needed as herders were sent by ship to Unalakleet on Norton Sound. Their destination was the newly established headquarters for the reindeer service, eight miles up the Unalakleet River. Eaton Station, named for General John Eaton, former commissioner of education and staunch Jackson supporter, was supplied with deer from the herd of the Swedish Evangelical Covenant mission at Unalakleet. The immigrants were pressed into service at once, herding deer, moving supplies, and building the station.[32]

Jackson decided to have as many herders as were needed drive the reindeer overland from Haines, south of Skagway on the Lynn Canal,

Reindeer at Woodland Park, Seattle, March, 1898. *Washington State Historical Society*

Hedley Redmyer, *MHS*

to the Yukon Valley between Circle City and the mouth of the Tanana River. There, where Jackson and Kjellmann had found beds of moss the previous year, the deer would be available for a variety of uses. This trip to the Tanana was the crucial and most difficult part of the plan.

To help execute it, Jackson hired a Norwegian Lapp, Hedley Redmyer, who was Kjellmann's cousin. Redmyer's experiences on the drive illustrate the tremendous problems Jackson's reindeer service had constantly to overcome while traveling through the wilderness: finding moss for the herd; watching the animals constantly to guard them from hungry wolves and to keep them from running away with their cousins, the caribou; finding supplies for the herders; and untangling government red tape which impeded rather than speeded their journey.

Redmyer was a good man for the job. Born in 1866, he emigrated in 1883 from Hammerfest with his father, Henry J. (a "tall, well-built" Norwegian), his mother Emilie (a Norwegian Lapp), his sister, and his cousin. By 1888 they had built a house at the mouth of the Cross River in Cook County. Hedley, hardy and capable like his father, short like his mother, and wiry, fished, sailed, built boats, operated a general store in part of the Redmyer house, and taught neighborhood children how to ski. Between 1888 and 1891 he was postmaster at the little settlement called Redmyer, which later became Schroeder.[33]

On Lake Superior's north shore in the 1890s, many settlers like the Redmyers weathered hard financial times by working at various jobs. From 1891 to 1897 Hedley and his father fished and hauled cargo in the "H. N. Emilie," a two-masted schooner they had built. Henry served as road supervisor for the western end of Cook County, and the men earned additional money by working on roads, building bridges, and doing other tasks for the county.[34]

Jackson had heard from Henry Redmyer in January, 1894, when the latter applied for the position of reindeer superintendent that was given to William Kjellmann, who was his wife's nephew. Henry had admitted that although he was over 50 years old, he was "in good health and can stand lots of hardships, and such a life would agree with me." By the late 1890s his son Hedley also had his eye on Alaska. The *Cook County Herald*, like newspapers all over the country, published well illustrated feature stories about the Klondike and Alaska, profiles of colorful and successful gold seekers, advertisements for maps of the gold region, and the names of local citizens who were outfitting to join the rush. On February 5, 1898, the *Herald* reported that Hedley Redmyer was "afflicted with Klondicitis" and planned to leave for the gold fields as soon as he could make "necessary arrangements."[35]

Hedley joined his cousin, William Kjellmann, in Seattle, hoping to join the Alaska expedition, but in what capacity it is not clear. It is probable that he expected only a temporary job that would pay his way to the gold fields, and he was hired for such a position as a supervisor and interpreter for the Lapps. When sickness altered Kjellmann's plans, Redmyer replaced his cousin as supervisor of the herders and reindeer scheduled to make the journey from Haines to Circle City. Redmyer's knowledge of Lappish, Norwegian, and English, his resourcefulness, hardihood, and endurance learned on the Minnesota frontier, and his willingness to extol the reindeer project for the press made him an asset of special value to Jackson.[36]

Redmyer's mission was threatened at the outset by circumstances beyond his control. The deer became weakened by their unfamiliar diet of grass at Woodland Park. Four died there, and eight more died on the sailing ship "Seminole," which took them from Seattle to Haines. When Jackson, Kjellmann, Redmyer, and the expedition landed at Haines on March 28, the herd numbered 526 deer. There they discovered that no orders had reached the military headquarters at Dyea to provide tents, camping equipment, and other supplies for the herders — or moss for the deer. The army, enmeshed in details of mobilizing for war, blamed the failure on irregular and unreliable mail service.[37]

While the herders camped for a week on the beach at Haines waiting for their outfits, the deer consumed the last of the Norwegian moss supply and started feeding on temporary rations of dried alfalfa. Herders watched them night and day to protect them from marauding sled dogs, but some of the deer died every day from the inadequate diet. The herd was moved — with great difficulty and some loss — to pastures 12 miles south of Haines, but there was not enough moss to restore the animals to strength for traveling. Redmyer and Jafet Lindeberg traveled up the Dalton Trail to find moss beds about 60 miles north on the Klehini River, a tributary of the Chilkat River, and decided to take the animals there.

The movement of supplies and reindeer to the Chilkat pasture occupied the men during most of April. Melting snow, rain, and early spring weather offered miserable traveling conditions, and every day of delay took its toll of animals. Jackson prepared to return to Washington, leaving Kjellmann to stay with the expedition until all the deer were safely moved to the mountain pasture. Before going, Jackson wrote letters of introduction for Redmyer to use if he should need extra sup-

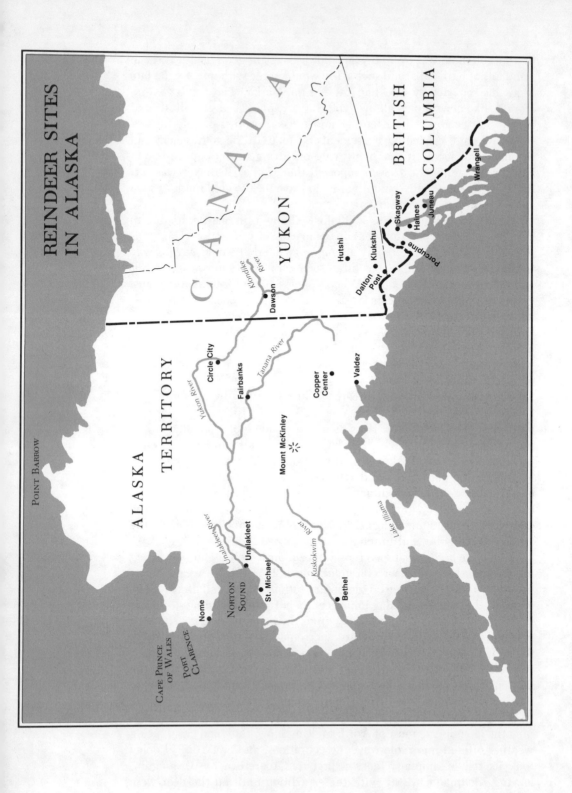

REINDEER SITES
IN ALASKA

POINT BARROW

ALASKA

TERRITORY

C A N A D A

YUKON

BRITISH
COLUMBIA

Cape Prince
of Wales
Port
Clarence

Nome

NORTON
SOUND

St. Michael

Unalakleet

Unalakleet River

Yukon River

Circle City

Fairbanks

Tanana River

Mount McKinley

Copper
Center

Valdez

Kuskokwim River

Bethel

Lake Illiama

Dawson

Klondike River

Hutshi

Klukshu

Dalton
Post

Porcupine

Skagway

Haines

Juneau

Wrangell

plies from trading posts on the way to Circle City. Then he met once again with the immigrants to tell them good-bye. In a touching farewell speech, Jackson told them to set a good example while living and working among the "heathen" in Alaska. William Kjellmann sang a Norwegian song in honor of the occasion.[38]

After supplies and rations for the overland journey finally reached Haines, the Laplanders loaded some bundles into four canoes procured from the Chilkat Indians and strapped others to the backs of the men for the move from the beach at Haines to the moss pasture. From April 8 to 11 the men, without the deer, moved up the Chilkat River Valley to the mouth of the Klehini River, where they established a temporary camp.

As death reduced the herd, Kjellmann decided that only 15 men would be needed for the drive to Circle City. Those he selected — 12 Lapps, 2 Norwegians, and Redmyer — stayed at the temporary camp while he and the rest of the herders returned to Haines to round up the deer and start them along the trail to the mountain pasture.

More frustrating delays took a tragic toll. By arrangement with Jackson, a number of military expeditions that were setting out that spring from Skagway expected to utilize some of the reindeer to pack their supplies. But when the military parties learned at Skagway of the weakened condition of the deer, the army ordered Kjellmann to keep the herd at Haines until it could be determined whether any of them had recovered enough to be used. During the enforced delay, from April 13 to 16, 124 deer died — 34 in one day. Finally, when the army decided to go on without the deer, Kjellmann was permitted to resume the march toward the moss beds.

The herders collected the deer in small bands and drove them northward, returning for stragglers, cutting down trees for the moss growing on them, collecting the moss in bags and carrying it to the slow-moving animals. Kjellmann went ahead to the moss beds with an Indian guide and 30 men, each pulling a sled loaded with rations. After unloading the supplies, the men gathered moss, piled it high on the sleds, and took it back down the trail to the deer. Then they divided into work crews, pulling sleds loaded with moss for the herd and supplies for the men who were to make the overland journey.

By May 6 the remnant of the herd had been turned loose in the moss fields near the north summit of Chilkat Pass. Of the 526 deer unloaded at Haines on March 28, only 185 survived. On that day Kjellmann turned over command of the reindeer expedition to Redmyer and started back to Haines with the rest of the herders, the surplus sleds, and other equipment. The men would join other immigrants for the steamboat trip to the new reindeer station near Unalakleet.

Redmyer and his crew moved to a spot they called Camp Pleasant, nearer the moss beds. They were not far from Porcupine Creek, where gold would be found that fall.[39]

On May 22 they attempted to move the herd onto the trail, but in their weakened condition the deer were able to travel only three miles that day. They could pull the sleds only at night when a crust had formed on the snow. By the end of the month the fast-melting snow was gone and Redmyer cached the useless sleds.

In camp Redmyer and his men made pack saddles, each to carry 25 pounds of equipment and supplies. This arrangement meant slower progress on the trail. As Redmyer explained to Jackson, "it is harder for an animal to pack than to pull." In addition, the deer continued to die of "starvation or disease caused by starvation" suffered during their detention at Haines; others succumbed to "a disease the Laplanders call in their language, 'sloopo;' it rots the hoof away." Three were killed in accidents. By the end of May the herd of 185 deer was reduced to 164.[40]

When it seemed that the journey to Circle City might take all summer, Redmyer estimated that he had provisions to last his 15 men only until July 31. He needed fewer men to manage the smaller herd, so he sent eight back to Seattle, where he hoped they could get transportation to Unalakleet.

Redmyer described his situation in a letter to Kjellmann. He and the men who remained with him hoped to break camp in a week or so and head for the White River, a tributary of the Yukon. "We are preparing ourselves for a hard and long travel," he wrote. Redmyer suggested that if Kjellmann had not heard from him by the end of September, perhaps it would be well to send men to Circle City to meet him with additional supplies. "Well," he concluded, "it remains for you to decide what to do. All I can say is that I'll push it through all right, so you need not fear; you can depend on me."

Redmyer's party now comprised five Laplanders and one Norwegian, all in their mid-twenties. The Norwegian, Emil Kjeldsberg from Kaaford, Norway, was 26 and among the higher paid of the immigrants — he earned $33.50 a month. Two of the Lapps, Per Johanneson Hatta, 26, and Per Nilsen Siri, 24, were from Kautokeino; the others, Klemet Persen Boini, 23, Hans Andersen Siri, 22, and Andrew Bahr, 25, were from Karasjok. Bahr thought that he understood reindeer language and that the animals understood him; one of his later employers claimed that he "had no peer among the deer men of Alaska in so far as an understanding of the animal was concerned." Bahr and the other young Lapps of Redmyer's party were to be paid $22.33 a month and, like all of the immigrants, they were guaranteed food, clothing, and other benefits for the duration of their contract with the United States.[41]

While the safe delivery of the reindeer to Circle City was Redmyer's first priority, he was not allowed to forget that reindeer herding and education were inseparable. "While in camp," Jackson instructed Redmyer, "drill the men in speaking English. Encourage them to try and use the English they may learn. Use it yourself as far as possible in conversing with them." If Redmyer's men learned as quickly on the trail as other immigrants did at the new reindeer station, their progress should have been gratifying. For some of them English was a third, fourth, or fifth language — most already spoke Norwegian and their own Lappish language and others spoke Swedish or Finnish as well.[42]

Progress along the route, however, was exasperatingly slow. The Dalton Trail was overgrown with brush and "underwood," and the Redmyer party was forced to travel on higher slopes to the west. For a time the men and deer crossed a valley "from one side to the other in order to find more level ground or a good mountain to travel on." Finally they reached mountains that were "nothing but needle points." Redmyer left Kjeldsberg in charge of the camp and went out alone to reconnoiter. He traveled some 40 miles ahead on the Dalton Trail and, finding less undergrowth, decided to take the expedition that way as far as the Canadian village of Hutshi.[43]

On September 1 Redmyer reported to Jackson from Lake Klukshu. "No disease has been among my men," he said, adding that "they, as well as myself, have had hard work, and our provisions are limited." He planned to go to Dalton Post, about 30 miles away, for more supplies. "We have provisions to last us to the 28th of October, but it might take a longer time to reach Circle City, and we want to be sure." Three of the surviving 144 reindeer were weak, but the rest were "in a splendid condition and are fat and healthy." Redmyer thought that the expedition could reach the Hutshi Valley by the end of September, when they would camp long enough to make sleds. The deer would move more rapidly in the snow. He promised that they would be brought safely to Circle City "if no unforseen mishap occur[s]." Just when, he could not say, but he concluded: "Hoping you believe me faithful to what I am intrusted with."

Beyond Klukshu Redmyer's expedition followed the Dalton Trail for more than a hundred miles. In October they halted at a small, unnamed lake while the men made toboggans and harness for winter travel. There Redmyer celebrated his thirty-second birthday. On November 3, with 141 deer, the men loaded the toboggans and set out again in the direction of the headwaters of the White River. At a place not named on their maps, they halted again for a week, waiting while ice formed so they could cross a large lake.[44]

The daily life of the expedition presented constant problems. When the deer were stampeded by wolves or mountain lions, the men were forced to chase through heavy underbrush and unbroken snow to collect them. Impassable mountain ranges blocked their path, compelling the expedition to turn around and try another route. Provisions ran out because of the delays, and the men had little to eat. They often had to sleep in wet clothing, which "froze upon their bodies." But the reindeer, Jackson and Redmyer agreed, "proved their ability to make a journey that could not have been made either with horses or dogs."[45]

The party finally arrived at the White River on November 20. They followed the river — "the crookedest stream in the world" — for 275 miles, reaching its junction with the Yukon on December 17. There they stayed until Christmas, then continued down the Yukon to the Indian River, another tributary south of Dawson. On this part of the journey several deer met fatal accidents — falling and breaking legs, strangling in tangled harness, killed by wolves, or shot by natives who thought they were caribou. At the Indian River camp the herd numbered 135.

At a trading post on the Indian River Redmyer purchased some supplies, then left the expedition in camp while he went to Dawson, a few miles to the north. Jackson had instructed him not to take the deer or the herders into the city, perhaps because no pasture was available. Miners had strewn the hills and valleys of the Klondike River and Bonanza Creek with tailings, rubble, and other debris, denuding the area near the city of all vegetation. But Jackson may have wanted to protect the herders from the lure of the city. Would the men want to go back on the trail once they had seen Dawson, the metropolis of the Klondike, the San Francisco of the North, the largest Canadian city west of Winnipeg?[46]

The late 1890s witnessed the brief heyday of Dawson, a modern city with electric lights, telephones, running water, moving picture theaters, well-appointed hotels, restaurants, hospitals, gambling parlors, dance halls, two banks, five churches, two newspapers, and any number of well-stocked stores where one could buy almost anything at a price — or five or six prices. Dawson was a gold rush city but by no means a lawless one. Under the firm control of the Canadian mounted police, its cosmopolitan population was estimated a few months before Redmyer's visit at 18,000 within town and some 5,000 prospectors in the nearby hills. All had survived the long journey to El Dorado and now all were enduring the bitter cold in the depths of the arctic winter and darkness. At the end of December and early in January the windows of Dawson were frosted over; thermometers recorded 50 degrees or more below zero. It was so cold horses could not be worked outdoors, and few people ventured onto the streets.

Redmyer transacted two items of business in Dawson. He bought provisions that he hoped would last his party until they reached Circle City, and he managed to be interviewed by Dawson's American-owned newspaper, the *Klondyke Nugget*. For the press Redmyer emphasized the positive aspects of his expedition in words worthy of Jackson himself. The reindeer, he said, could travel quickly through rough country, pull heavy loads, and feed off the land; they would "assist very materially in solving the question of communication on the Yukon in the winter time." The *Nugget*, impressed by what it called "in all probability one of the most difficult trips ever attempted into this country," described Redmyer as a "small man but strong and wiry and just suited for the task which he undertook. The U.S. government is to be congratulated upon its choice of a man for so difficult an undertaking."

Redmyer survived the blandishments of Dawson, and with his hardy men pushed on toward Circle City. A hundred miles down the Yukon, wolves again attacked the herd and killed more animals. On February 28 — exactly one year after the immigrants and the deer had disembarked at Jersey City — Redmyer, six men, and 122 deer reached Circle City, Alaska.[48]

Circle City, so named because it was thought to be on the Arctic Circle (it was actually 75 miles south of that line), was founded in 1893 as a distribution and merchandising center for the gold placer mines on

Birch, Mammoth, Mastodon, and Preacher creeks. Known as the "great-est log cabin town in the world," its two theaters, eight dance halls, 28 saloons, stores, library, church, newspaper office, and opera hall were constructed of round spruce logs from the nearby forest. Chinked with moss and roofed with sod a foot deep, the buildings sported grassy lawns, flower beds, and vegetable gardens on their roofs while the ground below was frozen many feet deep. In 1899, when Redmyer arrived, some prospectors were still working claims on creeks in the area, but most of Circle City's inhabitants had left for the new gold strikes on the Klondike.[49]

Redmyer's men were "used up" and the deer were in only fair con-dition. All needed rest. Redmeyer established them in a temporary camp about ten miles out of town, and before summer moved them to better pasture in the foothills of the mountains. He rented a log building that he called "Porcupine House" on Mammoth Creek for the herders' head-quarters and storage depot. Before the snow was gone, he bought enough provisions for five men to last through the summer and hauled them by sled to the log building. The deer would graze about fifteen miles from the headquarters until September. He expected only five men to remain with the herd; Kjeldsberg planned to leave government em-ploy in mid-June, and Redmyer himself wanted to quit on July 1.[50]

Although the deer did not recover their full strength before fall, Redmyer found opportunities to demonstrate their usefulness to the army officers stationed at Circle City. Traveling to a mining district in the hills, he "gave the deer a show of covering a few miles" for the army engineer who commanded the local military detachment. A second expedition, to explore the region between Circle City and the Tanana River, lasted a month. "This will be a trip outside of my orders," noted Redmyer at the outset, "and perhaps will bring no extra pay but I have done so much extra work for nothing that I may as well do this too." But glare ice, melting snow, and the loss of nine reindeer to a stampeding band of caribou turned the explorers back after three weeks of hard travel. The army had gained useful information; Redmyer had lost nine animals.[51]

Other matters required Redmyer's attention. He had to provide transportation into Circle City for a herder who became seriously ill and needed medical attention. Redmyer hired Kjeldsberg, who had resigned but had not left, to go with the sick man and two other Lapps. Jackson later disallowed the payment for Kjeldsberg's extra duty, saying that he was a "countryman of [the sick man] and therefore should charge noth-ing for his services." Redmyer had also to contend with the complaints of the agent at Circle City's trading post, who wrote Jackson, "We have extended every courtesy to Mr. Redmyer, and have supplied the Lap-landers with tobacco and similar articles of everyday use, as well as to Mr. Redmyer, which we understand is outside of the Government rein-deer account." The agent wondered when and by whom the bills would be paid.[52]

The greatest problem was what to do with the reindeer. Redmyer

207

thought they would be ready for work in September. Jackson hoped that they would be used for freighting or delivering mail, and a number of people wanted to buy them for such work. What was a deer worth? Purchased for $10 a head in Lapland, the deer had cost the government $68 each in New York, Jackson estimated. To a trading company and several mail contractors who wanted to buy animals and hire men as herders and drivers, Jackson had quoted a price of $125. Redmyer, instructed to sell them for that amount, refused. He was unwilling to accept that "rather cheap" price for deer that he, his men, and the government had spent so much time and effort preserving. Redmyer said he had been offered $300 by one person, and he would not sell the deer until Jackson had time to reconsider his order.[53]

In the meantime, Redmyer wanted to see Jackson. He traveled with Kjeldsberg down the Yukon River to St. Michael and arrived at Nome on July 16. Two weeks later he was on his way back up the Yukon with orders from Jackson to sell the expedition's equipment and as many deer as he could. He was to turn over the rest of the herd to the agent for the Episcopal mission at the mouth of the Tanana River. Redmyer had difficulty carrying out these orders — the trading company was not able to purchase deer, as it had expected, and he heard nothing from the mail contractors. Perhaps Redmyer was making only minimal efforts to find buyers, since Jackson still insisted on a price of $125. "Well, if it is left for me to decide, I will manage it all right, and without any loss to the Government," he reported. Eventually he sold the equipment to the Episcopal mission and turned over 92 reindeer to the mission's agent. With that business finished, Redmyer reported to headquarters at Eaton Reindeer Station and was discharged from government service on October 10, 1899.[54]

For the immigrants who stayed at the station plans had also changed. The Lapp immigrants were on the coast; the Lapp deer near Circle City. Jackson had made another reindeer-buying trip to Siberia soon after the immigrants arrived, but was able to purchase only 161 deer. The reindeer project now had many trained men and not enough deer to keep them busy.[55]

But again fortune smiled on Jackson and the reindeer project, as it smiled on Jafet Lindeberg. Only two weeks after Lindeberg had resigned from the reindeer project, he and a number of men from the Swedish mission at Unalakleet sailed on Norton Sound to Anvil Creek and Nome, where they found gold. Lindeberg helped organize the Nome mining district, was one of the incorporators of the Pioneer Mining Company, and led the fight of the legitimate owners against corrupt public officials and claim jumpers. By October of 1898 at least 44 immigrants and their families had resigned from government service to prospect for themselves or to work for Lindeberg's company. When an army unit went to the district to enforce order, reindeer from the mission station and immigrant drivers transported them and their military supplies. When food was scarce, Lapps with reindeer teams carried supplies from St. Michael to Nome "as an act of humanity and relief." In the fortuitous circumstances immigrants found work, and Lapps and reindeer gave succor to hungry (if not starving) miners and aided the army unit stationed at the gold fields. Thus the Lapp-reindeer expedition of 1898 ultimately achieved many of its objectives and, in Jackson's opinion, demonstrated his contention that the deer were a resource of great value to both white men and natives in the Arctic.[56]

Some 25 of the Lapps were not sufficiently impressed by Alaska to want to stay there, and when their contracts terminated in 1900 they returned to Hammerfest, Norway. As for the reindeer that had survived the long overland trek, they were transferred to the Episcopal mission in September, 1899, and put to pasture at Tanana. Since they were males trained to harness, numbers of them, with their Lapp drivers, were used to haul the U.S. mail. Their transfer to the mission was part of a complicated transaction in which they were substituted for deer at the government station on Golovin Bay which had been designated for the Episcopalians. "The exchange," wrote the commissioner of the Bureau of Education to the secretary of the interior, explaining the disposition of the deer, ". . . saved the expenses of driving the two herds, one west 100 miles, and the other east 800 miles." The solution, however, was not entirely satisfactory. As the Episcopal herd at Tanana included no females and therefore did not multiply, attempts to supply additional deer to that mission continued for several years.[57]

Many people have criticized the Lapp-reindeer expedition of 1898 as a fiasco, a monumental government blunder. Among those who attacked the project for faulty execution is Pierre Berton, whose *The Klondike Fever* contains a highly colored version of the journey from Haines to Dawson. There was "never really enough to eat" for man or deer, the writer asserts. "As the months wore on and the very dogs dropped in their tracks from hunger, the herders were reduced to picking up raw beans spilled on the trail by the gold-seekers ahead of them and stuffing them, filthy and frozen, into their mouths."[58]

It is doubtful that the men were driven to this extremity. Redmyer's letters of credit permitted him to buy supplies at a number of posts on the trail. And despite his dedication to the safe delivery of the herd, it is difficult to imagine that he would have allowed his men to be reduced to eating frozen, filthy beans while he had a stove, frying pans, and a herd of fat and healthy reindeer. The men could, and undoubtedly did, butcher the animals that died accidentally. Most of the deer that died, however, were victims of the disastrous ordeal at Haines, not of starvation along the trail. This was a failure of the government, not of Jackson, Redmyer, or the herders. And considering the massive problems the military faced with the deluge of thousands of gold seekers, and the conflicting demands made by the Spanish-American War, the snarls of red tape at Haines are perhaps understandable.[59]

The doughty Jackson continued to dream great dreams for the reindeer service, envisioning a chain of "reindeer settlements" at 100-mile intervals from the northernmost limits of arctic Alaska to tidewater areas on the Pacific. He rejoiced when native apprentices became owners of herds and the numbers of their deer multiplied, and when deer were used to haul freight, carry mail, and rescue and feed victims of shipwrecks. More success for the reindeer service came when deer could be butchered for cash sale without reducing the efficiency of herds, and when the number of native herders and apprentices in one area warranted their pooling interests and ordering supplies from the States in wholesale quantities. Canadians, impressed by the Alaskan reindeer project, were interested in importing reindeer and saw them becoming "the horse and the ox of our great northern land."

The reindeer service continued to purchase deer from Siberia until 1902, when the Russian government forbade their export. Of the 1,280 brought to Alaska by that time, probably the most valuable were the large Tungese deer from the Okhotsk region of Siberia, brought over the Bering Sea in 1901 and interbred with Alaskan herds to produce a superior animal.[61]

Hedley Redmyer, whose family moved to Washington state, probably spent some time with them before he returned to Cross River, where he opened a saloon. In 1904 he returned to the Alaskan reindeer service and took charge of 300 deer and four herders who were to travel overland from Bethel, on the Kuskokwim River, to Copper Center, north of Valdez. The journey, like the earlier trek, was longer and more difficult than anyone expected. "People who have had no experience with reindeer [except] only by reading," Redmyer observed, "are always led to believe the reindeer capable of more than they really are. They are in fact far ahead of any animals to go through a wilderness, but there is a limit to all." Finally, surrounded by wolf country, "needle point" mountains, and mossless territory, the expedition stopped at Iliamna Lake. For the next four years, Redmyer was superintendent of the reindeer station and school Jackson had established there.[62]

Redmyer left the service again in 1908, and his subsequent career apparently had little to do with Alaska or reindeer. He had married Mareth Rist before 1908, and the couple had two daughters; several years later, when they were living with Hedley's parents in Bow, Washington, they were divorced. In 1916, three years after his father's death, Hedley, his mother, and his daughter Ingeborg moved back to Minnesota. But an altercation with his neighbors over a bridge on his property (they tore it down while he was on a trip to Duluth) and the failure of his plans to go into the commercial fishing business convinced him to sell part of his land and return to Washington. There he fished, built boats, and did carpentry work. He died in Seattle in 1953.[63]

Sheldon Jackson also retired from government service in 1908 but continued his interest in Alaskan affairs. Only two weeks before his death in May, 1909, he spoke in behalf of missionary work in Alaska.[64]

Jackson had successfully weathered much controversy about the reindeer and other Alaska projects during his long tenure in the Bureau of Education. The conflict did not end with his death. Critics in and out of government — he never lacked them — found him ignorant of, and insensitive to, the nature of Alaskan natives and their way of life. It was condescending of him, they said, to think that he knew what was best for these people; he was being ethnocentric when he planned to "elevate" the "uncivilized" natives by means of reindeer herding.[65]

On the other hand, there was no question that Jackson's reindeer project, as an agricultural experiment, was a success. Climate and vegetation in the area were congenial to reindeer culture, and deer were used by white and native Alaskans for food, clothing, and cash income. Talented and imaginative men in the Bureau of Education, following Jackson's lead, encouraged reindeer culture, but not until 1920 did Congress appropriate funds for an experiment station, a move Jackson had long favored. The station was established by the U.S. Biological Survey at Unalakleet.

In 1922 the U.S. Department of Agriculture published *Reindeer in Alaska* by Seymour Hadwen and Lawrence J. Palmer of the experiment station staff. They reported that from the original herd at Teller, the reindeer population of Alaska had grown to an estimated 200,000 live deer; in addition 100,000 animals had been butchered for food and clothing. "Begun as an experiment, reindeer grazing in Alaska has amply proved its practicability and demonstrated its importance as one of the great future industries of the Territory," said the report. The authors estimated that Alaska had grazing areas sufficient to support between three and four million reindeer, and "The annual surplus from that number would yield a meat product each year worth more than the previous metals mined in the Territory and second only to the fisheries as a permanent income-producing asset." The experiment station was to continue studying ways of improving and managing the herds for meat and fur production and control of diseases and parasites. Other entrepreneurs who found a new use for the reindeer were entering the field, however, and the next chapter of the reindeer story was to prove as interesting as the first.

The Christmas Reindeer Shows
Entrepreneurs in Alaska and Minnesota
Take Reindeer and Santa on the Road for Fun and Profit

REINDEER REACHED MINNESOTA on the hoof and in the freezer during the 1920s. Members of the Lomen family, Minnesotans who helped develop the industry in Alaska in the first years of the 20th century, brought the animals to the Midwest in an effort to promote the consumption of reindeer meat. But they discovered that the appeal of the live animal far outweighed the local appetite for reindeer roasts, and Christmas Reindeer shows were born. The Lomens, and later Nicholas and Lillian Dimond, the Boostrom family, Hermund Melheim, and many other Minnesotans brought these shows to towns and cities in the Midwest and across the United States for a decade.

The Alaska bug bit 19-year-old Carl Lomen one day in 1900 when he was reading law in his father's St. Paul office. A veteran of the Klondike gold rush came to see Carl's father, Norwegian-born Gudbrand J. Lomen, who was an attorney and a former member of the Minnesota legislature. Carl, tantalized by the visitor's tales, borrowed library books and sent for folders from the railroad lines, which were then promoting travel to the West Coast and Alaska.

Young Lomen, born in Caledonia, Minnesota, and graduated from Central High School in St. Paul, was scheduled to continue studying law at the University of Minnesota. That plan became less and less attractive, and Carl told his father that he wanted to go to Alaska instead. The senior Lomen listened sympathetically, confessed his own fascination with the north country, and said, "I'll go with you." Later in the spring, father and son closed the law office, said good-bye to the family at Bald Eagle Lake, and set out on a vacation that stretched into a 40-year residence in Nome, Alaska.[66]

The Lomens reached Nome in the midst of the gold rush. People by the thousands poured into the little settlement on the Seward Peninsula that year, camping in tents on the beach or living in makeshift cabins or shacks. Lomen at once found work handling legal cases arising from contested mining claims. Carl tried prospecting with little success. After three years father and son were sure that they wanted to stay, and they persuaded the rest of the family to leave Minnesota and join them.

In Alaska they found opportunities for all. Gudbrand Lomen practiced law and became mayor of Nome, a United States attorney, and a federal judge. Sons Carl, Harry, Alfred, and Ralph established a photograph studio, a drugstore, and other enterprises, including warehouses, docks, and lighterage services (facilities for unloading ships where there is no harbor) at Nome and five other communities. Alfred and Ralph served in the territorial legislature. Carl and his sister Helen wrote books about Alaska.

Early in their days at Nome the Lomens became acquainted with Sheldon Jackson's reindeer project and with many of the Laplanders who had gone to Alaska as part of it. The deer had continued to multiply, numbering an estimated 57,872 in 65 herds in 1914. Some of the Lapp immigrants continued to work for the reindeer service. Others took part of their government pay in deer and started herds of their own.[67]

Carl, like Sheldon Jackson before him, saw the potential significance of reindeer culture to Alaska's economy. A well-cared-for herd could double in numbers in three years; careful breeding on scientific principles would produce superior stock; and Carl Lomen believed that without depleting the herds, 10 per cent of the male animals could be slaughtered each year to supply food and clothing for the Eskimo and other customers in and out of Alaska. Prepared to carry out such long-range objectives, the Lomens and Jafet Lindeberg, one of the Norwegian-Lapp immigrant gold miners, organized Lomen & Company. The firm would buy herds, build corrals and abattoirs, develop cold-storage and freezing facilities, and promote and market reindeer products. For Carl Lomen the reindeer became "the most interesting creature on earth."

Lomen & Company's enterprises, begun in 1913–14, were to be Carl's major concern for more than 20 years. To get started, the company bought herds from a number of the missions and from such Laplanders as Per Hatta and Andrew Bahr, two immigrants who were among Jackson's recruits in 1898. The Lomens hired Bahr and other experienced Lapps and Eskimos to manage their herds, and they learned about reindeer from them. In peak years the company employed as many as 579 full- and part-time Eskimo workers. It owned five herds on ranges of the Seward Peninsula, and on Nunivak Island it experimented with the crossbreeding of reindeer and the heavier caribou. The Lomens marketed meat, hides, and antlers; the latter were ground up for fertilizer or sent to the Orient, where they were prized as an aphrodisiac. The Lomens also produced reindeer-hide flying suits that were worn by pilots and explorers. The company even acquired and operated its own refrigerator ships for transporting meat to markets in the 48 states.[68]

Carl Lomen and his brothers devised various ingenious ways to promote the reindeer business. When Ralph Lomen visited Minnesota in 1925 he gave a dinner at the St. Paul Hotel featuring reindeer steak from the Lomen range. Interviewed by the *St. Paul Pioneer Press*, he observed that a herd of 20 to 35 caribou was said to be living in the woods of Koochiching County. There was no reason, he thought, why reindeer could not also thrive in Minnesota's caribou country, where natural food — reindeer moss — and "waste land" were available. The *St. Paul Dispatch*, commenting on Lomen's visit, said that meat-producing reindeer could make good use of northern Minnesota land, provided that Americans "took kindly to the venison on their tables."[69]

The Lomens' attempts in the late 1920s to promote reindeer meat on the menus of western trains were not highly successful. The Great Northern occasionally served the meat on its diners, but livestock interests, fearing competition with beef, discouraged large-scale promotion of the product. Subtler forms of educating the public about reindeer were carried on with more success.[70]

Undoubtedly the most colorful of the Lomens' efforts were their Christmas Reindeer promotions. In feet and yards of news copy these holiday adventures outclassed all other schemes that the resourceful family devised. The imaginative Carl could have invented a connection between reindeer and Christmas; but in fact, Santa Claus and his reindeer had been a part of the Christmas scene for more than a century. Washington Irving, writing under the pseudonym of Diedrich Knickerbocker, had created the jolly bearded character in his humorous *History of New York* (1809), when he transformed St. Nicholas and Kris Kringle into Santa Claus. In 1822 another New Yorker, Clement C. Moore, president of Columbia University, in a fanciful moment he was said to have later regretted, wrote a Christmas poem for his children to which he added the reindeer. In "A Visit from St. Nicholas," the jovial, rotund personage arrived on a sleigh drawn by eight tiny — named and tamed — reindeer.[71]

Some hundred years later, also in New York, Carl and Ralph Lomen gave a breath of new life to the old story. At lunch with two advertising-agency officials, the Lomens suggested the possibility of putting Santa Clauses into sleighs drawn by live reindeer and, with suitable pomp and pageantry, parading them up and down the streets of America. The advertising men were delighted; it was, one said, "the first new Christmas idea . . . since they took a fat man, hung chin whiskers on him, and called him Santa Claus!"[72]

The terms of a subsequent contract between the Lomens and the agency called for the advertising people to develop a program, produce copy for newspapers and radio, and sell the package to sponsors. The Lomens, supplying the agency with background information about reindeer and life in arctic regions, agreed also to train reindeer teams and ship them with native attendants to Seattle. The agency would then dispatch the teams to the various cities where they were to perform with locally recruited Santa Clauses.

The Lomens carried out their part of the agreement by selecting 100 young reindeer with well-shaped antlers and sending them to a camp at Golovin, Alaska, for special training. Lapp and Eskimo herders weaned the deer from their native diet to a mixture of moss and stateside food — oats, corn, wheat, or alfalfa tips. Teams of six deer were trained in harness for their new duties — the eight animals of Moore's imaginary team were judged too difficult a number to handle on the road.

Meanwhile the advertising program took shape. The agency prepared radio talks to be delivered by participants in the Christmas Reindeer pageants. It drafted letters and telegrams for promotion, offered suggestions for day-to-day schedules of events during Santa's local visits, and wrote news releases and background stories for the press. The first Christmas advertisements could be published in early November, "which meant an advance of Christmas shopping by thirty days," Carl Lomen noted. For a fee of $15,000, local newspapers, department stores, merchants' associations, or civic organizations from Oregon to Massachussetts became sponsors of Christmas Reindeer shows.

Carl Lomen's enthusiasm for the project was boundless. He envisioned short- and long-term benefits for the reindeer industry as well as the general public. "Santa would popularize the reindeer, which would then become less and less mythical, for it would be seen by millions of people. The children when they realized that Santa depended upon sales of reindeer meat to secure funds for toy materials, would boost the commercial industry." Would children who met and petted Santa's live reindeer want to eat deer butchered into steaks and chops? The question seems not to have occurred to Lomen. In fact, as the Lomens observed the pleasurable unfolding of the Christmas Reindeer drama in city after city, profits from the sales of reindeer meat became secondary to more heartwarming benefits.[73]

Carl's comments on the first Christmas Reindeer program, which was presented in Portland, Oregon, in October of 1926, may suggest why the project remained popular for a decade with both the Lomen family and the public. "This pageant," Lomen wrote, "brought joy to the children, increased good will and advertising lineage in the newspaper, developed a feeling of reality in the spirit of Christmas, and strengthened parental discipline. Visits were made to schools and hospitals where the reindeer could be petted by children. They paraded the streets and were seen and enjoyed by millions of people." The full measure of success, Lomen realized, depended on many persons and agencies. "Cities, businessmen, railroads and bus lines all recognized the unique value of having Santa and his reindeer in their areas and cooperated fully to make the gala event long remembered."[74]

There were some difficulties in carrying out the elaborate promotional scheme, particularly in the first year. But in most cases one or another of the resourceful Lomens was nearby to cope with problems. In Philadelphia, for example, a department store subscriber who had been promised exclusive rights to a reindeer program for the Christmas season discovered that a competitor was advertising Santa and a team of live reindeer. Investigation showed that the competing animals were not reindeer, but how could they be proven impostors? Alfred Lomen explained the problem in a telephone call to his old friend, Roald Amundsen, then in New York. Amundsen, a polar explorer and an arctic authority of unimpeachable credentials, agreed to help. He went to Philadelphia, saw the animal impostors, and pronounced them not reindeer but young elk. Viewing the Lomen team, he announced that *they* were authentic reindeer. In a day or so the fraudulent deer were quietly withdrawn from public view and the Lomen reindeer and their Santa reigned supreme on the Philadelphia scene.

One of the first Lomen Christmas Reindeer shows visited St. Paul in November, 1926. Santa and reindeer captured headline and feature space in the *Dispatch* and *Pioneer Press* for more than six weeks, competing with such other events as the visit to America of Queen Marie of Romania, the election of Melvin Maas to Congress, the death of magician Harry Houdini, the crash of a mail plane and the bailout of its pilot, Charles Lindbergh, and the ongoing debate over prohibition and the enactment of the Volstead Act. On October 29, a letter from a small girl had set in motion the series of events that brought Santa Claus and the deer to St. Paul. Gudrun Brewitz, who attended Phalen Park School and whose mother had grown up in Swedish Lapland, wrote to the editor of the *Dispatch*, asking to be reassured about the existence of Santa Claus.[75]

The paper's special "Santa Claus Editor" asked other children to help him answer Gudrun's letter. What did they know about Santa Claus? Did they believe in him? Letters from believers and disbelievers came to the editor in increasing volume during November and December, from the Twin Cities and from as far away as Wisconsin and the Dakotas. Disbelievers said Santa Claus was not a real person and chil-

215

dren who thought otherwise were "crazy." Santa Claus was "the bunk," said one writer. Hah, snorted another, "tell it to Sweeney," and wrote a third, "So's your old man." On the other hand, someone thought Santa Claus was a spirit. Another said he had a red nose and twinkling eyes. A spirit with a red nose? queried the editor. Anyone who did not believe in Santa was "naughty" wrote another little correspondent. When a nonbelieving youth asserted that Santa Claus was his father and mother and he had a black mustache, not a white beard, the editor wondered — a mother with a black mustache? It was all so complicated that he decided he needed an expert to answer Gudrun.

At this point Lomen and the advertising agency stepped in. The "Santa Claus Editor," nearly buried in letters, sent an emergency message to Alfred Lomen, the papers' special correspondent in Nome, and commissioned him to get the finest dog team he could find and go looking for Santa Claus. Lomen, the editor explained, was a reliable and "exceptionally resourceful" correspondent. He, if anyone, could find Santa, if indeed there *was* such a person. And, if Santa were found, Lomen was to invite him to come to St. Paul and make the city his Christmas headquarters for 1926.

After making this announcement, the papers began to publish photographs from a seemingly inexhaustible collection — Lomen and a dog team, reindeer in all sorts of places and poses, the midnight sun shining over a bleak landscape of snow and ice, the beach and Main Street in Nome, where Lomen lived, a group of Eskimos who had "quit Shamanism" and embraced Christianity (Lomen was said to know them), Eskimos in parkas, Eskimos with dogs, polar bears, and reindeer.

The paper offered children other good reindeer reading, both fact and fiction. During November the Sunday *Junior Magazine* published three feature stories, each well illustrated with photographs of reindeer. The theme was continued on the *Dispatch* comic page in "The Christmas Reindeer," an Alaska tale written especially for the paper by the famous author of children's stories, Thornton W. Burgess. The story began as a serial early in November and concluded the day before Christmas. The rotogravure sections of the Sunday papers published handsome pictures of young Christmas-letter writers, the deer, and scenes with Santa.

In the meantime, the resourceful Alfred Lomen and his dog team, searching through snow and storm over icy, wind-swept wastes, found Santa Claus and delivered the invitation from St. Paul. Santa was not sure whether he could leave his home and factory at such a busy season, Lomen reported, but the jolly man would decide in a few days. Then from his headquarters at Icy Cape he would send an answer by "racing reindeer" to Lomen at Nome.

Back in St. Paul, the editor complained that he was growing nervous. To be sure that the invitation was properly understood at Icy Cape, he called on WCCO radio for assistance. From its studio in the St. Paul Union Depot, the station obligingly broadcast the message and from that moment was a full participant in the 1926 Christmas Reindeer game.

Soon Lomen cabled the papers that Santa would accept the invitation, adding that the WCCO broadcast had come through "loud and clear." Santa would travel with six reindeer and sleigh overland to Nome and there obtain passage on a steamer for Seattle, where he and his entourage would take to the air for the journey to St. Paul. Tautuk, his Eskimo herdsman, would accompany him. The newspapers published a map of the northern regions showing the route Santa would follow.[76]

The *Dispatch* and the *Pioneer Press*, which had subscribed to the Lomen Christmas Reindeer package and were thus official hosts for Santa's visit, were delighted at the turn of events. "Despite the dignity of its 77 years of existence," wrote the editor on November 15, "the Pioneer Press feels very much like throwing its editorial cap in the air this morning and giving three rousing cheers." Santa Claus was coming to town "IN BROAD DAYLIGHT" with his reindeer and his Eskimo herdsman. "There IS a Santa Claus; he DOES drive a team of reindeer; he HAS an Eskimo herdsman, and they're all coming to see us." It promised to be "the very greatest Christmas St. Paul has ever had."

In preparation for their important guests, the hosts constructed two log cabins, an igloo, and a corral in Rice Park as headquarters for Santa, Tautuk, and the reindeer. Santa's luxurious sleeping quarters in the St. Paul Hotel's "Royale Suite," recently occupied by Queen Marie of Romania, overlooked the park. The newspapers celebrated the visit with a full-color medallion, produced by the thousands, depicting Santa flying through the air with sleigh and six reindeer. Printed excerpts from "A Visit from St. Nicholas," altered to suit the circumstances, substituted six for the usual eight reindeer. Downtown businesses displayed the medallions in their show windows and distributed them free to the public. Yet discerning young people protested the alteration to six reindeer. "Where are the other two reindeer?" the editor was asked. Either improvising or coached by a Lomen, the editor replied that Mrs. Santa Claus had kept two of the deer with her for company at Icy Cape. They would rejoin the rest of the team to pull the heavily loaded sleigh on Christmas Eve.

While Santa finished packing toys and putting names on gifts in preparation for his trip to Minnesota, his St. Paul hosts took steps to ensure him a cordial reception. Invited to participate were Secretary of State and former St. Paulite Frank B. Kellogg, polar explorer Richard E. Byrd, Representative Melvin Maas, Mayor Larry Hodgson, and C. Reinhold Noyes, president of the St. Paul Association. Unfortunately, Secretary Kellogg could not come; the paper explained that he was busy receiving foreign dignitaries in Washington. Instead, he sent a telegram: "Greatly regretting my inability to be present I desire in this manner to share in the welcome of Santa Claus to St. Paul from Icy Cape and to extend to the children of St. Paul my best wishes."

Byrd wrote that he would be delighted "to shake hands with Santa and pet his deer," if he had a chance to come. "Those friendly and frisky animals play an important part in life with[in] the Arctic circle," he noted, "and I think that aside from the sentimental value of such a

217

Christmas celebration it is a fine educational thing to bring to the boys and girls of St. Paul this touch of the Far North."

Santa's progress in his journey southward was mentioned daily in colorful reports to St. Paul by cablegram and radio. He had arrived in Nome and there boarded a steamer. The vessel encountered rough seas and the unfortunate Vixen became seasick. She wanted to get out and walk, a circumstance that allowed the editor to explain that actually reindeer were good swimmers, because their fur was buoyant with hollow compartments in the hairs. (Eskimos made life preservers from the hair the animals shed.) Vixen again made headlines when she kicked a cabin boy and when she accidentally swallowed a talking doll and was going about saying "Mama" without opening her mouth.

In good style the travelers disembarked at Seattle and took to the air. The final segment of their trip, however, had its anxious moments. At Great Falls, Montana, Santa was arrested for speeding at 100 miles an hour. Only a telephone call to the St. Paul newspapers saved him from jail, the papers said. Over the Little Missouri River the reindeer lost their way and wandered around in circles until they got their bearings and could continue over Bismarck, North Dakota, and Aberdeen, South Dakota.

At dawn on the day after Thanksgiving the little sleigh with seven reindeer — six pulling the sleigh and a little bonus fawn as cargo — dropped down out of the sky to land beside the log cabins and igloo at Rice Park in downtown St. Paul. Only one person, police officer Bill Meyer, was present to witness their arrival. Meyer stayed around to tell any doubting Thomases what he had seen and, later in the day, the papers said, "30,000 Smiling St. Paulites" welcomed Santa to the city.

Santa first made duty calls on Governor Theodore Christianson at the capitol, on Mayor Larry Hodgson at city hall, where he was given the ceremonial key to the city, and on his official host, C. K. Blandin, publisher of the *Dispatch* and *Pioneer Press*. At the WCCO studio he was given prime-time half-hour programs Monday and Wednesday at 5:15 P.M. In response to his chatty messages came a flood of letters, augmenting the swelling tide of "Santa" correspondence to the newspapers. Soon it was impossible to acknowledge individual letters, and day after day names and addresses of correspondents filled long columns of the papers.

Santa fans were spread over a wide range of radio and newspaper territory. The railroads offered reduced fares between December 2 and 6 from all points in Minnesota, Wisconsin, and North Dakota to St. Paul. The St. Paul Association promised a trophy to the town that sent the largest number of people. Visitors from such places as Bismarck, Fargo, Owatonna, Faribault, Wells, Bemidji, and Alexandria signed a guest register kept next to Santa's cabin.

The weeks before Christmas were packed with activity. Every day at Rice Park, from 10:00 in the morning until 8:00 at night, children could see and pet the reindeer and submit entries in a contest to name the little fawn. Often Santa and Tautuk were there to greet the children, but sometimes they visited hospitals and schools, taking one or two of the deer with them. Little Gudrun, who started it all, was not forgotten; hers was the first school Santa visited. The *Dispatch* interviewed her mother about Sweden, Lapland, and reindeer in general.

Parades during the noon hour and at night passed through the downtown business district under sparkling lights and great arches of evergreen. Early evening concerts in Rice Park featured an Eskimo quartet in parkas with megaphones. The Greybar Electric Company installed special loud-speakers in the park to broadcast organ music from the municipal auditorium. The *Dispatch* and *Pioneer Press* printed 18 carols on a flyer for community singing, and the Third Infantry Band from Fort Snelling presented a program of Christmas music. One Sunday at the auditorium Santa took part in an ecumenical Christmas program. He could not accept invitations from all the churches that sent them, so to show no favoritism he attended no other religious service.

The educational aspects of Santa's visit were not neglected. At the University of Minnesota's farm campus Tautuk made a short speech in the Eskimo language. At another school, with globe in hand, he presented a lesson in the geography of Arctic regions. No doubt mindful of the fiasco in Philadelphia, Tautuk explained the differences between elk and reindeer. His comments appeared in the newspaper beneath pictures of a reindeer and of an elk from the Como Park zoo.

A sudden bitter cold wave sweeping down from the Northwest closed the schools and forced Santa to curtail his activities. On December 14 the temperature was 38 degrees below zero in International Falls and 31 below in St. Paul — a 25-year record. Actually, Santa claimed, he and the reindeer felt quite comfortable and he was disappointed that some of his school visits were canceled. When the weather moderated, he visited Stillwater and White Bear Lake. Toward the end of his stay, Santa had a caller from across the Mississippi River. Mayor George Leach of Minneapolis, who took belated notice of the hullabaloo in St. Paul, made an official visit. Lacking his own reindeer, he arrived in a vintage coach drawn by four horses.

On December 24, government offices closed at noon and last-minute shoppers scurried about in new-fallen snow, which gave a "Final Touch of Splendour to St. Paul." WCCO arranged a live broadcast of Santa's final appearance at a jubilee in the St. Paul Auditorium. The station asked owners of loud speakers (there were an estimated 25,000 in St. Paul) to place them where the broadcast could be heard outdoors "so the immediate neighborhood may share in the music." In that way the "Christmas City" would be filled with the sounds of Christmas Eve.

Santa, Tautuk, and the reindeer were on the auditorium stage during the musical program that evening. As the last strains of the Christmas jubilee died away, there was sudden darkness throughout the big hall and the sound of pattering hoofs. When the lights came on again, Santa, Tautuk, the sleigh, and the reindeer were gone. "No Christmas Eve ever surpassed that of Friday," said the *Pioneer Press*.

A few days later St. Paul children on school holiday were seen out

219

in their neighborhoods building igloos like the one Santa had in Rice Park. The *Dispatch* and *Pioneer Press* gave the two log cabins in the park to the Boy Scouts. From Icy Cape came word that the reindeer had brought Santa safely back home, where he was recovering from his long journey, or perhaps from his exhausting schedule of activities in St. Paul.

The month-long Christmas Reindeer program was clearly a commercial enterprise. Its promoters obviously hoped it would increase newspaper and radio audiences and boost business for railroads and downtown stores. But the message was a gentle one; the key words were good will, children, concern for the unfortunate, and, of course, reindeer — in their most charming aspects.

In 1932 another Lomen Christmas Reindeer pageant was sponsored in St. Paul by the *St. Paul Pioneer Press*, the *Dispatch*, downtown merchants, and the Junior Chamber of Commerce. The city's brave interval of holiday joy in the darkness of depression followed much the same pattern as the earlier visit. Santa, his helper Tautuk, and the deer were quartered in a small log cabin with a corral beside Third and Cedar streets in downtown St. Paul. Santa visited orphanages and children's hospitals and made trips to White Bear Lake, Owatonna, and Albert Lea. Joining him in a grand parade was Governor Floyd B. Olson, who said he was "flabbergasted at the sea of youthful faces." The visit ended December 23 with a moving-picture show at the Paramount Theater. Twenty-five hundred children attended, each bringing a toy or a gift of food for the needy.[77]

While the Christmas Reindeer shows proliferated, the Lomens continued to promote reindeer business in more prosaic ways. On trips to Washington, D.C., Carl lobbied for his company's interests and for Alaska's needs. One happy result of these visits was his meeting with Minnesota Representative Andrew J. Volstead of Granite Falls and the congressman's daughter, Laura, who had been a boarding-school classmate of Lomen's sister in Minneapolis. In 1928 Lomen and Laura Volstead were married in St. Paul. Laura, who had been her father's office assistant and was a public speaker and writer of ability, became her husband's talented associate in reindeer promotion.[78]

Another Lomen venture, which captured wide public interest, began in 1928. The Canadian government, responding to the needs of Eskimo natives of the Northwest Territories, where white hunters and trappers had destroyed or driven off much of the wild game, decided to introduce domesticated reindeer and lessen the natives' dependence on imported food and clothing. The Canadians bought from the Lomens 3,000 deer, which were to be delivered on the hoof in two years. The "Great Trek" from Kotzebue Sound, Alaska, to the east bank of the Mackenzie River near Aklavik in Canada, covering 1,800 miles over mountains and river valleys on the rim of the Arctic, was not completed until March, 1935. Andrew Bahr, whom the Lomens had lured out of comfortable retirement in Seattle, was chief herder and supervisor of the twelve Lapps and Eskimos who made up the hardy crew. The expedition received wide coverage in the press, and Bahr, on his return to Seattle, was declared a public hero.[79]

The Lomens' success in the Christmas Reindeer business encouraged other midwestern entrepreneurs to enter the field. Most notable was Nicholas H. Dimond (1882–1935), a lawyer, Nonpartisan League organizer, and traveling salesman who had worked at various jobs from Wolf Point, Montana, to Escanaba, Michigan. Over six feet tall and weighing perhaps 220 pounds, Dimond was talented, well-read, and "a heavy weight personality," according to one of his associates. In 1926 he was employed at the stockyards in St. Paul, and he may have been inspired to go into the reindeer business by the spectacle of the St. Paul Christmas Reindeer program that year. Dimond organized the Northland Reindeer Company in 1927, and acquired a team of Alaskan reindeer. His first deer may in fact have been the very team that had starred in St. Paul. He quartered the animals north of Duluth on the old Vermilion Trail.[80]

In December, 1927, the Duluth Retail Merchants Association sponsored Dimond's first reindeer show with a dog team as an added attraction. The *Duluth News Tribune* and *Herald* and WEBC radio described Santa's adventures on the long journey so graphically that an estimated 10,000 children turned out to celebrate his arrival. The reindeer, housed in a shelter on Superior Street at Third Avenue, received visitors from noon to 10:00 in the evening. Often some or all of the deer were hitched to the sleigh for action-packed visits to schools, orphanages, hospitals, parties, or calls at the toy departments of downtown stores. Neighborhood gatherings, including gala events at West Duluth and Morgan Park, were sponsored by business and civic organizations.[81]

When it was all over, local merchants counted the tangible and intangible benefits of the Christmas Reindeer show. All branches of the retail trade reached new highs, according to one West Duluth spokesman. Duluth retail merchants told Dimond that they were "highly satisfied" with the show and felt that it had brought them much out-of-town business. The president of one of the department stores wrote to Dimond: "Without any doubt this was one of the outstanding civic successes put on in this community and brought much praise to your company for the successful manner in which you handled your part of it." The writer said that, viewed in a larger perspective, "such celebrations have a tendency to bring a community closer together and create a spirit that must and did tend towards building up friendly business relations." Dimond kept copies of the complimentary letters in a scrapbook with clippings from the *News Tribune* and *Herald* describing the events of the 1927 Christmas Reindeer program in Duluth. He used the book during the following years to help sell the show in other places.[82]

Soon after the Duluth show, Dimond began to look farther north for land with more moss for the deer. The editor of the *Cook County News Herald*, aware of Dimond's interest in the area, realized that a reindeer venture in Cook County would also advertise Grand Marais and draw tourists. In support of the possible venture the *News Herald* printed

221

several stories about opportunities for reindeer culture in the area. The articles pointed out the abundance of pest-free pastures of reindeer moss and speculated about the income from sales of hides and meat. Dimond and his employees willingly supplied some of the copy.[83]

Such promotional activity as this must have helped to convince Charles Boostrom of Clearwater Lake to join Dimond's reindeer enterprise. Boostrom had reindeer moss on his land and he had trained sled dogs, which Dimond had decided should be added to the Christmas shows. Just when Dimond and Boostrom agreed to work together is not clear, but Boostrom may have helped in some way with Dimond's shows in 1929. By the fall of 1930 the deer and an Ojibway Indian herder were in residence at Boostrom's place. In the Clearwater years between 1930 and 1933 Dimond called his business the Dimond Reindeer Ranch Company.[84]

Charlie Boostrom's contributions to the business were considerable. Boostrom (1888–1979) was born in Minneapolis of Swedish parents and he had lived in Milaca and Hinckley before 1911, when he settled in Cook County. He was a trapper, logger, carpenter, and builder of log cabins, a guide for fishermen, canoeists, and hunters, and, with his wife Petra, a resort operator at Clearwater Lake on the Gunflint Trail. Boostrom constructed a corral and a shed for the reindeer. He built sleds for the Christmas shows, provided a truck and trailer, and traveled with the shows for two or three years. He trained a white deer to shake her head from side to side when he laid his hand on it. When he scratched her, she would nod her head slowly up and down. With this act, the reindeer appeared to answer questions as to whether a child had been good or not. Children in hospitals and schools especially loved this deer.

Dimond enlarged the herd with purchases of trained deer from Alaska. Deer cost $7 each plus a charge of $57 for shipping to Grand Marais, according to Boostrom's son, but in 1933 Dimond paid $300 each for deer "Guaranteed Healthy & Tame," shipped from Seattle to the show in Chicago. When the reindeer were let out of their Clearwater corral, an Indian herded them, and as long as he was there the animals stayed nearby. Sometimes he would talk or sing to them and they seemed to like it. The deer were usually gentle, but when they were not in good humor they "raised heck" in the barn and kicked at people who came near. They ate some alfalfa and grain as well as the moss, which Boostrom's sons gathered for a dime a bag. During the hunting season the deer wore red-ribbon collars with bells and were kept in the corral as much as possible.[85]

When Dimond was at Clearwater he and his family camped out in an old school building; much of the time, however, he and another agent went out selling the shows for the Christmas season. They were so successful that in 1930 there were enough bookings to put three shows on the road. Rather than import actors from Alaska, Dimond used home-grown talent. He and his wife played the parts of Santa and Mrs. Claus in one of the shows. Boostrom, his brother Alec, his nephew Clifford Samuelson, who was a guide and trapper at Clearwater, Alfred Brissom,

Reindeer at Clearwater, Minnesota, October 14, 1930. *MHS*

Joe Thomas, an Ojibway family of father, mother, and son from Grand Portage, and a "Santa Claus" from Duluth were all employed in one or another of the traveling shows during Dimond's Clearwater years.[86]

What must have been one of Dimond's most successful engagements was in 1929 in St. Cloud, where the *Daily Times* sponsored the Christmas Reindeer show for three years. When the prancing deer hauled Santa and his helpers down the parade route lighted by red and green flares, it was reported that some 30,000 people (including 20,000 out-of-town visitors) roared their greeting. Merchants said all business records were broken as the greatest throng in the city's history invaded the downtown stores after the parade. The next year, after a successful repeat performance, *Times* publisher Fred Schilpin called Santa a "go-getter."[87]

One of the performers in the 1930 show, Clifford Samuelson, recalled some of the inside story of this and other Christmas Reindeer programs. The company was paid about $500 a day, of which the booking agent took 10 per cent. Samuelson earned $10 a day and expenses, a good wage for the time. The deer were carried in a truck and behind it was a trailer with the dog kennels and sleds. Other members of the troupe drove a car and a bus loaded with alfalfa and reindeer moss.[88]

Santa and his entourage reached St. Cloud on December 3 and established headquarters at Lake George. Driver-manager Samuelson — his show business name was "Scotty Girard" — had nothing to do with the publicity and he had no idea of what had been reported about his supposedly harrowing journey. "The first thing I did when I reached town," he remembered, "I looked for a paper to know where we came from!"

As usual, the newspaper publicity suggested a close relationship among Santa, Alaska, the reindeer, and the Lomens. After Dimond moved his herd to Grand Marais, newspapers extolled the Arrowhead as well, commenting that Santa was able to get reindeer moss there.

The schedule for the Dimond reindeer company at St. Cloud that year was a taxing one, calling for visits to a total of 35 nearby towns, including Royalton, Paynesville, Sauk Centre, Monticello, and Princeton. In a single morning Santa visited Waite Park, Sartell, Sauk Rapids, and an orphanage at St. Cloud; that afternoon he entertained children at St. Cloud's Lake George playground. On Sunday, Samuelson's free day, he drove the deer out into the country to give them a workout and to visit his family at their farm near Milaca. In St. Cloud, as in all other towns on the tour, the troupe stayed in hotels, the deer slept in the truck, where they had food and plenty of space to lie down, and the dogs remained in their kennels. The visit ended with a grand parade, which included business-sponsored floats that depicted children's rhymes and stories.

Meanwhile, Dimond and another troupe were playing to enthusiastic crowds at Watertown, Huron, Yankton, and Madison in South Dakota. But even with all the emphasis on the Arctic, the North Pole, and Alaska, Santa (Dimond) did not forget to speak of the Arrowhead country. He told reporters for the *Evening Huronite* that he was establishing his summer home in the Arrowhead region of northern Minnesota "where many reindeer live," and he invited everyone to visit him there. A week after visiting Huron, Santa told the *Daily Sentinel* at Madison that reindeer were destined to become a valuable economic factor in the northern tip of Minnesota, especially around Grand Marais in Cook County. A million deer could be raised there, he said.[89]

Samuelson worked on the Christmas circuit for two years, playing at Indianapolis, Bismarck, Chicago, Racine, Green Bay, and other places in Wisconsin, Illinois, Indiana, and Minnesota. Festivities in a town usually ended by about 8:00 P.M., he recalled. Then the show would pack up and drive four to six hours to the next town. The deer slept in the truck; members of the troupe slept a few hours after they arrived and then dressed and harnessed up for a round of activities the next day. Longer performances included a week in Kansas City, sponsored by Montgomery Ward, and another week in Chicago, sponsored by Sears Roebuck. The Santa party spent one day at each of seven Sears stores in Chicago.[90]

Problems with the deer sometimes altered the schedule. In Vincennes, Indiana, in 1931, authorities quarantined the deer because some had a skin disease. Dimond was said to have gone by plane to the next engagement at Libertyville, Illinois, and put on the show without the deer. One year two reindeer escaped from the corral at Clearwater just before a tour was to start. Three men tracked them in fresh snow for three days — with no time out for meals — before they were caught. One reindeer headed for water and the Canadian border, so the men went after it in a motorboat. When they caught up with the swimming animal, they tied an oar to its antlers and towed it to shore. True to its

Christmas Reindeer parade at Indianapolis. *MHS*

publicity, the deer's own buoyant fur kept the animal high enough in the water to reduce the risk of its drowning.[91]

The showmen, too, could run into unexpected trouble on the trail. One season Boostrom and Samuelson, who had never been to Alaska, each survived a face to face confrontation with an eagle-eyed Alaska hand. Boostrom evidently bluffed his way out of the encounter; Samuelson disarmed his critic by admitting that he was only a show-business Alaskan and had a pleasant chat with an old veteran of the Klondike.[92]

Before the 1933 season Dimond abandoned his deer at Clearwater and the Boostroms never heard from him again. Boostrom's sons said that Dimond left the deer in payment for debts owed their father, who was too easygoing to demand cash. Hermund Melheim, Dimond's next associate, suggested that Dimond left the deer because he could not get performers or engagements enough to keep more than one show on the road. Perhaps there is truth in both explanations.[93]

The Indian herder at Clearwater also seems to have disappeared at about this time. With no one to herd them the deer soon returned to the wild. They were seen farther out on the Gunflint Trail and as far as Tofte near Hedley Redmyer's old home. Chris Tormondsen saw an animal at Tofte he was sure was a reindeer because it had a red ribbon and bell around its neck and was friendly to people. Later in the 1930s, when Donald Boostrom was hunting, he shot an animal that he thought was a mixed-breed white-tailed deer and reindeer. It was much bigger than an ordinary deer and had reindeer-type antlers. No reindeer or mixed-deer descendants have been reported in Cook County since.

225

Although Dimond abandoned his herd at Clearwater, he was not yet finished with the reindeer business. In 1933 he acquired new deer, found another partner, and relocated his headquarters in a reindeer-moss area between Kabetogama and Rainy lakes near Ray, Minnesota.[94]

Dimond had met Hermund Melheim, his new associate, before the reindeer business ever started, when the two men were traveling salesmen in North Dakota. Melheim, born at Sogn, Norway, had immigrated in 1915 when he was 24, joining members of his family who had settled at Hanska, Minnesota. A handsome, thoughtful man, Melheim had educated himself in English and acquired book learning as well as a useful knowledge of human nature during his selling days. When Dimond searched him out and "talked him into" the reindeer enterprise, Melheim was working as a foreman at a General Motors plant in Detroit.

Melheim's duties as one of the proprietors of the business, now known as the Dimond Reindeer Company, were to help train the deer (although he had never seen one before), coach new members of the troupes in their roles, and put his other skills to good use. When the trailer burned at the end of the 1933 tour, he built a new 40-foot-long replacement, with room in the front for the deer and their food and bunks in the back for the employees. He also played Santa Claus one year, feeling that he was better able to perform the role than many of the local actors. The slim Norwegian "built up a big stomach," donned cap and bushy white whiskers, and put on a lively show. Instead of holding children in his lap, he stood up in the sleigh and told them about the toy factory at the North Pole, "the biggest factory in the world," about reindeer and the musk oxen he saw there, and a lot of other "big

Hermund Melheim unloading reindeer. *MHS*

Ping Pi Liu, who played an Eskimo herder. *MHS*

lies" — all in the show-business spirit. He encouraged them to ask questions, and then, in order to "get 'em alive," told them "I can't hear you." By the end of the show, they were singing songs and "hollering."

After 1933 Dimond and Melheim took only one troupe on the road and made other changes in operations. They continued to use dogs and they expanded the cast to include three wise men and a two-humped Siberian camel, rented for the season from a company at Lancaster, Missouri. The wise men, dressed in pajama costumes, were local people hired in each town. Those were Depression days, Melheim pointed out, and men were glad to work at any job for a couple of dollars a day. For the regular cast, Dimond and Melheim hired Finlanders John and Oiva Salmi, brothers who lived near Ray, as a handyman and "Eskimo," respectively. John Razor, an Ojibway Indian from west of Bemidji, Joe and Henry La Prairie and George Earth, Indians from the Duluth and Cloquet area, and Ping Pi Liu, a Chinese medical student at the University of Minnesota, also played Eskimo roles. Ping was the son of an affluent family in Manchuria, but the Japanese invasion of his homeland had cut off his means of support.[95]

In 1934 Dimond discontinued the practice of selling the show for extended visits of a week or more and began booking only short engagements. That year, the most ambitious of all the Dimond seasons, the troupe was booked in 64 cities and towns from Minnesota and North Dakota to Nebraska, Kansas, Colorado, New Mexico, Oklahoma, and Wyoming.

Dimond died the following spring in Duluth of complications from a ruptured appendix. He had not begun to sell the show for the new season. Melheim, who, with Mrs. Dimond, now owned the company, added booking-agent duties to his other responsibilities. By his own assessment, his personality differed from his friend's, but after two years with Dimond he had learned the show business, and his experience as a salesman gave him the necessary background in selling. He had no trouble booking the show for the full season in Iowa, North Dakota, and Minnesota.[96]

But the next season was a difficult one. A week and a half after the beginning of the tour, the deer began to die from moss poisoned by mildew. They were buried where they expired; Melheim saved the antlers of two and later gave them to the St. Louis County Historical Society. The other sponsors on Melheim's schedule agreed to let him present the show without the deer at a reduced fee, but the season was a financial disaster. "No one feels any worse about the death of the reindeer than does old Santa himself," explained the *Willmar Tribune* in the last engagement of the season, but the hardships of the journey proved too much for the animals. Nevertheless, a tremendous crowd gathered to watch Santa, his helpers, and the dogs parade through the downtown business district to the courthouse lawn, and merchants reported a "splendid holiday trade." It was a fine last show for the season, and although a few deer left at Ray survived the blight Melheim was unable to get any more from Alaska. It was the end of the road for the Dimond Reindeer Company.[97]

Melheim and Lillian Dimond married after 1935, and Melheim built a new log cabin in the woods near Ray. There he began a new and very successful career as a wood carver.

Melheim's problems in replacing the reindeer were a consequence of a drastic change in the whole character of the reindeer business in Alaska, which also brought about the end of Lomen & Company in the industry. Disputes in the 1930s between native and nonnative owners of reindeer and a new administration in Washington called into question some of the original premises of the program. Some said that if the reindeer were brought to Alaska at government expense for the benefit of the natives and were pastured on the public domain, then ownership of the deer should have been restricted to the natives. White owners should not have been allowed to profit from reindeer business. On the other hand, others said, it was only right for white men as well as natives to own herds. Large contributions of money and services from individuals and church organizations, augmenting modest public funds, had made possible the importing of deer and herders, and had supplemented federal appropriations for the operation of schools and apprenticeship programs. Laplanders, who had taught the natives how to care for the deer, were paid for their work in part with deer. When some of them had sold their herds to the Lomens, the animals became the nucleus of the Lomen reindeer business. Herds owned by natives and nonnatives could exist side by side, these people argued, to the benefit of each and the larger economic benefit of Alaska.[98]

Furthermore, said the Lomens, who owned by far the largest number of privately-held deer, ownership was not the only way the natives benefited from the reindeer industry. Those who wanted to have their own herds could do so. Those who did not want that responsibility could work for the Lomens, who were said to be the largest single employer of native labor in Alaska. The deer, no matter who owned them, provided meat and clothing for the natives. The Lomens provided markets outside of Alaska for the surplus deer from their own and native herds.

Critics of white ownership stressed the fact that it was difficult to separate the animals owned by natives from those of the Lomens when all were grazed on the open range. There was, too, much resentment of the Lomens' strength in Alaskan business and political affairs. The dispute raged from Alaska to Washington and forced both sides into extreme positions. In the end, Congress passed the Alaska Reindeer Act of 1937, which required nonnative owners to sell their herds, equipment, and facilities to the government for transfer to the natives. Henceforth only Alaskan natives would be permitted to own reindeer.

The decline of markets in the States during the Depression, the advent of World War II, overgrazing of pastures, and lax and inexperienced management during years of transition in ownership caused a dwindling of the Alaskan herds. In the 1950s, however, interest in reindeer culture revived, and by 1982, according to the *Alaska Farm Magazine*, the industry of reindeer herding was thriving "and could be the largest single renewable agricultural resource in the state."[99]

Of the 18 herds in Alaska in 1982 (comprising an estimated 30,000 deer), 14 were on or near the Seward or Baldwin peninsulas at such familiar places as Nome, Brevig Mission, and Teller; the others were on Alaskan islands. Surplus deer from these herds provided the nuclei of two new herds. A state-wide reindeer herders' association provided administrative and management services to the owners of the herds. The University of Alaska kept a herd on its Fairbanks campus, conducted reindeer health workshops, and had sponsored research in combating reindeer pests for more than 20 years. Thus some of the long-range advantages of raising reindeer envisioned by Sheldon Jackson and his supporters began to be realized, and the health of the industry was, as it was from the beginning, closely related to the educational system of Alaska.

Carl Lomen's statement of the economic case for the reindeer is as appropriate today as it was when he first became enamored of the fascinating creature: "We are convinced that the reindeer industry can once again prove [to be] of great value to the people of Alaska and the far North. A domesticated animal that can live without shelter in the Arctic the year around and feed itself, that lives free of disease and furnishes fine meat and beautiful skins to make the warmest garments ever developed for Arctic wear, is certainly worthy of further serious study and development by both government and private industry."[100]

And there is always a chance that some day a new generation of herders will send teams of six gentle reindeer prancing from Icy Cape down through the streets of St. Paul, Duluth, or St. Cloud to delight another generation of children at Christmas time.

Reference Notes

In the interest of brevity, the following abbreviations are used in the notes for this volume:

MHS — Minnesota Historical Society

NARG — National Archives Record Group

PREFACE

[1] Strachey, *Eminent Victorians*, v (New York, 1963).

A SOLDIER "DISGUISED" — Pages 1 to 22

The author wishes to thank the following people for their help in researching this story: Patricia Harpole, Stephen Osman, MHS; Sara D. Jackson, National Archives, Washington, D.C.; Rev. David King, Elizabeth, N.J.; Bruce M. White, St. Paul.

[1] The major source of information for this chapter is the record of the court martial of Phineas Andrews, File W31 in general court martial records, Office of Judge Advocate General (War), NARG 153. The file has three parts: a transcript of the Proceedings (hereafter Andrews, Proceedings); Andrews' Defense by Lieut. Nathaniel S. Harris (hereafter Harris, Defense); and the "replication" or reply of prosecutor Lieut. James McIlvaine (hereafter McIlvaine, Reply). The Defense consists of 17 numbered folios, each containing 4 unnumbered pages. Photocopies of these and many other military records hereafter cited are in MHS. The quotations in this paragraph appear in McIlvaine, Reply, 4; Andrews, Proceedings, 22. For "disguised," meaning intoxicated, drunk, or tipsy, see James A. H. Murray, ed., *The Oxford English Dictionary*, 750 (Rev. ed., Oxford, England, 1933).

[2] J. P. C. McMahan to Surgeon General, October 2, 1827, Letters Received, Records of the Surgeon General's Office, NARG 112. See also Ann Adams, "Early Days at Red River Settlement and Fort Snelling, 1821–1829," *Minnesota Historical Collections*, 6:97 (St. Paul, 1894).

[3] For examples of the treatment of enlisted men, see regimental orders 37, March 12, 1826, and 97, May 20, 1827, U.S. Infantry, 5th Regiment, Garrison Orderly Book (hereafter cited as 5th Regiment Orderly Book), original in Burton Historical Collection, Detroit (Mich.) Public Library, microfilm copy in MHS. For treatment of an officer see

Col. Josiah Snelling to Major T. Hamilton, August 10, 1827, copy in Josiah Snelling Journal, 13, in MHS; footnote 48, below.

[4] Harris, Defense, 5. As early as 1822 Col. Snelling did not care for Lieut. Andrews. Snelling wrote that Andrews was "not fit to be trusted" but he did not accuse him of drunkenness. See Snelling to Commissary General, November 1, 1822, Fort Snelling Consolidated Correspondence File, Records of the Quartermaster General, NARG 92.

[5] Andrews served in Samuel Waugh's militia company and under Capt. Daniel Ketchum in the 25th. For details of his early career, see Connecticut Adjutant General's Office, *Record of Service of Connecticut Men in the War of 1812*, 2:5 (Hartford, 1889); Andrews, Pension File 296, New York-Connecticut, War of 1812, in Records of the Veterans Administration, NARG 15; Francis B. Heitman, *Historical Register and Dictionary of the United States Army 1789-1903*, 1:166 (Washington, D.C., 1903). On Andrews' family, see Alfred Andrews, *Genealogical History of John and Mary Andrews*, 92, 93, 150, 260-262 (Chicago, 1872).

[6] On Andrews' later career, here and two paragraphs below, see Post Returns, Fort Edwards, January-June, 1823, and Fort Crawford, February, 1824-May, 1825 — both in Records of the Adjutant General, NARG 94; McIlvaine, Reply, 4. On Morgan, see Heitman, *Historical Register*, 1:726.

[7] McIlvaine's military record is summarized in Heitman, *Historical Register*, 1:668; see also Post Returns, Fort Crawford, June, 1824, NARG 94; Snelling to Gen. Edmund P. Gaines, September 22, 1822, Fort Snelling Consolidated Correspondence File, NARG 92. On his "infirmity" and Fort Snelling service, see McIlvaine, Reply, 6, 20; Harris, Defense, 17; Andrews, Proceedings, 53. On the plowing affair here and below, see Andrews, Proceedings, 6, 43, 56-62, 73; Harris, Defense, 10. On Joseph Baxley, see Post Returns, Fort Crawford, May, 1826, NARG 94; Andrews, Proceedings, 13, 74, 78; Heitman, *Historical Register*, 1:200. On John "Bailey" of Co. K, see Post Returns, Fort Crawford, May, 1826, NARG 94.

[8] Andrews, Proceedings, 47, 111; McIlvaine, Reply, 7. Cavan and Westernra are listed in Fort Crawford, Post Returns, March, 1825, NARG 94. See also note 16, below.

[9] On the Fort Armstrong stop, see Andrews, Proceedings, 34, 45, 104, 110; Harris, Defense, 6; McIlvaine, Reply, 6.

[10] Andrews, Proceedings, 46-48, 72, 111, 118-120. A cleves (clevis) was a U-shaped piece of iron with a pin or bolt through holes in its ends. On Burns, see note 43, below.

[11] Here and below, see Andrews, Proceedings, 45-56, 63-71, 111-116; Harris, Defense, 7.

[12] McIlvaine, Reply, 6.

[13] Andrews, Proceedings, 49, 64, 66, 113-116.

[14] Andrews, Proceedings, 51, 64, 67, 69.

[15] Andrews, Proceedings, 46, 50-53, 66, 68-70; Harris, Defense, 8.

[16] Andrews, Proceedings, 47, 65; Harris, Defense, 8; McIlvaine, Reply, 7. Nothing more is known about Westernra. Cavan (whose name is variously spelled) was court martialed after his capture and sentenced to hard labor, to wear an iron collar around his neck, and to pay a fine of $24, one dollar a month for every day of the 24 lost from duty. See Cavan, court martial file V7, 1825, in NARG 153.

[17] Andrews, Proceedings, 71; McIlvaine, Reply, 7-9.

[18] On McIlvaine's alleged threats against Andrews, see Harris, Defense, 5, 17; Andrews, Proceedings, 60. Cole was born in about 1800 in Scotland and when he enlisted in the army in 1823 his occupation was given as "surgeon"; see U.S. War Department Register of Enlistments, 3:277 (1823), in Records of the Adjutant General's Office, NARG 94. His testimony is in Andrews, Proceedings, 16-19. On Hamilton, see Heitman, *Historical Register*, 1:494, and Andrews, Proceedings, 32.

[19] Andrews, Proceedings, 16, 18, 23, 30, 31.

[20] On Sayres, see Andrews, Proceedings, 30-34, and note 34, below. The noncommissioned officers were Leger, Major, Adams, Day, Pike, Rose, and David. The enlisted men were Alcott (Allcott, Olcott) and Whitman. See Andrews, Proceedings, 13, 20-22, 24-26, 107, 118.

[21] Andrews, Proceedings, 31, 38; Harris, Defense, 3. On Allanson, see Heitman, *Historical Register*, 1:157.

231

[22] Andrews, Proceedings, 32, 37, 118; Harris, Defense, 3. Morgan was in command at Fort Snelling from June through December, 1825; Fort Crawford, Post Returns, 1825, NARG 94.

[23] Here and below, see Andrews, Proceedings, 13–15; Harris, Defense, 2. On Harney, see Heitman, *Historical Register*, 1:501.

[24] Andrews, Proceedings, 21, 107.

[25] Andrews, Proceedings, 10, 23–25, 31. Joseph Adams of Co. B, born in England, was 23 and a saddler by profession. The record of Adams' re-enlistment in 1824 is in Josiah Snelling File 8654–1825, Records of the 2nd Auditor, U.S. General Accounting Office, NARG 217. Adams was married in 1826 to Barbara Ann Shadeker, who as Ann Adams wrote "Early Days at Red River Settlement" (see note 2).

[26] Andrews, Proceedings, 23, 29, 37, 118; Harris, Defense, 3, 4. On Camp, see Heitman, *Historical Register*, 1:276.

[27] On the Denny episode here and below, see Andrews, Proceedings, 30–32, 36, 39; Harris, Defense, 3. On Denny, see George W. Cullum, *Biographical Register of the Officers and Graduates of the U.S. Military Academy*, 1:110 (Boston, 1891).

[28] For the charges and specifications, see Andrews, Proceedings, 1–9. On Green, see Heitman, *Historical Register*, 1:474.

[29] The arrest order has not been found, but Andrews is reported in arrest and confinement between October, 1825, and September, 1826, in U.S. 5th Infantry Muster Rolls, NARG 94. Order no. 19 authorizing the court martial was issued at Louisville, Ky., October 20, 1825; Andrews, Proceedings, 1. For Stone's testimony, see Proceedings, 100, 116.

[30] On Cruger, see Heitman, *Historical Register*, 1:342. His supply voucher no. 16 is in his Account 5569–1826, Records of the 3rd Auditor, NARG 217. See also Post Order no. 1, January 1, 1826, 5th Regiment Orderly Book; Andrews, Proceedings, 1–41. Snelling appointed to the court martial board captains Hamilton, Joseph Plympton, De Lafayette Wilcox, and Nathan Clark. Leger was court martialed, found guilty, and sentenced to ten days in solitary confinement with no whisky allowance, but after four days his company commander had his sentence remitted and a month later Leger was appointed a sergeant in Co. H; see Fort Snelling Post Orders no. 28 and 29 and Regimental Order no. 44, 5th Regiment Orderly Book.

[31] Snelling to Quartermaster General Thomas S. Jesup, March 1, April 23, 1826, in Fort Snelling Consolidated Correspondence File, NARG 92; Andrews, Proceedings, 36, 41, 116; Harris, Defense, 5. On Dr. Edwin James, see Heitman, *Historical Register*, 1:569; Andrews, Proceedings, 36.

[32] Andrews, Proceedings, 42, 120; Post Order no. 31, May 4, 1826, 5th Regiment Orderly Book. On Dr. Robert C. Wood, see Heitman, *Historical Register*, 1:1055.

[33] Andrews, Proceedings, 41–45, 90–92, 121; McIlvaine, Reply, 14.

[34] Regimental Orders no. 78, May 4, 1826 (Allanson), no. 97, May 20, 1826 (Sayres), 5th Regiment Orderly Book; U.S. 5th Infantry, Inspection Returns, April 30, 1826, NARG 94 (Denny); Andrews, Proceedings, 70–72, 77.

[35] Here and below, see Andrews, Proceedings, 85–88.

[36] On the "Eclipse" episode here and three paragraphs below, see Andrews, Proceedings, 91–97, 104; Harris, Defense, 16.

[37] Andrews, Proceedings, 107.

[38] Harris, Defense, 16.

[39] On Harris, see U.S. Military Academy Cadet Applications, 1820–21, File 129, NARG 94; Cullum, *Biographical Register*, 1:416; McIlvaine, Reply, 15. See also Post Order no. 2, January 7, 1826, and minutes and reports of council of administration, January 10–13, 1826, in 5th Regiment Orderly Book; Lawrence Taliaferro Journal, January 17, 30, May 9, 1826, Lawrence Taliaferro Papers, MHS.

[40] McIlvaine, Reply, 15. Andrews' request for orderly books and other documentary evidence was undoubtedly inspired by Harris; see Andrews, Proceedings, 85–88.

[41] McIlvaine, Reply, 1, 2, claimed Harris drew his literary allusions from a *Dictionary of Quotations* that McIlvaine brought to court; see Andrews, Proceedings, 89, 92.

[42] Andrews, Proceedings, 106, 111–116. Stewart (Steward) was a musician in Co. G; see Fort Crawford, Post Returns, March, 1825–May, 1826, NARG 94.

[43] Andrews, Proceedings, 118. Burns enlisted originally under the name of William Wager.

[44] On Charles Smith, a sergeant of Co. K, see Fort Crawford, Post Returns, April, 1826, NARG 94; Andrews, Proceedings, 79, 109, 119–121.

[45] For David Hunter (1802–86), see Cullum, Biographical Register, 1:290–293. Hunter was an 1822 graduate of the military academy and the son of an army chaplain. See also Fort Crawford, Post Returns, August, 1826–October, 1827, NARG 94. His court martial, File I39, NARG 153, is the source of the incidents described here and in the following two paragraphs; see p. 5, 8, 10, 12, 18, 21. The court martial board voted to "cashier" Hunter from the army, the appropriate verdict for his behavior, but recommended him in the strongest terms to the president for clemency. After review in Washington, his sentence was remitted by the president, and he went on to have a long and distinguished army career, retiring as a brevet major general in 1866.

[46] Here and nine paragraphs below, see Harris, Defense, 1–5, 7, 12–17; Andrews, Proceedings, 93.

[47] McIlvaine, Reply, 20. Press accounts of Andrews' defense have not been found.

[48] Here and four paragraphs below, see McIlvaine, Reply, 1–4, 6, 10, 11, 17, 18.

[49] Here and six paragraphs below, see Nathaniel S. Harris, Proceedings of a Court of Inquiry, File U54, NARG 153. On William Joseph Snelling, see Harris, Defense, 12; Adams, in Minnesota Historical Collections, 6:96; George D. Lyman, John Marsh, Pioneer: The Life Story of a Trail-blazer on Six Frontiers, 63 (New York, 1930); Edward D. Neill, History of the Minnesota Valley, 97 (Minneapolis, 1882). The younger Snelling is best known for his book Tales of the North West; or Sketches of Indian Life and Character (Boston, 1830).

[50] Report, August, 1826, in Records of the U.S. Army, Inspector General, NARG 159. A year later Snelling was less considerate. He offered Hamilton the choice of resigning with a year's furlough or standing trial as "no longer fit for the station you hold"; see Snelling to Hamilton, August 10, 1827, copy in Snelling Journal, 12.

[51] Andrews, Proceedings, 125; U.S. Infantry, 5th Regiment, Muster Roll, Co. B, October, 1826, NARG 94.

[52] Snelling Journal, 3; Phineas Andrews Account 12938, 2nd Comptroller File 7508, in Records of the 2nd Auditor of the Treasury, NARG 217.

[53] On Harris, see Rev. David R. King, historiographer, Diocese of New Jersey, to author, January 29, 1980, enclosing necrology of "The Rev. Nathaniel Sayre Harris," from the Journal of the Convention of the Diocese of New Jersey, 139 (N.p., 1886), in author's possession. Harris' report, Journal of a Tour in the "Indian Territory," Performed by Order of the Domestic Committee of the Board of Missions of the Protestant Episcopal Church, in the Spring of 1844, by Their Secretary and General Agent (New York, 1844), is cataloged by the Boston Public Library with Harris as author.

[54] See three letters from Capt. John Garland to Gen. T. S. Jesup, all dated October 12, 1827 (one marked "Private") and Garland to Jesup, September 26, 1827, all in Josiah Snelling Consolidated Correspondence File, NARG 92. Snelling's financial difficulties are suggested in memoranda in his Journal. By his own account he owed more than $1,600 to the former sutler on December 31, 1827, and various amounts to other persons. For references to duels, see Taliaferro Papers, February 6, 1826, and June 23, 1827; Adams, in Minnesota Historical Collections, 6:98; Neill, Minnesota Valley, 97; Hunter, Proceedings, 12, 27, 28; Snelling Journal, 16.

[55] Hunter, Proceedings, 28; Warren Upham, "The Women and Children of Fort Saint Anthony Later Named Fort Snelling," in Magazine of History, 21:34 (July, 1915). See also Adams, in Minnesota Historical Collections, 6:97.

[56] Here and below, see Snelling to Lieut. G. Low, September 10, 1827, copy in Snelling Journal, 16; 3rd Auditor to Josiah Snelling, June 18, 1828, in Miscellaneous Letters Sent, 1828, NARG 217; W. J. Snelling to Lewis Cass, February 16, 1833, in Josiah Snelling Consolidated Correspondence File, NARG 92. Snelling was indebted to the government some $740 at his death; how much he owed others can be guessed from the 1827 memoranda (see Snelling Journal, 3) and from file 117S-1828 in Letters Received, Main Series, NARG 94; the charges filed against Snelling by Alexander Johnston, David Hunter, and Anthony Drane, as well as the names of others, military and civilian, who would be called

233

as witnesses, are in this file, as are Hunter's "additional charges" from which the quotations are taken. General Order no. 46, NARG 94, announced his death. The *National Daily Intelligencer* (Washington, D.C.), August 21, 1828, announced arrangements for his funeral; he was 46 years old.

TRUTH TELLER AT LAKE CONSTANCE — Pages 23 to 54

The author wishes to thank the following people for their help in researching this story: Arthur and Nan Anderson, Lindstrom; Kenneth D. Bjork, Northfield; Kenneth L. Carley, Patricia Harpole, Marlin Heise, Deborah L. Miller, MHS; P. J. Casey, Stanley Hydeen, the Rev. David L. Parrish, Meeker County Clerk of Court and staff, Litchfield; Campbell Abstract Company, Mrs. Nellie Elliot, Sue Erickson, Mouraine Hubler, E. R. Mills, Marion Jameson, staff of Wright County Historical Society, Buffalo; Cottonwood County Clerk of Court and staff, Windom; Lu (Mrs. Lot) Jackson, Shafer; Sara D. Jackson, National Archives, Washington, D.C.; Selma Jacobson, Swedish Pioneer Historical Society, Chicago; Sigurd Westberg, Evangelical Covenant Church of America Archives, Chicago; Ruth Jefferson (Mrs. R. F.) Sando, Citrus Heights, Calif.; Lennart and Lilly Setterdahl, Växjö, Sweden; staff of Augustana College Archives, Rock Island, Ill.

[1] On Widstrand's early years at Lake Constance, here and below, see *Agathocrat* (Buffalo), September 8, November 17, 1876, January 31, February 19, 28, 1877; *Rothuggaren* (Litchfield), September, 1885. The only known file of Widstrand's paper *Agathocrat* (later *Truth Teller*) is in MHS Reference Library. Only 11 full issues of his *Rothuggaren* have been found; they are at Augustana College (Rock Island), North Park College (Chicago), and MHS. Although Widstrand did not own any animals, he sometimes borrowed a neighbor's horse; *Agathocrat*, August 21, 1877.

[2] Here and below, see Ulla Widstrand Jefferson, "Jocob Widstrand," 1–7, typescript in possession of Ruth Jefferson Sando, copy in Helen M. White, comp., Widstrand Family Research File (hereafter Widstrand File), in author's possession. Jocob, whose father was Eric Isaacson, took the name Widstrand from the parish (Wiby) where he was born and *Strand*, meaning shore; *Truth Teller*, July 2, 1877.

[3] "Frans Herman Widstrand," autobiographical sketch enclosed in Widstrand to Ignatius Donnelly, August 25, 1873, in Donnelly Papers, MHS; Widstrand to Alexander Ramsey, May 29, 1862, in Ramsey Records, Minnesota State Archives, MHS; *Truth Teller*, May 21, July 2, 1877.

[4] *Agathocrat*, August 21, 1876; *Truth Teller*, April 30, October 2, 1877; "Frans Herman Widstrand," in Widstrand to Donnelly, August 25, 1873, in Donnelly Papers.

[5] Here and below, see *Agathocrat*, August 21, September 8, 1876, February 19, March 29, 1877; Adolph B. Benson, ed., *America in the Fifties: Letters of Fredrika Bremer*, 235 (New York, 1924). He was influenced, too, by the writings of Gustaf Unonius; Ernst Skarstedt, "En misskänd samhällsdanarë," a biographical sketch of Widstrand, in *Präirieblommen Kalendar, 1908*, 125 (Rock Island, Ill., 1907), trans. by Marlin Heise in Widstrand File.

[6] Here and below, see *Agathocrat*, August 21, 1876, February 19, 1877; A. E. Strand, comp. and ed., *A History of Swedish-Americans of Minnesota*, 2:496 (Chicago, 1910); Donald C. Holmquist, "Pride of the Pioneers' Parlor: Pianos in Early Minnesota," in *Minnesota History*, 39:322 (Winter, 1965); Jefferson, "Jocob Widstrand," 6, 8.

[7] Here and below, see *Agathocrat*, August 21, 1876, February 19, 1877; *Truth Teller*, July 2, 1877; Widstrand to Charles Widstrand, January 1, 1866, copy in Widstrand to Donnelly, March 31, 1866, Donnelly Papers. U.S. manuscript census schedules, 1860, Buffalo, Wright County, show Emma, 25, living with F. H. Widstrand; Jefferson, "Jocob Widstrand," 12, says Emma was living in Minneapolis when she died. See also Widstrand to "Friend Ilstrup," July 25, 1864, in Wright County Historical Society, Buffalo.

[8] Here and below, see Widstrand to Donnelly, August 7, 1862 (which Donnelly noted as "a foolish letter"), and "Frans Herman Widstrand," in Widstrand to Donnelly, August 25, 1873, both in Donnelly Papers; *Agathocrat*, October 23, 1876.

⁹ Here and below, see *D. R. Farnham's History of Wright County*, 41–43, 73–85, 328, 407 (Reprint ed., Buffalo, 1976); William Watts Folwell, *A History of Minnesota*, 2:161, 283, 287 (Rev. ed., 1961); *Agathocrat*, February 19, 1877.

¹⁰ On Carl (Charles) Wilhelm Theodor Widstrand (1843–1898), see Jefferson, "Jocob Widstrand," 3, 6, 11; compiled service record, First Minnesota Volunteer Infantry, Records of the Adjutant General, NARG 94; Frances L. Widstrand (Frances L. Haha), Widow's certificate (pension), 865,380, Records of the Veterans Administration, NARG 15; *Minnesota in the Civil and Indian Wars*, 1:518 (St. Paul, 1890); Widstrand to Donnelly, March 31, 1866, in Donnelly Papers; Widstrand to Ramsey, May 29, 1862, in Ramsey Records. It is not clear exactly when Widstrand became a vegetarian, but in 1885 he said he had not used meat for 25 years; *Rothuggaren*, March, 1885.

¹¹ On Widstrand's Washington experiences, here and below, see *Agathocrat*, September 8, October 23, December 28, 1876, March 29, 1877; Widstrand to "Friend Ilstrup," July 25, 1864, in Wright County Historical Society; Skarsted, in *Präirieblommen Kalendar, 1908*, 127; "Frans Herman Widstrand," in Widstrand to Donnelly, August 25, 1873, in Donnelly Papers.

¹² Here and below, see Skarstedt, in *Präirieblommen Kalendar, 1908*, 127. Widstrand listed 34 "communistic" societies known to him in the United States in his circular, "The Farist Community," enclosed in Widstrand to Donnelly, February 8, 1866, in Donnelly Papers. He also expressed particular interest in the Shakers and the Amana and Fruitlands colonies; see *Agathocrat*, August 21, October 5, December 28, 1876, January 8, 1877; *Truth Teller*, April 20, May 21, July 2, 1877; Widstrand to Donnelly, March 31, 1866, August 25, 1873, in Donnelly Papers. For more on these 19th century colonies, see William A. Hinds, *American Communities and Co-operative Colonies*, 360–396 (Rev. ed., Chicago, 1908).

¹³ Here and below, see *Agathocrat*, August 21, 1876; *Truth Teller*, July 2, 1877; "The Farist Community," in Widstrand to Donnelly, February 8, March 31, 1866, in Donnelly Papers. In his circular Widstrand defined "Farity" as "a feeling at once of friendship, benevolence, justice, frankness, uprightness, dignity and expressive of principles: Do thy duty come what may; or do unto others, animals as well as mankind of all sexes, ages and races, as you justly and reasonably wish to be done unto."

¹⁴ Widstrand to Donnelly, enclosing copies of his correspondence with Charles, March 31, 1866, in Donnelly Papers.

¹⁵ *D. R. Farnham's History of Wright County*, 87, 92; *Agathocrat*, February 19, 1877.

¹⁶ Here and below, see State of Minnesota *v.* H. L. Gordon, April, 1867, Civil Case File A 139, in records of Wright County Clerk of District Court, Buffalo. On Hanford L. Gordon, see Warren Upham and Rose B. Dunlap, *Minnesota Biographies*, 266 (Minnesota Historical Collections, vol. 12, 1914).

¹⁷ *Agathocrat*, August 21, 1876, February 19, 1877.

¹⁸ Widstrand tried to explain the confusing transactions in *Rothuggaren*, May, 1881; see also *Agathocrat*, February 19, 1877.

¹⁹ The signers included Thomas Smithson, W. D. Leonard, Virginia [Prime] Gilbert, A[ugustus] Prime, John and Frances Varner. Varner had been among Widstrand's first friends at Lake Constance; author's interviews with Nellie Elliot and E. R. Mills, Buffalo, 1977, notes in Widstrand Family File. The petition is printed in *Northern Statesman* (Monticello), February 22, 1868, which also quotes and comments on the *Pioneer* article.

²⁰ Widstrand to Donnelly, March 27, 1868, October 27, 1870; "Frans Herman Widstrand," in Widstrand to Donnelly, August 25, 1873, in Donnelly Papers; *Agathocrat*, August 21, 1876, March 16, 1877; *D. R. Farnham's History of Wright County*, 108.

²¹ *Northern Statesman*, August 28, 1869.

²² *Northern Statesman*, December 4, 1869.

²³ Here and below, see *St. Paul Pioneer*, July 11, 1869; *Agathocrat*, February 19, 1877. Widstrand said that the tornado destroyed his house; the insurance report said that the house was struck by lightning and destroyed by fire; *Farmers Union* (Minneapolis), August, 1869, p. 2.

²⁴ *Agathocrat*, February 19, 1877.

[25] Perrine bought the farm at the sale, negotiated with Widstrand for a mortgage on 70 acres, and sold another part to Nilson; *Agathocrat*, February 19, 1877. On Perrine, here and below, see *D. R. Farnham's History of Wright County*, 338, 350; *Northern Statesman*, May 8, September 25, 1869, April 16, August 27, 1870, March 25, 1871; *Wright County Times* (Monticello), January 14, 1875, May 25, 1876; *Agathocrat*, March 29, 1877.

[26] *Agathocrat*, September 21, 1876.

[27] For example, Widstrand memorialized the legislature to pass a more stringent law regarding cattle running at large. Nothing came of his petition. See *Northern Statesman*, February 18, 1871; Minnesota, *House Journal*, 1871, p. 120, 165.

[28] On Widstrand's St. Paul sojourn, here and below, see *St. Paul Dispatch*, February 18, 19, 22, 1875; *Wright County Times*, February 4, 25, 1875; *Agathocrat*, August 21, 30, October 3, 23, 31, 1876. Wright County expenditures for the poor for the year ending April 1, 1875, indicate that "sundries" amounting to $8 were furnished Widstrand; *Wright County Times*, April 1, 1875.

[29] No copies of the *Agathocrat* before August 21, 1876, have been found, and Widstrand did not mention these preliminary issues in his later writings. Information about the early issues, here and below, comes from *Wright County Times*, December 9, 1875, January 13, 27, February 10, April 20, May 11, 18, 25, July 20, 1876. See also *Wright County Times*, August 3, 24, September 14, 1876; *Agathocrat*, August 21, November 17, 1876; *Truth Teller*, April 20, December 13, 1877.

[30] *Agathocrat*, August 21, 1876, August 21, 1877.

[31] *Agathocrat*, August 21, September 21, October 3, 1876; *Truth Teller*, April 20, April 30, May 21, October 2, December 18, 1877.

[32] *Agathocrat*, August 21, September 21, October 3, 1876; *Truth Teller*, July 2, 1877. For examples of advertising, see *Agathocrat*, April 30, May 21, December 14, 1876.

[33] *Agathocrat*, December 14, 1876; *Truth Teller*, December 13, 1877.

[34] *Rothuggaren*, May, 1881. For comments on the supreme council, see *Agathocrat*, October 3, 1876, March 29, 1877; *Truth Teller*, May 21, July 21, 1877.

[35] Here and below, see *Agathocrat*, August 21, 30, October 3, 31, 1876, March 29, 1877; *Truth Teller*, July 2, August 21, 1877; Widstrand to Donnelly, February 8, 1866, in Donnelly Papers.

[36] *Agathocrat*, August 30, October 3, 23, December 14, 28, 1876, March 29, 1877; *Truth Teller*, April 30, July 2, 1877.

[37] Widstrand to Donnelly, August 7, 1862, February 8, 1866, August 25, 1873, in Donnelly Papers; *Agathocrat*, September 21, October 31, December 14, 1876; P. W. Maglaren (McLaren) to Alexander Ramsey, June 16, 1880, Ramsey to Maglaren, June 18, 1880, vol. 104, in Ramsey Papers, Minnesota Historical Society. Ramsey told Maglaren that Widstrand was "a very excentric [sic] man, by many thought to be crazy. To humor him, I introduced his petition"; see also 43 Congress, 1 session, *Congressional Record*, 3420.

[38] On the Vidal language, see *Agathocrat*, September 21, 1876; *Scientific American Supplement*, November 28, 1885, p. 8248.

[39] For Widstrand's ideas on diet, here and below, see *Agathocrat*, August 30, September 8, December 14, 1876, February 28, 1877; *Truth Teller*, July 21, 1877.

[40] *Agathocrat*, September 8, October 3, November 17, 1876.

[41] Here and below, see *News Ledger* (Litchfield), October 1, 1891; *Agathocrat*, August 30, September 8, October 31, November 17, December 14, 28, 1876, March 16, 1877; Widstrand to Donnelly, August 7, 1862, in Donnelly Papers.

[42] *Agathocrat*, November 17, 1876; *Truth Teller*, April 20, 1877; "The Farist Community," in Widstrand to Donnelly, February 8, 1866, in Donnelly Papers.

[43] Here and below, see *Agathocrat*, August 30, September 21, 1876, March 16, 1877; *Wright County Times*, August 12, 1875; "The Farist Community," in Widstrand to Donnelly, February 8, 1866, in Donnelly Papers.

[44] *Agathocrat*, August 18, September 8, December 14, 1876; Widstrand's revised version of "Work Made Easy" is in *Rothuggaren*, March, 1885. Mrs. Lloyd's verses were reprinted from the *Newark* (N.J.) *Courier*, according to Widstrand.

[45] See for example *Agathocrat*, February 19, 1877; *Truth Teller*, May 21, 1877.

[46] *Agathocrat*, March 29, 1877; *Truth Teller*, April 30, May 21, 1877; *Wright County Times*, April 26, 1877.

[47] Here and below, see *Agathocrat*, February 19, 28, 1877; *Truth Teller*, October 2, 1877.

[48] *Agathocrat*, March 29, 1877; *Truth Teller*, May 21, August 21, 1877.

[49] *Agathocrat*, March 29, 1877; *Truth Teller*, April 30, May 21, 1877.

[50] *Truth Teller*, May 21, July 21, 1877.

[51] *Truth Teller*, May 21, 1877.

REFERENCE NOTES

[52] *Wright County Times*, May 10, 1877; *Agathocrat*, August 21, 1876. According to Widstrand to Donnelly, August 25, 1873, in Donnelly Papers, part of "The Pioneer's Shanty" had been sent to the printer, but no record of its publication has been found.

[53] *Truth Teller*, May 21, July 2, 1877.

[54] *Truth Teller*, July 2, 1877.

[55] *Truth Teller*, April 20, 1877; *Wright County Times*, January 4, April 26, 1877.

[56] Here and below, see *Truth Teller*, July 2, 21, August 21, October 2, 1877; *Agathocrat*, October 31, 1876.

[57] *Truth Teller*, August 21, October 2, 1877.

[58] Here and below, see *Truth Teller*, December 18, 1877; *Wright County Times*, June 14, 1877.

[59] *Northern Statesman*, August 27, 1870; *Wright County Times*, February 4, 11, 18, 25, 1875, September 21, 1876, January 11, 1877; *Truth Teller*, May 21, 1877 (quoting *Times*).

[60] *Agathocrat*, December 14, 1876, February 19, 28, March 29, 1877; *Truth Teller*, July 20, October 3, 1877.

[61] *Agathocrat*, August 21, October 23, 1876.

[62] *Agathocrat*, December 28, 1876, March 16, 1877; *Truth Teller*, April 20, 30, August 21, 1877.

[63] *Agathocrat*, January 17, 1877.

[64] Here and below, see *Agathocrat*, August 21, 30, 1876, March 16, 1877; *Truth Teller*, July 2, December 13, 1877.

[65] Here and below, see Skarstedt, in *Präirieblommen Kalendar, 1908*, 129–130, 133; *Svenska Amerikanaren* (Chicago), April 15, August 19, 1880, trans. by Nan and Arthur Anderson, in Widstrand File; *Rothuggaren*, December, 1885.

[66] *Rothuggaren*, September, December, 1885. For more on this paper, see note 1. A microfilm edition of *Uppslyningens Tidehvarf* at MHS includes copies of the paper from various sources. Signed contributions from Widstrand are, for example, in issues of April, August, 1879, and May, June, July, 1880.

[67] Skarstedt, in *Präirieblommen Kalendar, 1908*, 130–131, 135; [S. J. Fogelblad?], "Krig i Minnesota, 1881" ("War in Minnesota"), undated and otherwise unidentified article concerning the warfare of the "roosters" in Olof Ohman Scrapbook, John Andreas Holvik Papers, MHS, trans. by Marlin Heise in Widstrand File.

[68] Ernst Beckman, *Amerikanska Studier, Våra Landsmän i Amerika* (Stockholm, 1883), as quoted in Skarstedt, in *Präirieblommen Kalendar, 1908*, 136; his visit with Widstrand is described on pages 118–121. According to Frank B. Lamson, *Condensed History of Meeker County, 1855–1939*, 51 (Litchfield, [1939]), Widstrand was translating Thomas Paine's *Age of Reason* into Swedish during his last years. Such a translation, *Förnuftets Tidehvarf*, was published after Widstrand's death by C. J. Erickson (St. Paul, [1900]).

[69] Here and below, see *News Ledger*, October 1, 1891; *Litchfield Independent*, April 29, 1891; Skarstedt, in *Präirieblommen Kalendar, 1908*, 136. Records of the Emmanuel Independent Swedish Evangelical Church (later Trinity Episcopal) were examined with the permission of the Rev. David L. Parrish, Litchfield. Stanley Hydeen, secretary of the Litchfield Cemetery Association, located Widstrand's unmarked grave.

ELIJAH E. EDWARDS, CIVIL WAR CHAPLAIN – Pages 52 to 87

The author wishes to thank the following people for their help in researching this story:

237

Leona T. Alig, Indiana Historical Society, and Harriet Cohen, Indiana State Library, both at Indianapolis, Ind.; Faustino Avaloz, Kenneth L. Carley, Dennis Meissner, Stephen Osman, MHS; Virginia Brann, David E. Horn, DePauw University Archives, Greencastle, Ind.; Al Caldwell and staff, Garrett Theological Seminary Library, Evanston, Ill.; Lynn A. Grove, McKendree College Library, Lebanon, Ill.; Lillian Harwood, Evanston, Ill.; Sara D. Jackson, National Archives, Washington, D.C.; James R. Miller, Ord, Nebr.; Elizabeth Pinkepank, Mabel Tainter Library and Educational Society, Menominee, Wis.; Willard and Barbara Rogers, St. Louis, Mo.; Evelyn M. Sutton, Commission on Archives and History, United Methodist Church, Lake Junaluska, N.C.

¹ Major sources of information for this chapter are Elijah Edwards' writings. His Journal and Sketch Book, vol. 1, an edited typescript with additional notes by Theodore G. Carter, covers the period from June 29 to the end of November, 1864; it is in MHS. The handwritten Journal and Sketch Book, vol. 2, in the Elijah E. Edwards Papers, DePauw University Archives, Greencastle, Indiana, begins with a fragmentary note of December 2, 1864, page 71, suggesting that vol. 1 consisted of 70 handwritten pages before it was typed. The two volumes are hereafter cited as Edwards, Journal, by volume and page. For details of Edwards' journey south, see Edwards, Journal, 1:5–8; his commission and his discharge papers with physical description are in Edwards Papers, DePauw. Minor errors in spelling and punctuation have been corrected in quoting from the Journals, particularly vol. 1, which was typed by Edwards when his eyesight was failing and he often could not see what he had transcribed.

² Military records of William H. Burt, Henry (Frank) Folsom, Frank Pratt, and Theodore G. Carter are summarized in *Minnesota in the Civil and Indian Wars*, 1:370, 374, 384, 406, 695 (St. Paul, 1890). The collaboration of Edwards and Carter is revealed in their correspondence in Theodore G. Carter Papers, MHS; see, for example, Edwards to Carter, June 24, 1910.

³ Edwards, Journal, 1:3, 8.

⁴ Biographical information from correspondence, newspapers, Edwards Papers, and many other sources, in Helen M. White, comp., Edwards Family Research File (hereafter Edwards File), in author's possession; see, for example, Harriet Cohen, Indiana State Library, to author, February 18, 1974. Quotations are from [Ezra Lathrop], "Historical Remarks on Hamline University," 24, 25, in Methodist Episcopal Church, Minnesota Annual Conference Historical Society Papers, 1840–1909, MHS. Lathrop, a Methodist minister and Indiana Asbury graduate, was chaplain of the Tenth Minnesota Infantry; *St. Paul Pioneer Press*, June 10, 1916, p. 5.

⁵ On Crary, see *Western Christian Advocate* (Cincinnati), June 5, 1895, p. 355, 362–364. On Edwards' Hamline years, see [Lathrop], "Historical Remarks," 25; *Red Wing Republican*, November 13, December 11, 1857, February 5, June 11, 25, July 9, 1858; on his early Taylors Falls years, here and below, see, for example, *Taylors Falls Reporter*, November 29, December 6, 1860, February 14, March 6, April 28, 1861; *St. Croix Monitor* (Taylors Falls), March 28, July 18, August 23, 1863. Edwards, "Pen Pictures," sketchbook in Edwards Papers, DePauw, contains many Red Wing (25–31) and Taylors Falls (73, 84, 88, 90) sketches; see also "Edwards Painted St. Croix Scenes," in *Dalles Visitor* (Taylors Falls), Summer, 1973, p. 1, 6.

⁶ Here and below, see "Sternwheelers Made Round Trips to Falls Cities," in *Dalles Visitor*, Summer, 1974, p. 1, 5, 14, 15; Edwards to Carter, June 24, 1910, in Carter Papers; *Taylors Falls Reporter*, May 2, 23, 30, September 5, October 17, 1861. A narrative history as well as the rosters for the Seventh Infantry are contained in *Minnesota in the Civil and Indian Wars*, 1:347–385.

⁷ *St. Croix Monitor*, July 18, 1863; Edwards Family File; Helen M. White, " 'His World Was Art': Dr. Andrew Falkenshield," in *Minnesota History*, 47:184–188 (Spring, 1981). On Light, see *Minnesota in the Civil and Indian Wars*, 1:342, 370; Wyman X. Folsom to "Mother" (Mary Jane [Mrs. W. H. C.] Folsom), May 24, 1864, in William H. C. Folsom Papers, MHS; Carter to Edwards, August 11, 1909, in Carter Papers.

⁸ [Lathrop], "Historical Remarks," 25; Edwards, Journal, 2:297; John T. Axton, Jr., *Brief History of Chaplains in U.S. Army*, 5 (N.d., n.p.). William R. Marshall noted that Edwards was elected chaplain by the regiment; see his Diary, July 3, 1864, in Marshall

Papers, MHS. For Crary's service record, see *Minnesota in the Civil and Indian Wars*, 1:178.

⁹ Edwards to Carter, March 20, 1906, June 23, 1910, in Carter Papers; Edwards, Journal, 1:5, 2:371. The quotations are from Stephen Miller to United States Officers, June 24, 1864, Executive Record "B," Records of the Office of Governor, Minnesota State Archives, MHS. The U.S. Christian Commission, a service of volunteers under the sponsorship of the Young Men's Christian Association, distributed reading matter and performed many other services for soldiers; see Clifton E. Olmstead, *History of Religion in the United States*, 391 (Englewood Cliffs, N.J., 1960).

¹⁰ In the battle of Brice's Cross Roads on the Guntown Road, Forrest gave Union cavalry forces under Sturgis "one of the classic beatings of the Civil War"; Bruce Catton, *The American Heritage Picture History of the Civil War*, 516, 521 (New York, 1960). For Edwards' account of the Tupelo campaign, here and below, see Journal, 1:8–31, 50 (quotations p. 11–14, 16, 18, 50). For Carter's somewhat different view, see his "Note of Explanation," attached to Edwards, Journal, 1:2–5; see also Carter to Edwards, June 3, 1909, in Carter Papers; Edwards' letter about "gobbling," signed "Miles," in the *Central Christian Advocate* (St. Louis), February 15, 1865. Edwards also undoubtedly wrote "Gen. Smith's Battles Near Tupelo, Miss.," an article signed "E" in *St. Paul Pioneer*, July 31, 1864.

¹¹ Dr. Henry M. Murdock (1824–99), a member of the Eighth Wisconsin Infantry, was one of five Murdocks who practiced medicine at one time or another in Taylors Falls. He operated a drugstore at Stillwater in 1854 and in later life practiced medicine at New Richmond, Wis.; Dr. Robert Rosenthal, "Notes on the Doctors Murdock," undated manuscript in author's possession. For other references to Murdock, see Edwards, Journal, 1:10, 16, 24. On Edwards' horses, see Edwards to Carter, January 11, 1890, in Carter Papers.

¹² Edwards, Journal, 1:16. On Dr. Lucius B. Smith, see *Minnesota in the Civil and Indian Wars*, 1:370; Mrs. Smith to William R. Marshall, March 6, 1866, in Marshall Papers. His body was later removed to Taylors Falls for final burial; *Stillwater Messenger*, May 2, 9, 30, 1866.

¹³ Edwards, Journal, 1:21.

¹⁴ Edwards, Journal, 1:26, and Carter, "Note," 5; Edwards to Carter, May 5, 1906, Carter to Edwards, June 3, 1909, Carter to Seth Birdsall, June 26, 1904, in Carter Papers; *Minnesota in the Civil and Indian Wars*, 1:356. Marshall gave a more charitable view of Mower in a note on Mrs. R. A. Mower's letter to Marshall, August 8, 1894, in Marshall Papers. Mower was promoted after the battle of Tupelo; *St. Paul Daily Press*, November 6, 1864.

¹⁵ Edwards, Journal, 1:31, 33, 36. Ten men of the Seventh were killed and 52 wounded; *Minnesota in the Civil and Indian Wars*, 1:356. Edwards' figure of 7 dead does not include those who died later; Edwards, Journal, 1:5.

¹⁶ Edwards, Journal, 1:28.

¹⁷ Here and below, see Edwards, Journal, 1:5, 30, 34.

¹⁸ Here and below, see [Lathrop], "Historical Remarks," 26; Edwards, Journal, 1:105; Wyman Folsom to "Mother," September 12, 1864, in Folsom Papers; Francis A. Lord, *Uniforms of the Civil War*, 81–85 (New York, 1970).

¹⁹ H. Clay Trumbull, *War Memories of an Army Chaplain*, 3 (New York, 1898).

²⁰ Here and below, see Edwards, Journal, 1:34–37.

²¹ Edwards, Journal, 1:3, 32.

²² Here and below, see Edwards, Journal, 2:79, 170, 197, 295–297.

²³ Three of Edwards' reports escaped the wastebasket: those of January 31 (File 89E 1865), May 31 (File 374E 1865), and June 30 (File 449E 1865) all in Letters Received, Records of the Adjutant General, NARG 94. According to Olmstead, *History of Religion*, 392, a number of organizations published a variety of small pamphlets or tracts for the men in arms.

²⁴ Edwards, Journal, 1:1, 93, 160. Edwards' sketch of Brewer Mattocks is in Mattocks Papers, MHS.

²⁵ On the Oxford raid, see Edwards, Journal, 1:38–57; *Minnesota in the Civil and Indian Wars*, 1:357. The raid "comprised about 30 days, and 98 miles railroad travel, and

145 miles marching, and extended from Memphis to Oxford, Mississippi, and return"; *St. Paul Daily Press*, December 23, 1864.

[26] Edwards, Journal, 1:45.

[27] Edwards, Journal, 1:47–49; *Minnesota in the Civil and Indian Wars*, 1:358.

[28] Here and below, see Edwards, Journal, 1:50, 51, 57.

[29] Here and below, see Edwards, Journal, 1:57, 58, 2:189, 315. In Edwards' later version of events, the Seventh was detailed to unload stores from the steamboat, and the First Division (including the Seventh) but not the whole Sixteenth Corps was held accountable and penalized; Carter to Edwards, July 4, [1906], copy in Letterbook 12:442, in Carter Papers.

[30] On the journey to De Valls Bluff and Edwards' subsequent trip to Little Rock, here and below, see Edwards, Journal, 1:59, 61–66, 68; *St. Paul Daily Press*, October 7 (Edwards' letter signed "Miles"), 14, 1864.

[31] Here and below, see Edwards, Journal, 1:64–76, including medical orders opposite p. 66; Wyman Folsom to "Mother," September 12, 1864, in Folsom Papers.

[32] Edwards, Journal, 1:78, 82, and hospital discharge orders opposite p. 79.

[33] On Edwards' adventures, here and below, see Edwards, Journal, 1:84–105 (quotations p. 93–96, 99) and Edwards' orders (Special Order No. 1), November 2, 1864, opposite p. 94. McArthur's adjutant was an Indiana Asbury graduate; see Edwards, Journal, 2:171.

[34] Here and below, see Edwards, Journal, 1:104; *St. Paul Daily Press*, December 6, 28, 1864; *St. Paul Pioneer*, November 26, 1864.

[35] On the trip to Nashville, here and below, see Edwards, Journal, 1:106–118 (quotations p. 114, 117, 118). Edwards' description of the journey ends abruptly some 50 miles from Nashville, November 23–30, 1864. Edwards, as "Miles," also tells of the journey in *Central Christian Advocate*, December 21, 1864.

[36] Edwards, Journal, 2:71–74; *Central Christian Advocate*, December 21, 1864.

[37] Edwards, Journal, 2:77, 91–93.

[38] Edwards, Journal, 2:71, 78, 87, 95, 130.

[39] Edwards, Journal, 2:83, 84.

[40] Edwards, Journal, 2:85; *St. Paul Pioneer*, December 22, 1864.

[41] Edwards, Journal, 2:94, 98; *Central Christian Advocate*, December 21, 1864.

[42] Here and below, see Edwards, Journal, 2:99–101. For details of the Nashville battle, see Stanley Horn, *The Decisive Battle of Nashville* (Baton Rouge, 1957); Kenneth Carley, *Minnesota in the Civil War*, 101–121 (Minneapolis, 1961).

[43] For quotations on the battle, here and below, see Edwards, Journal, 2:102, 103, 106.

[44] Here and below, see Edwards, Journal, 2:109; Carter, "Flanking Hood at Nashville," in *Confederate Veteran*, December, 1904, p. 585; Horn, *Decisive Battle*, 99–101; Carley, *Minnesota in the Civil War*, 115. John P. Houston (Huston, Hueston) was a graduate of a college at Cannonsburg, Pa., and a member of Edwards' fraternity, Beta Theta Pi (Journal, 2:109, 129, 329); his military record is summarized in *Minnesota in the Civil and Indian Wars*, 1:282.

[45] Edwards, Journal, 2:110.

[46] On the second day of the Nashville battle, here and below, see Edwards, Journal, 2:111–116; Carley, *Minnesota in the Civil War*, 117–120; Horn, *Decisive Battle*, 109–141.

[47] Edwards, Journal, 2:112.

[48] Carter, quoting Marshall, said no orders were issued; Carter to Edwards, February 20 (copy), December 23, 1905, Edwards to Carter, May 4, 1906, in Carter Papers. See also *St. Paul Daily Press*, January 7, 1865; Horn, *Decisive Battle*, 113, 138.

[49] Edwards, Journal, 2:115.

[50] For Marshall's view of the events, here and below, see his letter to the *St. Paul Daily Press*, January 7, 1865.

[51] See, for example, Carter to Edwards, August 2, 1907, and to Joseph V. Ledoux, April 4, 1905, in Carter Papers; Carter, in *Confederate Veteran*, December, 1904, p. 586. Hubbard's name headed a list of 77 officers and soldiers who asked Marshall to be the Republican candidate for governor; *Stillwater Messenger*, August 8, 1865.

[52] Here and below, see Edwards, Journal, 2:120–123. Edwards was commended for his service by Lieut. Col. Bradley; *St. Paul Pioneer*, January 10, 1865; *St. Paul Daily Press*, December 25, 1864.

[53] *Minnesota in the Civil and Indian Wars*, 1:430–433, 466–469. The account in the *St. Paul Daily Press*, December 24, 1864, may have been the origin of the three-horse story; see also *Press*, December 30, 1864; Edwards to Carter, May 4, 1906, in Carter Papers. Hubbard's report, "Minnesota in the Battles of Nashville, December 15 and 16, 1864," is in *Minnesota Historical Collections*, 12:597–615 (St. Paul, 1908).

[54] *St. Paul Daily Press*, January 7, 1865.

[55] Edwards, Journal, 2:129. On Dr. Vincent Kennedy, who, like Edwards, was a graduate of Indiana Asbury, see *Litchfield Independent*, February 10, 1903.

[56] Here and below, see *Central Christian Advocate*, February 15, 1865.

[57] On the journey to Eastport, here and below, see Edwards, Journal, 2:131–189 (quotations p. 142, 153, 156, 157); *Central Christian Advocate*, February 15, 22 (quotations), 1865.

[58] On experiences at Eastport, here and below, see Edwards, Journal, 2:161–189 (quotations p. 170, 175, 176). For more on the rooster, an unofficial regimental mascot, see Edwards to Carter, February 22, Carter to Edwards, February 26, 1906, in Carter Papers; *Minnesota in the Civil and Indian Wars*, 1:364.

[59] Edwards to Adjutant General, January 31, 1865 (File 89E 1865), Letters Received, NARG 94; Edwards, Journal, 2:185.

[60] On the journey from Eastport to New Orleans, here and below, see Edwards, Journal, 2:190–218 (quotations p. 209).

[61] Edwards, Journal, 2:219–221; *Minnesota in the Civil and Indian Wars*, 1:363.

[62] Edwards, Journal, 2:221–232.

[63] Here and below, see Edwards, Journal, 2:232–237.

[64] Edwards, Journal, 2:237–248; *Minnesota in the Civil and Indian Wars*, 1:363–365.

[65] Edwards, Journal, 2:250.

[66] Edwards to Carter, May 1, 1906, in Carter Papers; Edwards, Journal, 2:254, 255. Wooden mortars are said to have been invented by a private in the Forty-ninth Illinois Infantry and first used at Vicksburg; undated newspaper clipping in Marshall Papers. The MHS has one of these wooden mortars, a gift from Edwards.

[67] Edwards, Journal, 2:255; *Minnesota in the Civil and Indian Wars*, 1:364.

[68] Here and below, see Edwards, Journal, 2:262–275 (quotations p. 266, 267, 269, 271).

[69] Edwards, Journal, 2:275; Wyman Folsom to "Folks at Home," May 8, 1865, in Folsom Papers.

[70] Edwards, Journal, 2:278, 282.

[71] Edwards, Journal, 2:280, 281, 285.

[72] Edwards, Journal, 2:285–288.

[73] Edwards, Journal, 2:288. On the experiences in camp at Selma, here and below, see Edwards, Journal, 2:289–348; *Minnesota in the Civil and Indian Wars*, 1:365.

[74] Edwards, Journal, 2:289, 303, 316.

[75] Here and below, see Edwards, Journal, 2:314, 323, 334–337.

[76] Edwards, Journal, 2:291, 308, 313, 321, 324, 344.

[77] Here and below, see Edwards, Journal, 2:309, 312, 316, 325, 334, 339 (quotation).

[78] Edwards, Journal, 2:299–301.

[79] Edwards to Adjutant General, May 31, 1865 (File 374E 1865), Letters Received, NARG 94.

[80] Edwards to Adjutant General, June 30, 1865 (File 449E 1865), Letters Received, NARG 94.

[81] Edwards, Journal, 2:342.

[82] Edwards, Journal, 2:319, 327–330, 343, 347.

[83] Edwards, Journal, 2:323–325, 338, 347, 348.

[84] *St. Paul Daily Press*, August 9, 1865.

[85] Here and below, see Edwards, Journal, 2:368–372; Edwards to Carter, September 29, 1913, in Carter Papers; *Taylors Falls Reporter*, August 26, 1865; Edwards File.

DR. THOMAS FOSTER — Pages 88 to 109

The author wishes to thank the following people for their help in researching this story: William A. Deiss, Janette Saquette, James A. Steed, and staff, Smithsonian Institution Archives, Washington, D.C.; David Gaynon, St. Louis County Historical Society, Duluth; James Harwood, Sara D. Jackson, Robert Kvasnicka, Lane Moore, William Sherman, National Archives, Washington, D.C.; Arthur Hecht, Washington, D.C.; Karen Peterson, St. Paul; Herman Viola and staff, National Anthropological Archives, Washington, D.C.; Alan Woolworth, MHS.

¹ William Darrah, *Powell of the Colorado*, 258 (Princeton, 1951).

² Foster, Soldiers Certificate no. 672,224, in Records of the Veterans Administration, NARG 15. The first quotation is from Ignatius Donnelly, Journal, January 22, 1872, Donnelly Papers, MHS; the others were reported by Foster in *Duluth Minnesotian*, April 2, 1870, January 6, 1872. For examples of Foster's temperament and philosophy, see Foster to Alexander Ramsey, September 25, 1849, July 22, 1850, Jared Benson to Ramsey, March 11, June 15, 1859, in Alexander Ramsey Papers, MHS; *Duluth Minnesotian*, May 28, June 25, July 23, 1870; H. P. Hall to Donnelly, June 12, 1870, in Donnelly Papers.

³ Foster to Richard Eames, March 26, 1871, in Richard Eames Papers, MHS; "Dr. Thomas Foster, Clerk," autobiographical sketch in MHS prepared in the 1890s for Henry A. Castle, sixth auditor, U.S. Treasury, for whom Foster worked. See also Foster, "Notes and Reminiscences," [August 19, 1898]; Pennsylvania Whig State Central Committee, Circular, [1848], probably written by Foster; details of his finances in Foster to Ramsey, October 19, 1849; Ramsey, "Abstract of Disbursements," [May 15, 1853] — all in Ramsey Papers.

⁴ Foster to Ramsey, August 7, 1849, July 22, 1850, in Ramsey Papers, and dates following in the summer of 1850 supply details of Foster's campaign for a position. Ramsey's "Report of the Minnesota Superintendency," is in U.S. Office of Indian Affairs, *Report*, 1849, p. 69 (Washington, D.C., 1849).

⁵ Foster to Ramsey, September 24, 28, November 7, 1850, in Ramsey Papers.

⁶ Foster to Ramsey, September 27, November 1, 7, December 19, 1850, February 10, 1851, in Ramsey Papers.

⁷ Foster to Ramsey, February 10, March 21, June 1, 1851, Dr. David Day to Ramsey, May 17, 1851, in Ramsey Papers.

⁸ Foster to Ramsey, March 21, November n.d., 1851, in Ramsey Papers.

⁹ The Dakota treaties signed at Traverse des Sioux and Mendota were approved by the Senate in 1852; the Ojibway treaty was rejected. See William W. Folwell, *A History of Minnesota*, 1:277–291 (Reprint ed., St. Paul, 1956); Foster to Ramsey, August 9, 1851, June 7, 1852, J. P. Bardwell to Ramsey, January 1, 1852, Foster, Treaty Journal, August 18–November 27, 1851, filed under the latter date — all in Ramsey Papers.

¹⁰ Foster to Ramsey, January 23, February 25, May 28, 1852, June 1, 1854, in Ramsey Papers. Bond accompanied the treaty party to Pembina; see *Minnesota and Its Resources*, 253–258 (New York, 1853).

¹¹ *Duluth Minnesotian*, April 24, 1869. On the treaty payments, for which Ramsey was later investigated by Congress, see Folwell, *Minnesota*, 1:292–304; Foster to Ramsey, August 9, 1851, Wallace B. White to Ramsey, June 22, [1852], Foster affidavit, August 4, 1843 — all in Ramsey Papers.

¹² Here and below, see *Minnesota Statesman*, March 22, 1859; Helen M. White, *Guide to a Microfilm Edition of the Alexander Ramsey Papers and Records*, 22, 44 (St. Paul, 1974); Foster, "Notes and Reminiscences," in Ramsey Papers; "Dr. Thomas Foster," in *Minnesota Historical Collections*, 10:264 (St. Paul, 1905); Donnelly Journal, November 29, December 1–3, 1866, in Donnelly Papers; Thomas Foster Quartermaster Consolidated File, Records of the Quartermaster General, NARG 92; Compiled Military Service Record, Union Staff Officers (Volunteer), in Records of the Adjutant General, NARG 94; Thomas Foster, Soldiers Certificate no. 672,224, NARG 15. On the lively Duluth years, see files of the *Minnesotian*, 1869–72; for examples, see May 28, June 25, July 23, 1870, January 6, 13, 20, 1872.

¹³ On Foster's support of Grant, see Foster to Donnelly, April 6, May 5, June 13, August 6, 1872, in Donnelly Papers. Here and below, see Foster to William Windom,

January 1, 1873, Thomas Foster File, Secretary of Interior Appointments Division, Commissioner of Indian Affairs Appointment Papers, NARG 48. Schoolcraft was appointed by the Secretary of War under an act of Congress, March 3, 1847, to "collect and digest such statistics and materials as may illustrate the history, the present condition, and the future prospects of the Indian tribes of the United States." His six-volume work, prepared under the direction of the Office of Indian Affairs and published and distributed by the government, was entitled *Historical and Statistical Information Respecting the History, Condition and Prospects of the Indian Tribes of the United States* (Philadelphia, 1851–57). See also Frances S. Nicholas, comp., *Index to Schoolcraft's "Indian Tribes of the United States,"* iv (Bureau of American Ethnology, *Bulletins*, no. 152 — Washington, 1954). The Minnesota delegation was composed of Senators Ramsey and Windom and Representatives John F. Averill and Mark Dunnell.

[14] Windom and others to President Ulysses S. Grant, January 9, 1873, in Foster File, Commissioner of Indian Affairs Appointment Papers, NARG 48; "Conference of the Board of Indian Commissioners with the Representatives of the Religious Societies," January 15, 1873, in Ramsey Papers; "Letter of Thomas Foster," in 42 Congress, 3 session, *Senate Miscellaneous Documents*, no. 39 (serial 1546). The newsprint edition of *Hints* quoted below is in Alexander Ramsey Miscellaneous Pamphlets, vol. 13, no. 11, in MHS Reference Library.

[15] Thomas H. Pressnell to Donnelly, February 8, 1873, in Donnelly Papers; "Letter of Dr. Thomas Foster . . . relative to the appointment of a Historiographer of the Indian Department," [1873], in Ramsey Miscellaneous Pamphlets, vol. 13, no. 6. On Smith, see Robert N. Kvasnicka and Herman J. Viola, *The Commissioners of Indian Affairs, 1824–1977*, 141–147 (Lincoln, Neb., 1979).

[16] Indian Office to James Harlan, February 17, 1873, in Letters Received Indian Division; Secretary of Interior to Harlan (copy), February 18, 1873, Record of Letters Sent, Indian Office Miscellaneous, 12:258 — both in NARG 48. See also Foster to Donnelly, March 3, 1873, in Donnelly Papers.

[17] The letters have not been found, but the matter was summarized in the commissioner's recommendation and note, May 21, 1873, in Department of Interior, Register of Letters Received, Indian Office, 2:425, NARG 48. See also Department of Interior, *Register, 1877–1881*, 69, NARG 48.

[18] Commissioner to Foster, June 2, 6, 1873, in Thomas Foster Account 702 (1874), Second Auditor, General Accounting Office Records, NARG 217. Foster lost no time in having these two letters set in type, and printed copies may be found in NARG 217. Two Minnesotans were Foster's bondsmen for the post: James H. Baker, former secretary of state, and Charles King, a law partner of John H. Sanborn of St. Paul; Bond no. 505, August 28, 1873, recorded in Bond Book 2, p. 136, NARG 217.

[19] Foster to Neill, June n.d., 1873, in Edward D. Neill Papers, MHS.

[20] Foster to Commissioner, June 14, 1873, F70, Letters Received Miscellaneous, 1873, in Bureau of Indian Affairs, NARG 75.

[21] Commissioner to Foster, July 9, 1873, copy in Foster Account 702 (1874), Second Auditor, NARG 217.

[22] Foster to Commissioner, August 30, 1873 (no file no.), Letters Received Miscellaneous, Indian Office, NARG 75; Commissioner to Foster, August 30, 1873, copy in Foster Account 702 (1874), Second Auditor, NARG 217; *Duluth Minnesotian*, September 20, 1873.

[23] Ramsey to Secretary of Interior, November 2, 1873, R437, Letters Received Miscellaneous, NARG 75.

[24] Foster Account 702 (1874), Second Auditor, NARG 217. His informants were "Baptiste," a Winnebago who had lived among the Iowa; Peter Manaige, mixed-blood interpreter; and Henry Foster, former trader turned prosperous farmer. The latter two lived in McPherson Township, Blue Earth County, according to U.S. manuscript census schedules, 1870. The interpreter who aided him in securing the story of the giants from "Little Dekorie" was Joseph Amelle. All of this information appeared in *Foster's Indian Record*, vol. 1, nos. 1–3; see page 101, below. On the borrowed books, see W. Hamilton to Commissioner, July 14, 1875, H974, Foster to Commissioner, July 11, 1876, F152, Letters Received Miscellaneous; Taylor Bradley to Commissioner, August 31, 1875, Letters Re-

ceived Winnebago — all in NARG 75. On the Winnebago removals, see Folwell, *Minnesota*, 1:318–320, 2:260.

[25] Foster Account 702 (1874), Second Auditor; Commissioner to Secretary of Interior, March 26, 1874; Secretary to Commissioner, March 27, 1874; Commissioner to Foster, June 19, 1874, in Foster Account 7199 (1877), First Auditor — all in NARG 217. See also Foster to Commissioner, December 29, 1873, F292, E. B. French to Foster, May 12, 1874, F177, Letters Received Miscellaneous; Commissioner to Foster, May 12, 1874, Letters Sent Finance, 117:289 — all in NARG 75.

TALE OF A
COMET AND
OTHER STORIES

[26] Jacket with endorsement, Foster to Commissioner, May 18, 1874, F185, Letters Received Miscellaneous, NARG 75; U.S., *Statutes at Large*, vol. 18, part 3, p. 141 (Washington, D.C., 1875).

[27] Foster Account 201,476 (1876), First Auditor, NARG 217; Foster to Spencer F. Baird, June 11, 1874, Office of the Secretary, Incoming Correspondence, Record Unit 26, Smithsonian Institution Archives (hereafter Smithsonian). The Fosters had three sons; see U.S. manuscript census schedules, 1860, Ramsey County, Ward 4.

[28] The original of Foster to Commissioner, June 25, 1874, has not been found, but extracts from it in Foster's handwriting are in Foster Account 201,476 (1876), First Auditor, NARG 217. A copy of his current account is in Foster to Commissioner, July 3, 1874, F250, Letters Received Miscellaneous, NARG 75.

[29] Foster Account 201,476 (1876), First Auditor, NARG 217; Foster to Commissioner, July 5, 1874 (no file no.), Letters Received Miscellaneous, NARG 75.

[30] Here and below, see Secretary of Interior to Commissioner, July 14, 1874, Commissioner to Foster, July 17, 1874, both in Foster Account 201,476 (1876), First Auditor, NARG 217. See also Foster to Commissioner, October 5, 1874, F429, November 22, 1875, F512, Letters Received Miscellaneous, NARG 75.

[31] Foster Account 7199 (1877), Second Auditor, NARG 217; Foster to Commissioner, September 30, 1875, F447, October 6, 1875, F456, Letters Received Miscellaneous, NARG 75. The latter was published in Indian Office, *Reports*, 1875, p. 377.

[32] Foster to Commissioner, November 22, 1875, F512, Letters Received Miscellaneous; Commissioner to Foster, December 16, 30, 1875, Letters Sent Finance, 219:369, 438 — all in NARG 75. Foster to Commissioner, January 3, 1876, F1, Letters Received Miscellaneous, is registered but not found.

[33] Clapp to S. A. Galpin, March 8, 1876 (no file no.), Foster to Commissioner, June 13, 1876, F140, Letters Received Miscellaneous; Commissioner to Foster, May 16, 1876, Letters Sent Miscellaneous, 130:351 — all in NARG 75. On Ramsey and Averill, see W. F. Toensing, comp., *Minnesota Congressmen, Legislators, and Other Elected State Officials*, 5, 99 (St. Paul, 1971); on Smith's removal, see Edward E. Hill, "John Q. Smith," in Kvasnicka and Viola, *Commissioners of Indian Affairs*, 149–153.

[34] Quotations here and below are from Foster to Commissioner, June 13, 1876, F140, Letters Received Miscellaneous, NARG 75. Shea's letter is mentioned in Commissioner to Foster, November 17, 1874, Letters Sent Finance, 121:337, NARG 75, but has not been found.

[35] Here and below, see Foster to Commissioner, August 7, 1876, F172, Letters Received Miscellaneous, NARG 75.

[36] Foster to Commissioner, August 18, 1876, F176, Letters Received Miscellaneous, NARG 75; U.S., *Statutes at Large*, 19:197 (Washington, D.C., 1877).

[37] This quotation and those in the four paragraphs below are from Foster to Acting Commissioner, September 1, 2, 1876, with a chart summarizing his expenditures, filed with Acting Commissioner to Secretary of Interior, September 8, 1876, F194, Letters Received Indian Division, NARG 48.

[38] Commissioner to Foster, August 19, 1876, Letters Sent Finance, 133:553; Secretary of Interior to Commissioner, August 31, 1876, I803, Letters Received Miscellaneous — both in NARG 75.

[39] Secretary of Interior to Commissioner, October 24, 1876, I990, Foster to Commissioner, December 19, 1876, H156½, Letters Received Miscellaneous, NARG 75; Acting Commissioner to Secretary, October 25, 1876, Letters Received Indian Division, NARG 48; Foster Account 7199 (1877), Second Auditor, NARG 217. The rooms were rented from William Foster, possibly a relative.

⁴⁰ Foster Account 7199 (1877), Second Auditor, NARG 217; Foster to Commissioner, December 19, 1876, H156½, January 16, 1877, F19, Letters Received Miscellaneous, NARG 75. The author has found only one complete original file of the *Record*, in the Library of Congress; photocopies are in author's possession.

⁴¹ Commissioner to Foster, December 14, 1876, Letters Sent Miscellaneous, 132:275; and Foster to Commissioner, December 19, 1876, H156½, Letters Received Miscellaneous — both in NARG 75.

⁴² Henry's letter of December 27, 1876, quoted in Henry to Whitney and Trumbull, December 30, 1876, Office of the Secretary, Outgoing Correspondence, 52:236, Record Unit 33, Smithsonian. On these three men, see *Dictionary of American Biography*, 8:550, 19:9, 20:169 (New York, 1932, 1936).

⁴³ Commissioner to Foster, February 20, 1877, quoted in Foster to Commissioner, February 21, 1877, F47, Letters Received Miscellaneous, NARG 75. The quotations in the paragraph below are from the February 21 letter.

⁴⁴ Whitney and Trumbull to Henry, January 6, 1877, Office of the Secretary, Incoming Correspondence, 163:287, Record Unit 26, Smithsonian.

⁴⁵ Henry to Secretary of Interior, February 20, 1877, H156½, Letters Received Miscellaneous, NARG 75.

⁴⁶ Secretary of Interior to Commissioner, February 21, 1877, H156½, Letters Received Miscellaneous, NARG 75.

⁴⁷ Commissioner to Foster, February 26, 1877, Letters Sent Accounts, 134:214, NARG 75.

⁴⁸ Carl M. Fuess, *Carl Schurz Reformer*, 198, 236 (New York, 1932); Acting Commissioner to Second Comptroller, May 11, 1877, Letters Sent Accounts, 134:326, NARG 75. On the $200, see U.S. *v.* Thomas Foster, District of Columbia Docket 6, Folio 206, Office of the Solicitor of the Treasury, NARG 206; Foster, "Dr. Thomas Foster, Clerk," 11; Foster to Ramsey, April 7, 1880, in Ramsey Papers.

⁴⁹ Here and below, see Darrah, *Powell of the Colorado*, 145, 160, 213, 215, 257, 269, 409, and "Down the Colorado," in *American Heritage*, October, 1969, p. 53–58, 83.

⁵⁰ Indian Office, *Report*, 1873, p. 41–46; Darrah, *Powell of the Colorado*, 194–204; Powell to Commissioner, May 3, 1877, P148, Letters Received Miscellaneous, NARG 75.

⁵¹ Commissioner to Secretary of Interior, January 6, 1875, Letters Received Indian Division, NARG 48; Indian Office, *Report*, 1875, p. 202–205.

⁵² J. W. Powell, *Introduction to the Study of Indian Languages*, vii (2nd ed., Washington, D.C., 1880).

⁵³ Darrah, *Powell of the Colorado*, 260; Acting Commissioner to Powell, October 13, 1875, Letters Sent Miscellaneous, 132:125, and Powell to Commissioner, May 3, 1877, P148, Letters Received Miscellaneous — both in NARG 75; Henry to Trumbull, December 8, 1876, Office of Secretary, Outgoing Correspondence, vol. 52, Record Unit 33, Smithsonian. See also Powell to Henry, October 2, 1876, and Henry to Powell, October 10, 1876, both in U.S. Department of Interior Geographical and Geological Survey of the Rocky Mountain Region, *Contributions to North American Ethnology*, 1:vi–vii (Washington, D.C., 1877).

⁵⁴ Powell to Commissioner, May 3, 1877, P148, Letters Received Miscellaneous, NARG 75.

⁵⁵ Gatschet emigrated to the U.S. in 1868 after studying languages at the University of Berlin. In 1877 Powell appointed him ethnologist on the Rocky Mountain Survey. His writings placed him in the front rank of scientists in his field. *Dictionary of American Biography*, 7:192 (New York, 1931).

⁵⁶ Commissioner to Secretary of Interior, May 29, 1877, is listed in Register, 4:23, but the original was not found in NARG 48; Secretary of Interior to Commissioner, June 9, August 25, 1877, I420, I582, Letters Received Miscellaneous, NARG 75.

⁵⁷ Powell to Commissioner, October 29, 1877, and his receipt, November 30, 1877, for 116 books, P485, Letters Received Miscellaneous, NARG 75. Not all of the books known to have been purchased by Foster are on Powell's receipt, and no list of the papers or of the documents accumulated by Foster has been found.

⁵⁸ Gatschet Account 3494 (1878), Second Auditor, NARG 217. The task was completed by Frederick Hodge in his massive two-volume *Handbook of American Indians*

North of Mexico (Bureau of American Ethnology, *Bulletins*, no. 30 — Washington, D.C., 1907–10).

[59] James Constantine Pilling, *Proof-Sheets of a Bibliography of the Languages of the North American Indians*, iii, v (Bureau of American Ethnology, *Miscellaneous Publications*, no. 2 — Washington, D.C., 1885); Foster's *Indian Record* is item 1321, p. 261.

TALE OF A
COMET AND
OTHER STORIES

[60] United States, *Statutes at Large*, 20:397 (Washington, D.C., 1879); Powell to Secretary of Interior, July 8, 1879, F71, Letters Received Miscellaneous, U.S. Geological Survey, NARG 48.

[61] Secretary of Interior to Spencer F. Baird, July 10, 1879, and to Powell, July 10, 22, 1879, in Letters Sent Miscellaneous, Letterbook 13:452, 484; Baird to Acting Secretary of Interior, July 17, 1879, F249, Letters Received Patents and Miscellaneous — all in NARG 48. See also Darrah, *Powell of the Colorado*, 254, 271, 351, 391. In 1894 the department became the Bureau of American Ethnology.

[62] Commissioner to Foster, March 29, 1877, and to Second Comptroller, May 11, 1877, Letters Sent Accounts, 134:268, 326, NARG 75; Hannah C. Foster *v.* Thomas Foster, Divorce File 670, St. Louis County District Court, May 30, 1877; Thomas B. Foster, "Recollections of Dr. Thomas Foster," 1947, in St. Louis County Historical Society Collection, Northeast Regional Research Center, Duluth; *Duluth Minnesotian*, August 22, 1874; *Superior* (Wis.) *Times*, August 22, 29, 1874.

[63] *Old Whig* (Bladensburg, Md.), January 1, 15, 29, 1878. The only known file of this paper was presented by Foster himself with the *Indian Record* to the Library of Congress; the author has photocopies. On Garrick Mallery, graduate of Yale, army officer, lawyer, and ethnologist, see *Dictionary of American Biography*, 12:222 (New York, 1933).

[64] Here and below, see Foster, "Recollections," 1; Foster, "Dr. Thomas Foster, Clerk," 11–12; W. A. Croffut, "A Minnesota Boss," in *Minneapolis Journal*, May 16, 1903, p. 11. Bessie Nicholls Croffut, "Memories of William Augustus Croffut," n.d., in Record Unit 7073, Smithsonian.

A CIRCUS GONE UP — Pages 110 to 127

The author wishes to thank the following people for their help in researching this story: Dean Anderson, Mrs. Clayton Anderson, North Branch; Faustino Avaloz, Duane Swanson, MHS; J. Daniel Draper, Robert L. Parkinson, Circus World Museum, Baraboo, Wis.; Marjorie Picotte Hackett, Minneapolis; Mrs. Agnes Hill, Tuppers Plains, Ohio; Gayle (Mrs. Maurice) Marthaler, Hampton; Carl E. Moore, Pomeroy, Ohio; Elizabeth (Mrs. Lemuel C.) Quillin, Brainerd; Sister Harriet Sanborn, Grand Rapids, Mich.; Leon L. Smith, Nisswa; Lee Smith, Lake Elmo.

[1] Unless otherwise indicated, details on the organization and operation of circuses were drawn from the columns of the *New York Clipper*, especially its annual circus supplements of March 31, 1866, April 8, 1871, April 13, 1872, and April 18, 1874. The Dallas (Tex.) Public Library and the Circus World Museum, Baraboo, Wis., have microfilm copies. On the springs at Mount Clemens, see Donald E. Worrell, Jr., "Mount Clemens's fabulous bath era," in *Chronicle* (Ann Arbor, Mich.), Summer, 1978, p. 4; *Clipper*, February 15, April 14, 1877.

[2] *Clipper*, February 17, 1877. On the Great Pacific Show, see Stuart Thayer, "Joseph E. Warner — Pioneer of the Three Tent Circus," in *Bandwagon*, January–February, 1970, p. 23; *Clipper*, January 22, February 19, July 8, 15, 1876.

[3] Other "Australian" circuses were mentioned in *Clipper*, June 4, 18, 25, July 9, 16, 1870, October 26, 1872, June 16, 30, August 11, 1883. Many circuses were forced to close for various reasons; for others "gone up" in Minnesota, see *Clipper*, September 10, 17, 1870, July 10, 1875, July 6, 1878.

[4] See also *Clipper*, April 28, 1877. On Castello (1860–1922), whose real name was Loughlin, see *Bannerline*, February 1, 1963, p. 6, March 5, 1968, p. 3.

[5] *Clipper*, February 17, April 14, 28, 1877.

[6] On Robie, see *Chisago County Post* (Rush City), January 13, 1875; this paper became

the *Rush City Post* in 1877. See also *North Branch Review*, July 29, 1892; *Rush City Post*, June 9, 1882; U.S. manuscript census schedules, 1880, Rush City, Chisago County.

⁷ The quotations here and below are from the *Post*, July 13, 1877. A number of male performers named Leopold and three women — Blanche and Geraldine, gymnasts, and Minnie, a rider — were mentioned in *Clipper*, June 18, November 26, 1870, June 15, 1872, April 18, 1874, April 17, 1875, July 15, 1882. A "Grace" Brockway, a rider, Mlle. Christine, and Eva Albertina were referred to in *Clipper*, March 31, 1877. On Worland, below, and her husband, Stewart L. Davis, a ringmaster and equestrian director, see *Clipper*, February 3, March 31, December 24, 1877, April 19, 1884, February 7, 1885. Nothing is known of Madame Gosh, but she is referred to in the *Rush City Post*, August 10, 1877.

⁸ On Edward G. Holland (1853–1939) and other members of this circus family, see *Clipper*, March 10, July 1, 1876; *Bannerline*, January 1, 1965, p. 2–4. Holland, Fields, and Sands were not listed among the Great Australian performers in *Clipper*, March 31, 1877. Fields is mentioned in *Rush City Post*, July 17, 1877; nothing more is known about him. Sands was, however, another famous name in circus history. An earlier Richard Sands invented the circus poster, and Sands and Nathans' Circus is said to have had the first circus calliope in 1859. See Marian Murray, *Circus! From Rome to Ringling*, 139–141, 167 (Westport, Conn., 1973).

⁹ On Quillin (1849–1925), here and below, see Leon Smith, "Notes on Smith and Quillin Families," compiled records of the Quillin Family; Agnes Hill, "Quillin Family Genealogy Chart"; author's interview with Dean Anderson, February 1, 1978; Carl E. Moore to author, February 12, March 20, 1978; Agnes Hill to author, January 20, 1979 — all in author's possession. Quillin's advertisements appeared on the want-ad page of the *Clipper*, March 8, November 22, 1873, February 28, 1874, September 4, December 18, 1875, March 4, April 1, 1876, February 17, 1877. Quillin's contract and testimony are in Great Australian Circus Company, Case File 412A, Chisago County District Court records, Minnesota State Archives, MHS. Hereafter these cases will be cited by file number and plaintiff's name, as Quillin, Case File 412A. A "First Clown" in the one-ring traveling circuses of this period was probably the forerunner of the modern "Producing Clown," who performs and supervises the other clowns of the troupe; author's interview with Robert L. Parkinson, Historian, Circus World Museum, May 19, 1983, notes in author's possession. For more on clowns' roles and duties, see Murray, *Circus!*, 301–309; *Clipper*, April 19, 1873.

¹⁰ Lulu was born on September 26, 1876; see death certificate, St. Paul, May 24, 1950, in St. Paul Bureau of Health, Division of Vital Statistics. On Quillin's costume, below, see description in Elizabeth J. (Mrs. Lemuel C.) Quillin to author, May 21, 1980, in author's possession. Clowns were responsible for their own costumes; Parkinson interview.

¹¹ The expression to "recruit up," used in the *Rush City Post*, August 3, 1877, was a common one of the period, meaning to renew or replenish health and vitality. On the hotel's contract, see Swenson, Civil File 416A; for the little that is known of Wilkes's arrangements, see Alva S. Titus, Civil File 422A.

¹² On North Branch, platted in 1870, and on Swenson (1848–1926), see Helen M. White, "North Branch Celebrates 100 Years," in *Dalles Visitor* (Taylors Falls), 1981, p. 1, 4, 25; for more on Swenson, here and below, see also *Rush City Post*, August 16, 1878, November 28, 1890; A. E. Strand, comp. and ed., *A History of the Swedish-Americans of Minnesota*, 384–386 (Chicago, 1910); U.S. manuscript census schedules, 1880, North Branch. Gustaf Unonius was pastor of St. Ansgarius, a Scandinavian Protestant Episcopal church in Chicago, and was well known in Sweden for his writings about America. The Swenson story appears in Nils W. Olsson, *A Pioneer in Northwest America, 1841–1858; The Memoirs of Gustaf Unonius*, 2:227 (Minneapolis, 1960).

¹³ Here and below, see *Rush City Post*, August 3, 10, 1877, November 28, 1890. On Wilkes, see U.S. manuscript census schedules, 1880, North Branch, Chisago County. According to the census, he was living in Minnesota as early as 1866.

¹⁴ *St. Paul and Minneapolis Pioneer Press*, August 7, 1877.

¹⁵ Here and below, see *Rush City Post*, August 10, 17, 1877; *Pioneer Press*, August 7, 1877. On Dent and his wife Linda, who was said to have been the first woman

admitted to the Minnesota bar (1887), see U.S. manuscript census schedules, 1880, Nessel Township, Chisago County; *Rush City Post*, December 26, 1890. Nothing more is known of B. C. (Burt) Newport; see *Taylors Falls Journal*, August 17, 1877. On Shaleen (1835–1901), Chisago County sheriff from 1870 to 1877, see *Chisago County Courier* (Lindstrom), November 2, 1901, p. 1, and *Chisago County Press* (Lindstrom), May 25, 1944, p. 8.

[16] Here and below, see Arthur Buckles (Beckles, Bickels), W. L. Merrick, Charles L. Meyatt (Mayett), S. R. Romer, Montanio, Swenson, Bignon, and Beckett, Case Files 410A, 411A, 413–418A, respectively. Warner's statement appeared in Quillin, Case File 412A. He was "master of horses" for J. E. Warner's Circus in 1873, according to *Clipper*, April 19, 1873.

[17] The timetable of events outlined here and below was based upon documents in Case Files 410–418A, which sometimes varied from the recitals given in the *Rush City Post*, August 3, 10, 17, 1877, the *Pioneer Press*, August 7, 1877. The St. Paul law firm representing the circus owners was headed by Cushman K. Davis, who served as governor of Minnesota in 1874–75. On O'Brien, see *St. Paul Pioneer Press*, August 28, 1922, p. 1. Gorman's father, former Minnesota Governor Willis A. Gorman, had also been a Davis law partner; *St. Paul Pioneer Press*, May 21, 1876.

[18] On Johnson, here and below, see *Rush City Post*, August 10, 1877. Johnson testified for Buckles, Merrick, and Bignon; Case Files 410A, 411A, 417A.

[19] Descriptions here and in the following 13 paragraphs were drawn from *Pioneer Press*, August 7, 15, and *Rush City Post*, August 3, 10, 17, 1877; see also *Taylors Falls Journal*, August 10, 17, 1877.

[20] *Rush City Post*, October 26, 1877; Quillin and Swenson, Case Files 412A, 416A.

[21] Wilkes information is in Titus, Case File 422A. On Judge Crosby (1830–1910), below, see MHS Scrapbooks, 59:96.

[22] Quillin and Swenson, Case Files 412A, 416A.

[23] Here and below, see *Rush City Post*, October 26, 1877, October 18, 1878; Downs (whose name may have actually been Edward J. Devine) and Whelan (Whallen) and Wagner (latter two combined), Case Files 421A, 496A. A "Whalen," a gymnast, was mentioned in *Clipper*, March 31, 1877; no information was located on the other two men. For a summary of court costs, see Quillin, Case File 412A.

[24] On Shaleen, see W. J. Toensing, *Minnesota Congressmen, Legislators, and Other Elected State Officials*, 108 (St. Paul, 1971); *Chisago County Courier*, November 2, 1901, p. 1. On Robie, see *Rush City Post*, July 29, 1892; on Wilkes and Swenson, see White, "North Branch Celebrates 100 Years," in *Dalles Visitor*, 1981, p. 4, 5.

[25] *Clipper*, January 19, February 23, 1878; *Rush City Post*, February 8, May 31, October 4, 1878; *North Branch Review*, December 16, 1892.

[26] *Clipper*, July 16, 1881, November 11, 1882, February 17, 1883; *Rush City Post*, May 5, 12, 1882.

[27] For Quillin's property, see Quit Claim Deeds, Lots 1–3, 10–12, Block 6, Chisago County Register of Deeds, Center City, Grantee Index, p. 628. On the Arlington Hotel and Opera Hall, see *Rush City Post*, November 28, 1890, January 8, 1892; *North Branch Review*, September 25, 1891, June 17, August 19, 1892, November 30, 1894, January 11, 1895. See also Smith, "Notes on Smith and Quillin Families," p. 2, 3. Three Quillin poems are published in Thomas W. Herringshaw, *Poets of America*, 754 (Chicago, 1890).

[28] *North Branch Review*, November 20, 27, 1891, April 22, 1892, November 23, 1894, January 4, 11, 18, February 8, April 5, 1895.

[29] *North Branch Review*, January 11, February 8, 1895, March 1, April 5, 1895.

[30] Anderson interview; *North Branch Review*, September 25, 1891. On the Quillin children, see "Quillin Family Genealogy"; author's interview with Gayle Quillin Marthaler, 1978, notes in author's possession; *North Branch Review*, June 6, 17, July 29, August 12, 1892, December 7, 1894, January 11, 1895.

[31] *North Branch Review*, December 9, 1904, p. 5; Smith, "Notes on Smith and Quillin Families"; St. Paul city directories; author's interview with Mrs. Clayton Anderson, January 21, 1978, notes in author's possession, and Dean Anderson interview.

The author wishes to thank the following people for their help in researching this story: Faustino Avaloz, Marlin Heise, June D. Holmquist, Deborah L. Miller, Lucile M. Kane, MHS; Olav Bjåland, Lars Romendal, Telemark, Norway; Algene Carrier, Polk County, Wis.; Audrey Cernohous, Lyman Johnson, New Richmond, Wis.; Jean (Mrs. Frank) Chesley, Harold Harrison, staff of the Goodhue County Historical Society, Goodhue County Clerk of Court and staff, Red Wing; Sue Collins, Stillwater Public Library, Stillwater; Carl D. Chrislock, Minneapolis; Joseph and Edna Grove, Oliver T. Kaldahl, staff of the Pope County Historical Society, Glenwood; Joyce Hemmestvedt (Mrs. Orville) Jensen, Mankato; George Joa, Cleng Peerson Institute, Stavanger, Norway; Rudolph Johnson, Matti Kaups, University of Minnesota, Duluth; Russell Magnaghi, National Ski Hall of Fame, Ishpeming, Mich.; Norman County Clerk of Court and staff, Ada; Howard Vezina, Percy Weinhardt, Edwin Zulliger, St. Croix Falls, Wis.; Thelma Strand Wegner, Moorhead; Gilbert T. White, Grand Marais; Henry Gilbert White.

REFERENCE NOTES

¹ Clubs are said to have been organized earlier at Berlin, New Hampshire, and Altoona, Pennsylvania; see Theodore C. Blegen, *Norwegian Migration to America; The American Transition*, 2:575 (Northfield, Minn., 1940). For quotation, see *Red Wing Daily Republican*, January 27, 1905, p. 1.

² Olav Bø, *Skiing Traditions in Norway, Det Norske Samlaget*, 11–38, trans. Helen M. Corlett (Oslo, 1968).

³ Here and below, see *Minnesota Pioneer*, February 3, 1853; Theodore C. Blegen, ed., *Frontier Parsonage; the Letters of Olaus Fredrik Duus, Norwegian Pastor in Wisconsin, 1855–1858*, 50–53 (Northfield, 1947); Ruby O. Bennett, "John Lewis Dyer: Snowshoe Itinerant," in *Ski*, November, 1956, p. 52; Blegen, *Norwegian Migration to America*, 2:574–575; *Northwest Magazine*, February, 1888, p. 34; *Minneapolis Tribune*, March 7, 1881; *Pope County Tribune* (Glenwood), Court House Edition, June 12, 1930, sec. 1, p. 7. *Illustrated Album of Biography of Pope and Stevens County, Minnesota*, 202, 242 (Chicago, 1888); *Red Wing Daily Republican*, January 27, 1905, p. 1.

⁴ Bø, *Skiing Traditions*, 39, 66, 68, 74; Olav Bjåland [or Bjaaland], *Ski Og Sudpol, Olav Bjaaland's Museum Morgendal-Telemark*, 37 (Skien, Norway, 1970), excerpts trans. by Deborah L. Miller, hereafter cited as *Ski Og Sudpol*.

⁵ Here and below, see *Ski Og Sudpol*, 35, 111; Bø, *Skiing Traditions*, 42, 56–57.

⁶ Bø, *Skiing Traditions*, 39, 42, 51, 56, 75; Jakob Vaage, *The Holmenkollen Ski Jumping Hill and the Ski Museum*, 8, 9 (Oslo, 1968).

⁷ Bø, *Skiing Traditions*, 86; notes on Hemmestveit (Hemmestvedt) family compiled by Olav S. Bjåland, enclosed in Lars Romendal to author, January 4, 1980 (trans. by Deborah L. Miller), in Helen M. White, comp., Hemmestvedt Family Research File (hereafter Hemmestvedt File), in author's possession.

⁸ Bø, *Skiing Traditions*, 84, 86; *The North* (Minneapolis), February 22, 1893.

⁹ *Ski Og Sudpol*, 75; "Sondre Norheim 'Father of Modern Skiing,' 150th Anniversary, 1825–1975," undated pamphlet in MHS Reference Library; Nancy Solum, ed., *Self Portrait of Marshall County: A History of One Minnesota County and Many People Who Made That History*, 201 (Dallas, 1976).

¹⁰ Thelma Strand Wegner to Joyce H. Jensen, February 27, 1980 (copy), Mikkel Hemmestvedt and Bergit Tveitane marriage certificate, October 31, 1886 (copy), and *Norman County Index* (Ada), January 21, 1887 (notes on issues for 1886–88 taken by Thelma Strand Wegner at Index office) — all in Hemmestvedt File; John Turner and C. Knute Semling, eds., *History of Clay and Norman Counties, Minnesota*, 1:527, 2:467 (Indianapolis, 1918); *St. Paul Pioneer Press*, January 26, 1887. Mikkel won the "Konge-pokalen" competition and second prize in "Drammensrennet" in 1886; *Norske Skiløpere*, 292, undated photocopied pages enclosed in George Joa to author, October 30, 1979, in Hemmestvedt File.

¹¹ *Norman County Index*, January 21, 1887, Wegner notes in Hemmestvedt File; Jakob Vaage, *Norske ski erobrer verden*, 174 (Oslo, 1952), excerpts trans. by Deborah L. Miller.

[12] *Northwoods Journal* (Taylors Falls), Winter, 1973, p. 1, 5; *St. Paul Dispatch*, January 9, 14, February 10, 1886, January 16, December 25, 1887; *St. Paul Pioneer Press*, January 16, 18, 31, February 10, 15, 1886.

[13] *Norman County Index*, January 21, 28, 1887, Wegner notes in Hemmestvedt File.

[14] Here and below, see *St. Paul Pioneer Press*, January 26, 1887. The Altoona skiers may have come with the Eau Claire club. The tournament was obviously a "governed" one, that is, one carried on with regulations, although Robert Scharff, ed., *The Encyclopedia of Skiing* ([New York, 1974]) credits Red Wing with the first governed tournament.

[15] *Norman County Index*, January 28, 1887, Wegner notes in Hemmestvedt File. Of the various spellings of Arntson's name, this one is used in the Aurora Club Minute Book, January 10, 1888, in Goodhue County Historical Society, Red Wing.

[16] *Norman County Index*, January 28, February 4, 1887, Wegner notes in Hemmestvedt File.

[17] On details of the club's organization, its constitution, and its activities, here and below, see Aurora Club Minute Book [1886–92], a club scrapbook, and a voluminous collection of midwestern ski tournament programs, yearbooks, photographs, and other memorabilia, in Goodhue County Historical Society; *St. Paul Dispatch*, January 18, 19, 31, February 7, 9, 1886; author's interview with Harold Harrison, Red Wing, 1980, notes in author's possession.

[18] Aurora Club Minute Book, April 29, May 6, 1887; *Red Wing Daily Eagle*, February 2, 1928.

[19] Here and below, see Aurora Club Minute Book, February 1, 1886; *Red Wing Advance Sun*, February 2, 8, 16, 1887; *St. Paul Pioneer Press*, January 31, February 7, 1886.

[20] *Red Wing Advance Sun*, February 16, 1887; *Red Wing Argus*, February 10, 1887.

[21] *The North*, March 12, 1891; Ole Mangseth, "My Skiing Days," in *National Ski Association of America, Inc.: Year Book* [1930–31], 30, in Goodhue County Historical Society; *Red Wing Daily Republican*, February 26, 1904, p. 1. For information on the manufacture of skis see note 34.

[22] *Norman County Index*, January 28, 1887, Wegner notes in Hemmestvedt File.

[23] *Taylors Falls Journal*, December 29, 1887; *St. Croix Valley Standard* (St. Croix Falls, Wis.), January 5, 1888.

[24] Author's interview with Percy Weinhardt, 1975, notes in author's possession; *St. Croix Valley Standard*, January 5, 12, 26, 1888; *Taylors Falls Journal*, January 12, February 9, 1888.

[25] Weinhardt interview. Another skier named Lee from Ada joined Hemmestvedt in the St. Croix Valley demonstrations; *Taylors Falls Journal*, February 2, 1888; *St. Croix Valley Standard*, January 12, 19, 1888.

[26] Elijah E. Edwards, "Dies Boreales or Life at the Dalles," 23 (1886), manuscript journal in Elijah E. Edwards Papers, DePauw University Archives, Greencastle, Indiana.

[27] *St. Croix Valley Standard*, January 19, February 2, 1888; *St. Paul Pioneer Press*, January 18, 1888; Vaage, *Norske ski erobrer verden*, 174–176. It is not known when the Dovre Club was organized.

[28] *La Crosse Republican*, December 5, 1887, January 19, 23, 1888. No other information about Mary Davidson has been found.

[29] *St. Croix Valley Standard*, February 2, 1888; *Taylors Falls Journal*, January 19, 1888; Vaage, *Norske ski erobrer verden*.

[30] *Minneapolis Tribune*, February 9, 1885, January 31, 1888. According to Martin Strand to Mrs. George Holmberg [Thelma Strand Wegner], September 26, 1946, copy in Hemmestvedt File, the Minneapolis Turner group was organized before 1883; Harold A. Grinden, comp., *History of the National Ski Association and the Ski Sport in the United States of America, 1840–1931*, 8 (Duluth, [1931]), says it was organized in December, 1885.

[31] Here and below, see Strand to Holmberg, September 26, 1946, in Hemmestvedt File; *Minneapolis Tribune*, January 31, 1888.

[32] The clock may have been the one Mikkel had in Norway when he was interviewed

in his old age; Vaage, *Norske ski erobrer verden*, 179. *St. Croix Valley Standard*, February 2, 1888, said the clock was marble and valued at $60.

[33] *St. Croix Valley Standard*, January 19, February 23, 1888; *Taylors Falls Journal*, February 9, 16, 23, 1888.

[34] Weinhardt interview; *Taylors Falls Journal*, October 25, November 1, 15, 29, December 13, 27, 1888; *St. Croix Valley Standard*, November 1, 1888. Although skis were being made at La Crosse, St. Paul, Ishpeming, Red Wing, and perhaps other communities where the sport became popular, the industry at St. Croix Falls seems to have been the first to adopt mass production techniques. See Grinden, comp., *History of the National Ski Association*, 13, 58; *Red Wing Republican Eagle*, December 16, 1945.

[35] *Stillwater Messenger*, January 23 (quotation), 30, 1886, January 19, 26, February 13, 22, March 3, 1889; *St. Paul Dispatch*, February 5, 1886, p. 3; *St. Paul Pioneer Press*, February 5, 1886.

[36] *Stillwater Messenger*, January 23, 30, 1886, January 15, 1887; *St. Paul Pioneer Press*, February 3, 5, 13, 1886, January 3, 1887.

[37] *Stillwater Messenger*, January 23, 1886.

[38] *Stillwater Messenger*, January 19, 1889.

[39] *Stillwater Messenger*, March 2, 1889; Sue Collins to author, May 22, June 13, 16, 1980, in author's possession.

[40] Vaage, *Norske ski erobrer verden*, 174. Mikkel made skis after hours in Boxrud's furniture factory. At St. Croix Falls, the Hettings offered skis for sale for another year, but it is not known how much longer they remained in business; see *Taylors Falls Journal*, February 7, March 7, 1889, January 20, 1890.

[41] U.S. manuscript census, 1900, Norman County, McDonaldsville Township, Enumeration dist. 134; Hemmestvedt File.

[42] Aurora Club Minute Book, November 19, 1889.

[43] *The North*, January 22, 1890.

[44] Here and below, see *The North*, February 5, 1890. For information about uniforms, see the Aurora Club Constitution and Aurora Club Minute Book, December 4, 1888, January 7, 14, 21, 27, 1890.

[45] Rebecca E. Blondell to Joyce Hemmestvedt Jensen, April 14, [1964], copy in Hemmestvedt File. The dance Mrs. Blondell remembered after the banquet may have been held at another time; *The North*, February 5, 1890.

[46] *The North*, December 3, 31, 1890, January 14, 1891; *Stillwater Messenger*, December 13, 1890.

[47] *The North*, January 7, 14, 21, 1891. The name of the club was changed later that year to the Ishpeming Ski Club; see Bill Berry, "Diamond Jubilee of the United States Ski Association," and Burton H. Boyum, "National Ski Hall of Fame," in Russell M. Magnaghi, ed., *Seventy-Five Years of Skiing 1904–1979*, 12, 21 (Ishpeming, Mich., 1979).

[48] *The North*, February 4, 1891.

[49] Blondell to Jensen, April 14, [1964], copy in Hemmestvedt File; Vaage, *Norske ski erobrer verden*, 174; Aurora Club Minute Book, November 19, 1889, December 26, 1890, January 5, 16, 1891. Little is known of Honningstad (Hunningstad, Onningstad), but on Hjermstad, who was later injured in a ski accident and became a dentist, see *Red Wing Advance Sun*, January 17, 20, 24, June 27, 1894.

[50] *The North*, February 4, 1891.

[51] Here and below, see *Ishpeming Daily Press* quoted in *The North*, February 4, 1891.

[52] Here and below, see *Stillwater Messenger*, December 13, 1890, February 6, 7, 9, 17, 18, 1891; *Stillwater Daily Gazette*, January 19, 24, 30, 1891; *The North*, February 25, 1891. Details of the club's participation in the Stillwater tournament are given in Aurora Club Minute Book, January 24, February 10, 13, March 1, 1891.

[53] Here and below, see *Stillwater Messenger*, February 21, 1891; *Stillwater Daily Gazette*, February 9, 17, 18, 1891; *The North*, February 25, 1891.

[54] Here and below, see *The North*, March 18, 1891; *Norman County Index*, March 13, 1891.

[55] *The North*, March 18, 1891.

[56] Joyce Jensen's handwritten notes on Thelma Wegner to Joyce Jensen, February 27, 1980; Blondell to Jensen, April 14, [1964], (copy); Jensen, "Hemmestvedt Family History," 4 (n.d.); correspondence between Jensen and author, from December 29, 1979, to April 7, 1980; Goodhue County, Clerk of District Court, Register of Deaths, 2:437 (copy) – all in Hemmestvedt File.

[57] U.S. manuscript census schedules, 1900, Norman County, McDonaldsville Township, Enumeration dist. 134; Jensen, "Hemmestvedt Family History," 3, in Hemmestvedt File.

[58] *Eau Claire Times*, February 12, 19, 1892.

[59] Johnson is in error on the date of the tournament in his reminiscences. Since Mikkel participated in his last U.S. tournament in 1892, his adventure could only have occurred in that year; *Red Wing Daily Republican*, January 31, 1928, sec. 3, p. 4; *The North*, December 20, 1893.

[60] *Red Wing Advance Sun*, January 4, 18, 1893; *Norske Skiløpere*, 292; *The North*, January 18, 1893.

[61] Here and below, see *The North*, February 15, 22, 1893.

[62] *The North*, February 22, 1893.

[63] Here and below, see *Stoughton Courier*, February 3, 17, 24, March 3, 1893; *Stoughton Hub*, February 17, March 3, 1893.

[64] *The North*, December 20, 1893; *Red Wing Advance Sun*, November 4, December 27, 1893; Goodhue County, Clerk of District Court, Marriages, 11:528.

[65] *Red Wing Advance Sun*, December 30, 1893; *The North*, February 8, 1893; Vaage, *Norske ski erobrer verden*, 178; Grinden, comp., *History of the National Ski Association*, 19, 57–58. Nansen's book is reviewed with comments on his use of skis in *The North*, December 31, 1890.

[66] On skiing in these communities, see *Hudson Star-Observer*, May 20, 1954, centennial edition, sec. 6, p. 5, sec. 11, p. 3, 7 (Hudson); *The North*, February 8, 15, 1893 (Ellsworth, Devils Lake); *Taylors Falls Journal*, January 17, 1889 (Winona); *St. Paul Pioneer Press*, February 5, 1886 (Northfield); *Red Wing Advance Sun*, February 14, 1894 (Cannon Falls); *Cook County Herald*, February 12, 1898 (Grand Marais); *Glenwood Herald*, March 27, 1947, p. 4, and *Pope County Tribune* (Glenwood), Court House Edition, sec. 1, p. 7 (Glenwood, Starbuck); "Trysil Club," undated typescript in Norwegian Activities File, Northeast Minnesota Historical Center, University of Minnesota, Duluth. For women on skis, see *The North*, March 4, 1891. A women's club was organized at Red Wing in 1903; *Red Wing Daily Republican*, January 6, p.[3], February 6, p. [3], 1903.

[67] *Red Wing Advance Sun*, March 8, 1893, January 6, 10, 13, 1894. *Norman County Index*, February 23, 1894, reported that Torjus, breaking his own record, had made a "tremendous jump of 120 feet" and was slightly injured on landing. No report of this event has been found in the *Red Wing Advance Sun*, and the report of the Aurora Club run, in the issue of February 21, does not mention Torjus as a participant. Vaage's report in *Norske ski erobrer verden*, 179, is taken from *Fremskridt*. The author has not been able to find this source or any firsthand report of the event.

[68] Here and below, see *The North*, March 15, 1893.

[69] U.S. manuscript census schedules, 1900, Norman County, McDonaldsville Township, Enumeration dist. 134; Norman County Heritage Commission and Norman County Historical Society, *In the Heart of the Red River Valley: A History of the People of Norman County, Minnesota*, 162 (Dallas, 1976); Jensen, "Hemmestvedt Family History," 5, in Hemmestvedt File. Summond returned to Norway in 1914; Bjåland notes in Romendal to author, January 4, 1980, in Hemmestvedt File.

[70] *Red Wing Daily Republican*, February 26, p. 7, 29, p. 3, 1904, January 26, p. 8, 27, p. 1, 28, p. 6, 8 – all 1905; Magnaghi, ed., *Seventy-Five Years of Skiing*, 8.

[71] A sketch on Hemmestvedt family history by Torjus' granddaughter, Joyce Hemmestvedt Jensen, is in Pennington County Historical Society, *Pioneer Tales: A History of Pennington County, Minnesota*, 217, 227 (Dallas, 1976).

[72] Pennington County Historical Society, *Pioneer Tales*, 217.

[73] Here and below, see *Red Wing Daily Republican*, February 6, 1928, p. 1. Other

newspaper items describing the tournament are in Viola Hofschulte Scrapbook and papers of Aurora Ski Club, both in Goodhue County Historical Society; see also files of the *Red Wing Eagle* and *Daily Republican*, January 6–February 6, 1928. Shipstad and Johnson, with Eddie's brother Roy, later founded the Ice Follies; Russ Davis, "Ziegfelds on Ice," in *Saturday Evening Post*, December 14, 1940, p. 35.

⁷⁴ Viola Hofschulte Scrapbook, 5.

[74] Viola Hofschulte Scrapbook, 5.

[75] *Norske Skiløpere*, 292; *Pioneer Tales*, 217; Bjåland notes in Romendal to author, January 4, 1980, in Hemmestvedt File; Jensen, "Hemmestvedt Family History," 7.

REFERENCE NOTES

THE TALE OF A COMET — Pages 152 to 187

The author wishes to thank the following people for their help in researching this story: Faustino Avaloz, Ruth Bauer, Patrick Coleman, John Dougherty, Dorothy Gimmestad, Wiley Pope, Ruby Shields, Alissa Wiener, MHS; Professor Kris Davidson, University of Minnesota, Minneapolis; Lucius Farish, Plumerville, Ark.; Father Barry Hagen, Portland, Ore.; Frederic B. Jueneman, Newark, Calif.

[1] On Donnelly, here and below, see Helen M. White, *Guide to a Microfilm Edition of the Ignatius Donnelly Papers*, 2–5 (St. Paul, 1968). The Donnelly Papers at the MHS, also available on microfilm, contain the letters, notes for speeches, diaries, and scrapbooks used in writing this chapter. Letters and speeches are filed chronologically except those that are part of Donnelly's Literary Scrapbook, vol. 127; citations to these letters and to all newspaper clippings from this source include microfilm roll and frame numbers.

[2] Donnelly, *Atlantis: The Antediluvian World* (New York, 1882). A revised edition edited by Edgerton Sykes (New York, 1949) contains bibliographical notes and commentary. Donnelly and other 19th-century writers found a constituency of people (in literary clubs, study circles, correspondence schools, and Chautauquas, for example) who were hungry for learning and received works of popular science with enthusiasm; Richard Hofstadter, William Miller, and Daniel Aaron, *The American Republic Since 1865*, 2:306 (Englewood Cliffs, N.J., 1961).

[3] Here and below, see Loren Eisely, *Darwin's Century*, 353 (New York, 1958). For examples of church reactions, see *Northwest Chronicle* (St. Paul), April 1, 1882 (162:42); advance sheet from *Harper's Monthly*, May, 1881 (162:32); *Christian Commonwealth* (England), September 21, 1882 (162:103).

[4] Details of the writing and publication of *Atlantis* are summarized in Martin Ridge, *Ignatius Donnelly, Portrait of a Politician*, 196–202 (Chicago, 1962). The quotation is in Sykes, ed., Donnelly, *Atlantis*, x.

[5] *New York Times*, August 30, 1881.

[6] Donnelly, *Ragnarok: The Age of Fire and Gravel*, 2 (New York, 1883). A recent photographically reproduced edition with an introduction (full of errors) by Paul M. Allen is *The Destruction of Atlantis: Ragnarok: The Age of Fire and Gravel* (New York, 1971).

[7] Here and below, see Donnelly, *Ragnarok*, 8–22, 44. The works by these scientists that Donnelly used are: Geikie, *The Great Ice Age and Its Relation to the Antiquity of Man* (London, 1874); Figuier, *The World Before the Deluge* (New York, 1866); Croll, *Climate and Time* (New York, 1875); Dawson, *The Story of Earth and Man* (New York, 1873); Dana, *Text-Book of Geology* (Philadelphia, 1863), an abridgement of his *Manual of Geology* (Philadelphia, 1863). On their careers, see Charles C. Gillispie, ed., *Dictionary of Scientific Biography*, 3:470, 552, 607, 5:338 (New York, 1971, 1972); *Encyclopaedia Brittanica*, 3:407, 4:450 (Chicago, 1975); Clarence L. Barnhart and William D. Halsey, eds., *Century Cyclopedia of Names*, 2:1554 (New York, 1954).

[8] Here and below, see Donnelly, *Ragnarok*, 23–42, 47, 58–62 (quotations p. 42, 47).

[9] Donnelly, *Ragnarok*, 43–57 (quotations p. 52, 56).

[10] Donnelly, *Ragnarok*, 80, 82–84. Donnelly was punning on "celestial," a word often used in the 19th century to describe the Chinese. In 1882 the U.S. Congress passed the Chinese Exclusion Act, designed to prevent immigration from China; see June D. Holmquist, ed., *They Chose Minnesota: A Survey of the State's Ethnic Groups*, 9 (St. Paul, 1981).

253

[11] Alexander von Humboldt, *KoΣmoΣ [Cosmos]: A General Survey of the Physical Phenomena of the Universe*, 1:108, 121, 122 (London, 1845). Donnelly had a German edition of *Cosmos* in his library; library list, 1909 (roll 132), Donnelly Papers.

[12] [William W. Payne], "The Comets of 1882," in *Sidereal Messenger*, 2:120 (June, 1883). For citations to Guillemin's *The Heavens: An Illustrated Handbook of Popular Astronomy* (London, 1866), see *Ragnarok*, 68–86, 100; Professor Kris Davidson of the University of Minnesota owns Donnelly's annotated copy. For references to Heinrich Schellen, *Spectrum Analysis* (New York, 1872), see *Ragnarok*, 69, 94, 104, 156. Donnelly may have been more indebted to Kirkwood's *Comets and Meteors: Their Phenomena in All Ages, Their Mutual Relations, and the Theory of Their Origin* (Philadelphia, 1873) than his single footnote (p. 136) indicates; he owned the book. His debt to an article on comets and meteors in the *Edinburgh Review*, October, 1874, is obvious; whole sections have been cut from Donnelly's copy of the magazine and are reproduced almost verbatim in the book (p. 78, 84, 85, 144, 311, for example).

[13] Here and below, see Lewis Boss, "Comets – Their Composition, Purpose and Effect upon the Earth," in *Sidereal Messenger*, 1:1-8 (March, 1882). For a description of modern theories relating to comets, see p. 168, below.

[14] On astronomical events of 1882 and 1883, see issues of *Sidereal Messenger* for those years; *Appletons' Annual Cyclopaedia*, 7:32–42, 8:20–30 (1882, 1883), hereafter *Appletons' Cyclopaedia*.

[15] Donnelly, *Ragnarok*, 80, 90.

[16] Here and below, see Donnelly, *Ragnarok*, 91–112 (quotations p. 95, 107, 108).

[17] Donnelly, *Ragnarok*, 121–131, 252. For Donnelly's discussion of folk literature, see *Ragnarok*, Part III, "The Legends"; italics in quotations are Donnelly's.

[18] Here and below, see Donnelly, *Ragnarok*, 154–166 (quotations p. 165, 166).

[19] Donnelly, *Ragnarok*, 287, 291, 310, 311, 339.

[20] Donnelly, *Ragnarok*, 316–340.

[21] Here and below, see Donnelly, *Ragnarok*, 141, 148, 152, 338. For his identification of the Irish with the Norsemen, see his St. Patrick's Day address, March 17, 1882.

[22] Here and below, see Donnelly, *Ragnarok*, 341, 360, 368, 375, 376, 404, 405.

[23] Donnelly, *Ragnarok*, 390, 391, 395, 399.

[24] Donnelly, *Ragnarok*, 84, 404.

[25] Donnelly, *Ragnarok*, 408–413.

[26] Here and below, see Donnelly, *Ragnarok*, 413–422, 430 (quotations p. 413, 414, 421, 422, 430). For a modern view of the causes and unprecedented destructiveness of the Peshtigo fire, see Robert W. Wells, *Fire at Peshtigo*, 199–208 (Englewood Cliffs, N.J., 1968); the blaze, when judged with the other fires of the same day, is considered the most deadly and probably the most extensive 19th-century forest fire in North America.

[27] Here and below, see Donnelly, *Ragnarok*, 437–441.

[28] Ridge, *Donnelly*, 206; Donnelly, Diary, July 8, 13, 21, 31, 1882. The New Haven scientist may have been Dana.

[29] Here and below, see Ridge, *Donnelly*, 206; Bunce to Donnelly, August 4, October 3, 1882, Donnelly to Bunce, August 8, 30, 1882, and to D. Appleton & Co., August 22, 30, 1882. For an example of a friend's comments, see Geo[rge] M. Giltinan to Donnelly, October 5, 1882.

[30] [U. S. Signal Service], *Monthly Weather Review*, August, 1882, *Scientific American*, 46:49, 47:53 (January 28, July 22, 1882), Royal Greenwich Observatory (Hurstmonceaux, England), *Observations*, 6:192, 39:214 – all as cited in Charles Fort, *The Book of the Damned*, 215, 216, 305, 332; C. S. Hastings, "Comet Cruls," in *Sidereal Messenger*, 1:172 (November, 1882); *Appletons' Cyclopaedia*, 7:34, 38; S. Hall Young, *Hall Young of Alaska: "The Mushing Parson,"* 260 (New York, 1927). For more examples of "falls" in 1882 and 1883, listed by date, place, and type of material, see Ivan T. Sanderson, *Investigating the Unexplained: Disquieting Mysteries of the Natural World*, 282, 284, 290 (Englewood Cliffs, N.J., 1972).

[31] Bunce to Donnelly, October 27, November 5, 1882; Knute Nelson to Donnelly, November 30, 1882; W. W. Windom to Donnelly, December 4, 1882.

[32] *St. Paul Dispatch*, n.d. (162:138); *Hartford Times* quoted in *Philadelphia Star*, December 20, 1882; *St. Paul Pioneer Press*, December 17, 1882 (162:144); *Philadelphia*

Bulletin, December 18, 1882 (162:142); *Boston Evening Traveller*, n.d. (162:158); *North American [Review]* (New York), December 20, 1882 (162:143).

³³ Ridge, *Donnelly*, 209.

³⁴ Hoerbiger, *Glazial-Kosmogonie* (Kaiserslautern, Germany, 1913); Velikovsky, *Worlds in Collision* (New York, 1950); Martin Gardner, *In the Name of Science*, 28–33, 37 (New York, 1952). The German edition of *Ragnarok*, edited by Axel Olrik, was published by W. de Gruyter (Berlin, 1922). William Whiston, a British mathematician and clergyman, had theorized in 1696 that "the original 'chaos' was the tail of a giant comet" and that comets had caused Biblical catastrophes, but there is no evidence that Donnelly saw his work; see Gardner, *Science*, 34.

³⁵ *Sky and Telescope*, 56:497 (December, 1978); Calder, *Comet*, 87–89, 124–126. Luigi G. Jacchia, an astronomer affiliated with observatories at Harvard University and the Smithsonian Institution, estimated that a meteorite he saw in 1972 over Jackson Hole, Wyoming, would have hit the Earth with the force of an atomic bomb; instead, it sliced through the atmosphere and "performed the unique trick of skipping back into space"; see *Sky and Telescope*, 48:4-8 (July, 1974).

³⁶ Urey, "Cometary Collisions and Geological Periods," in *Nature*, March 2, 1973, p. 32. Jueneman, *Limits of Uncertainty*, 185 (Chicago, 1975), cites radiocarbon/Bristlecone pine dendrochronology studies in the chapter titled "Tales of a Comet," which was first published in his column for the magazine *Industrial Research* (later *Industrial Research & Development*), October, 1973.

³⁷ Here and below, see Luis W. Alvarez, Walter Alvarez, Frank Asaro, and Helen V. Michel, "Extraterrestrial Cause for the Cretaceous-Tertiary Extinction," in *Science*, 208:1095 (June, 1980); Dale A. Russell, "The Mass Extinctions of the Late Mesozoic," in *Scientific American*, January, 1982, p. 58–65; "Birth of a continent linked to crash by meteroid," in Washington University (St. Louis) *Record*, 7:18 (February 2, 1982); *Science 82*, April, 1982, p. 10.

³⁸ John C. Brandt, *Comets: Readings from Scientific American* (San Francisco, 1981); Kris Davidson to Ann Regan, October 4, 1983, in author's possession. A journalist's popular view of cometary lore is Nigel Calder, *The Comet is Coming!: The Feverish Legend of Mr Halley* (New York, 1980).

³⁹ Donnelly, "St. Patrick's Day Address, Faribault, 1883." For characterizations of the 1880s, see Ray Ginger, *Age of Excess: The United States From 1877 to 1914* (New York, 1965); John A. Garrity, *The New Commonwealth, 1877–1890* (New York, 1968).

⁴⁰ Examples of these arguments are in Helen M. White, comp., 1883 Disaster File, in author's possession, which contains notes on St. Paul, Duluth, and Rush City newspapers for 1883; pertinent references to the *New York Times* and *Appletons' Cyclopaedia* for that year; references to Fort, *Damned*, and *Lo!* (New York, 1941), and to Jay Robert Nash, *Darkest Hours* (New York, 1976).

⁴¹ For examples of these arguments, see 1883 Disaster File; *St. Paul Pioneer Press*, July 31, August 22, 1883.

⁴² Donnelly, Diary, January 22, 1883; 1883 Disaster File, January.

⁴³ *St. Paul Pioneer Press*, January 4, 1883; *Duluth Daily Tribune*, January 6, 1883; 1883 Disaster File, January.

⁴⁴ *Winona Republican*, January 26, 1883; *Duluth Tribune*, January 26, 1883.

⁴⁵ *San Francisco Bulletin*, January 13, 1883 (162:180); *San Francisco Chronicle*, January 14, 1883 (162:180); *Hastings Gazette*, January 20, 1883 (162:196).

⁴⁶ Here and below, see *Dial*, January, 1883 (162:161); Donnelly, "A Review of a Review," n.d., memorandum filed at beginning of 1883 papers.

⁴⁷ *Popular Science Monthly*, February, 1883, p. 560 (162:204); *Pall Mall Gazette*, February 23, 1883 (162:256); *Daily News* quoted in *St. Paul Globe*, May 12, 1883 (162:282); *The Churchman*, February 17, 1883 (162:238).

⁴⁸ On book sales, see Bunce to Donnelly, January 15, 28, February 1, 19, March 9, 1883; J. B. Baldwin to Donnelly, March 12, 1883; Stan Donnelly to Donnelly, April 10, 16, 1883. On the Mardi Gras, see *Picayune* (New Orleans), February 7, 1883 (162:287); *Philadelphia Times*, February 7, 1883 (162:235); *Banbury Guardian*, April 26, 1883 (162:287); R. B. Matthews to Donnelly, March 6, 1883; Donnelly, Diary, February 11, 1883. For correspondence, see Arthur Gough to Donnelly, n.d. (probably early March),

March 9, 1883 (162:250, 262); Morris Goldwater to Donnelly, April 14, 1883 (162:283); Frank Daughty to Donnelly, June 18, 1883; Rasmus Anderson to Donnelly, January 6 (162:168), 15, 1883; Father Mir to Donnelly, May 1, 1883 (162:289).

[49] Here and below, see 1883 Disaster File, February, March, April, May; Nash, *Darkest Hours*, 599, 721.

[50] Here and below, see Donnelly, Diary, June 5, 6, 8, 19, 21–29, 1883; Bunce to Donnelly, June 2, 1883; Donnelly to R. C. Moore, June 1, 1883.

[51] Lionel Booth to Donnelly, June 25, 1883; Youmans to L. W. Hall, June 1, originally enclosed in Frank Daughty to Donnelly, June 18, 1883.

[52] 1883 Disaster File, June; *St. Paul Pioneer Press*, June 5, 1883.

[53] Here and below, see 1883 Disaster File, July; *St. Paul Pioneer Press*, July 19, September 9, 1883.

[54] 1883 Disaster File, July, August. On Ischia, see *Rush City Post*, August 3, 1883; *St. Paul Pioneer Press*, July 30, August 2, 1883.

[55] Here and below, see 1883 Disaster File, July, August; Fort, *Damned*, 104, 137; *Appletons' Cyclopaedia*, 8:20, 21, 26. The Mexican astronomer's report is translated and printed with the photograph in Trevor James Constable, *Sky Creatures: Living UFOs*, 235–239; see also Fort, *Damned*, 257.

[56] *London Standard* quoted in *Rush City Post*, August 3, 1883.

[57] Joel Bassett to Donnelly, August 13, 1883; AAAS to Donnelly, August 15, 1883; Donnelly to Kate Donnelly, August 12, 1883.

[58] Here and below, see *St. Paul Pioneer Press*, August 16, 20, 21, 1883.

[59] *St. Paul Pioneer Press*, August 17, 18, 21, 22, 1883.

[60] Donnelly to Bunce, September 30, 1883; *St. Paul Pioneer Press*, August 18, 1883.

[61] Wakeman to Donnelly, August 28, September 5, 1883; *Louisville Courier-Journal*, September 10, 1883 (162:297).

[62] 1883 Disaster File, August.

[63] On the Rochester tornado, here and below, see *St. Paul Pioneer Press*, August 23, 24, 1883.

[64] Helen Clapesattle, *The Doctors Mayo*, 242–244 (Minneapolis, 1941).

[65] Clapesattle, *Doctors Mayo*, 246; Iggy Donnelly to Donnelly, August 23, 1883.

[66] *St. Paul Pioneer Press*, August 29, 30, 1883.

[67] *New York Times*, August 24, 1883.

[68] 1883 Disaster File, August.

[69] Here and below, see Nash, *Darkest Hours*, 311–314; *Appletons' Cyclopaedia*, 8:286.

[70] *St. Louis Spectator* quoted in *St. Paul Globe*, September 14, 1883 (162:289); *Harpers Weekly*, September 29, 1883 (162:282); *Philadelphia Evening Star*, September 4, 1883 (162:294).

[71] Donnelly, Diary, September 3, 1883.

[72] Here and below, see Bunce to Donnelly, September 25, October 10, 17, 1883; Donnelly to Bunce, September 30, October 13, 1883. On the Baltimore Oriole, see Donnelly, Diary, September 17, 1883; Sarah [Donnelly] to Donnelly, September 18, 1883; Oriole Program (162:310–334).

[73] C. A. Young, "Astronomical Collisions," *North American Review*, 137:350–357 (October, 1883).

[74] Here and below, see Gillispie, ed., *Dictionary of Scientific Biography*, 6:564 (New York, 1972); *Dictionary of American Biography*, 9:393 (New York, 1932); Hunt to Donnelly, November 3, 24, 1883. Hunt's lecture on "Mineral Physiology," delivered at Poughkeepsie, N.Y., November 11, 1882, is in Donnelly Papers. No copies of Donnelly to Hunt, October 22, November 28, 1882, have been found.

[75] Here and below, see Donnelly, Diary, October 2, 26, 1883; notes for speeches, October 3, 25, 1883.

[76] Here and below, see 1883 Disaster File, September, October, November; Wright, *An Autobiography*, 55 (New York, 1943); John H. Bardon, "The Wreck of the Manistee" (February 4, 1932), typescript in Northeast Minnesota Historical Center, Duluth; *Rush City Post*, December 7, 1883.

[77] 1883 Disaster File, August–December; *Cook County Herald* (Grand Marais), No-

vember 25, 1898; *Philadelphia Star*, December 10, 1883, clipping in Donnelly, Diary, December 16, 1883.

⁷⁸ *Appletons' Cyclopaedia*, 8:525, 526; unidentified newspaper clipping in Donnelly, Diary, December 9, 1883; J. S. Gregg to Donnelly, December 28, 1883.

⁷⁹ *Rush City Post*, December 21, 1883.

⁸⁰ Donnelly, Diary, December 25, 31, 1883.

REINDEER PEOPLE — Pages 188 to 229

The author wishes to thank the following people for their help in researching these stories: Florence (Mrs. John) Alnes, Two Harbors; Mr. and Mrs. Richard Base, Engle Eide, John and Evelyn Eide, Mary Alice Harvey, M. N. Humphreys, Justine Kerfoot, Willis Raff, Ade Toftey, Chris and Matelda Tormondsen, Gilbert T. White, staff of the Cook County Register of Deeds, Grand Marais; Charles Boostrom, Silver Bay; Donald Boostrom, Schroeder; Edmund and Martha Bray, Philadelphia; Jeanne Brooke, Battleground, Wash.; Franklin W. Burch, Tim Hall, James Harwood, Sara D. Jackson, Renee Jaussaud, Robert Kvasnicka, and other staff members of the National Archives, Washington, D.C.; Lieut. Col. Neil Dimond, San Clemente, Calif.; A. Vernon Engelsen, Burlington, Wash.; Ben and Agnes Fenstad, Little Marais; Rudolph Johnson, Jim Vileta, University of Minnesota, Duluth; Lucile Kane, MHS; Milton Mattson, Beaver Bay; Edward McCann, Redwood City, Calif.; Hermund Melheim, Littlefork; Marie (Mrs. Irving) Olsen, Fort Yukon, Ala.; staff of the Presbyterian Historical Society, Philadelphia; Clifford Samuelson, Spring Lake Park; James Tulloch, Brinon, Wash.; Bruce M. White, St. Paul.

¹ On reindeer and the origins of reindeer culture, here and below, see Berthold Laufer, "The Reindeer and Its Domestication," and Gudmund Hatt, "Notes on Reindeer Nomadism," in *Memoirs of the American Anthropological Association*, 4:91–147, 6:75–133 (Lancaster, Penn., 1917, 1919). Hatt (p. 109) believes that the nomadic herding of reindeer is derived from reindeer hunting and dog driving and may have begun among stone-age people. The quotations are in Carl J. Lomen, *Fifty Years in Alaska*, 28 (New York, 1954). On reindeer and their response to music, see, for example, Sheldon Jackson, "[Third] Annual Report on Introduction of Domestic Reindeer to Alaska," in 53 Congress, 2 session, *Senate Executive Documents*, no. 70, p. 174 (serial 3160). Jackson submitted sixteen annual reports on the introduction of the domestic reindeer from 1890–91 to 1908. They were included in reports to Congress of the Bureau of Education of the U.S. Department of the Interior, but many were issued separately. The first citation to each report used here gives its number in the series and location in the government serial set; subsequent citations are to the series number and page only. More detailed bibliographical information on these and other basic source materials on Alaska may be found in James Wickersham, *A Bibliography of Alaskan Literature 1724–1924* (*Miscellaneous Publications of the Alaska Agricultural College and School of Mines*, vol. 1 — Fairbanks, Alaska, 1927), and William R. Hunt, *Alaska: A Bicentennial History*, 191–193 (New York, 1976).

² James and Catherine Brickey, "Reindeer Cattle of the Arctic," in *Alaska Journal*, 5:16 (Winter, 1975) give evidence to support U.S. Fish Commission zoologist Charles Townsend and Captain Michael Healy of the U.S. Revenue Marine Service as originators of the idea of importing reindeer.

³ For more on the Lomens and others, see "The Christmas Reindeer Shows," below.

⁴ On Jackson, here and below, see *Dictionary of American Biography*, 9:555 (New York, 1932); J. Arthur Lazell, *Alaskan Apostle: The Life Story of Sheldon Jackson*, 26–29 (New York, 1960); Robert L. Stewart, *Sheldon Jackson: Pathfinder and Prospector of the Missionary Vanguard in the Rocky Mountains and Alaska*, 66–69 (New York, 1908). Another book-length biography is John T. Faris, *The Alaskan Pathfinder: The Story of Sheldon Jackson for Boys* (New York, 1913). Although no full-length, scholarly biography of Jackson has been published, his papers, including scrapbooks and copies of official correspondence and reports, are in the Sheldon Jackson Collection of the Presbyterian Historical Society, Philadelphia (hereafter cited Jackson Collection).

⁵ Here and below, see Lazell, *Alaskan Apostle*, 31–33, 44, 48–50; Stewart, *Sheldon Jackson*, 101–106.

⁶ Lazell, *Alaskan Apostle*, 53–56.

⁷ Here and below, see Theodore C. Hinckley, "Sheldon Jackson, Presbyterian Lobbyist for the Great Land of Alaska," in *Journal of Presbyterian History*, 40:4, 20–23 (March, 1962); Stewart, *Sheldon Jackson*, 339.

⁸ On the damaging effects of whites and white culture on the Alaskan natives, see, for example, Hubert H. Bancroft, *History of the Pacific States of North America, Alaska, 1730–1885*, 538, 621, 624, 668 (San Francisco, 1886); Frederick Schwatka, *A Summer in Alaska*, 382 (St. Louis, 1893); *New York Sun*, December 6, 1888; *New York Times*, August 5, 1889; *Alaska Herald*, January 15, 1894. Newspaper clippings are in vol. 19, p. 40, 64, 37, respectively, in Jackson Collection.

⁹ Jackson, "[Third] Reindeer Report," 20, and "[Eighth] Annual Report on Introduction of Domestic Reindeer into Alaska," in 55 Congress, 3 session, *Senate Documents*, no. 34, p. 17 (serial 3728).

¹⁰ Karl Ward, "A Study of the Introduction of Reindeer into Alaska," in *Journal of Presbyterian History*, 24:255 (December, 1956); Jackson, "[Third] Reindeer Report," 20. For accounts of earlier proponents of reindeer culture, see Dorothy Jean Ray, "Sheldon Jackson and the Reindeer Industry of Alaska," in *Journal of Presbyterian History*, 43:74 (June, 1965); Brickey and Brickey, in *Alaska Journal*, 5:16; Lomen, *Fifty Years in Alaska*, 28. On reindeer culture, see W. H. Dall, *Alaska and Its Resources*, 514 (Boston, 1870); Paul B. Du Chaillu, *The Land of the Midnight Sun*, 1:126–130, 133, 2:175 (New York, 1882). Ray, an anthropologist, criticizes the reindeer experiment on cultural, not economic, grounds (p. 72, 79). She contends that while Jackson was sincere, he lacked understanding of native culture, that the Eskimo were not really in danger of starving, and that the reindeer made no difference in mortality rates among the natives. The fact remains that, while the Eskimo may have been in no more danger of starvation than usual, their sources of food, from season to season, were unpredictable and native people did sometimes starve. Ray criticizes the ineffectiveness of Jackson's efforts during the first few years of the reindeer program, before the herds had been established. The figures cited on p. 229, below, show the eventual success of the program, although it never grew to the size Jackson and others had hoped.

¹¹ Lazell, *Alaskan Apostle*, 90; Brickey and Brickey, in *Alaska Journal*, 5:16.

¹² Here and below, see Jackson, "[Third] Reindeer Report," 18; Lazell, *Alaskan Apostle*, 86, 90, 97–102; Stewart, *Sheldon Jackson*, 389–394.

¹³ Lazell, *Alaskan Apostle*, 111; Jackson, "[Third] Reindeer Report," 147–149, and "[Seventh] Annual Report on Introduction of Domestic Reindeer into Alaska," 55 Congress, 2 session, *Senate Documents*, no. 30, p. 49 (serial 3590).

¹⁴ Jackson, "[Third] Reindeer Report," 18, 155, 158–172. Other letters were published in Jackson, "[Fourth] Annual Report on Introduction of Domestic Reindeer into Alaska," 53 Congress, 3 session, *Senate Executive Documents*, no. 92, p. 94–96 (serial 3280).

¹⁵ Jackson, "[Third] Reindeer Report," 17.

¹⁶ Ray, in *Journal of Presbyterian History*, 43:87; J. Walter Johnshoy, *Apaurak in Alaska*, 24–26, 323 (Philadelphia, [1944]). On Kjellmann's recruiting mission, see Jackson, "[Fourth] Reindeer Report," 80. Luther Seminary was then in Robbinsdale; it is now Luther Northwestern Theological Seminary, located in St. Paul.

¹⁷ Johnshoy, *Apaurak in Alaska*, 26; *St. Paul Pioneer Press*, May 22, 1894; *St. Paul Dispatch*, May 22, 1894. The remainder of the Lapps' journey was equally eventful: floods west of the Rocky Mountains forced a rerouting of the train, fear of an anticipated attack of Coxey's army brought the protection of federal marshals, and a group of inquisitive Indians met the train at Kalispell, Montana. Brevig described the colorful meeting, noting that "The Lapps . . . were just as curious to know what kind of people Indians were" (Johnshoy, *Apaurak in Alaska*, 27).

¹⁸ Ray, in *Journal of Presbyterian History*, 43:82, 88, writes of the conflicts. Jackson, "Fourteenth Annual Report on Introduction of Domestic Reindeer into Alaska," 58 Congress, 3 session, *Senate Documents*, no. 61, p. 19 (serial 4764), and Ward, in *Journal of Presbyterian History*, 24:252, summarize statistics of the reindeer project. Jackson to the commissioner of education, January 25, 1906, in vol. 17, p. 316, Jackson Collection,

outlines the joint public and private responsibilities at mission stations for the reindeer project.

[19] Jackson, "Fourteenth Reindeer Report," 15.

[20] Jackson, "[Seventh] Reindeer Report," 28, and "[Eighth] Reindeer Report," 16, 32.

[21] Lazell, *Alaskan Apostle*, 157, 190–192.

[22] Lazell, *Alaskan Apostle*, 155–157; Jackson, "Thirteenth Annual Report on Introduction of Reindeer into Alaska," 58 Congress, 2 session, *Senate Documents*, no. 210, p. 171 (serial 4599); Ray, in *Journal of Presbyterian History*, 43:97–99.

[23] Here and below, see Lazell, *Alaskan Apostle*, 135–151; 55 Congress, 2 session, *Senate Documents*, no. 14, p. 3, 5, and no. 15, p. 1 (serial 3590); Pierre Berton, *The Klondike Fever: The Life and Death of the Last Great Gold Rush*, 112, 197 (New York, 1958).

[24] On the mission to Lapland, see Jackson, "[Eighth] Reindeer Report," 32–40, 103–119.

[25] The trip on the "Manitoban" is described in Lazell, *Alaskan Apostle*, 169–171; Jackson, "[Eighth] Reindeer Report," 39; diary of Wilhelm Basi (1869–1951), a Finnish-speaking Norwegian immigrant who joined the expedition and kept his diary in Finnish and Norwegian. It is translated into English and published as "Wilhelm Basi Diary on 1898 Yukon Rescue," in *Historical Tract Issue*, vol. 6, no. 4 (September, 1971), of the Finnish American Historical Society of the West (Portland, Oregon), hereafter cited as Basi Diary. Entries related to the sea voyage are on p. 2-4.

[26] Jackson, "[Eighth] Reindeer Report," 39; *St. Paul Pioneer Press*, March 4, 1898; Basi Diary, 10, 13, 18. On Balto, see Fridtjof Nansen, *The First Crossing of Greenland*, 11, 24–26, 442 (London, 1890).

[27] Jackson, "[Eighth] Reindeer Report," 40; *St. Paul Pioneer Press*, March 4, 1898; Basi Diary, 4. The Great Northern Railroad carried the expedition across the Northwest; on protests by the Northern Pacific over the granting of the contract, see "Reindeer for Alaska, routing," President's subject file 350, Northern Pacific Railway Company Records, MHS. The *St. Paul Pioneer Press* published other items about the reindeer on February 25, 28, March 2, 3, 7, and 13, 1898.

[28] Basi Diary, 6; Jackson, "[Eighth] Reindeer Report," 40; *Dictionary of American History*, 6:361 (New York, 1976).

[29] Lazell, *Alaskan Apostle*, 155; *St. Paul Pioneer Press*, March 2, 1898.

[30] Jackson, "[Eighth] Reindeer Report," 109, 145.

[31] For terms of the contracts, see Jackson, "[Eighth] Reindeer Report," 107.

[32] Basi Diary, 8, 12; Jackson, "[Eighth] Reindeer Report," 11.

[33] U.S. manuscript census schedules, 1900, Cook County, Enumeration dist. 201A; author's interviews with Chris and Matelda Tormondsen and Engel Eide, and with Ben and Agnes Fenstad, both October, 1979, and A. Vernon Engelsen to author, November 1, 1979, notes and letter in author's possession; *Cook County Herald*, March 19, 1898; index of Minnesota post offices, card file in MHS Reference Library. Emilie Redmyer's maiden name was Kjellmann ("Chalman"); see Hedley Redmyer, Certificate of Death 20203, Washington State Department of Health.

[34] For references to the "H. N. Emilie," see *Cook County Herald*, July 29, 1893, May 26, July 7, September 29, 1894, April 6, 1895; author's interview with William Raff, October, 1979, and Tormondsen-Eide interview, notes in author's possession; Emil Olund, Collector of Customs, Duluth, to Secretary of the Treasury, November 23, 1894, in Letters Sent, Collector of Customs, Port of Duluth, Bureau of Customs, National Archives Record Group (hereafter NARG) 36; certificates of enrollment for the "H. N. Emilie," no. 96150 (Redmyer, Frank Hicks, and M. M. Glasser, owners and masters), in Bureau of Marine Inspection and Navigation, NARG 41. References to road work appear in *Cook County Herald*, April 25, October 19, 1895, January 11, April 25, June 6, July 11, 19, 1896, October 17, 1897.

[35] Jackson, "[Third] Reindeer Report," 161. For Klondike and Alaska items, see *Cook County Herald*, August 7, October 2, December 4, 1897, February 5, June 4, October 15, 1898. William Kjellmann's father, Thorvald K., was employed as a mechanic, and his brother-in-law, Jens C. Widstead, was assistant superintendent; Ray, in *Journal of Presbyterian History*, 43:88.

[36] Jackson, "[Eighth] Reindeer Report," 41, 119. See also Hedley E. Redmyer, File

67676, AGO A 37, May 19, 1898, in Adjutant General's Office, NARG 94 (microfilm M698, roll 576, MHS); Secretary of War Record Cards, File 3272, May 13, 1898, Office of the Secretary of War, NARG 107. Redmyer was to be paid $75 a month and rations.

[37] Here and below, see Jackson, "[Eighth] Reindeer Report," 40–42; Basi Diary, 6, 7. Jack Dalton laid out the Dalton Trail for driving beef cattle to the Yukon in 1897. One of three routes to the Klondike, it is shown on the map accompanying Jackson's "[Eighth] Reindeer Report"; Patricia Roppel, "Porcupine," in Alaska Magazine, 5:2.

[38] Here and in the following paragraphs, see Jackson, "[Eighth] Reindeer Report," 42, 44, 120–123; Basi Diary, 7. E. C. Barnard, "Report of the Forty Mile Expedition," in 55 Congress, 3 session, Senate Documents, no. 172, p. 76 (serial 3737), describes the military expedition that was to travel with Redmyer's party. See also Jackson, "Ninth Annual Report on Introduction of Domestic Reindeer to Alaska," in 56 Congress, 1 session, Senate Documents, no. 245, p. 18 (serial 3867).

[39] Their camp was probably near Pleasant Camp, a post of the Royal Canadian Mounted Police. On the Porcupine Creek (then called Porcupine River) gold rush, see Roppel, "Porcupine," in Alaska Magazine, 5:2–10.

[40] Here and below, see Jackson, "[Eighth] Reindeer Report," 124, 131.

[41] Jackson, "[Eighth] Reindeer Report," 105–108; Lomen, Fifty Years in Alaska, 49.

[42] Lomen, Fifty Years in Alaska, 48; Jackson, "[Eighth] Reindeer Report," 123, "Ninth Reindeer Report," 14.

[43] Here and below, see Jackson, "[Eighth] Reindeer Report," 132.

[44] Redmyer's route is described in an interview published in the Klondyke Nugget (January 11, 1899) and reprinted in Cook County Herald, May 27, 1899.

[45] Here and below, see Jackson, "Ninth Reindeer Report," 18; Cook County Herald, May 27, 1899.

[46] Jackson, "[Eighth] Reindeer Report," 123. The description of Dawson in this and the following two paragraphs is from Berton, Klondike Fever, 296, 300, 302, 307, 366, 369, 394.

[47] Cook County Herald, May 27, 1899.

[48] Jackson, "Ninth Reindeer Report," 165.

[49] James Wickersham, Old Yukon Tales — Trails — and Trials, 46, 116, 122, 156, 473 (Washington, D.C., 1938); Jackson, "[Seventh] Reindeer Report," 28.

[50] Here and below, see Jackson, "Ninth Reindeer Report," 165.

[51] Jackson, "Ninth Reindeer Report," 165; George McManus, "A Reconnoissance [sic] between Circle City and the Tanana," in "Compilation of Narratives of Explorations in Alaska," 56 Congress, 1 session, Senate Reports, no. 1023, p. 751 (serial 3896).

[52] Jackson, "Ninth Reindeer Report," 116, 165, 167, 169. Kjeldsberg's claim for $100, June 24, 1899, was enclosed in Oliver Olson to the auditor's division, Department of the Interior, March 24, 1900, Alaska Division, Letters Received 4315, Bureau of Indian Affairs, NARG 75.

[53] Jackson, "[Eighth] Reindeer Report," 123, 126, 145, "Ninth Reindeer Report," 154, 165, 167. Jackson communicated with a number of people about selling the deer. See Jackson, "[Eighth] Reindeer Report," 126; R. Chilcott, Record Cards, File 2421 of 1899, Office of the Secretary of War, NARG 107; "Memoranda Concerning the use of Domestic reindeer in carrying the U.S. mails in Alaska (1897–1898)," in vol. 18, p. 325–328, Jackson Collection; St. Paul Pioneer Press, March 6, 1898; letters from Charles E. Roth, J. M. Teal, and others in Office of Secretary of Interior, NARG 48 (microfilm roll 5:344–402). When the herd was sold, Redmyer was to go to Unalakleet to be Kjellmann's assistant (roll 5:340).

[54] Basi Diary, 16; Jackson, "Ninth Reindeer Report," 12, 17, 116, 147, 159–161, 167–169.

[55] Jackson, "[Eighth] Reindeer Report," 48.

[56] Basi Diary, 9–11, 13–18; Jackson, "Ninth Reindeer Report," 12, 20, 21. On the Nome gold rush, see Leland H. Carlson, "The Discovery of Gold at Nome, Alaska," in Morgan B. Sherwood, ed., Alaska and Its History, 353–380 (Seattle, 1967); Wickersham, Old Yukon, 337–347, 350, 354.

[57] William T. Harris to Secretary of Interior, March 13, September 7, 1900, April 18,

1906, NARG 48 (microfilm rolls 7:155, 361, and 15:373); Jackson, "[Eighth] Reindeer Report," 109, and "Ninth Reindeer Report," 159–161.

[58] Berton, *Klondike Fever*, 200.

[59] On Redmyer's equipment, see Jackson, "Ninth Reindeer Report," 116.

[60] Jackson, "Ninth Reindeer Report," 170, "Fourteenth Reindeer Report," 13–24, and "Fifteenth Report on Introduction of Domestic Reindeer into Alaska," 59 Congress, 1 session, *Senate Documents*, no. 499, p. 34, 36, 74, 83 (serial 4931).

[61] Jackson, "Eleventh Annual Report on Introduction of Domestic Reindeer into Alaska," in 57 Congress, 1 session, *Senate Documents*, no. 98, p. 130–168 (serial 4230); Johnshoy, *Apaurak in Alaska*, 186.

[62] On Redmyer in Cook County, see *Cook County Herald*, April 18, August 8, September 19, October 3, 1903, February 27, May 7, 28, 1904. On his Alaskan work, see Jackson, "Fifteenth Reindeer Report," 160–163, 168–173; Jackson to Redmyer, October 25, 1905, in "Pioneer Presbyterian Missions," vol. 17, p. 279–281, Jackson Collection.

[63] Ingeborg Redmyer Tulloch, State of California Death Certificate 58708AC; A. V. Engelson to author, November 1, 1979, in author's possession; author's interview with Florence Alnes, October, 1979, and Fenstad interviews, notes in author's possession; *Cook County News Herald*, March 23, August 23, October 11, 1916; Deed Book, 4:154, 155, Records of Cook County Register of Deeds, Grand Marais; Hedley E. Redmyer, State of Washington Death Certificate 20203.

[64] Stewart, *Sheldon Jackson*, 412, 462, "Postscript" following p. 477.

[65] Here and below, see Seymour Hadwen and Lawrence J. Palmer, *Reindeer in Alaska*, 2, 4 (Department of Agriculture, *Bulletins*, no. 1089 – Washington, D.C., 1922; facsimile reproduction, Seattle, Washington, 1967). When deer from Norway were compared with the average deer from local herds in 1922, the Alaskan deer far outclassed the imported ones (p. 9). For two views of the reindeer project "within the framework of the Eskimo culture," see Ray, in *Journal of Presbyterian History*, 43:71–99 and Robert F. Spencer, *The North Alaskan Eskimo, A Study in Ecology and Society* (Bureau of American Ethnology, *Bulletins*, no. 171 – Washington, D.C., 1959). Spencer (p. 364, 468) considers reindeer a more practical and less expensive means of transport than dogs and "an economically and environmentally sound innovation" to which inland groups of Eskimos had adjusted successfully; maritime Eskimos, who did not want to be away from family and social groups for the periods of time required for herding, did not.

[66] Here and below, see Lomen, *Fifty Years in Alaska*, 3–5, 10, 19, 60, 65, 235; Brickey and Brickey, in *Alaska Journal*, 5:18; *St. Paul Dispatch*, June 20, 1924, p. 7; *St. Paul Pioneer Press*, June 1, 1934, p. 1. Helen Lomen's book is *Taktuk, An Arctic Boy* (New York, 1928).

[67] Here and below, see Lomen, *Fifty Years in Alaska*, 43, 57, 77, 78, 138, 295; Commissioner of Education, *Annual Report*, 1914, in 63 Congress, 3 session, *House Documents*, no. 1698, p. 638 (serial 6816).

[68] Brickey and Brickey, in *Alaska Journal*, 5:18–23; Lomen, *Fifty Years in Alaska*, 73, 87.

[69] *St. Paul Pioneer Press*, March 30, 1925, p. 1; *St. Paul Dispatch*, April 1, 1925, p. 12. Clippings of these stories and others regarding the Lomens are filed under Lomen names in the newspapers' morgue, St. Paul Public Library. Two publications, possibly not directly inspired by the brothers, nevertheless helped keep Alaska's reindeer in the public eye: Joseph W. Lamb's "Reindeer Rag Time Two-Step," published by the Stark Music Co., St. Louis, Mo., 1915, and James Oliver Curwood's *The Alaskan: A Novel of the North* (New York, [1923]), a fictional treatment of reindeer and Alaskan scenes with Carl Lomen as a principal character. Carl also wrote "Reindeer as a Source of Food," published in *Scientific American*, 141:105–108 (August, 1929).

[70] Brickey and Brickey, in *Alaska Journal*, 5:18; "Dining and Sleeping Car Department," in President's subject file 13039 (1929), Great Northern Railway Company Papers, MHS; Lomen, *Fifty Years in Alaska*, 213.

[71] For an account of the origins of Santa Claus and the Christmas reindeer connection, see Bill Vogt, "The deer that came in from the cold," in *National Wildlife*, 16:50–53 (October, 1977).

[72] Here and below, see Lomen, *Fifty Years in Alaska*, 192–202.

[73] Lomen, *Fifty Years in Alaska*, 192.

[74] Here and below, see Lomen, *Fifty Years in Alaska*, 200, 201.

[75] The Christmas Reindeer pageant of 1926 in St. Paul is described in the files of the *Dispatch* and *Pioneer Press* during November and December. A detailed index to all the references used on these pages is in the author's files. While a child's letter asking about Santa was the standard opening for a Lomen Christmas Reindeer program, Gudrun Brewitz was indeed a real person. St. Paul city directories show that she later worked for the Minnesota Mining and Manufacturing Co.

[76] "Tautook" was the name of an Eskimo apprentice herder at Golovin, Alaska. In 1904 Jackson described him as a good driver and trainer and the best reindeer manager of all the natives; see Jackson, "Fourteenth Reindeer Report," 23, 34.

[77] The Christmas Reindeer pageant of 1932 in St. Paul is described in the *Dispatch* and *Pioneer Press* from November 30 to December 23, 1932; for clippings of these stories, see "Santa Claus, 1932," in the papers' morgue, St. Paul Public Library.

[78] Lomen, *Fifty Years in Alaska*, 144, 148, 154, 203; *St. Paul Pioneer Press*, October 30, 1929, p. 10. Mrs. Lomen describes an article she wrote on reindeer that was published in *Vogue* magazine in the 1920s in Laura Volstead Lomen to Lucile Kane, July 3, 1965, in Andrew J. Volstead accessions file, 9938, MHS.

[79] For accounts of the journey, see Lomen, *Fifty Years in Alaska*, 248–273; Max Miller, *The Great Trek: The Story of the Five-Year Drive of a Reindeer Herd through the Icy Wastes of Alaska and Northwestern Canada* (New York, 1935); Allen R. Evans, *Reindeer Trek* (New York, 1946).

[80] Author's interviews with Hermund Melheim, Ray, and Clifford Samuelson, Spring Lake Park, November, 1979-January, 1980, notes in author's possession; *St. Paul City Directory*, 1926, p. 376; *Cook County News-Herald*, December 20, 1928, p. 6. According to Dimond's son, the deer were ordered from a man named Wachter in Seattle and kept at the Cloquet gravel pit, near Island Lake; Neil Dimond to author, April 6, 1980, in author's possession.

[81] Information on the 1927 Duluth reindeer show, here and below, is from the Dimond Reindeer Company Scrapbook, original in the possession of Hermund Melheim, photocopy in author's possession.

[82] D. Freimuth to Mr. N. H. Dimond, February 8, 1928, in Dimond Reindeer Company Scrapbook. The show was repeated with a minimum of fanfare the following year. See *Duluth News Tribune*, December 14, sec. 2, p. 1, December 19, p. 7, December 20, p. 13, December 23, sec. 1, p. 10, 1928.

[83] *Cook County News-Herald*, January 5, p. 4, February 2, p. 8, December 20, p. 6, 1928, September 4, 1930, p. 1.

[84] Information on Charles Boostrom, here and below, is from author's interviews with his sons Charles, Silver Bay, and Donald, Schroeder, October, 1979, notes in author's possession; *St. Paul Pioneer Press*, August 8, 1979, p. 13; Samuelson interview.

[85] *Cook County News-Herald*, September 25, 1930, p. 1; Charles Boostrom interview; Beatrice F. Ogren, *Gunflint Trailblazer*, 21 (Minneapolis, 1954).

[86] Neil Dimond to author, April 6, 1980, in author's possession; *Cook County News-Herald*, November 27, 1930, p. 4, January 1, 1931, p. 1; Samuelson interviews. The Grand Marais neighborhood attracted a number of other reindeer enthusiasts about the same time as Dimond moved to Clearwater. One Clyde Swale, said to be "prominent in Moose Lake Reindeer Feed Company circles," was selling stock in a reindeer "Incorpolation," according to the *Cook County News-Herald*, December 12, 1929, p. 4. Swale was said to have exchanged his company stock for several carloads of frozen herring. Since the deer in Swale's locality had been imported from Norway, the paper said, "no doubt he will use the herring for reindeer feed." How much was truth and how much spoof in the Swale tale is not known. Another herd of reindeer, imported from Finland by Michael Zoey, an "Assyrian," was in residence in 1930 at McFarland Lake. Zoey and Dimond at one time hoped to compete in a long-distance reindeer race from Grand Marais to Lake Placid, New York. Zoey's eight deer were eventually sold to Dimond (*Cook County News-Herald*, July 31, 1930, p. 1; Samuelson and Melheim interviews).

[87] The three St. Cloud Christmas Reindeer shows are described in the *St. Cloud Daily Times* for November and December, 1928 to 1930. A detailed index to all the articles used on these pages is in author's possession.

[88] Here and below, see Samuelson interviews.

[89] Clippings on these performances are in Dimond Reindeer Company Scrapbook. A post card with a reindeer photograph produced in the Arrowhead region probably dates from this time; a copy is in the possession of Hermund Melheim.

[90] Samuelson interviews.

[91] Samuelson interviews; *Cook County News-Herald*, December 31, 1931, p. 1.

[92] Samuelson interviews.

[93] Information used here and below is from Donald and Charles Boostrom and Melheim interviews; author's interview with Chris Tormondsen, Tofte, July 23, 1969, tape in MHS.

[94] Information on Melheim's involvement, here and below, is from Melheim interviews; Melheim to author, October 25, [November], [December], 1979, and Melheim's responses, handwritten on author to Melheim, January 1, 1980, all in author's possession.

[95] Ping Pi Liu subsequently was appointed a medical intern in New Jersey. University of Minnesota student records indicate that he received his medical degree, but they do not say where.

[96] Melheim interviews; Nicholas Dimond, Certificate of Death, 26623, Minnesota Division of Vital Statistics, St. Paul.

[97] Here and below, see Melheim to author, October 25, 1979, and Melheim's responses, handwritten on author to Melheim, January 1, 1980; *Willmar Tribune*, December 18, 1935; John M. Thomson, *Herman Melheim and His Hand-Carved Furniture* (Duluth, [1979]), a St. Louis County Historical Society pamphlet in author's possession. In 1983 Melheim was living in a nursing home at Littlefork. Some of his carvings were on display at Vesterheim Norwegian-American Museum in Decorah, Iowa, and a room at St. Louis County Historical Society museum in Duluth was filled with furniture he created. To some people in Duluth and in other towns and cities on the Christmas Reindeer circuit he was the "Reindeer Man."

[98] Here and below, see Brickey and Brickey, in *Alaska Journal*, 5:19–23; Margaret Lantis, "The Reindeer Industry in Alaska," in *Arctic*, 3:29–34 (April, 1950).

[99] Kathleen McCoy, "Reindeer Herding: An Industry on the Upswing," in *Alaska Farm Magazine*, vol. 2, no. 3, p. 30–32 (March, 1982).

[100] Lomen, *Fifty Years in Alaska*, 302. Lomen was overenthusiastic on one point. It should be noted that the reindeer are not entirely free of disease; see McCoy, in *Alaska Farm Magazine*, vol. 2, no. 3, p. 31.

Index

McMillen, Col. Willian, 77
Madison, Wis., 176, 185, 193, 194
"Magenta," steamboat, 79
Mail service, 36, 126, 129; regulations, 35, 44; use of reindeer, 197, 199, 200, 208–210
Maine, 177, 185
Malta, earthquake, 185
"Manistee," steamship, 185
"Manitoban," steamship, 197
Mankato, 96
"Mankato," steamboat, 52
Marie, queen of Romania, 215, 217
Maps, Fort Snelling, 7; Civil War, 57, 73; Alaska, 202
Marshall, Col. William R., 55, 63, 69–71, 87; issues orders, 58, 59, 67, 85; in battle, 74–77, 80
Marshall County, 131
Maryland, 176, 183
Massachusetts, 25, 177, 214
Mayo, Charles, doctor, 180
Mayo, Will, doctor, 180
Mayo, William W., doctor, 180
Mayo Clinic, founding, 180
Meeker County, 27, 50
Melheim, Hermund, reindeer promoter, 189, 211, 225–228; portrait, 226
Memphis, Tenn., 52, 55, 62–66, 68, 70
Merrick, W. L., in circus, 117, 119, 123
Meteors and meteorites, theories, 158, 163, 168, 255n35; sighted, 172, 174, 177, 181
Methodist church, 17, 64, 85; clergy, 53, 55, 58, 84
Metropolitan Hotel, St. Paul, 33
Meyer, Bill, policeman, 218
Mexico, 172, 177
Michigan, 128, 131, 143, 174–176, 226
Milaca, 222, 224
Miller, Stephen A., governor, 55, 63
Milwaukee, Wis., 172, 176
Minnehaha, etymology, 108
Minnehaha Creek, 10
Minneapolis, 25–27, 92, 170; skiers, 131, 133, 137, 138, 143, 145; fires, 172, 174, 185
Minneapolis and St. Louis railroad, 138
Minnesota, politics, 30, 33, 34, 154; economic growth, 169; reindeer herding, 222–226; reindeer shows, 215–224, 227, 228
Minnesota Historical Society, 34
Minnesota Sharpshooters, 27
Minnesota Territory, officials, 88
Mission Covenant church, 195
Missions, 189, 191, 193, 195, 199, 208–210
Mississippi, 55, 56, 58, 59, 64, 65, 77, 79, 108
Mississippi River, 1, 151, 189; travel, 3, 52, 66, 69, 79, 87; floods, 10, 174, 175

Missouri, 67–69, 87, 108, 227; storms, 175, 176
Missouri River, 69
Mobile, Ala., 79, 81
Montana, 175, 177, 179
Montanio, Signor, in circus, 117, 119, 123
Montgomery, Ala., 82
Monticello, 23, 27, 35, 42–45, 48, 224
Moore, Clement C., poet, 213
Moorhead, fires, 172
Morgan, Lt. Col. Willoughby, 3, 5, 6, 15
Morgedal, Norway, 129, 151
Morris, 184
Moselle River, floods, 172
Mott, Lucretia, 36
Mount Clemens, Mich., 110, 111
Mower, Gen. Joseph A., 60, 66, 68; sketched, 61
Mower County, 131
Murdock, Dr. Henry, 58, 60
Music, band, 82, 113, 123, 134, 135, 143, 151, 219; vocal, 122, 134, 188
Myram, A. H., skier, 133

NANSEN, FRITJOF, author, 149, 197
Nashville, Tenn., battle, 69–77; camp sketched, 71
Natchez Indians, 99
National Hotel, Washington, D.C., 27, 97
National Ski Association, 143, 149, 150
National Ski Hall of Fame, Ishpeming, Mich., 151
Nebraska, 96, 175, 176, 227
Neill, Rev. Edward D., 94, 102
Nelson, Knute, governor, 194
Nelson, Peter, legislator, 134
New Great Australian Circus, performers, 110–117, 119–121, 123–125; finances, 114, 116, 117; lawsuit, 117–125
New Hampshire, earthquake, 174
New Jersey, 165, 174, 197
New Mexico, reindeer shows, 227
New Orleans, La., 79, 114, 173, 175
New York, 174, 176, 181, 189
New York Clipper, 110, 111, 112, 113, 125
New Zealand, meteors, 177
Newberry, J. S., professor, 178
Newport, B. C., lawyer, 117
Newspapers, technology, 34, 44, 99; editors, 32, 34–41, 43–47, 50, 55, 88, 99; in Civil War, 64, 77; reindeer promotions, 214–221. See also individual papers
Nicaragua, 176
Nelson family, 31, 41, 42, 43, 47
Nininger, 153, 170, 176, 186; depicted, 154, 171
Ninth Minnesota Volunteer Infantry, 56, 63, 77

U.S. Navy, 195
U.S. Revenue Cutter Service, 193
U.S. War Dept., 108, 199
University of Alaska, 229
University of Minnesota, 212, 219, 227
Unonius, Gustaf, pastor, 114, 234n5
Utopianism, 28. *See also* "Farist" colony
Urey, Harold C., chemist, 167

VANDERBURGH, CHARLES E., judge, 30
Varner, John, 42
Velikovsky, Immanuel, 167
Vermilion Trail, reindeer, 221
Verne, Jules, author, 166, 172
Vidal language, 37
Viking Ski Club, Minneapolis, 138
Villard, Henry, railroad man, 182
Virginia, 81, 108
Volcanoes, 160, 174, 176, 181, 185
Volstead, Andrew J., congressman, 220
Volstead, Laura, promotes reindeer, 220
Volstead Act, 215

WABASHA COUNTY, tornado, 180
Wagner, Charles, in circus, 124
Wakeman, Edgar L., 179
Warner, R. L. (Gus), circus employee, 117
Warner, J. E., circus owner, 117
War of *1812*, 2, 79
Washington, George, name, 102
Washington, D. C., 27, 31, 96, 104, 191, 196; army headquarters, 17, 18, 22, 71; lobbyists, 89, 220
WCCO, Minneapolis, radio station, 150, 216, 218, 219
WEBC, Duluth, radio station, 221
Weinhardt, Isaac, ski maker, 136
Wells, reindeer show, 218
West Point, *see* U.S. Military Academy, West Point, N.Y.
West Virginia, storms, 175
Westernra, Sgt. Roderick, 3–5, 13
Whelan, Thomas J., in circus, 124
Whig party, 89
White Bear Lake, reindeer show, 219, 220
White River, Alaska, 204, 205
White River, Ark., 66
Whitman, Walt, 173
Whitney, William D., linguist, 101, 103, 105
Widstrand, Frans Herman, family, 24, 25, 29; career, 24–29, 31, 50; political views, 24–27, 30–34, 36, 43,

48; diet, 27, 28, 33, 37; utopianism, 28, 30, 38, 45, 49; social views, 28, 31, 33, 36, 39–41, 47; legal battles, 29, 42, 44, 50; financial problems, 30–32, 44; labeled insane, 32, 33, 47, 51; newspapers, 34–41, 44–47, 50; religious views, 38
Widstrand, Charles, 25, 27, 29
Widstrand, Claes, 24, 25, 29
Widstrand, Emma, 25
Widstrand, Gustava Annell (Mrs. Jocob), 24, 25
Widstrand, Jocob Isaacson, 24
Wilkes, Benjamin, businessman, 114, 116, 118, 124, 125
Wilkes, Chloe (Mrs. Benjamin), businesswoman, 114, 116, 125
Willmar Tribune, quoted, 228
Wilson, Gen. James H., 83
Winchell, Alexander, geologist, 172
Windom, William, senator, 92, 94
Winnebago Indians, 89–91, 96, 98, 101, 102
Winona, 87, 149, 170
Winona County, tornado, 180
Wisconsin, 13, 172; skiers, 128, 129, 131, 133, 137, 149; storms, 175, 176; reindeer shows, 218, 224
Women, rights discussed, 28, 33, 36, 39–41; skiers, 130, 134, 137, 143, 149, 150, 252n66
Wood, Robert, assistant surgeon, 11, 12
Woodland Park, Seattle, Wash., 198, 199
Worland, Annie (Annette), in circus, 113
World War II, 229
Wright, Frank Lloyd, architect, 185
Wright County, 23, 48, 50; politics, 26, 31, 47; disasters, 27, 29, 31; relief, 29
Wright County Times (Monticello), 32, 43, 47
Wyoming, 125, 227

YANKTON, S.D., 125, 224
Yellowstone Park, 179
Youmans, Edward L., professor, 173, 175, 183
Young, Alexander, lawyer, 118, 122
Young, C. A., astronomer, 183
Yuchi Indians, 98
Yukon River, 195, 200, 204, 205, 208
Yukon Territory, gold rush, 196

ZUMBRO RIVER, 179